Handbook of
SHORT-TERM
THERAPY GROUPS

Handbook of SHORT-TERM THERAPY GROUPS

Edited by
MAX ROSENBAUM, Ph.D.

JASON ARONSON INC.
Northvale, New Jersey
London

THE MASTER WORK SERIES

First softcover printing 1996

Library of Congress Cataloging-in-Publication Data

Handbook of short-term therapy groups / edited by Max Rosenbaum.
    p. cm. — (The master work series)
   Originally published: New York : McGraw-Hill, 1983.
   Includes bibliographical references and index.
   ISBN 0–7657–0045–X (alk. paper)
   1. Group psychotherapy. 2. Brief psychotherapy. I. Rosenbaum,
Max, 1923–   . II. Series.
RC488.H362   1997
616.89'152—dc20
                                    96–35207

Printed in the United States of America on acid-free paper. For information and catalog write to Jason Aronson Inc., 230 Livingston Street, Northvale, New Jersey 07647-1731. Or visit our website: http://www.aronson.com

Contents

III. Working with Women

IV. Working with Couples

V. Working with the Aged

VI. Working with Patients in a Hospital Setting

VII. Working with People in Crisis

Preface to the Softcover Edition

Since this book was first published there have been major changes in the United States relating to health care. The use of short-term psychotherapy approaches quickened after the 1970s as managed care techniques became part of the delivery of mental health services. Studies at the Kaiser-Permanente managed care facilities in California indicated a significant drop in patients' use of all areas of medical care when their emotional problems were addressed. The next step was to ascertain whether time-limited approaches, both individual and group, were effective. Again, brief therapy techniques were found to be valuable and they accelerated the pace of psychotherapy.

In this age of managed care, brief approaches to psychotherapy are being emphasized. Also, there has been a recent push for psychological treatments that have adequate empirical support (American Psychological Association, 1995).

Managed care did *not* motivate this writer when this book was being formulated. Nor did managed care motivate this writer when he co-founded and co-directed a short-term therapy center in midtown Manhattan in New York City. It was rather a desire to reach more people in need of psychotherapy, especially those who would not or could not commit to long-term psychotherapy. The hope was that once movement began in short-term therapy, the momentum would pick up quickly. An early figure in psychodynamic psychotherapy, Alfred Adler, noted that once a patient reached one goal, however minor it appeared, it served as an incentive to move further.

In Freud's final paper, "Analysis Terminable and Interminable" (1937), he discussed the efficacy and limitations of psychoanalytic technique. He stated, probably with some pessimism, that " . . . psychoanalytic therapy . . . is a lengthy business . . . " (p. 377). Before Freud's final paper, Otto Rank and Sandor Ferenczi sought to improve psychoanalytic treatment with an emphasis on the use of the therapy as a present experience rather than a reliving of past experiences (Rank & Ferenczi, 1925). Over five decades later, Merton Gill (1979) stressed a focus on the "here and now." So there is a long history of clinicians who stated that attention should be given to the immediate interaction. This predates the current emphasis on the patient's defensive and adaptive mode of interacting with the therapist and group members in a group therapy session or an individual therapy session.

It was after World War II that Franz Alexander (1956) published a book that challenged many approaches to psychotherapy, especially the long-held belief that a transference neurosis must develop if psychotherapy is to be at all successful. He went so far as to state that a psychotherapist's efforts to develop a transference neurosis with the patient resulted in lengthy if not interminable psychotherapy.

Alexander stressed the importance of confronting the current day-to-day issues of life. He would change the frequency of therapy as well as continually pressure the patient to apply what had been learned in psychotherapy. Constant developments in the field of short-term psychodynamic psychotherapy have challenged many of the parameters of psychoanalytic theory that numerous clinicians accepted as absolutes.

Bordin (1979) proposed that patients have their own concept about how and what they want to change. The patient's concept of change in psychotherapy may be radically different from the psychotherapist's concept. Recognition of what the patient's goals are is a given in short-term approaches, whether they are psychodynamic, cognitive, or behavioral. Different schools of psychotherapy (psychodynamic, cognitive, or behavioral) note that differing stress responses, especially after varied types of psychological trauma, require different forms of intervention. The folk adage, different strokes for different folks, is very much to the point.

America's "loss of innocence" (Raine, 1995) demands that psychotherapists intervene immediately and effectively. On the morning of April 19, 1995, the Alfred P. Murrah Federal Building in Oklahoma City was blown up by terrorists. In February 1993, terrorists conspired to blow up the World Trade Center in New York City. Even after the conviction of the conspirators in New York City, the United States remains threatened by those who would engage in terror. The disaster that occurred in Middle America did not occur in the Middle East or Chechnya (Russia).

As the pace of modern life increases, as calamities strike, mental health professionals must intervene quickly and effectively. Short-term approaches resolve the reality of people who need immediate attention. A British psychotherapist summed up brief psychotherapy succinctly when she noted that the focus of brief psychotherapy is the end (Ashurst, 1995). She also noted that Donald Winnicott cautioned psychotherapists who might overtreat. A clergyman once commented to this writer: "Faith may be the ultimate answer, but how do I get through the next half mile?"

Consumer Reports (November, 1995), the publication of Consumers Union, conducted what they described as "a ground-breaking survey," indicating that psychotherapy usually works (pp. 734–739). Cognitive therapy for depression, a major problem for many who suffer mental or emotional distress, has been well established as an effective short-term treatment for unipolar depression (Beck et al., 1979). In the near past, such patients would have been rushed to electric shock therapy. Our clinical interventions are refreshingly challenged and short-term approaches accept the challenge.

Finally, I note that as the twentieth century comes to a close, there is a dramatic worldwide shift in the proportion of younger to older persons. At the time of this writing 13 percent of the United States population is 65 years of age or older. According to the U.S. Bureau of the Census (1991), by the year 2030, 20 percent of the population will be 65 and older. The older population is living longer. By the year 2000, almost 50 percent of the elderly will be 75 years of age or older. We must find ways to work with the emotional problems of the elderly, without medicating them to obeisance.

In a conference and training institute organized by this writer and held some years ago in Mexico, a group of youngsters was in the same audience as conference registrants as we all watched Mexican folk dances. The youngsters were intrigued by the badges worn by some of the conference registrants that identified them as participants in a short-term therapy training institute. One boy, seated next to his friend, asked him, "What is short-term therapy?" His friend replied, "Well, that's for older people. You know they don't have much time left to live." Nor do any of us.

MAX ROSENBAUM

REFERENCES

Alexander, F. *Psychoanalysis and Psychotherapy*. New York: W.W. Norton, 1956.

American Psychological Association. Training in and dissemination of empirically validated psychological treatments: Report and recommendations. *Clinical Psychologist*, 1995, *48*, 3–23.

Ashurst, P. The end is the beginning. *Group Analysis*, 1995, 28, 443–452.

Beck, A. T., Rush, A. J., Shaw, B., & Emery, G. *Cognitive therapy of depression*. New York: Guilford, 1979.

Bordin, E. S. The generalizability of the psychoanalytic concept of the working alliance. *Psychotherapy: Theory, Research and Practice*, 1979, *16*, 252–260.

Freud, S. Analysis terminable and interminable. *International Journal of Psycho-Analysis*, 1937, *18*, 373–405.

Gill, M. M. The analysis of the transference. *Journal of the American Psychoanalytic Association*, 1979, *27*, 263–288.

Raine, H. The buried sounds of children crying. *U.S. News and World Report*, May 1995, *10*, p. 10.

Rank, O., & Ferenczi, S. The Development of Psychoanalysis, trans. C. Newton. New York: Nervous and Mental Diseases Publishing Company, 1925.

Preface

Group psychotherapy is considered a major treatment modality for all types of emotional difficulties. The new treatment manual which accompanies the recently issued DSM III accepts group psychotherapy as a recognized treatment procedure. Every kind of patient has been treated with group psychotherapy. It has been used in every type of setting ranging from crisis intervention clinics, prisons, hospitals, schools, convents, monasteries—the list of possible settings grows every day. Under the rubric "group psychotherapy" are grouped interactional group psychotherapy, "traditional" analytic group psychotherapy, transactional group psychotherapy, gestalt group therapy, behavioral group therapy, network group therapy, psychodrama, existential group therapy, family group therapy, client-centered group therapy, encounter groups, self-help groups, art group therapy, music group therapy, training groups. Every age group is covered—although to my knowledge infants have not as yet been placed in therapy groups, although new mothers and fathers have been. Group therapy is used throughout the world with every type of patient problem—neurotics, psychotics, narcotic addicts, alcoholics, terminally ill, newly or about to be divorced, gender identity problems, sexual offenders, child molesters, wife beaters, husband beaters, rapists. The list is endless.

This comprehensive book covers many of the settings where group therapy is used. It is directed to those who want to know about groups led by a trained professional. This trained professional believes that the group experience will help the patient, even more than a dyadic experience and the clinical evaluation is that the patient will be able to cope with the group experience. The therapy groups consist of people who agree on some recognition and definition of their problems. This is what brings them together with the group leader.

There exists an implicit or explicit contract which recognizes the group leader as the trained professional, the patient as someone in distress. The group experience is at first accepted as a *possible* way of relieving the patient's distress. The hope is that the group experience will lead to a new and more comfortable way of responding to the pressures of every day life. There is planning and thought given to the composition of the group, and while there is constant innovation, it can only be carried out if it is in the best interests of the group member(s).

So much then for the value of group therapy. *But why short-term group therapy?* Isn't it enough that the dyadic experience has been enlarged so that there is more efficient use of professionals and more people in distress can be served? There exists, as yet, mental health professionals who still have reservations about the validity of the group experience and attack this modality as surface and only transient in effectiveness. The literature will answer their criticisms as to effectiveness. But will the short-term group therapy experience merely cater to the magical fantasies of psychotherapists who seek instant gratifications. Is this merely "hype" and a "hard sell?" I think not. The history of psychodynamic therapy validates that there has always been a desire to expedite the length and time of treatment. There were members of the group of psychoanalysts surrounding Freud who believed that the process of psychotherapy could be shortened (Ferenczi & Rank, 1925; Stekel, 1940).

After World War II, Franz Alexander and Thomas French published a book which questioned the idea that long-term psychotherapy insured deeper exploration of problems and in this book specific suggestions were offered as to how to shorten psychotherapy (Alexander & French, 1946). Alexander was European trained and after he came to the United States became a seminal figure in the founding of the Chicago Institute of Psychoanalysis—clearly in the heartland of America. French was American born and trained. Both Alexander and French were concerned about the integration of learning theory and psychoanalytic concepts. They stressed that treatment must consist of a selection and focus on the patient's most central difficulties in living. This in turn was related to careful delineation of suitability for psychotherapy and a joint plan by patient and therapist to arrive at goals and strategies for getting to those goals. In the early history of dynamic psychotherapy, the byword was the neutrality of the therapist. But now the therapist was encouraged to be more active, and to provide an emotional climate and experience that was corrective in nature by the nature of its positive approach. Most dynamic psychotherapists dismissed the Alexander and French approach as too manipulative although I have often speculated that their antagonism was based on their rigid commitment to the idea that longer is better.

Over the last twenty years, with increasing emphasis upon cost effectiveness and the demand that psychotherapy justify itself, psychotherapists became interested again in short-term approaches. There is a huge community of people who need mental health services and it is critical that we find ways to reach these people, else "quack" techniques will take over. According to Gresham's law—in a vacuum, the "bad" will take over in the absence of anything else.

All forms of short-term dynamic psychotherapy focus on early and careful diagnosis, delimiting the problem area, and avoiding the possibility of fostering regressive and dependent behavior. Whether the emphasis is upon a strongly supportive approach with elements of direct encouragement or the establishment of a positive transference where the therapist is perceived as helpful, interested, and warm, or clarification, interpretation of the patient's behavior, and confrontation with the patient's defenses, all approaches are oriented toward doing the job more quickly. Hans Strupp, the researcher in results of psychotherapy, has stressed the importance of psychotherapy effectiveness, but, more importantly, the *discriminant* use of the variety of psychotherapy approaches that are available so that different patients are able to have their needs and problems resolved.

More than ever, psychotherapists are concerned with a focus in psychotherapy. Whatever the name given to the type of psychotherapy—whether short-term or time-limited—or even the use of the term STAAP (short-term anxiety-arousing psychotherapy), the emphasis is upon focusing the treatment. The various contributors to this book describe different approaches to focus but all approaches are devoted to helping the patient get to a fruitful and easier life without disabling anxiety. Whether the contributors are aware of it or not, somewhere they have followed Alexander and French's statement in 1946— encourage, request the patient to do the things that have been avoided in past life, and to move beyond failure and pursue success.

This book is then an effort to follow Strupp's statement: the application of psychotherapy discriminantly to patients with different problems of living.

MAX ROSENBAUM

REFERENCES

Alexander, Franz & French, Thomas M. *Psychoanalytic Therapy: Principles and Application* New York: Ronald Press, 1946.

Ferenczi, Sandor & Rank, Otto *The Development of Psychoanalysis* New York: Nervous and Mental Disease Publishing Company, 1925.

Stekel, Wilhelm *Technique of Analytic Psychotherapy* Eden and Paul, trs. New York: Norton, 1940.

Handbook of
SHORT-TERM
THERAPY GROUPS

I

WORKING WITH PARENTS

1

Filial Therapy:
A Group for Parents of Children
with Emotional Problems

Michael P. Andronico, Ph.D.

A clinical psychologist in private practice in Somerset, New Jersey, MICHAEL P. ANDRONICO is also adjunct associate professor of psychiatry at the New Jersey University of Medicine and Dentistry, Piscataway, and a field instructor at the Graduate School of Applied Professional Psychology at Rutgers University, New Brunswick.

Filial therapy is a method of teaching parents to conduct play-therapy sessions with their children in their own homes. It was originated by Bernard Guerney, Jr. (B. G. Guerney, 1964). The first filial therapy group was conducted in 1963. Although play therapy can be taught to individual parents or a parental couple, this article will describe the application of filial therapy in groups of parents. Most of the experience to date, especially the research data, has been derived from parents who have been in filial-therapy groups. The basic premise of a filial therapy group is that the parents are taught the roles of play therapists while at the same time experiencing group therapy for themselves (Andronico & Blake, 1971; Andronico et al., 1967; Andronico & B. G. Guerney, 1967, 1969; Fidler et al., 1969; Ginsberg, 1976; Ginsberg et al., 1978; B. G. Guerney,

1976; B. G. Guerney & Andronico, 1969; B. G. Guerney et al., 1966; B. G. Guerney et al., 1972; L. Guerney, 1976, 1980; Stover & B. G. Guerney, 1967).

Selecting the Children

The bulk of the experience in filial therapy has been with neurotic children. Although some work has been done in applying filial therapy techniques to retarded, schizophrenic, and brain-damaged children, certain modifications have to be employed, and more research needs to be conducted with these populations. The patient population to be discussed here is neurotic children between the ages of 2 or 3 and 10. In working with very young children, below the age of 2 or 3, it is difficult to ascertain whether their problems are the result of emotional difficulties, cerebral deficit, or other factors. It is also rare that children so young are referred to mental health personnel.

The procedure for selecting children for filial therapy should include an interview with the child's parents and some form of direct diagnostic evaluation of the child. During the parent interview the therapist should obtain a comprehensive case history of the child and the family, including developmental information on the child. The diagnostic session with the child should include psychological testing to rule out the possibility of mental retardation, brain damage, or perceptual impairment. After the gathering of all this information, and assuming that the child is diagnosed as neurotic, the recommendation for filial therapy can be made. It is my conviction that filial therapy is the treatment of choice for most children of play-therapy age.

Once the interpretation of the diagnostic evaluation is communicated to the parents and the recommendation for filial therapy is made and accepted, the parents are told that they will join a group of other parents whose children also have emotional problems, some of which will be similar to and some different from those of their child.

As with many forms of psychotherapy, filial therapy can be approached in various ways, each offering advantages and disadvantages. The choice of approach depends, of course, on the preferences and circumstances of the therapist. For example, if the therapist has the opportunity of forming several filial therapy groups at one time, he can choose to have groups of parents whose children are of the same age or of different ages. Organizing a group for parents whose problem children are approximately the same age forestalls complaints from parents who claim they have little in common with other parents whose children are of different ages from theirs. Homogeneous age grouping, however, reduces the opportunity for parents of younger children to benefit from the experience of parents of older children. Heterogeneous age grouping, further, encourages parents of older problem children to think more about the problems of their younger children (if they have any), to whom they may not have paid enough attention because of their preoccupation with their problem child.

Even more of an issue in homogeneous versus heterogeneous grouping is whether the therapist should combine parents whose children have similar or different symptoms. Parents of children with similar symptoms can certainly acquire a quicker understanding of one another's plight, but developing an understanding of someone with dissimilar problems, especially when parents learn that the same play-therapy techniques work with dissimilar problems, may be more helpful. It also helps parents to better comprehend the underlying principles of play-therapy techniques and enables them to utilize those principles in their daily lives, outside of the play-therapy sessions.

For children who are slightly older than 10 but who are emotionally immature, filial therapy is usually appropriate. These immature 11- or 12-year-olds still relate to play and can derive much benefit from expressing their feelings through play.

For bright, overly responsible children of 9 or 10 who have already stopped playing with toys, filial therapy is particularly recommended. The unwillingness of these children to play with toys is usually an indication of emotional constriction and lack of spontaneity that can be overcome through play therapy. It is particularly helpful to point out to the parents of these children that it is important for these children to learn to express themselves through play and to make up a phase of their emotional development they missed earlier. In my experience, children of this sort readily get involved in play with toys if their parents believe it is helpful. The children probably have "misunderstood" parental or societal messages, interpreting them to mean that growing up quickly and giving up play was a valued form of behavior. In fact, this reaction has actually impeded rather than facilitated their emotional development.

Composition of Parents' Groups

My filial-therapy groups usually number from seven to ten parents and meet weekly for an hour and a half. Some therapists feel more comfortable with two-hour groups. An important consideration is the anxiety level of the therapist. Many therapists beginning to lead filial-therapy groups are temporarily overwhelmed by the amount of didactic and emotional material that is involved in the first few sessions and prefer to lengthen the group meetings. It might be pointed out to these therapists that there is an important parallel between individual therapy, group therapy, and filial therapy—namely, that there is always an overwhelming amount of material to be dealt with and that the most significant material, if not all of it, eventually gets dealt with. This work is never completed in a few sessions.

In general it is highly desirable for both parents to take part in filial therapy.

Because both parents learn together and therefore understand what is being done and why, they are more likely to be supportive of each other and of the home play sessions. They are also equally knowledgeable and can discuss the play and group sessions with each other.

Of course, not every couple is willing or able to attend group meetings. In these cases, the willing or able parent can be included in a mixed group, along with couples and other parents whose spouses are not participating as well as with single parents who are separated, divorced, or widowed. The mixture of these different types of parents offers several advantages. The couples can observe the difficulties that single parents have and learn to appreciate even the limited help they get from their spouses. The group members can benefit from the "mistakes" of the other parents in the group and learn more positive ways from couples who get along well together, especially when the group progresses into the group-therapy phases of filial therapy.

It is possible and highly desirable for separated or divorced couples to participate in filial-therapy groups, either together or in separate groups. In this way, both parents are aware of, and cooperate in, the treatment of their child or children. It also gives them a common ground on which to coordinate their respective parenting efforts, since they are likely to agree on the theoretical and practical approaches that are being taught to them in the filial therapy group.

In cases where one parent is not going to attend the filial therapy group meetings, these parents may be encouraged to at least attend during the training period, which lasts for four to eight weeks. Some nonparticipating parents who attend the training meetings will change their minds and remain in the group. Those who attend only the training meetings are still more likely to be encouraging and supportive of the spouses who continue to attend the filial therapy group and conduct the play sessions at home.

For those parents who neither participate in the ongoing group nor attend the training meetings, it is worthwhile for the therapist to offer a single meeting, either individually or in a group with other parents whose spouses are going to participate in a filial therapy group. A group setting is preferable for this single meeting because of the supportive nature of a group and the opportunity to have other people reduce some of the initial resistances and hostilities toward the therapist. It is important that the therapist accept resistances on the part of these parents while at the same time explaining with conviction the purposes and nature of filial therapy and what the spouses of these parents will be doing in the filial therapy groups and in the play sessions at home.

The Initial or Training Phase of Filial Therapy

Since most neurotic children under 10 years of age do not require therapy for more than one year, especially if their parents are also actively involved in their treatment, a filial therapy group is generally projected to last one year. This time is divided into three phases or stages. The first is the training phase, during which most of the time in the group meetings is devoted to teaching the parents how to conduct play sessions. They do not begin their home play sessions until they have successfully learned to do this. The initial phase takes from four to eight weeks. The middle phase, lasting approximately eight to ten weeks, is a transitional period involving close supervision of the home play sessions and group therapy for the parents. The conclusion of this phase has the parents moving flexibly from discussions of the home play sessions to discussions of their feelings about their children, their spouses, and other group members. The last and longest phase entails a flexible combination of supervision of home play sessions and group therapy, with the group and the therapist using their own judgment as to how much time to spend on supervision and how much on personal dynamics.

Introducing the Group Members

It is advisable to begin the first group meeting by having the parents briefly introduce themselves and tell why they are in the group. The therapist may begin with a brief opener like: "As all of you know, my name is _____ [using the first name to establish an informal and comfortable atmosphere]. I would like to outline for you what we'll be doing here. I want to teach you how to have play sessions at home with your children. This teaching will take a few weeks and then you'll start your sessions at home. After that you'll continue to come here every week and we'll discuss the play sessions, your children's reactions to them, your own reactions, and your reactions to other things. In brief, then, the play sessions will be a chance for your children to deal with their issues, and these group meetings will be a chance for you to deal with your issues. Now maybe we can take a few minutes to introduce each other and say why we're here."

As the parents introduce themselves, the therapist has an opportunity to set the stage for both the training period and future meetings. There is generally a tendency on the part of most groups to get into personality dynamics during the first discussion and spend a great deal of time doing so. Parents will often, for example, say that they are there because their 7-year-old son gets into too many fights with the neighborhood children, and one parent may say, "Yes, and if my husband was stricter with Johnny, he wouldn't get into so many fights" or "If my husband wasn't so strict with Johnny, he wouldn't get into so many fights." The husband might then respond, "I'm only lenient because you're too strict" or "I'm strict because you pamper him too much." If the parent relating this story is not there with a spouse, someone else in the group may respond. In either situation, the therapist is confronted with two options, neither of which is desirable. If the budding fight becomes full-blown, a great deal of time will be consumed and too little time left for the main business of the first meeting. It will also set the stage for the rest of the group, who have not yet introduced themselves, to get into lengthy discussions and perhaps fights about their issues.

On the other hand, if the therapist steps in too soon and cuts off the discussion, he sets a precedent for not dealing with feelings and group interactions; this precedent might slow the group's progress later on, after the training period, when it is desirable to have spontaneous expressions of feelings by the group members.

Each therapist must find his own comfortable balance between these options. My own way of dealing with this problem is to allow a certain amount of interaction and emotional expression initially. If this begins to become excessive, I say, "You both really seem very angry about that issue. Obviously, it's quite important to each of you, and I agree that it does have an impact on your child. I think that's worth exploring at length, but right now, because I do want to hear from the rest of the group, I'd like to continue with our introductions and get back to this important issue later." The message here is that the therapist recognizes the importance of the material in which the parents are emotionally involved, wants to deal with it, but is temporarily postponing doing so. Also, there is the message that emotional materials of a personal nature are important and worthwhile for the group to work on in the future.

In the rare instance that a group is slow in interacting or in presenting emotionally laden material in this first round of introductions, the therapist may serve as a catalyst and provide the message that it is appropriate to deal with emotional materials in the parent meetings. For example, he may point out that one group member smiled when someone said something or that another had a sarcastic expression while his or her spouse was talking. Often this will stimulate enough emotional material to set a precedent for dealing with feelings in the group. If it stimulates too much of an emotional response, the previously discussed method of temporarily limiting discussion may be utilized.

Presenting Didactic Material

With the initial introduction of the parents to each other, the stage is set for the didactic presentation of the theory of play therapy, which is the main business of the first meeting. Before the meeting, I give or mail to all members an eight-page parent training manual (L. Guerney et al., 1976) that briefly introduces the concepts of nondirective play therapy in simple language. As a result, parents come to the first group meeting with some familiarity with the theory and practice of play therapy. It is important to communicate most of the basic didactic material during the first meeting so that a demonstration of an actual play session can be given at the second meeting. A demonstration is a far more effective teaching device than verbal exposition. If all the didactic material is not covered during the first meeting, it can be completed at the start of the second meeting with time still remaining for a demonstration play session and a group discussion.

The theory employed is that of nondirective play therapy. Although it may be possible to utilize other dynamic forms of play therapy, these would take a great deal of time to teach. It has been demonstrated that parents can effectively learn the filial therapy method in six to eight sessions (Stover & B. G. Guerney, 1967), and for this reason the nondirective method is advocated. The parents are briefly told that their role is to establish a warm and accepting atmosphere in which their children can express their feelings without fear of being hurt or criticized. No interpretation of the child's play is made to the child by the parents. Occasionally, the therapist will interpret for the parents the symbolic meaning of the child's play. When he does so, he tries to give examples, relevant to the parents' own experiences, of the value of warm, uncritical acceptance and how this enables the child to resolve his problems.

During this didactic presentation, it is advisable to utilize a nondirective or Rogerian style of teaching. Since the model of the play sessions is nondirective, the therapist can serve as a role model for the play sessions by adopting a generally nondirective stance, eliciting from the group itself as many as possible of the ideas he wants to present to them. This is also a very effective teaching method. Of course, here again different professionals have different orientations and styles, and each therapist must decide for herself which style to use, taking into consideration her own comfort and background. It is also important to realize that therapists, as well as the parents who are going through the training period, often evolve from one position to another, and what may initially feel awkward and foreign can become comfortable and familiar, especially when one experiences success while doing it.

Dealing with Emotional Issues

One of the most important problems that arise during the training period is the incidents of emotional reaction on the part of parents during the didactic presentations and discussions, which may be frequent at the beginning but gradually decrease as time goes on. For example, an overcontrolling parent may have a very strong emotional reaction to the idea that her child will have an opportunity to punch a bop bag at will during the play sessions. This parent may argue: "The reason we brought Johnny here in the first place is because he fights with the boys at school. If we encourage him to hit this punching bag, he'll think we think it's all right, and he'll get worse, not better!" If this reaction is one of ignorance, it may suffice simply to explain that the child's "acting out" is a result of a lot of internalized tensions that he can no longer control but that these tensions can be drained off by allowing the child to release them in a sheltered atmosphere. If, however, the issue is of a deeper, more unconscious nature, the parent will not accept this explanation and will argue further or express her anxieties by some such statement as: "I'm not sure you really understand my Johnny. He's really a nasty kid. I'm afraid that if I allow him to hit that punching bag, he's going to go wild and I'll never be able to control him." The therapist could go into a lengthy exploration of these feelings, but doing so would, at this point, take more time away from the didactic presentation than is desirable. The therapist might, instead, begin to explore these feelings and then return to the didactic material, or acknowledge the feeling and encourage the parent to pursue it in future meetings and then go on with the didactic presentation. The former reaction might involve a statement such as "Your son's fighting really bothers you," followed by a brief discussion. The latter approach might involve a similar but more structured statement, such as: "I can see that your son's fighting bothers you, and I think it is important for you to pursue those feelings. Now, however, I'd like to return to what I was saying about the value of allowing a child to express his feelings during the play session."

Another parent may respond, "That sounds all right to me because I can control him, but I'm afraid that if Johnny sees a punching bag in a session with my wife he'll go amuck because she can't control him. She never has!" This can stimulate an argument between the parents that could go on for quite a while. If it were not for the necessity of covering the didactic material, this argument might be worth pursuing. Here again a statement that both reflects and interprets the parents' behavior might be made, such as: "Johnny's fighting certainly is upsetting to both of you and I can see how, based on both of your reactions here, his fighting leads to your getting into fights with each other. I think that's worth following up on. These are the kinds of issues we want to discuss in a few weeks when you folks better understand the materials I'm teaching you. Right now I'd like to say a few words about how you parents might deal with the few rules we have in the sessions, since we're talking about controls and losing control."

As can be seen from the preceding illustration, it is important to be able to find a balance between the dynamic and didactic elements, especially in these first few training sessions. The dynamic or emotional component will interfere with the learning of the didactic material if it is not sufficiently attended to. (A more detailed discussion of this issue is presented in Andronico et al., 1967). On the other hand, it is necessary to cover the didactic material in a short period of time. If the group takes three or four sessions to cover the didactic material and does not get to the actual demonstration of a play session by the second or third session, the didactic material tends to be heard by the parents as very abstract, and motivation on their part diminishes.

Each therapist must find his own comfortable and effective balance between these two pressures. The balance may be—and probably should be—a shifting one as the group progresses, since the amount of didactic material to be presented is most pronounced in the first session and gradually diminishes. My rule of thumb, which is applicable in all situations involving the combination of teaching and emotional reactions, is to proceed with the teaching as long as the voice the parents hear coming from me is louder than the voice they hear coming from inside themselves. That is, a person will be receptive to hearing and learning so long as his emotional reactions are below a certain level. Once his feelings rise above that level, it becomes very difficult, if not impossible, for him to listen to and absorb new materials. At this point the therapist must put aside the didactic material and deal with the emotional reactions of the parent in question. Once the emotional reaction has been dealt with sufficiently to allow the "inner voice" of the parents' emotions to be reduced in volume below the voice of the therapist, the therapist can resume her teaching role.

Where exactly is the point at which the voice of the therapist and the parents' "inner voices" meet? How much time and therapeutic attention must be given to someone whose inner voice has become a shriek to enable it to settle down to a whisper? These are crucial questions, yet they are impossible to answer on an absolute basis. The therapist's clinical judgment is the best tool to evaluate these situations, and each therapist arrives at her own way of deciding when to intervene therapeutically and when to proceed didactically. Experience, of course, is very helpful, and the more experience one has with this approach, as with most others, the more proficient one usually becomes.

The Demonstration Play Session

By the end of the first group meeting the didactic material usually has been covered. The therapist can suggest at that time that some parent bring in a child the following week for a demonstration play session with the therapist. Usually several parents will volunteer their children, giving the therapist a choice. She will by this time have seen some of the children, read all their cases, and met their parents, so she is in a good position to choose a child likely to provide an active or quiet session, as she prefers.

Assuming that all or most of the didactic material has been covered in the first group meeting, the second meeting can begin with the completion of the didactic material or a brief review, followed by a demonstration play session of 20 or 30 minutes depending on the amount of time left. It is important to leave an additional 20 or 30 minutes after the play session for the parents to discuss it.

The demonstration play session can be held in a variety of settings. If the parent group is meeting at a community mental health facility, the play session can be held in a standard playroom with observation facilities. These include an adjacent room with one-way glass and sound transmission from which parents can observe and hear the play session. If the facility does not have these accommodations, two adjacent rooms can be used and an attempt made to approximate the one-way glass and sound transmission by building a wooden frame to fit the doorway between the playroom and the adjacent observation room and stretching over it an inexpensive gauze material. With the light in the observation room off, most of the light from the playroom will be reflected back, while the sound will go directly through the cloth. This arrangement can also be used in a private office where the therapist has an adjacent room, such as a waiting room.

In those rare circumstances when there are neither two adjacent rooms available nor any alternative such as videotape or closed-circuit television a large office room will have to suffice. The parents can be placed at one end of the office while the play session is held at the other. Children are initially inhibited by this arrangement, but after a few minutes—once they get involved in their play—they tend to ignore the observing parents. It is helpful under these circumstances to have the play-session portion of the room lit and the portion where the parents are observing unlit.

The therapist should mention the observing parents when he explains the play session to the child. I generally say something like: "Hi, Jennifer, I'm Dr. Mike. You and I are going to be playing here for 30 minutes. This is going to be a different kind of play. Your parents don't know how to play in this new way, and that's why they are coming here. They want to learn this new way of play so they can play this way with you at home. These other parents are also coming here to learn this so they can play this way at home with their own children. This is going to be your session. I'm not going to tell you what to do or how to play. In here, you can do almost anything you want to do. If you have any questions, feel free to ask me. I'll tell you when there are five minutes left and when the session's over."

This begins the demonstration play session. When the session is over, the therapist discusses the session with the parents. Parents usually have many questions and observations. For some parents, the session provides answers to questions: "Now I know what you mean when you say that allowing the child free expression doesn't lead to worse behavior, because after he spent five minutes hitting that punching bag he moved over to the puppets and had one puppet hold the other in a very affectionate manner." For other parents it serves as a means of getting their questions clarified: "When Jennifer kept looking at the dart gun, all you said was 'You're looking at the gun' and 'You're looking closely at the gun.' Why didn't you say it was all right to play with the gun or tell her to play with the gun, since that's what I thought she wanted to do?" The therapist can then explain that suggestions and directions are not part of play therapy, that the child will get more from self-discovery, and that in this instance Jennifer benefited more from deciding for herself that she wanted to use the gun than if the therapist had decided for her.

Following the questions, the therapist might briefly interpret or explain portions of the session: "As some of you probably noticed, Jenifer did take a lot of time deciding to pick up and shoot the dart gun. She was probably afraid of my reaction if she did it, or was waiting to see if I would suggest to her that she play with it. By my reflecting to her that she was looking at it and staring at it, I indirectly gave my permission and was consistent with the idea that this was her session and that I would not tell her what to do. Once she got up the courage to try it, she seemed happy, which I also reflected by saying, 'You're happy now that you've picked up the gun' and later, 'You're really enjoying shooting the gun.' This is a good illustration of how the accepting atmosphere of the play sessions allows a child to discover and explore his feelings. It also illustrates how allowing the child to express these feelings reduces their intensity and thereby reduces the possibility of their expression outside the session." It is helpful here to stress that the parents do not have to accept acting-out behavior outside of the play sessions. This helps the child to differentiate between appropriate and nonappropriate settings where he can and cannot express these feelings.

The second group meeting ends with the didactic material having been covered and the parents having had a chance to see the theory put into practice. The therapist can now select another child for the demonstration portion of the third group meeting. He can ask the parents to decide, or he can himself make the decision. It is usually best to get a child with a different style to provide a contrast, so a younger, aggressive boy might follow a session with an older, more passive girl.

The same procedure is usually followed during the third group meeting. After a brief review of the didactic material, the therapist might ask the parents of the child at the previous week's demonstration play session what the child's reactions were on the way home and during the week. Following this discussion, the therapist again has a demonstration play session. The same introduction is given to this child by the therapist, and this play session is also discussed by the parent group.

Parent Demonstration Play Sessions

By the end of the third group session, at least one parent is usually eager to try a play session herself. If the therapist concurs, based on his observation of the parent's participation in the first three group meetings, that parent may be asked to bring her child the next week. If the therapist is dubious about this parent, he may hesitate and ask if any other parents would like to have a play session during the next week's meeting. If other parents volunteer, the therapist may select one of them and suggest to the parent who originally volunteered that this second parent's child would be more appropriate (easier to work with, etc.) for a first demonstration session and that the original volunteer might have the play session the week after.

By this fourth session, the therapist has a pretty good idea how well group members understand the theory of the play sessions. The therapist may elect not to review the didactic principles at the beginning of the fourth session if he thinks the group has learned them sufficiently well, or he may choose to review these principles again if he thinks the group needs more review.

It is important for the therapist to be supportive of the parent who is going to conduct her first demonstration play session. He can say something like: "Don't worry about it, you'll make mistakes but that's all right, you'll do fine," or "If I thought you could have a session without a mistake, you wouldn't need to be here to learn, you would be home doing it already." It is particularly helpful to point out that there may be many different reflections that one might make during the play session and if one worries too much about having said something slightly inaccurate or not having said something soon enough, one is likely to have difficulty making good reflections the next few times, since the action can proceed rapidly in a play session.

The therapist should continue to be supportive of this parent after the play session. He might point out all or most of the positive points of the play session before making suggestions for changing or modifying certain behaviors. The other parents are usually supportive as well, which is also helpful to the parent who conducted the play session. If a parent is not supportive but attacking, this may be indicative of the feelings that these two group members have toward each other, or at least that the attacking member has for the other. The therapist may use this as a way of beginning to spend more time on group interactions by saying something like: "John, you really seem to be very critical of Bill," or "You two seem to be continuing with the feelings you expressed last week."

If the therapist thinks that more discussion of the play session is important, he may put a temporary hold on the members' interactions by saying: "John, you really seem angry at Bill, and I can see that you also have feelings on this, Bill. Right now, I'd like to spend some more time discussing the play session, and if we have time later perhaps we can pursue this more or, if not, you two may want to discuss this further next week."

At the end of the fourth meeting, the group may take one of many different directions. The parent who had the play session, if it was a good one, may be given the option of having a play session at home and discussing it the following week. In that case, the parent must purchase the play-session toys for the home play sessions, as the group had discussed in the didactic sessions. She will return the following week with her notebook, in which she will have written notes following (not during) each play session and discuss these notes so that other parents and the therapist can make comments and suggestions.

If the therapist feels that the parent should wait another week or two before starting at home, the therapist can say that. In those rare instances when the therapist has strong misgivings about a parent's beginning the play sessions at home, the therapist can suggest to this parent that they have another play session during the parent group with a simple supportive statement like: "I think you'd get more out of another demonstration play session before you get started at home. Maybe you can bring Ellyn back next week or the following week and have another play session with her here and then start at home."

Another choice that the therapist has at the end of the fourth meeting is to have two demonstration play sessions during the fifth meeting. These can be 20 to 30 minutes in length and can be variously arranged: one child may have one session with the therapist and a second session with her parent; or one child may have separate sessions with each of her parents; or two different children may each have one session with a parent. At this point the therapist's judgment of the progress of the group is important. If he feels that the group is moving slowly in picking up the didactic material and applying it, he may opt to have fewer and longer demonstration play sessions. He may even decide to give more demonstration sessions himself with more children.

On the other hand, if the group is progressing rapidly, the therapist may choose to have two demonstration sessions in the fifth meeting and two in each of the meetings thereafter until all the parents have had opportunities to be seen by the therapist and the other parent. It is highly recommended that each parent be given an opportunity to have a play session observed by the therapist and the other parents before he or she begins home play sessions.

Some therapists may prefer to have the entire group conduct demonstration play sessions before any begin the home play sessions, while others may allow parents to begin home sessions after they have had successful demonstration sessions in the group. The latter course has the advantage that there are not so many initial home play sessions to concentrate on in one group meeting because the home sessions are begun in staggered fashion.

The fifth, sixth, and subsequent meetings in the initial training phase of the filial-therapy group gradually lead into the middle phase. It is not possible to delimit the training phase by number of sessions, since some groups are smaller than others, some spend more time on personal issues in the first few meetings, and some need more teaching and demonstration time than others.

The Middle Phase of Filial Therapy

As the parent group moves from the training phase into the middle phase, all the parents will have had at least one demonstration session that has been observed by the therapist and the other parents. This is important in the middle phase because the therapist has seen the interaction between each child and her parent and is therefore better able to supervise the parents' home play sessions. The most characteristic part of this middle phase is the beginning of the filial therapy group's evolution into a combination supervisory and therapy group. During the first few meetings in this phase (from approximately session eight or ten to session thirteen or fifteen), the emphasis is usually on the supervision of the home play sessions while some time is kept available for the group-therapy aspect of the meetings.

Supervision of the Home Play Sessions

As has been previously mentioned, the parents take notes after each of their home play sessions. They are told to number and date each session and are encouraged to review their notes periodically to see if they notice any trends developing in the sessions. For example, a parent might say: "I was wondering why Sally had the alligator bite the mother's head off so vehemently last week, and when I looked over my notes I began to realize that she has been showing some form of anger at the mother puppet for the past three or four sessions, starting with her shooting it with the dart gun four sessions ago."

Most therapists experienced in supervising beginning practitioners in play therapy, or any form of psychotherapy, can find supervising parents a refreshing change. There is usually very little competition with the therapist because the parents readily acknowledge her as their teacher and have very little at stake in trying to outdo her. There is little competition among the parents themselves because they usually have a supportive group feeling; they are all trying to learn how to conduct the play sessions and improve their own skills while helping others to improve theirs. A positive attitude on the part of the therapist is essential to the establishment and continuance of this feeling of group cohesiveness and mutual support. An additional note in supervising parents is that it is easy to grasp what is happening in the home play sessions by listening to how the parents read their notes as well as to what the notes contain. Parents do not know enough to be able to conceal their mistakes and omissions. Furthermore, most parents are not interested in hiding their mistakes. They sincerely want to develop their play-therapy skills so that their children can improve more quickly.

In general, most therapists can get a clear picture of the home play sessions by listening attentively to the parents' presentations and discussions of them. If some questions remain, the therapist may ask a parent to take very detailed notes at the next home play session or two. If questions still remain after this, the therapist may ask the parent to bring the child to the next group session and have a play session there, at which the therapist and the other parents may come up with insights into the problem. Of course, the therapist can elect at any time to suggest that a parent bring in a child for a play session during the parent group meeting. Some therapists have play sessions as a regular part of their ongoing parent groups or have play sessions at every other meeting. I prefer to utilize this time for more group therapy interaction among the parents, but here again each therapist must make his own decision based on his own clinical judgment.

I recommended that parents give all children of play-therapy age in their families separate play sessions. This is helpful in removing the stigma of "problem child" from the initially referred child. It is also desirable from a preventive point of view since it prevents or reduces the probability of problems occurring in the other children. Moreover, it helps alleviate and reduce problems that are beginning to develop in some of the siblings but have been unnoticed because of the more pronounced problems of the referral child.

The Group-Therapy Aspect of the Middle Phase

As the parents get more comfortable in their roles as play therapists at home with their children and the therapist sees that the parents are improving their play-therapy skills in acceptable ways, more time can be spent discussing the parents' reactions to their children, to each other, and to other aspects of their lives. When a couple attends a filial therapy group, issues concerning their relationship with each other come up fairly quickly, especially through the play sessions. When a child is having play sessions with both parents, these parents will often use the sessions as a focus for their own anger toward each other. A father, for example, may accuse his wife of not being firm enough with their aggressive son: "If you would put your foot down with Dave, he wouldn't be getting into trouble." This child may be inhibited in his play sessions with his father and express a lot of hostility in his play sessions with his mother. The father may take this as proof that he is appropriately firm with the boy whereas the mother is too lenient: "You see, it's just what I've been saying all along, you're his problem, and if you were stricter outside the play sessions Dave wouldn't be showing such hostility during the play sessions." The wife may reply that the father is too strict and, if it weren't for her "appropriate" approach, the boy would have worse problems. The group aspect of filial therapy becomes important here because other parents begin to react to these situations. Other parents may take one side of the argument or the other, saying something like: "John, you're too strict. If you got off your wife's and son's backs, you all would be better off" or "Mary, why don't you listen to John, he's right after all."

This may also stimulate other couples in the group. One mother recently said to the father mentioned above: "John, why don't you stop it? You remind me of my husband, who's always complaining about my handling of my daughter." Her husband in turn defended John, and the debate was on. As in other group-therapy situations, the intervention of other group members can often be more valuable than the intervention of a spouse. One father, for example, was very disappointed and angry that his son was drawing flowers in his play sessions and generally not following his father's wishes outside the play sessions. This father recounted a play session in which he related very well to his son in his role as play therapist but, as soon as the session had ended, began to order his son about tyrannically. Another parent in this group, a mother who had interacted positively with this father in previous meetings, said to him: "You know, Erik, when it comes to your son, you're really a bastard!" This father got much more upset when she said that than when his wife, sitting next to him, said similar things. He became defensive and, turning to the therapist, insisted, "He said I can do anything I want to outside the play sessions as long as I follow the rules in the play sessions."

Here is a big advantage of the group-therapy aspect of filial therapy. The therapist agreed with this father and supported him, saying that at this time in the group all that was required was to learn to play the therapist's role. A few weeks later this man's wife reported that her husband was beginning to relate better and less harshly to their son, and the husband himself confirmed this. This illustrates how the group-therapy aspect can allow for a direct challenge from other group members that would be difficult for a therapist to make, and it also places the therapist in a supportive role.

The Third Phase

The third phase of filial therapy is basically an extension of the middle stage, with the opportunity now to include some additional options, especially more didactic material. The format of the third phase combines group supervision of the home play sessions with group therapy for the patients, with increasing stress on the latter element. Since the parents have had several months to learn and practice play therapy, the supervisory element becomes less crucial and more time can be spent on group therapy. Some of the material for group therapy is provided by the parents' reactions to the play sessions. A mother, for example, said in one meeting, "I used to think that I didn't pay much attention to Billy because I was busy with the baby and I had a lot of housework to do. Now, however, when I have the 45 minutes set aside for the play session and my husband is watching the baby and there are no distractions, I still find it difficult to pay attention to what Billy says and does. At first I thought it was because I was learning how to conduct the play sessions, but now I realize that I have a lot of trouble paying attention to Billy. I'm going to have to start giving that kid more of my time." Another parent responded, "I'm glad you said that, Jane, because I've begun to feel that I like my play sessions with Sally; but when Jimmy has his sessions I daydream an awful lot and have to work real hard to concentrate on making accurate reflections. I wonder why we're having so much trouble with our sons."

At this point a third parent said, "I'm surprised you said that, Milly. I could see that Jane felt that way a few weeks ago when she had her play session here in front of the group, and I even said it then, but I didn't see anything like that with you. Besides, you two worry too much. Let the kids take care of themselves." This started a heated debate with both of the other parents retorting that this parent didn't care enough for her own child and that she should pay more attention to her son.

Expanding the Therapy Role to Include Spouses

By this time, the parents have learned the techniques of empathically relating to their children during the play sessions according to the nondirective Rogerian therapy principles they have been taught. The focus has been on the empathic reflection of feelings that the children express in the play sessions, primarily around the play of toys. During the course of the training meetings and the middle phase of filial therapy, some parents will jokingly comment that they themselves should be having these play sessions or something similar.

Since these parents already possess the basic knowledge and skills of empathic listening with regard to their children, it is possible, if the therapist so desires, to teach these parents to modify what they have learned in order to have therapy sessions for and with each other. This kind of therapy is best suited to the couples in the group. Each spouse take the empathic listening role and reflects whatever feelings her mate expresses for the "therapy" session of 30 minutes. Then the spouses exchange roles, and the mate who was expressing her feelings now listens empathically and reflects the feelings expressed by her mate (B.G. Guerney, 1977). Other parents whose spouses are not in the group can also learn this adaptation of the skills they have already learned by practicing empathic listening with another group member.

Additional Didactic Material

Once the basic model of the empathic role has been taught to the parents in a filial therapy group, the therapist can introduce additional didactic material, such as behavior modification techniques. These techniques are particularly effective in conjunction with filial therapy since the children's emotional reactions to a behavior modification program can be readily dealt with in play sessions.

For example, a parent wanted her son to brush his teeth regularly, but he resisted. When a behavior modification program was begun, the boy stubbornly refused to brush his teeth unless he was prompted. After a few play sessions in which the boy expressed much rebellion and anger, however, the boy began to respond rapidly to the behavior modification program and the problem was soon eliminated.

The parents' resistances to utilizing these techniques can be dealt with in their own group sessions. What the therapist chooses to teach a particular group will of course be determined by his clinical judgment.

Ending the Filial Therapy Group

By the time one year has elapsed, the parents in a filial therapy group should have covered a great deal of material. They should have become proficient in the conduct of the home play sessions. They should have had ample opportunity to discuss and otherwise deal with their own feelings about their children. They should also have had ample opportunity to discuss and deal with their feelings about themselves, other parents in the group, and other important aspects of their lives. Their children should have been substantially improved by this time.

For those children and parents whose progress has been sufficient, the end of therapy can be planned for the end of one year. These parents can be encouraged to keep the time set aside for play sessions and to spend it with their children, using a modified play-session approach. This approach consists of empathic reflection but without the toys. It is basically a more informal time together in an activity of the child's choosing, such as going for a walk, playing a game, etc. In this way, even though formal therapy ends with the cessation of the play sessions and the parents no longer attend the parents' group, the children and the parents have the opportunity of continuing a therapeutic dialogue.

For those children who have not progressed as well as could be hoped, an additional few weeks or months of home play sessions might be the answer. This determination is made if a child appears to be progressing steadily, or if a child got off to a slow start but now appears to be progressing satisfactorily. The therapist may combine the parents of these children with some from another group or two and conduct this new group for a few more weeks or months. This is usually difficult in private practice, but it is practical in an agency setting where several groups may be going on at the same time.

In some instances, the problems of the children may be resolved but the parents may want to continue therapy for themselves. These parents may join parents from other filial therapy groups who feel the same way, or they may be referred to a short-term or an ongoing psychotherapy group.

Another way of terminating therapy is to encourage those parents who are ready to stop in less than one year to do so. These can then be replaced by new parents just beginning filial therapy. The beginning parents can benefit from the experience of the more advanced parents in the group and can derive encouragement from their progress. In turn, the advanced parents can benefit from quick reviews of the didactic materials, and they are encouraged by the realization of how far they and their children have come when they see the beginning parents and their children.

References

Andronico, M. P., & Blake, I. The application of filial therapy to young children with stuttering problems. *Journal of Speech and Hearing Disorders*, 1971, *36*(3), 377–380.

Andronico, M. P., Fidler, J., Guerney, B. G., Jr., & Guerney, L. The combination of didactic and dynamic elements in filial therapy. *International Journal of Group Psychotherapy*, 1967, *17*(1), 10–17.

Andronico, M. P., & Guerney, B. G., Jr. The potential application of filial therapy to the school situation. *Journal of School Psychology*, 1967, *6*(1), 2–7.

Andronico, M. P., & Guerney, B. G., Jr. A psychotherapeutic aide in a Headstart program. *Children*, 1969, *16*(1), 14–22.

Fidler, J., Guerney, B. G., Jr., Andronico, M. P., & Guerney, L. Filial therapy as a logical extension of current trends in psychotherapy. In B. G. Guerney, Jr. (Ed.), *Psychotherapeutic agents: New roles for nonprofessionals, parents, and teachers*. New York: Holt, Rinehart & Winston, 1969.

Ginsberg, B. Parents as therapeutic agents: The usefulness of filial therapy in a community psychiatric clinic. *American Journal of Community Psychology*, 1976, *4*(1), 47–54.

Ginsberg, B. G., Stutman, S. S., & Hummel, J. Notes for practice: Group filial therapy. *Social Work*, 1978, *23*(2), 154–156.

Guerney, B. G., Jr. Filial therapy: Description and rationale. *Journal of Consulting Psychology*, 1964, *28*(4), 303–310.

Guerney, B. G., Jr. Filial therapy used as a treatment method for disturbed children. *Evaluation*, 1976, *3*(1-2), 34–35.

Guerney, B. G., Jr. *Relationship enhancement: Skill-training programs for therapy, problem prevention, and enrichment*. San Francisco: Jossey-Bass, 1977.

Guerney, B. G., Jr., & Andronico, M. P. Comments on commentary concerning a psychotherapeutic aide in a Headstart program. *Children*, 1969, *16*(2), 86–87.

Guerney, B. G., Jr., Guerney, L., & Andronico, M. Filial therapy. *Yale Scientific Magazine*, 1966, *40*, 6–14.

Guerney, B. G., Jr., Guerney, L., & Stover, L. Facilitative therapist attitudes in training parents as psychotherapeutic agents. *Family Coordinator*, 1972, *21*(3), 275–278.

Guerney, L. Filial therapy program. In D. H. Olson (Ed.), *Treating relationships*. Lake Mills, Iowa: Graphic Publishing, 1976.

Guerney, L. F. Filial therapy. In R. Herink (Ed.), *The psychotherapy handbook*. New York: New American Library, 1980.

Guerney, L., Stover, L., & Guerney, B. G., Jr. Play therapy: A training manual for parents. In C. E. Schaefer (Ed.), *Therapeutic use of child's play*. New York: Jason Aronson, 1976.

Stover, L., & Guerney, B. G., Jr. The efficacy of training procedures for mothers in filial therapy. *Psychotherapy: Theory, Research and Practice*, 1967, *4*(3), 110–115.

NOTE: The author wishes to express his gratitude to Barbara Dazzo, M.S.W., for her editorial comments.

2

A Group for Parents of
Autistic Children

Carol J. Samit, M.S.W.

CAROL J. SAMIT is senior psychiatric social worker and assistant coordinator of the Family Crisis Program within the division of Child and Adolescent Psychiatry at North State University Hospital–Cornell Medical Center in Manhasset, New York.

Infantile autism is characterized by deviant behavior and uneven development. It manifests varied and severe symptomatology throughout life (Ornitz & Ritvo, 1976). The condition is probably present at birth; symptoms usually become obvious before 30 months of age. A higher incidence of males than females are diagnosed, and in a small number of reported cases there has been more than one autistic child in the same family.

There are nine basic symptoms: (1) impairment of social relationships, exhibited as gross withdrawal or undifferentiated attachment to persons; (2) lack of communicative language with distortions in development of speech, which may be delayed, echolalic, or perseverative; (3) preference for and preoccupation with inanimate objects that are used in a ritualistic manner; (4) extreme resistance to change, with an obsessive desire for maintaining the sameness of the environment; (5) lack of personal identity, failure to respond to name, inability to identify body parts or boundaries; (6) abnormal perceptual experiences, poor eye contact, sensitivity to loud noises and changes in temperature, and insensitivity to pain; (7) distortion in mobility, often seen as the use of the body in a fragmented or disjointed way; (8) frequent illogical anxiety; and (9) overall mental retardation with islets of normality or superior mental functioning (Creak, 1964; Kanner, 1942–43).

Autistic children differ in the number and severity of symptoms they exhibit. With increasing age, some aspects of the handicap may improve (Wing, 1974). However, long-term studies have shown prognosis to be poor (Kanner, 1971), with at least 90 percent of autistic children functioning on a retarded level as adolescents and young adults (DeMyer et al., 1973). To date, it has not been determined that improvement of the condition is related to any one form of therapy. Spontaneous improvements as well as regressions are likely to occur despite the treatment modality (Schopler & Reichler, 1976). Prognosis appears better for the child who develops speech before the age of 5, has an IQ of at least 60, and has the least number of symptoms (Ornitz & Ritvo, 1976).

The parental decision to institutionalize the child or maintain him at home appears to depend on four factors: (1) the degree of retardation; (2) the adverse effect the child has on the integrity of the family, particularly in view of the emotional needs of siblings; (3) the availability of familial and community supports; and (4) the behavioral-management skills of the parents.

The need for parental education, emotional support, and behavioral-management training cannot be overemphasized. For many years, parental handling was considered to be the cause of autism (Ornitz & Ritvo, 1976). More recently, the parents' difficulties have been viewed as reactions to the stressful family situation rather than the causative factors of the child's deviant functioning. Regardless of the etiology, it can safely be said that the autistic child upsets the family equilibrium. Coping with the child can tax the best of parents to the point where they experience anxiety and confusion. This will happen concurrently with expressions of concern with how they can help their child.

The Parents' Group: Objectives, Methods, Limits

This article describes a group for parents of autistic children conducted from 1975 to 1979 at Bellevue Psychiatric Hospital in New York City in conjunction with a psychiatric nursery unit under the direction of Magda Campbell, M.D., to which severely disturbed young autistic children were admitted for treatment. The children, ranging in age from 2 to 6 years, were admitted for a comprehensive diagnostic workup and a trial of intensive treatment. The treatment milieu included a highly structured nursery program consisting of special education, dance, music, and occupational therapies. Psychopharmacology and behavioral therapy were the major treatment interventions.

The object of the parents' group was to improve the parents' ability to cope with the manifold personal and family stresses occasioned by the presence of the autistic child and to arrive at a resolution or acceptance of the problem. It sought to do this in two ways. First, it provided a forum for the sharing of concerns and experiences with other parents of autistic children and for open discussion with the professional staff. These exchanges reduced the parents' feelings of isolation, guilt, and despair. Second, it afforded the staff an opportunity to train the parents in behavioral-management techniques so that they could assume greater control in managing the daily lives of their children. The literature supports the belief that parents can be successfully employed as agents of change in the development of their autistic children (DeMyer, 1979; Fenichel, 1974; Gajzago & Prior, 1974; Mahon & Battin, 1978; Paluszny, 1979; Schopler & Reichler, 1971; Whittaker, 1975). At the same time that increased parental competence benefits their children, it allays the parents' hopelessness and stress and contributes to their movement toward resolution or acceptance.

The parents' group was composed of mothers, fathers, and (occasionally) extended-family members and of staff—psychiatric residents, nurses, aides, teachers, and social workers. No parent was excluded from the group, regardless of his or her mental health status. The group, which met weekly, was fluid; parents entered as their children were admitted to the hospital and terminated when their children were discharged. Generally, there was a nucleus of six to eight parents, mostly mothers, who continued to meet for 10 to 12 weeks. The interdisciplinary staff members who were actively involved in the group contributed their expertise, experience, and guidance.

A social worker and a nurse functioned as group leaders, encouraging the emergence of parent leaders. The topics for discussion were generally chosen by the group leaders in response to the parents' needs and the staff's suggestions. These usually revolved around promoting each child's maximum independent functioning. During the course of these discussions, leaders usually encouraged examination of parental feelings as they related to the handling of difficult and disturbing situations. But they avoided probing deeper problems that would be better treated in individual therapy.

Because parents joined the group to learn how to help their children, the main object of group discussion was to instruct the parents in the techniques of behavior management. Feister and DeMyer (1961) demonstrated that the limited repertoires of previously unreachable autistic children could be extended through the use of behavior modification. Behavioral techniques used in the treatment of autistic children include positive reinforcement; extinction; time out; aversion conditioning; and shaping.

Food, candy, or affection is used as a *positive reinforcer* to encourage the continuance of a desired behavior. In the nursery it was used to encourage behaviors such as the naming of objects in a book, identifying parts of the body, or repeating words as instructed.

An undesired behavior may be *extinguished* by ignoring the child. This technique was used in a situation in which a child repeatedly removed his clothing during nap time. In this situation, it was more beneficial to ignore the behavior than to interfere with the establishment of a rest-period routine.

Time-out, also commonly employed, requires the isolation of the child after each occurrence of an undesired behavior, such as screaming or temper outbursts. This usually necessitated the child's removal from the stimulating situation to a chair at the edge of the nursery's playroom. During the initial occurrences, a nurse's aide was generally required to sit behind the child to maintain compliance. Often, within a few trials, the child learned the routine and the undesired behavior was moderated and then eliminated. Consistency is essential for successful modification of behavior using this technique, especially in regard to temper outbursts.

Aversive conditioning is employed in the form of a sharp "No!" to intervene in a behavior that requires an immediate response. This behavioral technique is used when a child is engaged in a potentially dangerous activity, such as attempting to climb onto a shelf, hurting another child, or running away. Aversive conditioning may also require holding a child firmly so he/she cannot complete the action. It may be employed in treating a child who is involved in self-mutilating behavior.

Shaping a child's behavior is a much-employed behavior modifier. A child's behavior may be shaped by modeling, a procedure commonly used to teach various skills such as throwing a ball or playing with a toy appropriately. By holding the child's face so that eye contact can be made, the child can be taught to mouth and then repeat the words spoken by the teacher.

Behaviors that are particularly amenable to a behavior modification approach are the acquisition of social, self-help, and language skills. The development of motor skills and appropriate play behavior can also be taught by the behavioral approach.

Following group sessions, the parents were invited to participate in the nursery program where the teaching and nursing staffs modeled skills and reinforcement techniques that the parents could continue to employ at home. A specific behavioral objective had been formulated for each child. For example, a behavioral objective for one child engaging in stereotyped movements might have been to teach that child an adaptive skill. To accomplish this, a parent would be encouraged to intervene in the child's stereotyped activity, such as hand flapping or spinning of an object. By placing his or her hand over the child's, the parent could guide the child into an adaptive activity such as stacking blocks, inserting a peg in a hole, or drawing a circle with a crayon. The child's self-stimulating behavior was decreased, and the parent was reassured to learn that he or she could be an effective teacher.

Stages to Resolution or Acceptance

The parent who assumed a teaching role could develop some hope that, although the child was limited, he or she could profit from treatment and training. The process by which the parents reached that understanding was not an easy one. Awareness of the severity of the disability, and acceptance of the child as he or she was, required parents to move through various stages of a grief process. These stages were neither separate entities nor sequential in nature. Rather, they overlapped and recurred with varying frequency and duration. The very nature of autism, namely, its unevenness, contributed to these recurring stages. A question posed by a mother illustrates the potential for despair. Her child, a 9-year-old boy, was being seen for a reevaluation three years after he had been discharged from the hospital. At the time of the child's follow-up interview, the mother asked, "It's never-ending, isn't it?"

To arrive at the stage that closely resembled acceptance or resolution required that the family experience the stages of shock, denial, shame, guilt, anger, and depression; shock appeared to be the only stage that was time-limited.

Shock or Disbelief

Generally, there was a common order of events which finally led to the parents' arrival at the unit seeking aid. A number of the parents had sensed that something was wrong with their child since infancy. Commonly, the height of their concern occurred when the child was 2 or 3 years old and the parents were upset by the child's delayed development, particularly with regard to communicative speech. Up to that time, the more subtle symptoms may have been overlooked or denied. The child may have been described as appearing to be "in a world of his own," with parents tending to interpret this withdrawal as the result of a hearing loss. Early consultations with family, friends, and members of the medical community often were not reassuring. The parents may have been counseled to "wait and see, he'll outgrow it," or told that they, as parents, were "overconcerned and anxious." This advice was hardly a comfort to the distressed parents.

In their pursuit of an answer, parents may have sought a hearing evaluation, a neurological consultation, and a psychiatric examination. Confirmation of the diagnosis of autism may be too threatening an experience for some parents; they may reject it and look for a "better diagnosis." This, a not-uncommon experience, can be exemplified by the case of Mrs. T, whose 3-year-old son had been referred to the psychiatric nursery by the hospital's Department of Pediatrics. Mrs. T was reluctant to observe the therapeutic nursery program when she was invited to do so. Maintaining that her child's mannerisms did not bear any resemblance to the behaviors exhibited by the other children, she withdrew him from the chair in which he was rocking and held him close to her. She was guarded and defensive, declaring she could not understand why it was suggested that her child be evaluated in the psychiatric nursery. She was determined to enroll him in a day-care program where "he would be understood."

Some parents were so overwhelmed that they were eager to relinquish child-care responsibilities altogether. Bewildered by their children's behaviors and overwhelmed by the energy and patience required to care for them, these parents admitted their children to the psychiatric nursery unit without apparent hesitation. These burdened parents, eager to turn over custodial responsibilities to the nursing staff, frequently opted for the inpatient hospital status rather than day-patient status. Upon the child's admission, and for a period following, they visited their children on an irregular and infrequent basis.

Without doubt, a child's admission to a psychiatric hospital was an anxiety-provoking period for the parents (Adams, 1976). The admission was viewed by many parents as their last hope for a cure or recovery. The stressfulness of the situation was too much for some parents to bear without having serious effect upon their own mental health. A small number of parents we saw were themselves admitted for psychiatric treatment or referred to an appropriate mental health clinic shortly after diagnosis.

Mrs. K, a Hungarian-born science teacher, had arrived in this country with her husband four years earlier. Her family and friends remained abroad. She was unable to secure employment commensurate with her level of education and had difficulty making new acquaintances because she felt that she could not speak English well. She looked forward to the birth of her child, hoping to settle down to family life in her new country and make friends with other young mothers.

From her son's early infancy, Mrs. K recognized that he was not developing normally and she sought professional help for him. As he grew older and his developmental problems became more apparent, Mrs. K spent less time in the neighborhood park, avoiding neighbors whose friendship she had earlier craved. She was removed from family and friends and felt isolated in her new country because of her deviant child. After visits to various professionals, Mrs. and Mr. K were referred to the psychiatric nursery unit. Jay, their child, was 27 months old at that time. Lacking in affect, Mrs. K described her child's behavior in detail. In response to any questions that evoked feeling, she replied that she did not understand, although her command of the English language was apparently very good. Her comments focused on Jay's deviance. She handled him in a rigid and detached manner, as if he were an object. She did not talk to him because he did not speak or respond to her. She said she felt that he did not know her as his mother.

Jay was admitted to the nursery unit as a day patient. Mrs. K eagerly joined the parents' group, intently asking questions. She emphasized her son's deviance, while staff and other parents pointed to improvements he had made, such as learning to drink from a cup and feeding himself with a spoon. As she brought Jay daily to the hospital, it was noted that her own appearance was deteriorating. She complained of loss of appetite, an inability to sleep, a lack of interest in housekeeping, and an overwhelming fear that her husband would get sick and then she would have no one. Her family doctor prescribed medication, she received individual counseling from the social worker, and she continued to attend the parents' group weekly. In time, she began to express her concern and contribute to the discussion more actively.

Within six weeks of Jay's acceptance into the unit, Mrs. K's mental health had significantly improved. She resumed taking an interest in her appearance and began to experience a full range of emotions. She also began to express some hope for the future. At one group meeting, she reviewed what she had originally experienced as a state of shock. Following numerous visits to professionals in search of an understanding of her child's problems, Mrs. K viewed Jay's admission to this psychiatric hospital day-care program as a symbol of her hope for cure or recovery, but also as a signal of the severity of the problem. She was unable to cope with the stress of the situation; his diagnosis of mental illness was too much for her to bear. With the supports available, her anxiety gradually lessened, and the feelings of isolation and hopelessness diminished. She began to mobilize her resources. She was able to participate fully in the nursery program and to learn techniques to teach her child. She recognized that movement on his part was slow but possible. She adjusted her expectations to more realistic goals. She came to view Jay as a developmentally delayed child, but she no longer focused only on his deviance.

The Ds represent another family experiencing a disabling reaction to their child's admission to the hospital. Since David was an infant, Mrs. D had observed that he failed to make eye contact or smile responsively. His body stiffened when she attempted to cuddle him. He appeared startled by outside noises (trucks, airplanes, fire engines), but failed to respond to his parents' voices. As a toddler he would sit in front of the television set watching "Sesame Street," and would scream incessantly in a high-pitched shrill voice when the television set was turned off. Mrs. D. recalls "knowing" that something was wrong since infancy. She blamed herself for David's deviance, believing that he had inherited her mental illness. His bizarre behavior was a constant reminder of her own breakdown in adolescence. Successful treatment for him represented her last hope for recovery for both of them. Shortly after David's admission to the therapeutic nursery, Mrs. D suffered a psychotic episode and was hospitalized. After Mrs. D's release from the hospital, she and her husband attempted to care for David while he continued in treatment as a day patient in the nursery. They were not able to manage, and following David's discharge he was placed in a long-term residential treatment facility.

Denial

Parents had a need to deny the severity of their child's disability, as well as the negative feelings it aroused in them. Minimizing the problem permitted them to engage in fantasy. The implications of the illness were sometimes too severe to be accepted all at once. This denial was often reinforced by the child's normal appearance. Family and friends may have been critical of the parents' handling of the child, thereby contributing to a need to deny the problem and defend the parents' performance.

Denial was manifested in numerous ways within the parents' group. Parents arrived late, missed meetings, or positioned themselves outside the group when they did attend. They did not want to see their child's limitations as being as severe as those of the other children.

Mrs. M, for example, failed to attend the first few meetings of the parents' group. During the following weeks she arrived late or sat on the side, seldom participating in the discussion except to register complaints. She minimized the significance of Paul's disturbance by declaring that his problems were limited to his slow-developing speech. She insisted that "correct" treatment would make him better. Neither the group leaders nor the other parents confronted Mrs. M. Her very presence at the meetings and her son's admission to the psychiatric nursery unit were indications that denial was not gross. In her description of her son, she maximized and exaggerated his learning abilities. She identified unintelligible sounds as specific words. She reported being successful in her attempts at establishing a toilet-training routine while minimizing the significance of frequent bowel movements on the furniture.

She described her 7-year-old daughter's attention to her brother as loving devotion. Mrs. M reported with pride that her daughter enthusiastically volunteered to spend her time teaching Paul. While attending to her own homework assignments, Janice would donate a pencil and sheets of paper and demonstrate the letters of the alphabet to her brother. The group commended her daughter's patience and efforts and queried the mother about whether she could do the same for her son. The group dealt delicately with Mrs. M's attempts to relinquish some of her child-rearing responsibilities to her young daughter.

Mrs. M's description of her children's interaction contrasted with those of the other parents, who related incidents describing the difficulties their normal children had in coping with their autistic siblings. Behavioral problems caused by the unsatisfied needs of the siblings were reported. Other parents described the embarrassment and shame their nonautistic children felt and how they avoided bringing friends into their homes. Parents also examined the burdens felt by their nonautistic children who shared in the supervisory and teaching responsibilities for the autistic sibling. Many parents related changes in the behavior of the nonautistic children due to the limited attention they received from their parents. The autistic child required the majority of the parents' attention. They related the fears expressed by some of the nonautistic children that they too would require hospitalization. During a family visit to the nursery a parent reported that her older child had asked, "When will it be my turn?"

Fathers, as well, showed evidence of denial. Mr. C brought his 3-year-old blond, blue-eyed daughter to the nursery daily. She closely resembled the "angelic looking" autistic child described in the literature. She was "normal" and healthy looking. As her father questioned, "Who would guess there was anything wrong with her?" When she was first admitted to the therapeutic nursery, Mr. C seemed compelled to convince the staff members that she would be a "good student" because she was an eager learner. He intervened whenever his wife would attempt to clarify the nature of their child's disturbance. As Gail exhibited echolalic and perseverative speech patterns, Mr. C stressed, "See, she's smart, she can speak. Just teach her the right things to say and to stop rocking and pay attention to us, then she'll be alright, right?"

Mr. C's need to deny the severity of his daughter's illness while his wife attempted to express her concerns, and Mrs. M's overwhelming need to present her family's functioning in idealistic terms served to help the other parents develop adequate reality testing and examine the effect of their children's autism on their family life. As Mrs. M began to attend the meetings more regularly, staff members focused on helping her to develop teaching skills for her child. As her son responded favorably to the teacher's consistent approach, Mrs. M began to seek staff assistance for specific behavior problems. Mr. C held on firmly to the hope for recovery, but in time this expectation was tempered with bargaining: "It's alright if she's not a teacher, there are other jobs." Though he could not easily express his concerns, he permitted his wife to do so for both of them.

Shame and Guilt

Shame and guilt could immobilize constructive action. Despite wider acceptance of the view that an autistic child's problems were not reactions to inadequate parenting, parents felt responsible. They reasoned that if it was not their parenting, then it had to be their genes that had caused the problem. They were ashamed for having produced such a child and felt guilty for having such a reaction. At the same time, they frequently had an emotional investment in a "well" child and it was difficult to accept a less-than-perfect child. The onset of symptoms was confusing and heartbreaking for the parent. In an attempt to achieve a positive response from the child, parents tried various approaches with minimal, if any, success, and often felt that what they were doing was wrong because no one supported their efforts or told them otherwise. The immediate result was to keep the child out of public view, thereby avoiding criticism and need for explanation.

Mrs. H, for example, traveled daily by bus to the nursery program with her 6-year-old daughter, Nancy, whose behavior was often characterized by inappropriate laughter and face-slapping. Mrs. H was too embarrassed to restrict her daughter's hand movements firmly and instruct her to "stop" the behavior; she would, instead, suddenly leave the bus pretending the child was ill, announcing, "Oh my, Nancy, you don't feel well today." This type of social embarrassment was commonly described by parents. They had similar experiences on family outings. Mrs. H, who had received conflicting advice with little family support, had not been successful in extinguishing inappropriate behavior and most often reacted inconsistently to her child.

The case of 6-year-old Teddy illustrates another response. His twin sister was a healthy, functioning first grader. Teddy had first been treated in the hospital when he was 3 years old. As he grew older his behavior became more stereotyped and his appearance more bizarre. He tossed his head to the side in a tic-like motion, and there was a constant drool from his mouth. He continued his tiptoe walking and hand-flapping movements. Despite the contrasting development between her two children, Mrs. O felt her son's disability was well concealed. With amazement she related to the group that while seated at a lunch counter with her son, the person to the right had bent over and whispered to her, "Oh, I know what it must be like, I have a disturbed son also." Angrily she questioned, "Of all the nerve, how could she say that?" Sadly, she added, "I didn't think it was so obvious."

The parents often felt cheated and inadequate. "Why me, why my child?" was an expression of the disappointment and anger felt by parents who were attempting to understand what had happened. They were angry at the child for being disappointing and unresponsive; they were ashamed they had produced such a child, and felt guilty for having such a reaction. As has been illustrated, an inability to express anger and disappointment inhibited the parents' ability to act as effective agents of change. They experienced difficulty in setting limits, and often infantilized the child, whom they viewed as "helpless." They did not want to show themselves as unloving parents. It was often easier for parents to blame each other than to openly express angry feelings toward the child.

Mr. and Mrs. B, for example, had great difficulty managing their 5-year-old, severely retarded autistic son, Tom. Mrs. B was depressed and tearful as she described Tom's impulsive and destructive behavior. He broke furniture, disrupted his sibling's play, hit and bit his mother. He refused to hold his mother's hand outdoors, and would dash off. He required constant supervision. Mrs. B described the difficulties she had setting limits and managing Tom's behavior when he was home on weekend passes. While she described the chaotic home life, it was apparent that Tom was more in control of his mother's behavior than she was in control of his. He would have temper tantrums, which subsided only when she beat his older brother. Tom appeared to enjoy these episodes.

It took a long time for Mrs. B to recognize her inability to express her anger at Tom. She was very angry at what she viewed as her husband's lack of involvement for not assisting in the child's care. He, in turn, accused her of being a "religious fanatic," relying on rituals, looking for a miracle. The group leaders served to lend permission for the parents to express angry feelings.

They accepted disappointment as being a normal response. Parental interaction and peer support permitted Mrs. B to express her intense fear and anxiety. She pleaded love for her helpless child and expressed her concern about how he would fare without her. She slowly moved toward understanding these feelings and how they affected her handling of her child.

Depression

Depression was an inevitable stage of the grief process that was characterized by sadness, withdrawal, and feelings of inadequacy. Repressed anger rendered the parent immobile. The parent felt helpless. The depressed feelings were an appropriate reaction to the child's poor prognosis. Parents could lend much support to one another during this stage. Grief was shared. Depression with a concomitant expression of sorrow was an extremely painful stage (for staff members as well as parents). Time was needed to express these feelings until the individual showed a readiness for movement toward acceptance or resolution. The grieving process allowed the parents to mourn for the "wished-for child," while moving toward the acceptance of the child as he or she was. This was the goal of supportive counseling. The group leaders aided in the parents' expression of sorrow.

Mr. J was an active group participant. He chastised his wife for not being firm with their son. In his view, her lack of limit-setting permitted the boy's temper outbursts to go unchecked. Mr. J was quick to point out that he had better control of the child, declaring that when he uttered a powerful "No!" the boy's behavior was inhibited. While outdoors, he went on to relate, he insisted that the child hold onto his hand and thus prevented the child from pulling away and dashing off. He questioned his wife's motivation and accused her of being an inadequate parent. She tearfully acknowledged that, indeed, he was better able to manage their son, but she pointed out that he was involved with the child only for brief periods of time. She expressed anger at her husband for not being available to her and for blaming her for their son's predicament. How could he charge her with not caring, she retorted, after all the endless hours she spent with the child. She envied his ability to get away from the problem by throwing himself into his work. This exchange allowed Mr. J to respond to his sobbing wife and share his sorrow with her: "I can't be around anymore than I am, it hurts too much. I need to get away from the pain." Mrs. J was able to understand that her husband too was suffering and that his attacks upon her reflected his inability to cope with their life's circumstances and his need to protect himself from the pain. The group process permitted this couple to open up a dialogue which was helpful to all.

As emphasized earlier, the stages of the grief process are recurrent. This is especially true during the initial phase of depression. The process permitted the parents to accept the child as he or she was and also engendered hope that the child could make some progress and was not hopeless. Although the parents' recurring sorrow was recognized by the group leaders, parents were encouraged to focus on the child's growth, no matter how minimal. The parents' efforts in working with their child despite their often only limited success were always reinforced.

At a follow-up interview, some months after her son's discharge, Mrs. L reflected upon her struggle to wean her 3-year-old son from a bottle and teach him to drink from a cup. With considerable support from the staff, Mrs. L had endured hours and days of screaming by "keeping her eye on the goal." Her confidence grew as she saw changes and improved functioning. However, the long, hard struggle was concrete evidence to her that her son was indeed retarded and disturbed.

Parents often said, "I work so hard, but I see so little change." The leaders' interventions guarded against parents being pushed too hard to develop management skills because they might begin to suffer loss of self-esteem or feel anxious and inadequate. It was not uncommon for rivalry to develop between parents and staff members when staff demonstrated behavior improvements that parents up to that time had been unable to accomplish. Soliciting information from parents in order to clarify a behavior problem served to open the lines of communication between staff members and parents. This tended to break down the almost inevitable feelings of rivalry and freed the parents to discuss problems and seek guidance. Leaders stressed that parenting a disturbed child was a very difficult task, requiring endless patience, structure, and consistency, and still might not result in modifying behavior. It was essential for parents to have a sense of control in what could be done to help their child.

The parents needed hope; they were nourished by it. The task of maintaining a balance between hope and unrealistic optimism was delicate. As parents began to recognize the significance of the prognosis, they might bargain, "If only he would grow up to be a carpenter, that's all I ask for . . ." or "If I work very hard, maybe he'll recover." Professionals needed to be extremely sensitive not to encourage unrealistic hope by minimizing the severity of the problem. Although a parent might not internalize all that was said at the time, it was important for one to describe the child realistically, as he or she was. If parents felt helpless and ineffectual, they might depend upon a "miracle cure." This could result in an endless and fruitless search for a recovery through medical gimmickry or religious fanaticism. The parent might suffer from a chronic state of depression. In efforts to help parents become more effective in managing and planning for their child, support systems needed to be encouraged. Help had to be provided in choosing and developing appropriate treatment programs.

Many families were unable to cope with their heartbreak and disappointment. Parents who failed to offer mutual support suffered great disruption and often headed toward separation and divorce within a few years of the child's diagnosis.

Acceptance or Resolution

Few parents reached full acceptance of their child's disability within the short period their child was on the unit. However, the beginning of acceptance could be seen when parents could focus on the goal of promoting their child's development with confidence and renewed energy. They assumed a greater sense of control in managing the daily life of their child. They began to recognize the child's limitations and to make realistic plans for an immediate future. They examined what they expected of themselves as parents and the impact of caring for their child on their family life. They began to understand how their feelings could interfere with the management of their child's behavior.

One parent described the process toward acceptance poignantly. Ms. T was an attractive, articulate women, the mother of Don, a 6-year-old, nonverbal autistic boy. She discussed her early need to defend herself and deny the severity of her child's deviance because of overwhelming guilt and shame. Though aware of Don's abnormal development from infancy, it took her time to admit her fears openly. As long as she had a need to protect herself, she said, she was unable to help her child. She summed up the process as long and tedious. It took her approximately three years to accept the fact that her son was retarded and disturbed. She emphasized that as long as parents are unable to talk about their child's disability or face the problems, they really cannot help him or plan for his future. She stressed that valuable time is lost. Coming to terms with Don's disability allowed her to structure his environment. The rigorous work and limits she placed on him helped in many ways. Temper tantrums were controlled; Don became a more acceptable family member who could join in family outings. He also developed self-care skills and adaptive play. His improvements were evidence of good management. Ms. T reported that the results were gratifying because they demonstrated that she could be effective in her child's growth and development.

Coming to terms with what it means to have an autistic child develops over a period of time. In the author's experience, this is a lengthy process that may take years. Not all parents are successful in reaching resolution; some may never accept the implications of the severity of their child's handicap or recognize its impact on the family life. The parent group focused on mutually shared concerns and the development of skills that enabled each parent to participate more fully in promoting his or her child's improved functioning.

Conclusion

The recognition and understanding of the progression of emotional responses that family members experience as they begin to examine the significance of the child's disability is essential for those involved in training parents to work with their children. The parent's readiness to utilize the techniques taught depends to a large extent upon the knowledge and sensitivity of the professional staff. This readiness can be enhanced by the skill of the trained workers, who should recognize that improved parental coping ability is related not only to a working through of feelings concerning their child, but also to the support systems available through the family and the community. Enabling a parent to become a more competent teacher and advocate for his or her child's welfare has significant benefits. Professionals must respond directly to the parents' expressed desire to develop specific management training skills.

References

Adams, M. A. A hospital play program: Helping children with serious illness. *American Journal of Orthopsychiatry*, 1976, *46*(3), 416–424.

Creak, M. Schizophrenic syndrome in childhood. *Developmental Medicine and Child Neurology*, 1964, *6*, 530–535.

DeMyer, M. K. *Parents and children in autism*. New York: Halsted Press, 1979.

DeMyer, M. K., Barton, S., DeMyer, W. E., Norton, J. A., Allen, J., & Steele, R. Prognosis in autism: A follow-up study. *Journal of Autism and Childhood Schizophrenia*, 1973, *3*(3), 199–246.

Feister, C., & DeMyer, M. The development of performance in autistic children in an automatically controlled environment. *Journal of Chronic Diseases*, 1961, *13*, 312–345.

Fenichel, C. Special education as the basic therapeutic tool in treatment of severely disturbed children. *Journal of Autism and Childhood Schizophrenia*, 1974, *4*(2), 177–186.

Gajzago, C., & Prior, M. Two cases of "recovery" in Kanner syndrome. *Archives of General Psychiatry*, 1974, *31*(2), 264–268.

Hingtgen, J. N., Sanders, B. J., & DeMyer, M. K. Shaping cooperative responses in early childhood schizophrenia. In L. P. Ullmann & L. Krasner (Eds.), *Case studies in behavior modification*. New York: Holt, Rinehart & Winston, 1965.

Kanner, L. Autistic disturbances of affective contact. *Nervous Child*, 1942–43, *2*(3), 217–250.

Kanner, L. Follow-up study of eleven autistic children originally reported in 1943. *Journal of Autism and Childhood Schizophrenia*, 1971, *1*(2), 119–145.

Lovaas, O. I., Litrownik, A., & Mann, R. Response latencies to auditory stimuli in autistic children engaged in self-stimulatory behavior. *Behaviour Research and Therapy*, 1971, *9*(1), 39–49.

Mahon, E., & Battin, D. Therapeutic nurseries. In B. B. Wolman (Ed.), *Handbook of Treatment of Mental Disorders in Childhood and Adolescence*. Englewood Cliffs, N.J.: Prentice-Hall, 1978.

Ornitz, E. M., & Ritvo, E. R. The syndrome of autism: A critical review. *American Journal of Psychiatry*, 1976, *133*(6), 609–621.

Paluszny, M. J. *Autism: A practical guide for parents and professionals*. Syracuse, N.Y.: Syracuse University Press, 1979.

Rutter, M. Concepts of autism: A review of research. *Journal of Child Psychology and Psychiatry,* 1968, 9(1), 1–25.

Schopler, E., Brehm, S. S., Kinsbourne, M., & Reichler, R. J. Effect of treatment structure on development in autistic children. *Archives of General Psychiatry,* 1971, 24(5), 415–421.

Schopler, E., & Reichler, R. J. Developmental therapy: A program model for providing individual services in the community. In E. Schopler & R. J. Reichler (Eds.), *Psychopathology and child development: Research and treatment.* New York: Plenum Press, 1976.

Whittaker, J. K. The ecology of child treatment: A developmental/educational approach to the therapeutic milieu. *Journal of Autism and Childhood Schizophrenia,* 1975, 5(3), 223–237.

Wing, L. *Autistic children: A guide for parents.* Secaucus, N.J.: Citadel Press, 1974.

3

A Parent-Training Group in a Preschool Mental Health Project

Annette U. Rickel, Ph.D., and
Grenae Dudley, Ph.D.

ANNETTE U. RICKEL is associate professor of psychology and director of the Preschool Mental Health Program in the psychology department at Wayne State University, Detroit, Michigan. GRENAE DUDLEY is a psychologist working with abused and neglected children and their families at the Children's Center of Wayne County Group Home, Detroit.

For the past several years, the authors have been involved in developing and evaluating a preventive mental health program for Title I preschool children and their parents in the Detroit Public Schools. The Preschool Mental Health Project is designed to provide early screening, diagnosis, and remediation to children evidencing difficulties such as learning, acting out, or withdrawal problems (Jones et al., 1980; Rickel & Lampi, 1981; Rickel & Smith, 1979; Rickel et al., 1979). In conjunction with the intervention project for preschool-age children, the authors introduced a group parent-training program aimed at reducing dysfunctional parenting behavior in these lower income, chronically stressed parents (Berman & Rickel, 1979; Rickel et al., 1980).

Participants in the parent-training program were recruited by letters carried home by their children inviting them to attend parenting sessions. In most cases, parents were paid $3.00 per hour to attend. A total of 59 parents became involved in the groups, which ranged in size from 8 to 15 members. The majority of the participants were black women of low socioeconomic status; 54 percent were single parents, 68 percent had completed high school, and 70 percent received support from Aid to Dependent Children (ADC). All parent sessions were held at the neighborhood school during school hours. These hours were convenient for child-care arrangements, since older siblings were in school and babysitting was available at the schools for the younger children. The program sessions were made as pleasant and congenial as possible with refreshments being served.

Problem Parenting

The need to modify inappropriate parental attitudes and behaviors is based on the importance of the "parenting role" in influencing the optimal development of children. A report by the Group for the Advancement of Psychiatry, Committee on Public Education (1973), pointed out that from a physical, psychological, or social point of view the importance of adequate parenting for a child's healthy personality development cannot be overemphasized. The committee stressed the sociological aspect of the family and the contention that the child's earliest and most influential experiences take place in the context of parent-child relationships.

Child abuse is an area where dysfunctional parenting is often cited as a primary contributor. Faith in the myth of the maternal instinct and the widespread notion that everyone loves and protects innocent children have lulled public awareness and obscured the true extent of child abuse (Blumberg, 1974). The true incidence of child abuse is not available, since many cases are not reported or go unrecognized. Conservative estimates indicate that each year from 1.4 to 1.9 million children are subjected to forms of abuse (Starr, 1979). There are numerous studies on the nature, dimensions, and epidemiological components of child abuse; yet there are relatively few studies on therapeutic intervention for the treatment of the child abusing parent(s). Therapy, for the most part, has centered on the physical needs of the child. The urgent need for an effective treatment plan for the parents is based on the number of abused children who are returned home. According to Blumberg (1974), there are two reasons for returning the child to the home: (1) the belief that leaving the child in an abusive family environment may cause less serious consequences than the emotional trauma of separation and placement either with another family or in an institution; and (2) the contention that correction of the many pejorative consequences of childhood displacement is an impossible task. The abusing parent is a psychiatric emergency by the very nature of the fact that the child's future rests with the parent's emotional equilibrium. Efforts must be made so that the parent's crumbling controls over his or her potential destructiveness are reestablished.

Another need for parent training and involvement is reflected in a recent increase in teenage parents. The incidence of young, inexperienced, naive "parents" assuming responsibility for the socialization of another human life is alarming. Teenagers' pregnancies account for one out of every five births in the United States; an estimated 570,000 children are born annually to teenagers (Edelman, 1981). A large proportion of these births (70–85 percent) are unplanned. About 4 in 10 mothers are married; 3 in 10 are unmarried, and 3 in 10 marry before giving birth or soon after (Sorensen, 1978). Very few of these teenage parents are adequately prepared to assume the full responsibilities of parenthood, emotionally or functionally.

A number of studies have shown that behavior problems in children may stem from problems in their familial environment. Ross (1974) reviewed several studies regarding the "unsocialized delinquent" and concluded that the acquisition of behavior controls that seem weak or absent in the unsocialized delinquent seems to require the following: consistency in the consequences parents bring to bear on the child's behavior; clear guidelines as to what is acceptable behavior; positive regard; good role models; and conditions under which social approval can acquire secondary reinforcement potential. When these conditions are absent, the probability that a child raised in such an environment will come to be identified as a delinquent appears greatly increased.

The attitudes and behaviors of parents can greatly influence the attitudes and behaviors of their children. With regard to behaviors exhibited by parents, many behaviorally oriented psychologists (Bandura, 1971; Berkowitz & Graziano, 1972; Wahl et al., 1974) have pointed out the significant effects of parental behavior on the child's behavior. They indicate that parents may inadvertently contribute to acting-out behaviors in their children by reinforcing negative behaviors. Their data suggest that the reinforcement serves the purpose of giving the parent temporary relief from the deviant behavior. The drawback, however, is that it increases the probability of the child's future deviant responses.

Ferguson and Allen (1978) also found that children who exhibit deviant social behavior generally come from families characterized by marital dissatisfaction and discrepant parental attitudes. Griest et al. (1979) supported this contention, but pointed out that parental adjustments may affect parental perceptions of behavior problems in their children. Therefore, the need to intervene at some early developmental level and provide ways for helping parents deal more effectively with their children is manifest (Belle, 1980; Hetherington et al., 1977).

Using Parents as Change Agents

The objective of the parent-training program was the utilization of parents as change agents for their children's inappropriate behaviors. Working with parents to modify children's behaviors by helping them to modify their own represents a relatively new approach for dealing with the problems of children and their parents. It provides greater access to the natural environment of children, which more often than not is composed primarily of family. The parents can, therefore, become not merely recipients of therapy but also active behavior co-therapists (Berkowitz & Graziano, 1972). Traditionally, experts have attempted to directly influence the child and change his/her behavior. However, according to Glogower and Sloop (1976), behavior change may be brought about more effectively by controlling the child's environment through the manipulation of behavioral contingencies. Parents, who are the primary socializing agents of the child (Baumrind, 1978), are in a better position to bring about change than are professionals who see the child for only a few hours each week.

Mash et al. (1973) conducted a study using a group of mothers to modify their children's deviant behaviors. Their focus was on the modification of maladaptive mother-child interactions. They found that the altered response repertoires of the mothers resulted in behavior change on the part of their children. They pointed out that their results supported the usefulness of working with the child-care agents as vehicles for modifying children's behavior. Other studies have demonstrated positive results using parents as change agents and indicated that they were very effective in eliciting positive changes in children who exhibited a wide range of behavior problems (Johnson & Katz, 1973; McPherson & Samuels, 1971; O'Dell, 1974; Reisinger et al., 1976; Tavormina, 1974). These problems included antisocial and immature behavior, speech dysfunction, school phobias, encopresis and enuresis, seizures, self-injurious behavior, and oppositional behavior. The authors, however, pointed out that the success of therapeutic intervention by parents depends on the ability of a backup therapist to produce reliable changes in the behavior of parents toward their children.

Our work with parents has focused not only on the remediation of problems but also on a preventive mental health approach. This strategy teaches parents more effective ways to deal with child rearing and child management issues and consequently stands in contrast to the more traditional approaches oriented toward child or parent therapy (Tavormina, 1974).

Methods for Modifying Inappropriate Child-Rearing Attitudes and Behaviors

There have been essentially two methods employed in working with parents, one a more traditional reflective approach and the other a behavior modification approach. The reflective approach emphasizes parental awareness, understanding, and acceptance of the child's feelings. This model uses cognitively mediated variables as a means of altering the parent-child interactions. The behavioral approach attempts to eliminate cognitive variables and emphasizes actual behavior. Training is directed toward teaching parents to manipulate their responses to the child in order to affect the child's subsequent behavior (Tavormina, 1974).

The reflective approach is best exemplified by Hereford (1963), Auvenshire (1974), and Swensen (1970), who were able to produce significant changes in the attitudes of parents through use of parent discussion groups. Stearn (1971) and Hanley (1974) demonstrated that the use of Parent Effectiveness Training (P.E.T.), a reflective method, yielded substantial changes in attitudes. They found that parents became more accepting of their children and their behavior, and developed more democratic attitudes toward their families.

The behavioral approach has also been shown to be effective in changing inappropriate attitudes and behaviors. Zeilberger et al. (1968) showed that parents could control undesirable behaviors in their children through the use of differential reinforcement contingencies. O'Leary et al. (1973) also involved parents in the treatment of their children and produced important therapeutic changes. Their focus was on consulting with parents concerning how they could change their children's behavior through systematic shaping of inappropriate behavior, timing of punishment, modeling appropriate behavior, and the establishment of incentive systems. Patterson (1974, 1980) and his associates (Taplin & Reid, 1977), in one of the most extensive parent-mediated child treatment programs for aggressive boys, obtained significant reduction in targeted deviant behavior through parents' use of behavior modification procedures.

Variations of the reflective and behavioral approaches have met with both success and failure. Johnson (1970) conducted an interesting study in which she compared mother groups versus child groups and traditional versus behavior modification procedures in the treatment of disobedient children. She found the behavior groups for both mother and child showed slight increases in general adjustment from post- to follow-up testing, while the reflective group showed a slight decrease during the same periods. Tavormina (1975) evaluated the relative effectiveness of a behavioral and a reflective group counseling procedure. He found that both types of counseling had beneficial effects relative to the untreated controls but that the behavioral method resulted in significantly greater improvement. He concluded that the behavioral technique was the treatment of choice for counseling parents because it provided them with an understandable, consistent, and effective way to deal with the specific problems they were facing in raising their children.

An Assertiveness-Training Approach for Parents

The procedure employed in our parent-training groups was an assertiveness-training behavioral technique. The origin and development of assertiveness training is attributed to Joseph Wolpe. Wolpe (1973) defines assertive behavior as the proper expression of any emotion other than anxiety toward another person. Since its inception, many professionals have used this technique and report that it has been successful and therapeutic (Alberti & Emmons, 1970; Lange & Jakubowski, 1976; Lazarus, 1971; Smith, 1975; and Wolpe, 1973).

The assertiveness-training program used in this study was designed by Berman and Rickel (1979), who incorporated the procedure used by Lange and Jakubowski (1976) as well as other approaches. Its goals were to: (1) encourage parents to treat children and other family members as individuals with personal rights; (2) develop a democratic atmosphere in the home for the child; (3) foster self-esteem and self-respect in the child; (4) view the child, the parent, and other family members in a positive way; (5) teach the difference between assertion and aggression and between nonassertion and politeness; (6) help people identify and accept both their own personal rights and the rights of others; (7) reduce existing cognitive and affective obstacles to active assertiveness, e.g., irrational thinking and excessive anxiety, quiet, or anger; (8) develop assertive skills through active practice methods; (9) understand what is typical and atypical behavior in their children.

This particular approach not only encourages the appropriate expression of anger and standing up for one's rights, but also heavily encourages the expression of positive feelings and behaviors. Hersen et al. (1973) and Lazarus (1971) felt that behavior-therapy literature devoted a disproportionate amount of space in assertiveness training to the expression of anger and the need to be able to contradict and verbally attack other people. They further pointed out that many clients are able to contradict and attack, or to criticize and defend, but are completely incapable of voluntary praise and approval, or of expressing love and affection. They stated that almost none of the research on assertiveness training was devoted to an examination of the most effective methods for helping clients express their positive feelings.

The present procedure encompassed both these approaches to assertive behavior, combining them in order to improve two-way communication between parents and their children. This procedure used six structured sessions. These sessions included training in (1) the expression of positive assertions; (2) listening; (3) making requests and expressing anger; (4) discipline techniques; (5) problem solving; and (6) follow-up. Handout sheets outlining the most important points discussed in each session were given to each parent for future reference.

The training was conducted within a group setting and utilized several major behavioral techniques associated with assertiveness training. These included behavioral rehearsal and role playing, modeling, cognitive reshaping, homework assignments, and videotape feedback. Since these were new experiences for parents, every effort was made to make them feel comfortable in discussing their thoughts and feelings and to develop support systems. Sensitive issues such as child abuse and violence between adults were likely topics to surface, requiring leaders who did not inhibit or intimidate participants. In examining the above approach, it is important to review the utility of these techniques in modifying behavior.

The use of behavioral rehearsal and role playing during each session emphasized the basic concept to be learned and transformed the parents into participant observers instead of nonparticipant observers. This allowed the parents to become involved in the treatment process. McFall and Marston (1970) investigated the use of behavioral rehearsal in assertiveness training and found that the behavior rehearsal procedures employed resulted in significantly greater improvements in assertive performance than did their control conditions. They also found a nonsignificant tendency for behavior rehearsal coupled with performance feedback to show the strongest treatment effects.

The group leaders served as models for the parents, utilized the role playing, and gave examples representative of the techniques being discussed. An added feature of this program was the use of cognitive restructuring. This is generally not used in assertiveness training because the emphasis has been on the modification of direct overt behavior. However, Lange and Jakubowski (1976) described a cognitive behavioral program that not only trained people to behave more assertively but also helped them to deal with their anxiety about change by identifying and challenging their irrational belief systems. For the most part, this aspect of assertiveness training has been ignored. Thorpe (1975) found that both self-instructional training (a procedure modeled on rational-emotive therapy) and modeling-plus-behavior-rehearsal emerged superior to controls on self-report and behavioral measures. Wolfe and Fodor (1977) found support for the efficacy of modeling-plus-behavior-rehearsal and modeling-plus-behavior-rehearsal-plus-rational-therapy in the treatment of assertiveness difficulties in women.

Homework assignments were given to parents to ensure practice of the techniques at home with their children and to enhance learning of the principles discussed during each session. Parents were also encouraged to discuss these concepts with their spouse or the person with whom they lived. This was done to generalize what was learned from the sessions to home situations. Videotape, a relatively new feedback procedure in behavioral research, was also employed. It provided a basis for observing differences and served as a reinforcement for assertive behavior. Parents were able to view changes in themselves and in other group members.

Description of Weekly Sessions

Session 1: Positive Assertions

The first part of this session was spent in introductions and getting to know one another. Parents told a little about themselves, their children, and the activities they enjoyed with their families. In hearing how others had fun with their children, parents gained ideas about how to increase the variety of pleasurable activities they could enjoy with their own children. They also learned from this sharing that having fun with their children increased children's liking for the parents. The leaders pointed out that children who liked their parents were more likely to want to please them.

The notion of assertive behavior was introduced. The leader explained the difference between assertive, nonassertive, and aggressive behavior. Examples were presented of daily life situations that could most effectively be responded to with assertive behavior. Some of those situations were: a child helping his mother make the beds, a child helping her younger sister get dressed, a child setting the table. The leaders pointed out how important it was for parents to *first* comment on what they *liked* about their child's behavior; parents should *praise* their child's *efforts*, as in the above examples, even though the job was not done perfectly. The point was stressed that parents needed to look for the positive aspects of their children's behavior for two reasons: (1) parental praise increases the child's feelings of self-esteem and (2) praise can increase the frequency of appropriate behaviors. Leaders discussed how often parents paid more attention to their children when they misbehaved. This tended only to increase the misbehavior, since children wanted their parents' attention and would attempt to get it in whatever way they found successful.

A specific technique of praising was demonstrated by the group leader. The parent was taught to say the child's name, establish eye contact, describe exactly what she liked about the child's behavior, and state how she felt about this behavior. For example, the parent would say, "Billy, I like the way you picked up your toys without my asking you to do it. I'm really pleased when you help me like that." Parents were then asked to think about what their child did that they *liked,* and the group role-played praising their child for that behavior.

These positive assertive techniques, it was explained, are not only helpful with children but also benefit relationships with friends and loved ones. The basic premise is to look for positive behavior and praise it in order to increase its occurrence. This technique can be used whether it relates to your child doing well in school, your friend talking to you when you're down, or your husband taking his turn doing dishes.

Homework. At the end of each session, parents were given a task related to that day's session to be done at home and reported on at the next session. At the end of this first session, parents were asked to praise their child at least once each day. This practice was intended to help the parent become accustomed to looking for positive behavior. It was also suggested that parents work at increasing their total number of pleasurable activities—with their spouse, their children, and the family as a whole. Parents were asked to observe their behavior and that of others to see if they were acting assertively, nonassertively, or aggressively.

Session 2: Listening

During this session, leaders discussed the importance of listening to children; as Gordon (1970) stressed, "Children should be heard." Group leaders recommended that parents spend at least ten minutes each day listening to their children. For example, parents were encouraged to ask about their children's day when they came home from school. It was suggested that it is not necessary to give advice, simply share the experience.

An important part of listening is *how parents respond* to what is being said. Leaders urged that parents take their children's questions seriously and use them as opportunities to teach their children self-reliance and assertiveness. For example, when a child asked a question, the parent was encouraged to ask, "What do *you* think?," "What do *you* want?," "What do *you* feel?"

Similarly, parents were instructed to listen to their children's feelings of happiness, fear, hurt, sadness, joy, and anger, and to respond empathetically. For example, when a child expressed feelings of anger toward parents, siblings, friends, or teachers, the parent was encouraged to ask the child, "What are you angry about?," instead of telling the child he *shouldn't* be angry and thereby elicit guilt feelings (Ginott, 1965). Fear of allowing a child to express anger in relation to loved ones seemed to be a particular problem for these parents. The group leader stressed the difference between *feeling* angry and *acting* aggressively. The leader also pointed out that a child can be angry, for example, with his brother and still like his brother. The child is angry only about his brother's behavior. Examples of a child expressing negative feelings were presented and the parents role-played aggressive, assertive, and nonassertive responses to the child's expression.

When the parent is in a conflict situation, an empathetic assertion was suggested. In the empathetic assertion, the individual states the other person's position, thus displaying one's understanding of the other's feelings and desires. Parents were instructed to think of conflict situations with their children and to practice using empathetic assertion.

Homework. Parents were asked to practice listening to each one of their children for ten minutes each day and to practice responding with empathy to each child's thoughts and feelings.

Session 3: Making Requests and Expressing Anger

During the first part of the session, the group leader demonstrated appropriate and inappropriate ways of asking children to do something. An example the leader used was requesting that a child stop watching the television and pick up her toys. The group leader demonstrated a nonassertive request by yelling ineffectively from the other room. The leader then demonstrated an assertive request by walking over to the child, establishing eye contact, and saying in a calm voice, "John, let's pick up the toys." The physical aspects of assertiveness—eye contact, posture, voice volume, and gestures—were discussed in detail. A hostile, aggressive request was also demonstrated. The group leader then asked for the parents' responses to each type of request.

The group leader pointed out alternative ways of handling the above example. The leader suggested that if the child wished to finish watching the TV program before he picked up the toys, this would be appropriate so long as he agreed to clean up when the program was over. It was pointed out that children had the right to have their own needs taken into consideration. Second, the leader encouraged parents to tell their children what they wanted in advance. The leader pointed out that telling the child in the above example that clean-up time was in ten minutes would give her time to finish the activity and could help avoid conflict.

In the second part of the session, the leader demonstrated several ways of expressing anger. The leader role-played an adult who was angry because her children had walked across the floor with muddy feet. The leader demonstrated an aggressive response: "You stupid kids, how could you be so dumb? You're no good and you'll never be any good." Then the leader expressed her anger assertively: "I'm really angry. I worked so hard to clean this floor. I feel furious." Finally, demonstrating a nonassertive expression of anger, the leader muttered to herself and said nothing directly to the children. Group members were asked to compare the three methods of expressing anger. It was suggested that when parents used "I" statements to describe their feelings and state how the situation affected them, such as in the assertive example, they could express their anger without damaging the relationship with their child (Gordon, 1970). Conversely, it was stated that when parents use "you" statements and attacked the other person's personality instead of dealing with the specific situation, as in the aggressive example, the expression of anger was alienating.

After this demonstration and discussion, the parents role-played expressing anger to their children in assertive, nonassertive, and aggressive manners.

Homework. Parents were encouraged to practice making requests assertively, paying special attention to their use of eye contact, voice volume, and body posture. They were also encouraged to practice using "I" statements in their expression of anger at home.

Session 4: Conflict Resolution

A four-step technique for conflict resolution was presented in this session. First, the parents were told to find time to sit down and talk about the problem when all the family members involved were calm. Second, it was suggested that each person state what he or she wanted. Third, each member was to state what he or she thought the other member wanted (empathic assertion). Fourth, possible solutions were to be discussed and agreed upon. Penalties for not carrying out agreements could also be decided. Group leaders stressed that, while using this technique, there must be no putdowns and no dealing with the past; all discussion should deal with the present, specific situation. Further, the leaders stated that the use of "I" statements and assertive expressions of feelings, as discussed in the last session, were appropriate in resolving conflict situations. After group leaders had demonstrated this technique, parents practiced it by role-playing a discussion they might have with their children about some problem they were having with the children at home.

Toward the end of this session, the group leader dealt with a special type of conflict resolution—dealing with children's fights. It was pointed out that the technique used depended somewhat on the age of the child. For example, with younger children, parents were encouraged to intervene by stopping the fight and helping each child *state* her angry feelings. With older children, it was suggested that parents stand back and let them work out the situation themselves. If the children were not successful, then parents could model the four-step technique for conflict resolution and encourage the children to deal calmly with the issue at hand.

Homework. Parents were requested to practice using this conflict-resolution technique at home with special attention paid to empathic assertions.

Session 5: Discipline

This session dealt with the concept of discipline as a method of teaching children to become more cooperative and more productive. As had been stressed in previous sessions, the point was made that the best method of teaching a child was to give him attention when he was behaving appropriately. If a child required correction, group leaders pointed out that it was best for parents to talk calmly to the child and address the specific behavior, *not* the total personality of the child. It was stressed that using positive assertions with children demonstrated respect for them, thus increasing the child's willingness to change his behavior.

Group leaders also discussed some techniques in dealing with situations that frequently occurred with children. The following examples and suggestions were taken from Abidin (1976) and Dreikurs and Grey (1970). *When a child makes a mistake, he can correct it and then practice a new response.* For example, if a four-year-old child spills his milk, he is asked to clean it up, and then the parent shows him how to pour it correctly. Parents were asked to role-play the application of this technique to a child who had misplaced his mittens. *When a child refuses to assume responsibilities, give the child a choice of assuming them or having a loss of privilege that is reasonable and directly related to the misbehavior.* For example, when a small child refuses to pick up her toys, the mother can say, "You have a choice, you can pick them up now, or I'll pick them up and you won't be able to play with them for two days." Parents then role-played using this technique. *When the child is engaging in a power struggle, the parent can disengage and decide what to do.* For example, the child has a temper tantrum because his mother won't give him a cookie. The parent says, "I'm not going to listen to this. I'm going to my room and read. When you're quiet, I'll come out." Parents were asked to apply this technique when the parent is driving the car and the children are very noisy. *Children learn best when they experience the natural consequences of their mistakes.* For example, the parent is looking out the window and sees his child acting very bossy with the neighborhood children. The parent does not interfere and allows the child to be rejected by the other children. Later, he might talk to the child about it. Parents were asked to apply this technique when the child forgets her lunch.

Parents were encouraged to present problem behaviors that existed with their children, and to role-play some of the above-suggested techniques as possible solutions to the problems. Other parents were requested to give positive and negative feedback on the role-play.

Homework. The parents were asked to practice using the above techniques when disciplining their children. The group leader strongly encouraged the parents to adopt the concept of discipline as a teaching tool and to deal with their children calmly and positively.

Follow-up Session

A follow-up session five weeks later was designed to evaluate how successful the parents had been in using the techniques they had learned. Parents discussed the specific techniques they had incorporated into their behavior at home, and any problems they had with them. Some of the techniques that parents had forgotten or were having difficulty with were briefly reviewed. They also discussed what they had gained from the training program as a whole, and what parent skills they would still like to develop. Parents were encouraged to develop their own support groups to help others deal with the stresses of child rearing and thus become more effective parents.

Parental Response to the Program

Parents were very enthusiastic about the program. Many stated that they had never had an opportunity to discuss these kinds of issues before. They reported that the discussions helped them feel better about themselves as parents and spouses. Often, we found that these parents were having so many problems with their spouses or boy friends that, before they could concentrate on improving their relationship with their children, we had to help them improve adult relationships. Some parents reported that they were criticized by others for using some of the positive techniques, which made them more difficult to practice. However, they later felt more confident and therefore were able to handle specific problems with their children more effectively.

As an example, Mrs. R was a hostile parent who was unable to relate effectively to her preschooler. She found his active childish behavior annoying and responded to him in a callous manner. She would allow her son's negative behavior to escalate until it was intolerable and then would lash out at him impulsively. Mrs. R was aware of her behavior and came to the group to learn how to deal with her son more effectively. As a result of her active participation in the parent workshop, she was able to become more assertive and less aggressive with her son. She found him to be more likable and felt more comfortable with him. Mrs. R was also able to see that it was primarily her behavior and her attitudes toward her child that had changed.

In another example, the preschool teacher had observed Mrs. K slap and push her son on a number of occasions. She was concerned about this behavior and encouraged Mrs. K to attend the parent workshop. Mrs. K appeared to be intolerant of her son's acts of independence. She was defensive regarding her behavior and proved to be a difficult group member initially. However, through the efforts of the group leader and the group members, she was encouraged to be more tolerant of her son's appropriate acts of independence and assertiveness. Her attitudes were modified and she became one of the most productive group members. The preschool teacher also noted that her aggressiveness toward her son decreased after about the third session of the workshop. A follow-up with this particular family several weeks after the sessions had ended showed that Mrs. K continued to be less aggressive.

In addition, the children seemed very pleased that their parents were coming to school once a week, and they enjoyed sharing new activities with their parents. The parents, as a group, reported a happier atmosphere at home, became closer with each other, and developed a more positive association with the school.

Results and Discussion

The effectiveness of our training program has been evaluated with an attention placebo control discussion group format using center-city versus suburban parents, with positive results. At pretest, center-city parents were significantly more restrictive (expecting conformity to external demands) than suburban parents on Block's Child Rearing Practices Report (1965). There were no significant differences at pretest between the center-city and suburban parents on the dimension of nurturance. From pretest to post-test, all parents in the experimental training group showed a significant decrease in restrictiveness (a dimension associated with dependency, conformity, and low-achievement behavior in children) and a significantly greater change was noted for parents in the center city.

Demographic Influences

A look at the demographic information may contribute to an understanding of the results found regarding a higher restrictiveness dimension among center-city parents at pretest. The parents in this program may be described as working class. As members of the working class, these individuals face certain restrictions and inherent problems that directly affect their concepts of parenting. The differences between middle-class and working-class parental values are probably a function of the entire complex of differences in life conditions characteristic of the two social classes (Kohn, 1972). For example, the types of jobs working-class parents have often require that the worker follow explicit rules set down by someone in authority. They are conforming to externally imposed standards and tend to apply the same principles to their children. Stressing obedience to parental commands is part of their dynamics of parenting. The concept of a totally democratic family system directly conflicts with already established, learned concepts that, in turn, make parents more resistant to change. For example, the issue of spanking was discussed in several of the assertiveness training groups. The original position one of the group leaders upheld was that spanking was not to be employed with preschool children. A number of parents were quite alarmed and argued vehemently with the group leader. They indicated that either they were spanked growing up or they had raised a number of children and spanked every one of them. They did not feel that they or their children had any serious problems as a result of it.

Additionally, as previously stated, 54 percent of the parents were unmarried, divorced, or widowed. This allows for maladaptive parenting responses which can take two extreme forms: (1) parents may insist on total control and demand adherence to all parental dictates, or (2) parents try to overcompensate by not imposing reasonable expectations or restrictions on the child's behavior. Another effect of being a single parent is the difficulty one has in retaining one's own individual identity. Dresen (1976) investigated the effects of being a single parent and pointed out that single parents tend to assign priority to the children's needs and desires when they are in conflict with their own. This had direct relevance to the assertiveness training of the present program, which emphasizes personal rights as well as the rights of the child.

As mentioned, there were no significant differences at pretest between the center-city and suburban parents so far as the nurturance subscale was concerned. Explanations for this could be that center-city parents are becoming more aware of parenting skills and valued behavior through the media and from mental health professionals who go into the field, raise questions, and offer advice. Furthermore, a great deal of information is given to parents without their actively seeking it. This is sometimes done by teachers and social workers through referrals of children with problems to the school psychological services or outside agencies that provide education and support.

Adhering to external demands, which is what the restrictiveness dimension implies, does not exclude parents from also being nurturant. Parents in the center city often discussed the negative aspect of spoiling children or letting them have their way. They indicated that it was important for them to maintain and exhibit control over their children, especially in public places. However, parents also discussed how important it was for them to support their children and encourage them to make it where they may have failed (socially, educationally, etc.). Control of the child's behavior may be necessary in order for the child to circumvent the environmental conditions that conspire against him or her. The results suggest that parents wanted to show they were in control and therefore restrictive but, at the same time, supportive and nurturant.

Enhancing the Training Program

In order to effectively enhance the power of the training procedure, a closer examination of the assertiveness training program is warranted. The parents who actively participated in the groups were for the most part mothers. A source of variance which was not accounted for was the influence of fathers. Even though 54 percent of the children were from single-parent homes, 46 percent were from homes where fathers were present. Hughes and Haynes (1978) critiqued the methodological issue of structured laboratory observation in the behavioral assessment of parent-child interactions. They pointed out that the omission of the fathers in this type of programmatic research prevents the assessment of a large source of variance in the child's environment and thereby reduces the power and generalizability of the results. A suggestion would be to include fathers in both the training and assessment phases of the program.

Assuming that the parent acquires the basic skills for modification of the child's behavior, other issues emerge. In order for training to be effective, parents' skills must generalize outside the training situation and be maintained after training (Kiecolt & McGrath, 1979). A heavier emphasis on the homework assignments and monitoring may serve to persuade parents to practice the skills at home. The increased use of videotape equipment may also serve to generalize the basic skills. For purposes of feedback, the equipment could be used several times during the course of the assertiveness training. Parents could be videotaped interacting with their children, and the tapes would serve as feedback of their behavior. This would provide a vehicle through which the group leaders and the other parents could point out positive changes and use positive assertions to reinforce progress. Parents would be able to apply their learning and skills directly to their children, thus building an assertive repertoire. Including the fathers in these sessions would further serve to generalize the techniques throughout the family.

Another possible addition to the program incorporates training the preschool teachers in assertive behavior. In this way, teachers can serve to reinforce the efforts of the parents, along with providing some consistency for the children. Patterson (1980) indicates that parents are necessary agents in the socialization process, but other key socializing agents interacting with the child, such as teachers, can be taught those skills necessary to reduce deviant behavior and increase more adaptive forms of interaction.

The advantage of behavioral intervention strategies to educate, inform, and use parents as change agents becomes self-evident when one examines the direction preventive mental health is taking. There is a growing demand for child and family intervention. The fact of too few professionals for too many cases curtails the use of traditional psychotherapy with children characterized by a one-to-one therapist-child relationship. Solutions to these problems lie with recent and future innovations that make active use of parents in the treatment process.

References

Abidin, R. R. *Parenting skills.* Vol. 2, *Workbook.* New York: Human Sciences Press, 1976.

Alberti, R. E., & Emmons, M. L. *Assert yourself . . . It's your perfect right.* San Luis Obispo, Calif.: Impact Publishers, 1970.

Auvenshine, W. R. The parent discussion group: An additional dimension to the role of the school counselor. *Dissertation Abstracts International,* 1974, *34,* 3859A.

Bandura, A. Psychotherapy based upon modeling principle. In A. E. Bergin & S. L. Garfield (Eds.), *Handbook of psychotherapy and behavior change.* New York: Wiley, 1971.

Baumrind, D. The contribution of the family to the development of competence in children. *The Schizophrenia Bulletin,* No. 14. Washington, D.C.: U.S. Department of Health, Education and Welfare, Public Health Service, Alcohol, Drug Abuse and Mental Health Administration, 1978.

Belle, D. Mothers and their children: A study of low income families. In C. L. Heckerman (Ed.), *The evolving female: Women in psychosocial context.* New York: Human Sciences Press, 1980.

Berkowitz, B. P., & Graziano, A. M. Training parents as behavior therapists: A review. *Behaviour Research and Therapy,* 1972, *10*(4), 297–317.

Berman, S. F., & Rickel, A. U. Assertive training for low-income black parents. *Clinical Social Work Journal,* 1979, *7*(2), 123–132.

Block, J. H. *The child rearing practices report.* Berkeley: University of California, Institute of Human Development, 1965.

Blumberg, M. L. Psychopathology of the abusing parent. *American Journal of Psychotherapy,* 1974, *28*(1), 21–29.

Dreikurs, R., & Grey, L. *A parent's guide to child discipline.* New York: Hawthorn Books, 1970.

Dresen, S. The young adult adjusting to single parenting. *American Journal of Nursing,* 1976, *76,* 1286–1289.

Edelman, M. W. Who is for children? *American Psychologist,* 1981, *36*(2), 109–116.

Ferguson, L. R., & Allen, D. R. Congruence of parental perception, marital satisfaction, and child adjustment. *Journal of Consulting and Clinical Psychology,* 1978, *46*(2), 343–346.

Ginott, H. G. *Between parent and child: New solutions to old problems.* New York: Macmillan, 1965.

Glogower, F., & Sloop, E. W. Two strategies of group training of parents as effective behavior modifiers. *Behavior Therapy,* 1976, *7*(2), 177–184.

Gordon, T. *Parent effectiveness training.* New York: Peter H. Wyden, 1970.

Griest, D., Wells, K. C., & Forehand, R. An examination of predictors of maternal perceptions of maladjustment in clinic-referred children. *Journal of Abnormal Psychology,* 1979, *88*(3), 277–281.

Group for the Advancement of Psychiatry, Committee on Public Education. *The joys and sorrows of parenthood.* New York: Mental Health, 1973.

Hanley, D. Changes in parent attitudes related to a parent effectiveness training and a family enrichment program. *Dissertation Abstracts International,* 1974, *34,* 7044A.

Hereford, C. F. *Changing parental attitudes through group discussion.* Austin: University of Texas Press, 1963.

Hersen, M., Eisler, R. M., & Miller, P. M. Development of assertive response: Clinical measurement and research considerations. *Behaviour Research and Therapy,* 1973, *11*(4), 505–521.

Hetherington, E. M., Cox, M., & Cox, R. The aftermath of divorce. In J. H. Stevens & M. Matthews (Eds.), *Mother-child, father-child relations.* Washington, D.C.: NAEYC, 1977.

Hughes, H. M., & Haynes, S. N. Structured laboratory observation in the behavioral assessment of parent-child interactions: A methodological critique. *Behavior Therapy,* 1978, *9*(3), 428–447.

Johnson, C. A., & Katz, R. C. Using parents as change agents for their children: A review. *Journal of Child Psychology and Psychiatry,* 1973, *14*(3), 181–200.

Johnson, S. A. *A comparison of mother versus child groups and traditional versus behavior modification procedures in the "treatment" of disobedient children.* Urbana: University of Illinois Press, 1970.

Jones, D. C., Rickel, A. U., & Smith, R. L. Maternal child-rearing practices and social problem-solving strategies among preschoolers. *Developmental Psychology,* 1980, *16*(3), 241–242.

Kiecolt, J., & McGrath, E. Social desirability responding in the measurement of assertive behavior. *Journal of Consulting and Clinical Psychology,* 1979, *47*(3), 640–642.

Kohn, M. Social class and parent-child relationship: An interpretation. In S. I. Harrison & J. F. McDermott (Eds.), *Childhood psychopathology: An anthology of basic readings.* New York: International Universities Press, 1972.

Lange, A., & Jakubowski, P. *Responsible assertive behavior.* Champaign, Ill.: Research Press, 1976.

Lazarus, A. A. *Behavior therapy and beyond.* New York: McGraw-Hill, 1971.

Mash, E. J., Lazere, R., Terdal, L., & Garner, A. Modification of mother-child interactions: A modeling approach for groups. *Child Study Journal*, 1973, 3(3), 131–143.

McFall, R. M., & Marston, A. R. An experimental investigation of behavior rehearsal in assertive training. *Journal of Abnormal Psychology*, 1970, 76(2), 295–303.

McPherson, S., & Samuels, C. Teaching behavioral methods to parents. *Social Casework*, 1971, 52(3), 148–153.

O'Dell, S. Training parents in behavior modification: A review. *Psychological Bulletin*, 1974, 81(7), 418–433.

O'Leary, K. D., Turkewitz, H., & Toffel, S. Parent and therapist evaluation of behavior therapy in a child psychological clinic. *Journal of Consulting and Clinical Psychology*, 1973, 41(2), 279–283.

Patterson, G. R. Retraining of aggressive boys by their parents: Review of recent literature and follow-up evaluation. *Canadian Psychiatric Association Journal*, 1974, 19(2), 142–158.

Patterson, G. R. Mothers: The unacknowledged victims. *Monographs of the Society for Research in Child Development*, 1980, 45, 1–64.

Reisinger, J. J., Ora, J. P., & Frangia, G. W. Parents as change agents for their children: A review. *Journal of Community Psychology*, 1976, 4(2), 103–123.

Rickel, A. U., Dudley, G., & Berman, S. An evaluation of parent training. *Evaluation Review*, 1980, 4(3), 389–403.

Rickel, A. U., & Lampi, L. A two-year follow-up study of a preventive mental health program for preschoolers. *Journal of Abnormal Child Psychology*, 1981, 9(4), 455–464.

Rickel, A. U., & Smith, R. L. Maladapting preschool children: Identification, diagnosis, and remediation. *American Journal of Community Psychology*, 1979, 7(2), 197–208.

Rickel, A. U., Smith, R. L., & Sharp, K. C. Description and evaluation of a preventive mental health program for preschoolers. *Journal of Abnormal Child Psychology*, 1979, 7(1), 101–112.

Ross, A. O. *Psychological disorders of children: A behavioral approach to theory, research, and therapy.* New York: McGraw-Hill, 1974.

Smith, M. *When I say no, I feel guilty.* New York: Dial, 1975.

Sorensen, J. L. Outcome evaluation of a referral system for juvenile offenders. *American Journal of Community Psychology*, 1978, 6(4), 381–388.

Starr, R. H., Jr. Child abuse. *American Psychologist*, 1979, 34(10), 872–878.

Stearn, M. B. The relationship of parent effectiveness training to parent attitudes, parent behavior and child self-esteem. *Dissertation Abstracts International*, 1971, 32, 1885–1886B.

Swensen, S. S. Changing expressed parental attitudes toward childrearing practices and its effects on school adaptation and level of adjustment perceived by parents. *Dissertation Abstracts International*, 1970, 31, 2118–2119A.

Taplin, P. S., & Reid, J. B. Changes in parent consequences as a function of family intervention. *Journal of Consulting and Clinical Psychology*, 1977, 45(6), 973–981.

Tavormina, J. B. Basic models of parent counseling: A critical review. *Psychological Bulletin*, 1974, 81(11), 827–835.

Tavormina, J. B. Relative effectiveness of behavioral and reflective group counseling with parents of mentally retarded children. *Journal of Consulting and Clinical Psychology*, 1975, 43(1), 22–31.

Thorpe, G. L. Short-term effectiveness of systematic desensitization, modeling and behavior rehearsal, and self-instructional training in facilitating assertive-refusal behavior. *European Journal of Behavioral Analysis and Modification*, 1975, 1(1), 30–44.

Wahl, G., Johnson, S. M., Johansson, S., & Martin, S. An operant analysis of child-family interaction. *Behavior Therapy*, 1974, 5(1), 64–78.

Wolfe, J. L., & Fodor, I. G. Modifying assertive behavior in women: A comparison of three approaches. *Behavior Therapy*, 1977, 8(4), 567–574.

Wolpe, J. *The practice of behavior therapy.* New York: Pergamon Press, 1973.

Zeilberger, J., Sampen, S., & Sloane, H. N., Jr. Modification of a child's problem behaviors in the home with the mother as therapist. *Journal of Applied Behavior Analysis*, 1968, *1*(1), 47–53.

NOTE: The Preschool Mental Health Project, a research and service endeavor, has been supported by grants from the McGregor Fund, the Eloise and Richard Webber Foundation, the David M. Whitney Fund, and by the Detroit Public Schools, for which the authors express grateful appreciation.

WORKING WITH CHILDREN
AND ADOLESCENTS

4

An Activity Group for Preadolescent Boys

Beryce W. MacLennan, Ph.D.

A clinical and community psychologist specializing in group psychotherapy with children and adolescents, BERYCE W. MAC LENNAN is presently mental health adviser to the U.S. General Accounting Office and clinical professor at the Center for Medical and Behavior Science at George Washington University, Washington, D.C.

"Preadolescent" children—roughly, children of elementary school age—range from 6 to 13 years. This cohort divides into two broadly overlapping groups. In the younger group, children are particularly concentrating on ego development. This includes the affirmation of the self; improvement in self-esteem; identification with adults, generally of the same sex, as coping models; and skill development through experience and through matching self against peers. It is essentially a period of doing, of activity, contrasting sharply with teenagers' tendency to "hang out" and talk.

While preoccupation with sexuality starts earlier today, typical 6-to-9-year-olds are still more concerned with cognitive learning, physical development, and experience. They relate to peers as companions and rivals in activity, and work for self-affirmation within the family. Nonpsychotic problems involve self-esteem, authority, sibling and peer rivalry, physical and cognitive skill development, social relations, impulse control, and management of emotions. Magical thinking is still powerful. When rejected, children frequently fantasize not belonging to their families and think about being changelings or adopted. If a parent dies, they easily attribute this to powerful negative wishes.

In the latter part of preadolescence, physiological sexual development creates major changes in the individual. Sexual identity may become a major preoccupation with some children, who show intense interest in comparing their sexual selves with peers and adults of the same sex. Major moves to separate from the family are not usual until early adolescence.

Short-Term Therapy Groups for Children

Short-term children's groups have been conducted in inpatient and outpatient settings, in schools and camps, and in correctional institutions. The majority of groups have been run by mental health professionals in clinics, although some short-term groups have been conducted in schools, particularly by teachers and counselors interested in behavior modification or confluent education.

Although short-term groups, as defined in this book, do not exceed one year in duration, the number of hours and sessions can range broadly within this limit—from a one-session diagnostic group lasting 1½ to 2 hours to weekly or more frequent sessions continuing a whole year. Group sessions may be as short as 15 minutes or they may continue for an entire day or weekend, as in some workshops and marathon groups. They may also be set within the context of 24-hour residential treatment.

Many short-term groups are reality-oriented. They focus on a specific problem or set of problems and explore feelings, reactions, and solutions. Other short-term groups are experiential and abreactive, resolving specific emotional hang-ups and offering experiences of a different way of being accepted or of perceiving the world.

Short-term groups generally function within a rather low-key transference, although some intensive, experiential groups are conducted even with latency-age children. Therapists are usually more active in helping individuals, and the group works on designated issues because time is too short for unfocused discussion. Therapists' tasks are to set an effective working climate and to maintain the limits and boundaries of the group. Their interventions serve to guide the group and to clarify points that are made. Therapists may also provide information for the group and models for identification.

The selection of children as members of short-term groups must be determined by the goals of the groups and the methods employed. In short-term groups, the problem is sometimes paramount. For instance, all the children may belong to families that have recently experienced divorce, or they may all have gone through a disaster such as a fire or flood. Under these circumstances, the personalities, psychosocial backgrounds, and ages of the children will be less important because the group will focus on the problem, the children's reactions to it, and their options in learning how to cope with it and remake their lives. On the other hand, some short-term groups are particularly concerned with how the children may change some aspect of their behavior—become more assertive or less argumentative, become more comfortable with peers or with authority, overcome a particular fear. In these circumstances, developmental age becomes an extremely important selection criterion.

The literature on short-term group therapy with preadolescent children is very scattered and quite hard to find. Although a number of authors—for example, Frank and Zilbach (1968), MacLennan (1977), Schamess (1976) and Scheidlinger (1977)—have reviewed children's group psychotherapy, they have not concentrated on short-term treatment. Nor did Slavson and Schiffer (1975), in their comprehensive book on children's group psychotherapies, describe or critique all the different short-term methods.

Several authors have described the use of short-term diagnostic groups with preadolescent children. All these have used play or a combination of play and discussion. Redl (1944) was the first. Twenty years later, Daniels (1964) reported trying to create a situation in which children could play as freely as if unobserved. Ganter and Polansky (1964), Churchill (1965), and King (1970) all used four-session groups for diagnostic purposes.

Many short-term groups are conducted around specific incidents or issues. Groups dealing with post-traumatic stress and disasters, accidents, and other frightening events have often made therapeutic use of activity—for example, the coloring books developed by the Omaha Tornado Project (1976) and art therapy used by Landgarten et al. (1978) after a neighborbood shoot-out. These groups strive for abreaction, working through loss and grief, and dealing with survivor guilt.

Groups have been formed in child guidance and family clinics and in schools which deal with transitions in the lives of preadolescent children (Anderson & Marrone, 1977). Major transitions for such children include family breakup through death, divorce, or separation; moves from one part of the country to another; and changes within the school system. Effron (1980) describes a short-term group in an elementary school for preadolescent children following parent divorce in which she used affective-education techniques over a 12-week period. Pasnau et al. (1976) and Barsky and Mozenter (1976) used creative drama to help children recognize and deal with their feelings. Role-playing and sociopsychodrama have been particularly useful in helping children as well as adults prepare for new roles, cope with new situations, and understand the reactions of others.

Behavior modification groups have been used for a number of different types of problems, such as overcoming specific fears, reducing hyperactivity, controlling aggressiveness, and motivating antisocial children to work on their problems. A number of authors describe using contracting methods and reward systems to reduce hyperactivity in the classroom. Brundage-Aguar et al. (1979) review the literature on such techniques.

Many behavior modification groups are run within day or 24-hour treatment programs where the groups form part of token economy milieus. One of the most successful of these was at Achievement Place in Philadelphia, a group home for delinquent children, in which peers monitored and reinforced one another (Pappenfort & Levitt, 1980). Bardill (1972) and Brunning and Stover (1971) also describe using behavior modification techniques in residential settings.

Groups for seriously mentally disturbed children have been run on a short-term basis in inpatient settings, although most groups for psychotic children are long-term. Williams et al. (1978) describe using fantasy-provoking and expressive materials such as puppetry, drama, and music in such groups.

There have been many adaptations of Slavson's activity-group therapy for children in preschool years. Most of these have been long-term, but a few have been short-term and focused. Green and Fuller (1973) and MacLennan and Rosen (1963) have described groups focused on dealing with issues related to sexual identity. Karson (1965) describes 30 groups organized for children with behavior problems. Lovasdal (1976), Strunk and Witkin (1974), and Rhodes (1973) used combinations of activity and interview therapy.

Activity-Group Therapy

Activity-group therapy is a method of treatment developed in the 1930s at the Jewish Board of Guardians in New York City by S. R. Slavson (Slavson & Schiffer, 1975). Emphasis is on the quality of the interactions experienced by the children and their therapist within the group. Four to six children of the same sex who have been referred to a mental health clinic or child-guidance department are invited to attend a club where they will get to know other children, make friends, play games, and have fun. The children are carefully selected both in terms of their personality characteristics and problems and in regard to how they will relate to one another. The group meetings, which take place once a week for two hours, are relatively unstructured: a range of toys and games is available to the children; there is a refreshment period during which the children sit around a table; and occasionally the group will arrange to go on a trip. The therapist must be well-trained in the mental health treatment of children and must understand the psychodynamic processes at the level of both the individual child and the group and be able to respond to both levels.

The group progresses through the characteristic stages of dependency, testing the leader, competition for position in the group, work on individual and group tasks, movement toward group cohesion, individuation of members, and ultimately termination and separation. As the group develops, the children become more intimately concerned with one another and take increasing responsibility for the conduct of the group. Adult authority is split between the institution and the outside world on one hand and the leader on the other. The former sets the ultimate permissible boundaries for the group, while the leader serves as benign authority, protector against serious harm in the group, identifier of reality, and a model of a perceptive, caring, responsible person.

Treatment in activity-group therapy is primarily on an ego level, and the problems dealt with are ego problems: self-esteem and clarification of identity; capacity to deal with authority and peers; coping with sibling rivalry; winning and losing; taking responsibility for self and others; mobilizing psychic energy to solve problems; accepting and working through loss and change and separation. While regression is not encouraged, the loose structure of the group, particularly in the early stages, does create some anxiety. For that reason, children with very poor ego controls, such as psychotic children or those with organic disorders, are not selected, nor are children who have difficulty learning from experience, such as many mentally retarded youngsters. As the group develops, different themes are worked through and there are periods of greater and lesser emotional intensity. It is important that the therapist understand and cope with his or her own feelings that are aroused by the group pressures.

The lack of initial structure in the group creates anxiety among the children. They begin to cope with this in characteristic ways and, as the group progresses, they reveal and act out their problems. The leader responds differentially to these problems and soon the other members emulate him or her. Thus the group brings pressure on the individual to feel and act differently. As members work through a particular problem, the level of emotional intensity in the group is raised. For instance, a child may spend one or two sessions in a phase of intense dependency, demanding help from the therapist every few minutes. The therapist may decide that it is important for the child to experience the fulfillment of this need. After one or two sessions, the demandingness and dependency lessen and the child is able to become more self-confident and self-reliant. In the meantime, however, this attention may have triggered feelings of sibling rivalry in other members, and they too become very demanding. In activity therapy, the therapist is likely to respond nonverbally, giving attention to each child according to its demands. In a more verbal group, the fact may be discussed that attention to one very needy member is given at a particular point in time and does not mean that others are not also loved or will not receive attention when they are needy. Sometimes, after the urgency of one set of problems has been reduced, there is a period of calm and stability before other problems are tackled.

Group composition—selecting children to ensure the desired climate and level of activity produced by the interaction of personalities—is as important in short-term as in long-term activity-group therapy. This contrasts with most focused and problem-oriented short-term groups, where group balance is not a factor. In those groups, the therapist is more active, and more structure is built into the group sessions. Group balance is always important when the experience is to be the major therapeutic factor and structured interventions are to be minimized.

Several factors must be taken into consideration when selecting children for a particular group. Most importantly, the personalities and coping skills of the children are evaluated. Those selecting the children attempt to predict from previous behavior how the children will behave in the group: Do they take the initiative? Are they withdrawn, passive, shy, fearful, overly compulsive, defiant, aggressive? Do they relate to children or adults or to no one at all? Generally, an age range is set of not more than two years: for instance, one may select boys or girls between the ages of 7 and 9 or 10 and 12. The maturity of the child, taken in conjunction with size and personality, is important. A very large, aggressive boy in a group of smaller, younger children will have too much power and will force the therapist to intervene too frequently. On the other hand, a large, passive child might fit in quite well. Very fearful children should not be placed in a group that includes a preponderance of aggressive children who are likely to start with outbursts of defiance or fighting. Consideration should be given to whether the children are entering puberty or are still in latency. Ten- and 11-year-old children often vary greatly in this regard.

The aim in supplying materials for activity-group therapy is to stimulate activity and interaction between the children at an ego level. Opportunities for both solitary and group activities are provided: balls, skittles, checkers, cards, clay, materials for lanyard-making, leathercraft, and carpentry, as well as crayons and paper, tempura paint, and some age- and skill-appropriate models. These groups are not designed to stimulate fantasies and the uncovering of unconscious material, so fantasy-stimulating materials such as puppets, finger paints, water pistols, and clay made from powder are not included. These all tend to be too exciting and regressive. Dollhouses are not usually provided, but we did so in the particular group to be described in this article because we thought it would be useful for one of the boys who had a conflict around his sexual identity. However, while we sanctioned the doll play, we did not explore the meaning of the family fantasies expressed through it.

In general, activity-group therapy has been conceived as a long-term method in which most members remain in treatment for at least two years. However, this therapist has used the method in a more focused way, establishing a contract for 36–40 group sessions with review at the end of that time. The groups have usually begun in the fall at the start of the school year and terminated in the spring at the end of the year. The groups are conducted like ordinary activity-therapy groups, in which the nature and quality of the experience are critical, although the therapist may at times intervene in a more focused way than is usual in activity-group therapy. Scheidlinger (1965) and others have described similar modifications for different purposes when they have been treating children with very weak ego control.

In the short-term activity groups conducted by the author, goals are set in family evaluations prior to referral to "the club." These are explicitly established with parents and children, in contrast to the practice in conventional activity groups, where reasons for treatment and desired goals are often only implicit. Goals are ego-oriented, often behavioral, such as "learning to get along better with other children and have friends," "being able to stand up for myself," "feeling good about myself," "getting along better with my parents," "finding school more interesting." These goals are based on what the children would like for themselves.

The group to be described here and others like it were conducted in mental health and child-guidance clinics. However, similar groups have been run in family agencies and in school guidance departments. It is important that there are enough children available so a group can be formed that will develop therapeutic interaction. If all the children are very passive and withdrawn, the therapist will be forced to take on too much responsibility for initiating action. On the other hand, if all the children are very aggressive and defiant, the group is likely to get out of control. Although some children may be eager to defy authority, others must have stronger superegos, at least initially, in order to support the positive directions of the group and to place some restraints on the acting out.

Children and their parents who are referred to the clinic are evaluated in three different ways. In some clinics, the family goes through a regular intake process of several interviews and a diagnostic assessment is made. In one clinic, attended only by rather literate middle-class families, the author and others developed a questionnaire exploring the history of the family, the identified problems, and the psychological and social adjustment of the child at home, at school, and with peers. From this questionnaire, which the family filled out before the first interview, it was possible to select children suitable for the group on a quite reliable basis, and a treatment program was immediately worked out with the family.

In another clinic, this author used single two-hour group sessions to aid in diagnosis. Intake started with a telephone conversation with a mental health professional who had accepted the application and ascertained that there was no immediate emergency and no psychosis in the family. Parents were then given appointments for themselves and their children. They came at the same time for a parents' group and a children's group, and then families returned for individual and family interviews. The rationale for using these different modalities was that the staff wished to observe the children and their parents under different circumstances.

The aim of the children's group session was to observe how the boys and girls coped with a new and unfamiliar situation and related to peers and adults in a group. Two therapists met with four or five children in a large playroom. A wide variety of toys and games was provided. At the start of the session, the children were introduced to each other, and the group was explained as an opportunity for them to become acquainted with the therapists and clinic and for the therapists to get to know them. Then a period of free play was announced and the children were allowed to take the initiative. This was the moment when the children felt most anxious—in a strange place, with strange people, not sure what they were supposed to do. Reactions varied considerably. Some children approached the adults, others engaged their peers. Some of the children moved immediately into an activity or a game. A few children did nothing and withdrew into themselves. The therapists intervened only to calm or reassure overactive or fearful children but otherwise allowed the children free play. This gave the therapists an opportunity to evaluate how the children related to each other and to note their expectations of authority in a novel situation. It also permitted the therapists to study their physical coordination and their tendencies to engage in concrete, collaborative, or creative activities or to indulge in fantasy.

After the play period, the group met around a table for refreshments and discussion. The therapists could now observe how the children came to table for a meal and how they handled food. This can be very revealing. Whereas most children are rather polite at a first session, there are some who cannot control their impulse to grab and still others who are unable to eat in front of strangers. The refreshment period gave the children an opportunity to talk about themselves, to tell what they liked and didn't like to do. The play activity having broken the ice, they felt freer to exchange information about their schools, neighborhoods, and families.

After the refreshments, crayons and water-based paints were provided and the children were asked to draw a person and a scene from their lives. To complete the session, the children created a group picture. The individual art works were again revealing through the choice of subject, the choice of medium and color, and the children's capacities to project their ideas into art. The group picture revealed the capacity of the children to relate to each other and their willingness to take the initiative as leaders and organizers or to follow and share an activity.

The group session was followed by an individual and family interview on another occasion, and these contacts usually provided sufficient information to develop a diagnosis and a treatment plan. Sometimes, in these very few hours, it was possible to resolve minor family problems, such as misunderstandings between children and their parents.

One Group's History

The following group of preadolescent boys was selected by means of a questionnaire and a family interview at which goals for both the children and the parents were established. The children met in the group for 30 sessions over nine months. The setting was a large group room about 24 by 30 feet leading out onto very pleasant grounds and trees. There was a table for refreshments and a work table, closets and shelves for materials, and a washroom adjoining. The children could come to the group room without having to go through the main part of the clinic. It is very important for preadolescent children that there is enough space for them to play actively and that the room is somewhat insulated for other parts of the institution so that noise does not disrupt other functions. It should also be possible to lock up the possessions of the group, such as half-finished models and treasured paintings, so these can be carried over from meeting to meeting. While the room should be left tidy, floor, walls, and furniture should be of materials that are not easily damaged. The therapist should not have to inhibit the children for the sake of protecting the room.

Group Members

The group consisted of five boys ranging in age from 9 to 11:

Sam was a very upset and angry boy who, although 11 years old, could read at only the second-grade level. He was poorly coordinated, clumsy, and did not do well in sports. Most of the time he presented a blank expression, but occasionally he gave way to explosive rages. His family, which had moved five times during Sam's first year in school, was very competitive. Sam had been surpassed in the second grade by his brother, who was 11 months younger. The brother was well coordinated and also a fine athlete. Sam's father was particularly disappointed in Sam and nagged him constantly. Sam spent most of his time dreaming hostile fantasies. His goals in the group were to get along better with his father, do better in school, and make some friends.

Tom's father had died six months previously and, as the eldest child, Tom, also 11, was now assuming the role of "man of the house." Although he was concerned and responsible, he was depressed, his schoolwork had fallen off, and every now and then he got himself into trouble impulsively. It seemed as if his unconscious anger and guilt came to the surface and he made trouble for himself. His goal was to stop "messing up."

Chris, age 10, was the only son of a frustrated athlete who wanted his boy to live out his dreams. He wanted his son to be supermasculine and a top-flight ballplayer. Chris's mother was the dominant figure in the family, and there were three daughters who were closer to her than Chris was. Chris reacted negatively to the pressure to be masculine. He did not really feel he could live up to his father's image of him, and he thought it was much nicer to be a girl. He very provocatively played with dolls, cooked, swept the kitchen floor—all of which infuriated his parents and aroused much anxiety in his father. Chris did not articulate a goal for himself in coming to the group, since he came under protest and somewhat defiantly. However, our goal for him was to accept being a boy as a reality and obtain more enjoyment from that role. We worked concurrently with the parents to reduce the pressure placed on him.

George, also 10, was a large, flabby boy, bright and intelligent but fearful and overprotected by his mother. He would get into difficulty with peers, then run to his mother for protection. As a tattletale he was very unpopular with other children and had no friends. His goal was "to make friends with some other children."

Bob, age 9½, had a very strict father toward whom he was passively resistant. He could not defy his father openly, but he did not apply himself at school and was a follower with other children. He had difficulty expressing any anger and was afraid of asserting himself. His stated wish was "to do better in school."

Sam was the heaviest, but Tom was stronger in that he was thin and wiry whereas Sam was not athletic. While Sam might have been inclined to bully the younger children if he had been the strongest in the group, Tom was concerned for other children and usually kept the peace. George was well-built but became fearful if challenged aggressively and initially sought protection from the adult. Bob was smaller than the others but of normal build for his age and quite strong and sturdy. He did not initiate aggressive actions but very soon was able to stand up for himself in the group. Chris, slim and well-coordinated, avoided confrontations and at the beginning of the group assumed an effeminate walk and manner.

Sam's and Chris's parents participated in a parents' group that met every two weeks in the evenings. George's mother brought him each time and attended a mothers' guidance group. Tom's mother was in individual psychotherapy to help her remake her life following her husband's death. Bob's parents were not willing to be in treatment. However, it was possible to visit the family several times during the year and through these visits to persuade his father to be somewhat less harsh with him.

The group was run as a classic activity group except that, as these were articulate boys, the therapist did make some interpretations when the meaning seemed quite clear. As the group progressed, the boys spent more time than usual talking together at the table at the end of the meal.

Early Meetings

The therapist was in the meeting room early for the first meeting. She was laying out materials when Sam came in, the first to arrive. Pale and expressionless, he was overweight and looked flabby. He clutched several comic books and immediately sat down and held one before his face as if for protection. He did not respond to the therapist's greeting.

Bob was the next to arrive. He was a sturdy little boy with an engaging smile. He greeted the therapist and then sat down next to Sam and picked up a comic book. He did not take off his coat. George arrived next. He shook hands with the therapist and sat down next to her. He did not say anything but watched her sort out some lanyard material. Bob became restless. He got up and went over to the shelves, spotted some soldiers, and asked if he could play with them. He began to build a fort.

Chris, pale and slim, now entered. He sat down at the table and picked up the comic book that Bob had left on the table. All this time Sam paid no attention to anyone, and the boys did not speak to each other. Tom now came in, greeted the other boys and the therapist, and sat down. Almost immediately, however, he got up, went over to the closet, picked up a suction-cup gun with rubber-capped darts, and started to shoot them into the floor. Sam got up and joined him but had difficulty fitting the dart into the gun. Tom showed him how. Tom then found a tin target. When he shot the gun, the darts hit the tin with a loud noise. Each time, Tom looked at the therapist rather apprehensively as if he expected to be scolded. She paid no attention and he soon relaxed.

At the beginning of this session the boys showed how they characteristically reacted to anxiety. Sam took cover behind the comic book, as did Chris. George ranged himself close to the adult. Bob and Tom explored the room, selected aggressive toys, and started to play, Tom more actively than Bob. The aggressive shooting mobilized Sam, who in joining Tom with the guns showed his lack of coordination. Tom gave indications of his relationship at home with his mother in his expectation of reprimand when noisy.

Tom and Sam began to talk and Tom told him that he was in the sixth grade. Sam had to admit that he was only in the fourth. Later, when Bob told the others that he was only in the third grade, Sam exclaimed, "Baby!," indicating his own feelings about his poor school performance.

As the session proceeded, Bob initiated a game of cops and robbers in which all but Chris played. Chris took some of the lanyard material and started to work on it. Then he helped the therapist set out the meal, looking at her to see if she would comment. At the meal the boys exchanged stories about school and Scout Club. Chris told how his den mother made him undo a project on which he had worked pretty hard because they finished too quickly. The therapist commented that he must have been angry. He said, "I quit after that. I just didn't go back."

After the meal, all the boys went outside except Chris, who returned to lanyard making. Sam followed the others, pretending to stalk them and telling the therapist that he had learned how to stalk from an Indian friend. He climbed onto a carousel and tried to keep Bob from mounting, but Tom came along and the two boys pushed their way on. Then Tom climbed a tree. He had difficulty climbing down and confided to the therapist that he was always getting into difficulty.

As the meeting wore on, the boys exhibited some of their problems. Sam indicated his tendency to bully. Tom got himself into difficulty over the tree. Chris showed his distrust of women, expecting them to be unkind and destructive. Sam, Tom, and Bob particularly enjoyed active shooting games.

By the third session, the boys showed their problems more clearly. George began to provoke the others, particularly Tom, but would back down and run behind the therapist if the boys turned on him. Chris and Bob spent much time playing with the dollhouse. They giggled a lot and looked at the therapist provocatively as if expecting her to disapprove and to try and stop them. Later in the meeting, Chris drew a girl's head on the blackboard and then, when he saw the therapist looking, erased it. Again, she did not comment.

Tom showed his ambivalence about aggression and danger by shooting darts without the caps on and becoming very upset when he nearly hit Sam in the eye. He became contrite and commented that he was always doing stupid things. The therapist picked up the dart and put the cap back on. Tom and George invented a game jumping out of the window and called the others chicken when they would not follow. Since the room was on the first level, there was no real danger. Sam stuck cap guns in his belt and fantasied that he was the sheriff seeking out cattle thieves and bank robbers. He cornered all the guns and boasted about this. In consequence, he was chased by Tom and Bob and George. Chris stood on the sidelines commenting on what was going on. As they closed in on Sam, Sam became nervous and his voice became high-pitched and anxious. He was relieved when Bob changed sides to help him.

To lower the tension, the therapist served the meal and the boys rushed to the table. Sam and George grabbed most of the cookies, but George gave some of his away to Bob, who had got only one, and to Tom, who had not tried to grab.

Later Meetings

By the twelfth session Chris was clearly involved with his feelings about being a boy. When he entered the room, he complained how untidy it was and asked the therapist to tell the girls' club which met before that they should not leave it in such a mess. He and Sam wondered whether they would be the only ones at the meeting and talked about the fact that George's mother was going to have a baby. Chris remarked that he would like a brother; he had only sisters. Sam said he would like a sister; he had only a brother. Later, Chris told the therapist that his birthday was in March and that he wanted a watch—a boy's watch, anything but a girl's watch. He told her that he was doing well in school. He also said that he could have gone to a party that day but chose to come to the club instead. Later, he cleaned the blackboard with wet paper, obviously enjoying the mess, and played with the dollhouse, putting a double bed in the bedroom and the cradle in the dining room. He and Bob told stories of their fathers' bravery in the war, and he seemed pleased that his father was going to pick him up after the club. However, when the boys were playing cops and robbers again, he still played a neutral role, informing on both sides and avoiding an active part.

Sam also seemed concerned with his sexual identity. He boasted of having a girl friend in the seventh grade, showed interest in comparing the size of Coke and Pepsi bottles, and boasted that he was going to be in charge of the house when his father went to Europe—his mother wanted him to help her. He continued to express his aggression by bringing in cards with aggressive jokes on them. He used these to divert attention when Tom and Chris were talking about their excellent performance in school. Later, working on a model, he became anxious when he found a defective part. When he had difficulty completing the model he gave up and shot at furniture in the dollhouse. However, when Tom wanted the boys to chase Sam, Sam was now able to express his fear that they would beat him up and agreed to the game only when Tom reassured him that they would not.

Tom became very anxious when the other boys started talking about their fathers during the meal. He tried to start an active game and, when the others did not want to join in, he evolved another game for himself, shooting at a paper cup of water. Afterward, he sought reassurance from the therapist that she did not mind his playing such a messy game. He sought the therapist's approval by telling her of his excellent performance at school. Tom was the leader in the group. Sometimes he initiated the most daring activities, but at the same time he was concerned about what the therapist would think of them.

Bob continued to participate in all the active, aggressive games. Although he was not the group's leader, he was respected by the others and sometimes perceptive of their needs—for instance, going in support of Sam when Sam became panicky. Although the smallest and youngest, he was able to stand up for himself. The group support and a place to ventilate his feelings seemed to free him, and he began to perform better in school.

At the fifteenth session, Sam seemed quite depressed and angry. He stood at the work table, jabbing into some clay with a pencil. The therapist stood beside him and said quietly that he seemed upset. He told her that he would like to make a bomb and blow up the world. She was aware that his midterm grades had been poor and chose to comment on his apparent interest in chemistry, suggesting that he might like to be a scientist one day. He seemed to listen, so she continued that she thought he was intelligent (he had an IQ of 120) and that he could have a successful career when he grew up if he got some help with his reading and math. Would he like her to help arrange this?

He nodded. Later, she talked to his parents about this and for the rest of the year Sam received individual tutoring as well as participating in the group, and his skills rose from second- to fifth-grade level.

The seventeenth session was the turning point for George. Tom had come late to the group and had been rather subdued throughout the meeting. Evidently, something had upset him at school. As he got up from the table, George tripped him up and immediately Tom turned on George and started a fistfight. George called to the therapist, "Help me, help me!" but she was over by the bookshelves and pretended not to hear. Very quickly Tom gave George a punch on the nose and then broke away, his anger dying down quickly.

George stood in the middle of the room, raging at the therapist because she had not come to his rescue. Tom was looking rather guilty. The therapist replied that George was a big boy, equal in size to Tom. He had started the fight, which was a fair one, and she had not thought he needed any help. She thought he could take care of himself. She handed him a tissue to wipe his nose and suggested he might want to put some cold water on it.

George went to the door saying that he was going to leave the group and never come back. He wanted his mother. *She* would stand up for him. He ran out into the reception area but could not find her, for she was in group and he could not reach her. He came back still raging and saying that he hated the group and would never come back. Bob said they liked him but George would have to do what he thought best. Tom was upset at George's threat to leave the group. He said he was sorry that he had hurt his nose but that George had started it.

George hesitated in the doorway, threatening to leave, and the other boys stood around repeating that they would like him to stay but that it was his decision. The meeting ended with George still unsure what he was going to do. He did return to the group, and after this seemed much more confident. He ceased to run to the therapist for protection and shared the leadership of the group with Tom. At the twenty-fifth meeting, the boys were playing outside. George was standing next to the therapist acting as umpire in a game of baseball. A small child got into a car and then got out again several times as if hesitating whether to stay or leave. George turned to the therapist and said, with a broad grin, "We all know about mixed feelings, don't we, Mrs. Mac?"

At the twentieth meeting the boys again talked about their fathers as they ate their snacks. This time they did so in a more insightful way. Chris and Sam shared how their fathers wanted them to be great athletes and how they hated this. Bob told how his father was always pushing him to do well in school and would beat him if he didn't. It made him unable to think properly and then he didn't want to try, although he really did want to do well. Tom said, "I know. You want your success to be your own."

Tom then began to talk about his father. He felt so badly because the last two years when his father had been ill he had resented the time his mother had spent with him. He felt guilty about this and also because he had not wanted to share his mother. His father had been away much of the time before his illness and Tom had been "the man of the house." Sometimes Tom had not wanted him to come back, but now he missed him terribly. He wondered whether his bad feelings had helped make his father ill. He knew this really wasn't so, but he still felt bad about it.

Sam said he also was glad sometimes when his father was away because then he could relax with his mother. Chris also agreed that he sometimes liked to be home with just his mother and the girls. They all acknowledged that they had good and bad feelings about their parents. The therapist said that this was natural. Everyone had mixed feelings about their parents even when they loved them very much. This did not mean that feelings could kill. Tom seemed much relieved by this discussion, and his need to "mess up" and do dangerous things began to die away.

Most of the boys, with the exception of Chris, had participated in active, aggressive shooting and chasing games during the first few sessions. Sam had frequently been the object of the chase. However, he gradually was able to stand up for himself and he and Bob became quite friendly. In the middle phase of the group, the boys spent much time making models. At first, Sam was very clumsy and became upset and aggressive when he could not put things together. The therapist conveyed confidence in his ability to succeed.

George asked for a lot of attention from the therapist initially but she did not encourage his dependency and he gradually became more self-reliant. Chris and Bob spent a lot of time in so-called "feminine activities," testing to see if the therapist would become upset and reprove them. When she accepted their games quite calmly, activities such as doll play became less interesting to them. Tom too tried to arouse the therapist's anxiety by his "messing up." None of these escapades were really dangerous and she nonverbally expressed confidence that he would not and did not really need to hurt himself. In other ways he was a positive leader in the group as he was fundamentally a fair and friendly boy.

Closure

During the last few sessions, the boys spent much time playing baseball in the grounds. Sam's coordination improved and he became less clumsy. George also ceased to be afraid of physical contact. Even Chris joined in the games and gave up his "lounge lizard," provocatively feminine walk. He and George and Tom became good friends.

At one of the last sessions, the boys were talking about their summer. Chris spoke of having to go to camp. He confessed he was nervous as he had never been away before. He was afraid of stepping on snakes or scorpions if he had to go to the john at night. Bob and Tom, who had been to camp, reassured him and suggested he take a flashlight to see where he was going. They told him they too had been anxious about going to camp but had enjoyed it when they got there.

All the boys made considerable gains over the year. Both Sam's and Bob's schoolwork improved, Sam's most dramatically. He was able to become more relaxed and confident and ceased to be a bully. He made one or two friends in school and was appointed a traffic monitor, of which he was very proud. Bob's ability to express aggression in the club, and the acceptance and support accorded him by the other boys, enabled him to take more initiative in school and to attack his work more aggressively. He became less afraid of his father.

George also learned to rely on his own strengths, ceased to run to his mother for protection, and made good friends at school and in his neighborhood. Tom was able to give up his sense of overresponsibility and guilt and to grieve normally for his father. He ceased to get into trouble. Chris accepted himself as a normal boy and ceased provoking his parents with feminine behavior. While he continued to be more interested in intellectual and artistic things, he was also willing to participate in sports and enjoyed his summer at camp. He made some good friends among the boys as well as continuing to enjoy the company of girls. He no longer felt that women were destructive creatures whom he could not trust.

Evaluation

The role of the therapist in this group was to be accepting of the boys. She genuinely liked and enjoyed them all. She sought to understand and respond to each boy's individual needs. When Sam became anxious because the boys were crowding him, she moved in closer or diverted them initially, until Bob began to come to Sam's support. When George sought protection unnecessarily, she withheld it, conveying the idea that he did not need it. She tried to help Tom feel less guilty about his actions, did not blame him when he "messed up," but made sure he did not try anything that was too dangerous. She neither approved or disapproved of Bob's attempts to provoke her by acting out in "feminine" ways. She treated this as natural and so it ceased to be interesting. She accepted and liked the boys as they were and encouraged them to become what was most natural for them. She did not interpret conflicts but rather exuded confidence that the boys could manage to overcome their difficulties and achieve their goals.

Traditional activity groups have been run for one-sex patients, either boys or girls, and conducted by a therapist of the same sex. However, the predominance of latency-age boys attending child-guidance clinics and the large numbers of female child therapists led to experimentation with female therapists leading boys' groups. In this particular group it was probably quite useful to have a female therapist. While the sex of the therapist did not really matter for Tom, Sam, and Bob, George was able to deal with his reliance on an overprotective mother through his experience with a very different maternal figure in the shape of the therapist. Chris too, while resisting his father's pressure to become masculine, had at least partly adopted a feminine identity because of his fear of his father's power and domination. It was safer to be feminine. Thus it was particularly useful for him to experience a more permissive and accepting woman whom he could trust.

None of these boys had really begun to enter puberty. They did not show the reluctance to accept feminine authority described by the author in another paper (MacLennan & Rosen, 1963). In two groups described there, composed of 11- and 12-year-old boys, the peer leaders began to develop an "I am the all-powerful male" syndrome, well-known in fifth-grade classes in America. They began to exhibit curiosity about their budding sexuality and wished to turn the therapist from their mother into their love object. In one of these groups, this phenomenon was dealt with by adding a male therapist, which initially infuriated the boys. However, they soon accepted him and identified with him, transferred the female therapist back into a mother figure, and sought their love objects outside the group. In the other group, the therapist converted the process into an activity-interview group in which the curiosity about homo- and heterosexuality and what it was like to grow up into a young man could be dealt with directly in discussion. Both methods worked well.

The group described in this chapter worked therapeutically because, in the relatively safe and accepting environment, the boys could reveal and work on their difficulties. They could gain support from each other, share mutual problems, understand that mixed feelings were inevitable and appropriate. As they gained confidence in themselves and rid themselves of pent-up aggressive and unhappy feelings, they were able to perform more effectively physically and intellectually. They were also able to care more for others and to become desirable and popular as friends. They felt less need to provoke and annoy their parents and consequently received more love and approval from them. A positive cycle of feeling and interaction was established.

In the early days of the group, the members looked to the therapist to sanction their behavior and to protect them from each other. As the members grew more confident in themselves and more trusting in each other, they were able to make their own group decisions and to function more cooperatively.

None of the boys in this group had very severe psychopathology. However, without intervention, the consequences for all could have been serious. Both Bob and Sam were failing in school, and Sam in particular had considerable difficulty in controlling his aggression. He was living a solitary life, isolated in his own aggressive fantasies. Tom was not able to deal with the loss of his father and his guilt about his negative feelings and was repeatedly getting into trouble. Chris was likely to continue to have difficulty with both men and women and to be unable to resolve his sexual identity if he did not get help. Although doing well intellectually, George was overattached to his mother and unable to make friends. These interpersonal problems were likely to handicap him seriously as he grew up, both in his relationships with colleagues and in his heterosexual relationships. Following up these boys over a year revealed that all continued to do well.

This group was particularly well balanced and, while it was designed as a 30-session group, progressed very rapidly and probably could have been terminated at about the twenty-fourth session. In today's climate of cost containment, it is important to design economic forms of treatment, and well-planned activity groups can be effective in resolving many preadolescent problems on a short-term basis. However, it is important that the therapist be well-trained. Therapists should understand child development and child psychopathology. They should be trained in both individual and group psychodynamics. They must understand the strengths and weaknesses of the children and the ways in which they defend themselves against anxiety and hurt. Some activity groups can go through periods of intense emotional pressure, and the therapist must know his or her feelings and reactions in order to be able to respond therapeutically. There is no rote way to conduct activity-group therapy. The therapist is the tool in working with the children to create a therapeutic climate and in helping each child work through individual problems.

The institutional setting must also be permissive enough to allow for mess and noise in the group room and secure enough to be able to be the outside authority in containing the group when it threatens to overrun its boundaries. Consequently, while such groups can and have been run in school settings, it is preferable to conduct them in a more neutral milieu, such as a recreation center, a child-guidance clinic, or even a church basement. The games and crafts are merely the pegs on which to hang the treatment; it is the quality of the climate and interaction that matters, not the quality of the physical environment.

References

Anderson, N., & Marrone, R. T. Group therapy for emotionally disturbed children: A key to affective education. *American Journal of Orthopsychiatry*, 1977, 47(1), 97–103.

Bardill, D. R. Behavior contracting and group therapy with preadolescent males in a residential treatment setting. *International Journal of Group Psychotherapy*, 1972, 22(3), 333–342.

Barksy, M., & Mozenter, G. The use of creative drama in a children's group. *International Journal of Group Psychotherapy*, 1976, 26(1), 105–114.

Brunning, R. M., & Stover, D. O. *Behavior modification in child treatment.* New York: Aldine, 1971.

Brundage-Aguar, D., Forebard, R., & Caminero, A. R. A review of treatment approaches for hyperactive behavior. *Journal of Clinical Child Psychology*, 1979, 6(1), 3–10.

Churchill, S. R. Social group work: A diagnostic tool in child guidance. *American Journal of Orthopsychiatry*, 1965, 35(3), 581–588.

Daniels, C. R. Play group therapy with children. *Acta Psychotherapeutica*, 1964, 12(1), 45–48.

Effron, A. K. Children and divorce: Help from an elementary school. *Social Casework*, 1980, 61(5), 305–316.

Frank, M. G., & Zilbach, J. Current trends in group therapy with children. *International Journal of Group Psychotherapy*. 1968, 18(4), 447–460.

Ganter, G., & Polansky, N. A. Predicting a child's accessibility to individual treatment from diagnostic groups. *Social Work*, 1964, 9(3), 56–63.

Green, R., & Fuller, M. Group therapy with feminine boys and their parents. *International Journal of Group Psychotherapy*, 1973, 23(1), 54–68.

Karson, S. Group psychotherapy with latency age boys. *International Journal of Group Psychotherapy*, 1965, 15(1), 81–89.

King, B. L. *Diagnostic activity groups for latency age children*. New York: Community Service Society, 1970.

Landgarten, H., Junge, M., Tasem, M., & Watson, M. Art therapy as a modality for crisis intervention: Children express reactions to violence in their community. *Clinical Social Work Journal*, 1978, 6(3), 224–229.

Lovasdal, S. A multiple therapy approach in work with children. *International Journal of Group Psychotherapy*, 1976, 26(4), 475–486.

MacLennan, B. W. Modifications of activity group therapy for children. *International Journal of Group Psychotherapy*, 1977, 27(1), 85–96.

MacLennan, B. W., & Rosen, B. Female therapists in activity group therapy with boys in latency. *International Journal of Group Psychotherapy*, 1963, 13(1), 34–42.

Omaha Tornado Project. *Final report to the Federal Disaster Administration*. Omaha: Eastern Nebraska Human Services Agency, 1976.

Pappenfort, D. M., & Levitt, J. L. *Achievement Place: A behavioral-treatment program in a group home setting*. Washington, D.C.: U.S. Dept. of Justice, Law Enforcement Assistance Administration, National Institute of Juvenile Justice and Delinquency Prevention, 1980.

Pasnau, R. O., Meyer, M., Davis, L. J., Lloyd, R., & Kline, G. Coordinated group psychotherapy of children and parents. *International Journal of Group Psychotherapy*, 1976, 26(1), 89–103.

Redl, F. Diagnostic group work. *American Journal of Orthopsychiatry*, 1944, 14(1), 53–67.

Rhodes, S. L. Short-term groups of latency-age children in a school setting. *International Journal of Group Psychotherapy*, 1973, 23(2), 204–216.

Schamess, G. Group treatment modalities for latency-age children. *International Journal of Group Psychotherapy*, 1976, 26(4), 455–473.

Scheidlinger, S. Three group approaches with socially deprived latency-age children. *International Journal of Group Psychotherapy*, 1965, 15(4), 434–445.

Scheidlinger, S. Group therapy for latency-age children: A bird's eye view. *Journal of Clinical Child Psychology*, 1977, 6(1), 40–43.

Slavson, S. R., & Schiffer, M. *Group psychotherapies for children: A textbook*. New York: International Universities Press, 1975.

Strunk, C. S., & Witkin, L. J. The transformation of a latency-age girls' group from unstructured play to problem-focused discussion. *International Journal of Group Psychotherapy*, 1974, 24(4), 460–470.

Williams, J., Lewis, C., Copeland, F., Tucker, L., & Feagan, L. A model for short-term group therapy on a children's inpatient unit. *Clinical Social Work Journal*, 1978, 6(1), 21–32.

5

A Structured Group for Undersocialized, Acting-out Adolescents

Billie F. Corder, Ed.D.

BILLIE F. CORDER is co-director of psychological services in the Child Psychiatry Training Program at Dorothea Dix Hospital in Raleigh, North Carolina, and a member of the clinical faculty of the University of North Carolina School of Medicine, Department of Psychiatry.

Therapists who must develop treatment programs for undersocialized, acting-out adolescents from low socioeconomic backgrounds quickly discover the inadequacies of traditional psychotherapeutic modalities. These patients are particularly difficult to treat in psychotherapy groups. Restive and intellectually limited, they have restricted vocabularies, speak in slang phrases and obscenities, and have great difficulty formulating ways to verbalize their concerns and feelings.

The present paper describes a type of structured psychotherapy group that has proved highly effective with these difficult patients. The specific techniques employed include: (1) development of group goals; (2) a pretherapy training program; (3) a group therapy contract; (4) a therapeutic game designed to structure initial sessions; and (5) techniques for assessing group progress.

Background

The Therapist's Background

As a staff psychologist at Eastern State Hospital in Lexington, Kentucky, in the early 1960s, I was assigned to develop therapy groups for the small number of adolescents committed to the facility. My interest in group therapy for adolescents expanded in later work at the Child Guidance Clinic in Lexington. For many of the adolescents referred to these groups, selection criteria recommended for conventional therapy groups were not applicable, since the patients were severely deficient in the verbal and social-interaction skills normally considered requisites for group psychotherapy. While most group-therapy training programs and the literature suggest that one might include one, or at most two, of these limited, acting-out adolescents, my training did not prepare me for working with an entire group of patients perceived as marginally functional in group-therapy situations. Later, at the Area C Adolescent Crisis Intervention Center in Washington, D.C., where I was director of day care services, treatment programs were required for an even more difficult group: aggressive, often violent adolescents whose participation was coerced and who were often highly resistive to any intervention.

Such experiences begin to convince a therapist of the futility of traditional individual psychotherapy approaches, and attempting a traditional group-therapy approach with five to eight of these youngsters is more likely to traumatize the therapist than to aid the clients. Over the years, I began to develop a number of more structured, intrinsically interesting approaches to groups for this kind of adolescent. In 11 years at Dorothea Dix Hospital in Raleigh, North Carolina, along with coworkers and trainees I have completed a number of research projects that have produced the materials employed in these structured groups.

The Institutional Setting

The Child Psychiatry Training Program is a part of the psychiatric training programs of the University of North Carolina School of Medicine and Dorothea Dix Hospital, a regional state mental hospital. The program's outpatient clinic offers a broad range of services relevant to the training needs of residents, fellows, and graduate trainees in psychiatry, psychology, and social work. Its clients represent varied socioeconomic levels and diagnostic problems.

The outpatient, adolescent group described here was one of a series held in a large group-home facility in Raleigh that served orphaned children and others from indigent or temporarily nonfunctioning families for whom the North Carolina Department of Social Services had ordered extended or temporary respite care. Adolescents living in the home attended school and/or worked in the community.

Group Members

Group members were referred by the group-home staff. They were described as showing significant levels of disturbed or acting-out behavior within the community, school, or group-home setting. This particular group consisted of five adolescents (two male, three female) ranging in age from 13 to 17. Intellectual functioning was within the average range, and all had lived in lower socioeconomic environments prior to group-home residence (family incomes were slightly higher than the state's poverty level). None had individual therapists, and as a group they showed the following personality and behavioral characteristics: low frustration tolerance, mildly antisocial acting out (stealing, truancy, fighting), and poor verbal skills. The group was led by me together with a male staff psychologist from the Child Psychiatry Training Program's outpatient clinic.

Membership in the group was voluntary, and sessions met weekly for one hour over eight months. There were few absences and no dropouts. This may be attributed to the following facts: Being referred to the group had a kind of status within the group-home setting. Members missed part of their required study period to come to the group. There was no transportation problem since members had to walk only a short distance from the home. We strived to make group meetings intrinsically interesting, and the youngsters enjoyed their association with "the doctors from the medical school training program." We also served refreshments after group meetings on such special occasions as a member's birthday, Halloween, Christmas, etc. None of these factors alone would account for the youngsters' cooperation, but in combination they provided a highly motivated group. In another group in the same setting, when we removed a group member from the group for two weeks because of acting-out behavior within the group, he complained to the residence staff and would wait at the meeting-room door, demanding to be allowed back into the group.

Group Goals

The goals of the group were based primarily on a study of "curative factors" in adolescent groups modeled after Yalom's (1970) work in establishing characteristics and functions of adult psychotherapy groups that were perceived as helpful by group members and on our own similar study of adolescents (Corder et al., 1981a). In the latter study, adolescent group members in a number of different treatment settings were asked to rank 60 cards containing statements

TABLE 5-1

Curative Factors Chosen as Most Helpful by Adolescents*

Item no.	Category	Percent of Subjects	Item statement
7-35†	Catharsis	44	Being able to say what was bothering me instead of holding it in.
7-34†	Catharsis	38	Learning how to express my feelings.
12-60†	Existential factors	38	Learning that I must take ultimate responsibility for the way I live my life, no matter how much guidance and support I get from others.
4-18†	Interpersonal learning (input)	38	Other members honestly telling me what they think of me.
9-43	Family reenactment	31	Being in the group was, in a sense, like being in a big family, only this time, a more accepting and understanding family.
2-10	Group cohesiveness	25	Belonging to a group of people who understood and accepted me.
5-24	Interpersonal learning (output)	25	The group's giving me an opportunity to learn to approach others.
3-12	Universality	25	Seeing I was just as well off as others.
1-5	Altruism	25	Helping others and being important in their lives.

*Table includes all items chosen by 25% or more subjects for Category I—most helpful, or Category II—extremely helpful.

†Items which were also chosen by adults for these categories.

describing Yalom's curative factors in group psychotherapy into categories ranging from "most helpful to me in group" to "least helpful to me in group." Results of the rankings are shown in Tables 5-1 and 5-2. Curative factor items ranked as the ten most helpful by adults are shown in Table 5-3 (Yalom, 1970).

The adolescents' low ranking of insight category items, compared to higher rankings by adults, can be attributed to the higher level of defensiveness maintained by adolescents against recognition and expression of repressed conflicts and to the more indirect techniques used by many adolescent-group therapists, which may not emphasize direct interpretation of focus primarily on underlying conflicts (Masterson, 1958; Sugar, 1975).

The results of our study appeared to support the assumptions of Shapiro et al. (in Sugar, 1975), who describe the importance of developing self-perception through peer feedback and recapitulating family experiences through group experiences. The importance attributed to these interpersonal learning experiences suggested to us that increased use of techniques that actively structured and ensured opportunities for peer feedback about behavior, such as role playing and psychodrama, might enhance group perception of positive movement

TABLE 5-2

Curative Factors Chosen as Least Helpful by Adolescents*

Item no.	Category	Percent of subjects	Item statement
10-49	Insight	60	Learning that I react to some people or situations unrealistically with feelings that somehow belong to earlier periods in my life.
7-33	Catharsis	40	Expressing negative and/or positive feelings toward the group leader.
8-40†	Identification	33	Finding someone in the group I could pattern myself after.
4-20	Interpersonal learning (input)	27	Learning that sometimes I confuse people by not saying what I really think.
6-28†	Guidance	27	Group members telling me what to do.
8-36†	Identification	27	Trying to be like someone in the group who was better adjusted than I.
10-50	Insight	27	Learning that how I feel and behave today is related to my childhood and development.
12-58	Existential factors	27	Recognizing that no matter how close I get to other people, I must still face life alone.

*Table includes all items chosen by 25% or more subjects for Category VI—less helpful, or Category VII—least helpful
†Items which were also chosen by adults for these categories.

TABLE 5-3

Curative Factors Chosen as Most Helpful by Adults*

Item no.	Category	Rank	Item statement
10-48	Insight	1	Discovering and accepting previously unknown or unacceptable parts of myself.
7-35†	Catharsis	2	Being able to say what was bothering me instead of holding it in.
4-18†	Interpersonal learning (input)	3	Other members honestly telling me what they think of me.
7-34†	Catharsis	4	Learning how to express my feelings.
4-16	Interpersonal learning (input)	Tie 5	The group's teaching me about the impression I make on others.
7-32	Catharsis	Tie 5	Expressing positive and/or negative feelings toward another group member.
12-60†	Existential factors	Tie 5	Learning that I must take ultimate responsibility for the way I live my life no matter how much guidance and support I get from others.
4-17	Interpersonal learning (input)	Tie 8	Learning how I come across to others.
7-37	Catharsis	Tie 8	Seeing that others could reveal embarassing things and take other risks and benefit from it helped me to do the same.
5-22	Interpersonal learning (output)	10	Feeling more trustful of groups and of other people.

*Item rank of 60 item statements represents rank order of helpfulness as perceived by adult subjects with 1 = most helpful, 60 = least helpful
†Items also chosen for these categories by adolescent subjects.

toward change. It also suggested that a pretherapy training program that actively taught techniques for constructive expression of feelings and for giving and receiving feedback about behavior might enhance and increase these interpersonal learning experiences early in the group process. The high rankings given to opportunities for cathartic expression of feelings prompted the researchers to concentrate on the development of other techniques that might encourage this expression without developing intolerable levels of group tension and anxiety, which are easily reached in volatile adolescent groups. The techniques developed are described in the account of the group that follows.

Group Preparation

Social Skills Training

In previous groups in this setting, some adolescents had proved severely deficient in basic social and communication skills, as measured by the Devereux Adolescent Behavior Scale (Spivak et al., 1967) and as observed at clinical interviews. Such adolesents, when referred to the therapy group, were required to complete a social skills training program involving three to four months of weekly one-hour sessions, during which they followed a highly structured manual (Corder et al., 1981b).

The training provided specific social and behavioral skills, such as "Successful and Unsuccessful Behavior" (problem-solving skills, feedback about behavior), "Etiquette Olympics" (etiquette for basic daily skills such as table manners and social introductions), and "How to Make a Friend" (basic communication skills, recognizing social cues). Each session involved group discussion, role playing of structured "scenes" illustrating the skills to be learned, and practice for each member, progressing from the simplest to more difficult and complex tasks (recognizing body cues, initiating a conversation, learning to negotiate in problem solving, learning to verbalize anger in an acceptable manner).

In most cases, adolescents began group-therapy sessions after practicing these social skills and being rated as improved in them.

The Therapeutic Contract

Adolescents referred to the group were interviewed individually by the cotherapists, who explained the general purpose of the group and developed with the adolescent an individualized, written contract for group-therapy involvement and responsibilities (Corder et al., 1980a). The therapy contract (Exhibit 5-1) concretely describes group-therapy techniques, expectations for the adolescent's behavior, and methods of handling confidentiality issues, and it sets up some positive expectations for therapy. The adolescent is required to set at least two goals for himself, which may be changed or expanded later in therapy.

Exhibit 5-1

GROUP THERAPY CONTRACT FOR ADOLESCENTS, PARENTS AND THERAPISTS

This contract is written to help improve understanding, agreement, and communication by (1) the adolescent and the group, (2) parents and guardians, and (3) the therapists, about the goals of therapy, the type of therapy offered, handling of confidential information, and appropriate expectations and responsibilities on the parts of those involved.

Treatment Goals. In group therapy, the adolescent will have the opportunity to learn to talk, think about, and solve problems that he agrees to work on with the help of the therapists and other group members. He will be expected to help his fellow group members in the same way that they are expected to help him. Members are not forced to talk about anything that they do not wish to talk about. Though we cannot work on anything the adolescent is not willing to work on, the group is available to help him change the things about himself that he does want to change. For those who are willing to work and try, small changes are usually seen after 12 to 16 sessions (once weekly). Usually people get to know and trust the group and begin talking about important issues in eight sessions. Lasting differences usually don't show for six months to a year; it took people a long time to be the way they are, and it takes a while to learn to be a different way. In therapy groups, therapists do not give much direct advice and do not give commands. Rather, they use relationships in the groups and techniques to help people understand themselves, their problems, other people, and the ways that they can go about changing themselves.

Expectations and Responsibilities of Adolescents and Parents. The adolescent is expected to come regularly once a week to the group, to talk about feelings and problems, to listen to others, and to try to help them. If he has to miss a session, he is expected to call beforehand to give the reason, since others in the group will worry about him. He has to pick some problem areas to work on, though these may change somewhat later, and be willing to discuss these in the group. Parents and guardians should not expect the group to change anything the adolescent does not want to change, though it often happens that the feedback the person receives from the group will influence him to want to change some of the same things parents would like to see him change. Parents and guardians will be expected to provide transportation for their adolescent, to pay bills on a regular basis unless the adolescent can agree to take responsibility for paying all or part of his bills, and to be involved in collateral parent therapy if this is available. Parents are expected to contact the therapists if they have questions or concerns about the adolescent's experience in therapy.

Confidentiality. Parents will receive letters periodically from the group, written by the therapists, group members, and their adolescent, which tells in general how he is getting along and what kinds of things the group thinks it would be helpful for them to know. All specific things said in the group are secret and confidential between the group, and will not be shared with parents unless the adolescent agrees to it. The only exception to this rule is when the adolescent tells something which may result in danger or harm to himself or to others. Then the therapists have an obligation to tell parents and/or take other action. The parents can contact the therapists for information or discussion at any time within the limits described.

Individual Goals. Some of the things I want to work on in the group are: (Adolescent writes in own goals statements and must select at least two goals)

We have read and understand and agree with the therapy plan described. *SIGNED:* (Parents/Guardians, Adolescent, and Therapists)

The contract was read word for word with each adolescent. Members approached the contract with extreme seriousness. They enjoyed the formal signing—one even asked if we were going to have it notarized. They viewed the contract as an adult, respectful form of asking for their involvement and recognizing their control over it.

Pretherapy Training

After initial interviews with the co-therapists and the development of the therapy contract, group members were introduced to the group-therapy process by a brief pretherapy training program involving the use of a 45-minute videotape and a printed orientation information packet. The pretherapy training program has increased positive expectations for treatment, speeded development of group cohesion, reduced time spent in "pasttime discussions" in early sessions, and decreased verbalized concerns over confidentiality. It has also facilitated the growth of patient skills in giving and receiving feedback earlier in the group process (Corder et al., 1980a).

In preparing the topics and issues covered by the videotape, we interviewed adolescents in a number of different treatment settings about their initial concerns and misconceptions about group therapy. These subjects were addressed in the videotape, which dramatizes the entry of an adolescent into a psychotherapy group, beginning with the initial interviews and therapists and including a dramatized scene from an early group session. In the interview scene, the actor-patient discusses the issues and fears that had been identified by the adolescents surveyed. The group-session scene is structured to illustrate as many as possible of the guidelines for group behavior contained in the orientation information packet. Following the group-session scene, the therapists on the tape review the group's behavior with reference to specific guidelines for giving and receiving feedback and participating in role playing, and they discuss the therapists' role and function in the group.

The written guidelines (Exhibit 5-2) for group participation contained in the orientation information packet had been discussed in earlier interviews and illustrated by the videotape. These guidelines were developed primarily from clinical experience and from a reformulation of material suggested by Gauron and Rawlings (1975) and Beier et al. (1971) in work with adults. Members were asked to review the simply written material, which emphasizes the need for listening, urges responsibility for bringing problems to the group, and covers the need for practicing positive behaviors and changes in behavior outside the group. The training guidelines are read aloud for the group members in the videotape.

Exhibit 5-2

GROUP PARTICIPATION GUIDELINES

1. It's a waste of time to talk about things about yourself that you think it's impossible to change ("I can't help my temper . . . that's the way I am.") You can change anything about yourself you really want to change.

2. When someone else is talking, listen and try to understand what they are saying about themselves. It might also apply to you, and they need your view of what they are talking about. This is as much a part of your job as talking about yourself.

3. *Sometimes* suggesting a way of solving a problem is helpful to others. But most of the time, it is more helpful to help them find out why they didn't do the right thing in the first place. People usually know what they should do . . . they just have trouble doing it.

4. You're supposed to practice what you talk about in here. Just talking won't change people much. You have to practice the changes you think about in here in your everyday life. Then be willing to let the group know about how things went when you practiced new ways outside the group.

5. You have an obligation to tell the group about things that are worrying you. The therapists and the group can't read your mind. They will *help* you talk, but you have to make yourself talk about things that concern you.

6. You have an obligation to tell others in the group what you think about the things they say. You have agreed to help each other, and you can do it by telling others in a kind way how they come across to you in the way they act and talk.

7. Try to be as honest as you can. We can't read your mind, and hiding stuff won't help us help you. Try to talk straight about your feelings and thoughts.

8. When something important is happening to you, inside or outside the group, be willing to let the group know about it.

HOW TO TELL OTHER PEOPLE WHAT YOU THINK ABOUT
WHAT THEY SAY AND DO (FEEDBACK)

1. Telling someone else what you think can be done in a kind way that is also honest. There's a real difference in attacking someone and in letting them know how they're coming across to you.

2. It's usually better to talk about things you actually see people doing and saying in the group; then you have the real thing to report on.

3. Tell the person how what they did or said made you feel, or what you thought about it without using bad labels (don't say, "You acted like an idiot" or "That was dumb") or name calling. Instead you might say, "What you did makes me think you were madder than you admit" or "What you said made me think you were making fun of me and hurt my feelings."

4. Don't talk about people in a general, fuzzy way ("He always makes trouble," "She's just like that"). Talk about the actual things they do and say ("You sounded like you did not hear what I said"). Be as specific as you can and don't wait a long time to say what you thought about what is happening in the group.

5. Tell people how you feel about good things you think they say and do. People also need to know when they come across in a good way to others.

HOW TO ACCEPT WHAT OTHERS SAY TO YOU ABOUT
WHAT YOU SAY AND DO (TAKING FEEDBACK)

1. Be willing to talk about what they say to you.

2. Try not to get angry when people have to say things you don't like. You are here to learn how you affect others and how they affect us.

3. You don't have to agree with what people say about you. But you should be willing to accept that this is how it looks and feels to them.

4. If you don't understand what somebody is saying, say so.

5. Ask people to tell you about how they feel about what you do and say. If you take their ideas reasonably, they will be more likely to give them attention.

Aspects of the Group

Introductions

During the initial sessions of the group, members were asked to pair themselves with the person seated on the right, to separate briefly from the group, and after a short discussion with their partners to return to the group and introduce each other. Specifically, these were their instructions: "You are going to introduce each other to the group. Find out what the other person wants you to say about him or her to the group. It should include something brief about what some of the things are that he wants to work on in the group, and something about what he would like other people here to know about him. Individuals should say only as much as they want to say right now, but enough to try to help us get to know them."

Here is an example of one member's introduction of another: "Well, ——
— says she has a sister and a brother who are here too, and one sister who is
married and lives in ——. She said she never gets to see her mother, though,
because she is married again, and they don't get along, even when she goes
to see her on Christmas. And she says that the social worker said she could
come to the group because she had a lot of trouble with the houseparents. But
she said it was usually not her fault and she wants to talk about how unfair
they are to her. And her favorite group is Kiss."

The pairs also included the co-therapists, who had some of the group members introduce them and who introduced group members. One group member
introduced a co-therapist this way: "Well, she says she is a psychologist and
she likes to work with kids our age in groups because she likes to see us work
on things and learn how to get along good. She wouldn't tell me anything really
about herself, except I know she is married and lives in Raleigh. She said the
group is about us, and not about her."

"The Life Game"

To lower anxiety levels and encourage positive group interaction, the therapists utilize some structured group-activity materials for at least half of the
hour during the first four or five sessions, and continue the use of structured
activity until there is a gradual increase in the unstructured portion of the
session along with acceptable levels of tension and positive interaction. This is
usually accomplished within two months, even with groups that are most difficult in terms of the wide ranges in abilities and motivation levels.

One type of structured activity is "The Life Game," which has been used
in a number of treatment and residential settings (Corder, 1977; Corder et al.,
1977). The object of the game is to facilitate the integration of groups with
wide ranges of intellectual and social skills, limited verbal skills, and little or
no previous experience in psychotherapy.

The game consists of a cardboard gameboard with squares labeled to cor-
respond to "item" cards, which are stacked in the middle of the board in areas
labeled "Knowing Yourself," "Understanding Each Other," and "Problem
Solving." These areas relate to specific adolescent developmental tasks: "Knowing Yourself" deals with verbalization of feelings and feeling states; "Understanding Each Other" deals with development of communication and interaction
skills; "Problem Solving" deals with discussion and role playing. The "items"
on the cards are questions or tasks divided into five levels (lettered A to E) of
intimacy, self-disclosure, and group cohesion required to handle them. Level
A contains warm-up, fairly neutral items; level E calls for intimate material
about self and others and problem solving in specific, intimate areas. These
items were developed from modifications for age and interest levels of ideas
from a variety of group discussion and interaction aids (James & Jongeward,

1973; Simon et al., 1972; Frye & Rockness, 1974; Gardner, 1959) and from an earlier, more simplistic therapeutic game (Corder, 1975).

Each player in turn moves his gamepiece (a poker chip with his name attached on a gummed label) around the board according to the number of spaces indicated by a dice roll, and answers the question or performs the task indicated on the card corresponding to the space on which he lands. The items themselves are written to require group interaction and discussion. Time spent on each item usually increases dramatically as the group progresses. Various items, representative of the three areas and the five levels, are shown in Exhibit 5-3.

Exhibit 5-3

SAMPLE ITEMS FROM "THE LIFE GAME"

KNOWING YOURSELF

Level A, item 6:   What is the best and worst thing about the school you go to? Ask the person on your right the same question.

Level B, item 4:   Tell the things about yourself that are like your mother, and the things that are like your father. Have the person on your left answer the same question.

Level C, item 5:   What do you think you will be like 10 years from now? What kind of job, family, and lifestyle do you think you will have? Ask 3 other people in the group the same question.

Level D, item 8:   What do you think is the most unfair thing that ever happened to you? Did you do anything that made it happen? Have any two other people in the group answer this question.

Level E, item 6:   What was the meanest thing you ever did to someone? What made you do it? How do you feel about it now? Would you handle it differently now? How? Have the person on your right answer this question for him/herself.

UNDERSTANDING
EACH OTHER

Level A, item 7:   Stand in front of each person in the group and tell him/her something about the way he/she looks, or anything that you think is pretty or nice (one thing per person).

Level B, item 8:	How can you tell when a person's feelings are really hurt? What do you usually do when your feelings are hurt? Ask the person on your left to tell you what he/she usually does when his/her feelings are hurt. (How they act, and how they show their feelings).
Level C, item 4:	If you had a bad reputation and decided to change your life, how could you go about showing other people you wanted to be different and get across to them that you wanted to change?
Level D, item 9:	Who in this group always has the most trouble telling about their feelings? What ideas do you have about how the group could help them? Ask the person on your right for his/her ideas.
Level E, item, 3:	Do you know anyone who committed suicide? Why do you think people usually kill themselves? Have you ever thought you might hurt yourself? Why do you think you had those feelings, and what did you do about them? Ask the person on your left these questions also.

PROBLEM SOLVING

Level A, item 5:	Should you tell other people that you come to group therapy? Ask the other members of the group what they plan to do about this.
Level B, item 7:	Suppose your 13-year-old sister planned to run away from home. What kinds of things would you tell her, and what kinds of advice would you give? Have a person of the opposite sex in the group answer this question.
Level C, item 3:	ACT OUT: You are working at a fast-food restaurant and the manager fusses at you about your work in front of everyone. Let the group help you assign roles, and then show how you would probably act. Then discuss the ways you usually handle your feelings when things like that happen.
Level D, item 9:	Suppose you don't want to do any kind of drugs or smoke pot, but several of your friends keep worrying you to do it. How would you handle this? Ask someone in the group of the opposite sex the same questions.
Level E, item 8:	What is a boy's responsibility if his girlfriend gets pregnant? Have the whole group discuss this question.

Group Process

Gradually, the time spent on structured activities such as "The Life Game" decreased as the group required less structure and developed signs of cohesion (launching quickly into personal material as the session began, demonstrating empathy for others in their verbal exchanges, etc.). Group discussion in the early sessions tended to begin with members' cathartic expressions of anger, resentment, and confusion over their present situation and move on to home placements and tenuous future plans during the first three months. The group concentrated on exploring present interpersonal relationships and difficulties during the last four to eight months. In the latter part, members tended to focus on their emotional and behavioral responses to loss, on attempts to feel some control over their environment, and finally on gaining some practice in concrete problem solving and planning for the immediate and sometimes more distant future.

Summaries

Each group session—which comprised both structured and unstructured portions—concluded with summaries performed in various ways by the group members. The members usually were instructed to "go around" and summarize what they thought had happened in that session and how they felt about the experience. Specifically, they were asked, "(1) Tell anything about yourself or your feelings that you didn't get a chance to say but felt was important. (2) Tell what you enjoyed about the group today and what you did not enjoy. (3) Tell anybody in the group something you wanted to tell them but didn't get a chance to say."

A touching example of one of these summaries, in an early session, was provided by one of the most withdrawn, least verbal members of the group, a boy who had little or no association with peers in the group residence: "There wasn't nothing I didn't like. What I did like was, I liked hearing —— talk about her Daddy and Mother and all. I guess I just liked setting here and being with the others. I didn't have nothing else to say. I don't like to talk much—they know that—but I like to set here and listen to the others and afterwards —— and me walk back together to the house."

Later in the sessions, a girl who had a history of expulsions from school for attacking other students and threatening them with weapons summarized her feelings using some of the transactional analysis concepts introduced briefly to the group in earlier sessions: "Well, today at first I thought I might have to whip ——'s ass, because she knows what she said was a lie. But then after we talked some more and I knowed how she thought that, I kept my temper. I was really on my adult part, you know. And what I didn't like was when — —— wouldn't stay on his adult part, just acted like a child. We ought to have some more rules in this group. Somebody ought to do something when a person keeps on acting on their child part."

The co-therapists always took their turns summarizing each session along with the group members. In a late session, one co-therapist said: "Today I really liked the way everyone really let ———— know that we understood what she was feeling. ———— even put her arm around her, to let her know we cared about how much she missed her mother. And I liked the way everybody shared with her some of their own feelings like hers. One thing I didn't get time to say, because we were feeling so much for ————, was that I did notice we didn't get to spend much time on ————, and he wanted to tell us about some things that happened at school. Can we talk about that next week, or can it wait till then?"

This exercise served a number of purposes: It allowed the group to practice giving and receiving feedback from peers about their group behavior; it provided practice in assessing group process and progress; and it allowed the group therapists, in their summary turns, to model techniques for giving and receiving feedback within the group and to reinforce the group for work on behavior targeted by group and individual goals.

Evaluation and Results

Evaluating the Group Process

For the first 15 minutes of every other group session, a videotape replay of portions of the previous session led to a structured discussion. Significant differences in the level of intimacy of verbal content and the frequency of feedback about behavioral content were noted. Where videotape equipment is available, this can be highly useful in assessing group progress (Corder et al., 1980b).

The letter from group members to parents and staff, described in the therapy contract, was also a useful tool in assessing group progress as well as providing feedback to parents and staff within confidentiality guidelines. In inpatient groups, this letter became a part of the patient's record; in the outpatient group described here, the letter was sent to the member's caseworker and was used, together with the caseworker's behavioral observations to assess behavioral progress and to assist in program planning.

The letter was written at approximately two-month intervals. Portions were written by the therapists, by the group, and by the individual member himself (Exhibit 5-4). Generally, the therapists wrote their comments prior to the group session and read them aloud during the meeting, recorded the consensus from the group about each member, and recorded the individual's own comments about his or her progress.

Exhibit 5-4

THE EVALUATION LETTER

Dear Treatment Team and Parents or Guardians:

As a report back to you about how group therapy is progressing, we will be sending you this letter every _____ . The letter will be filled out by the group therapist, the adolescent group members, and by your own adolescent, who is a member of the group. We will be checking about general areas of concern and about progress on individual goals; no confidential group material will be included, unless, as we have previously agreed, some material may be outside the limits of confidentiality (possible self-harm, severely destructive behavior towards others). If you have questions about this letter, please contact the therapist at _____ , or the Unit Administrator at _____ . All conferences about the letter will be discussed with the group member concerned.

TO BE COMPLETED BY GROUP THERAPISTS:

In general he/she shows, by his/her level of involvement and participation in group _____

_____

Within the group and with the other young people in the group, he/she shows the following level of frequency of verbal input to the group: _____

_____

Response to limit setting in the group: _____

Ability to give and receive feedback from the group: _____

Ability to discuss and deal with everyday problems: _____

Ability to bring up and discuss things which are truly important to him/her:

_____

Ability to understand responsibility for his/her own behavior: _____

(Check Appropriate Lists)

TO BE COMPLETED BY THE GROUP MEMBERS WITH ASSISTANCE OF THERAPISTS:

SHOWS GOOD ACHIEVEMENT

Polite & attentive _____

Gives feedback to others in a helpful way _____

Talks about important things _____

Is willing to talk about feelings _____

Shows "adult" behavior most of time _____

NEEDS IMPROVEMENT

Interrupts others _____

Criticizes others in a hurtful way _____

Does too much playing and chitchat in group _____

Is seldom on time _____

Shows "child" behavior much of the time in group _____

TO BE COMPLETED BY GROUP MEMBER INDIVIDUALLY

Of the specific problem areas which I selected to work on in the group I feel I have been working on: _____

_____

_____

I can describe how I think I have been doing in the group as: _____

_____

_____

The things I want to continue working on in the group are: _____

_____

_____

SIGNED _____   _____
                    Group Member   *Therapist*

DATE _____

The group members approached this task very seriously. The structured opportunity for giving a group consensus about the behavior and progress of another group member afforded a nonthreatening opportunity for peer feedback that was quite valuable and that proved an impetus for intense positive group interactions.

Some legal advocates believe that periodic sharing of information about aspects of the treatment program in this manner, along with the initial therapy contract, not only increases the therapeutic alliance with the family but provides an additional safeguard against development of misunderstandings and confusions regarding expectations for treatment, which often lead to discharge against medical advice and/or litigation between patients and mental health programs (Corder et al., 1976).

Group Results and Follow-up

Although the group members might not have been considered suitable candidates for a more traditional group-therapy approach, due to their limited abilities to form a therapeutic alliance, low levels of verbal skills, and prevalence of acting-out behaviors, the group-home staff reported some consistent gains in their behavior within community, school, and group-home settings. Amanda was able to be placed with another foster home, and remained there at follow-up four months later, longer than in any previous placement. Patsy appeared most improved, and the decrease in her violent, acting-out behaviors led to her placement in a part-time job in the community on a work-study program in which she took great pride, with no further suspensions from school throughout the remaining school year. Debbie showed the fewest changes, but house parents reported a decrease in verbal and physical conflicts with peers. Ronnie remained quiet and a loner, but was able to remain in group sessions and began to participate minimally in some extracurricular activities with another group member. David was placed for the summer with a member of his extended family who had been unwilling to accept him earlier as a result of his impulsive behavior. Later he was transferred to another group home that would not have accepted him earlier, when his behavior record failed to meet admission criteria.

The treatment of such youngsters in group therapy can be effective and can produce the limited but positive results I have described. But modification of traditional approaches is crucial in most treatment settings where the group mix is highly variable, where therapists must deal with a wide range of functioning, and where the adolescents themselves are deficient in the verbal and interactional skills necessary for effectively utilizing the group process.

A pretherapy training program and the use of structured modifications of typical group-therapy approaches seem critical for many of these types of groups, and their use appears to reduce the high levels of frustration, confusion, and anxiety that may sabotage initial group-therapy sessions with adolescents before they can achieve the positive feedback and cohesion necessary for continuing an ongoing group where attendance is not mandatory.

References

Beier, E. G., Robinson, P., & Micheletti, G. Susanville: A community helps itself in mobilization of community resources for self-help in mental health. *Journal of Consulting and Clinical Psychology*, 1971, 36(1), 142–150.

Corder, B. F. *The life game.* Chapel Hill: University of North Carolina Press, 1977.

Corder, B. F., Haizlip, T. M., & Spears, L. D. Legal issues in the treatment of adolescent psychiatric inpatients. *Hospital and Community Psychiatry*, 1976, 27(10), 712–715.

Corder, B. F., Haizlip, T., Whiteside, R., & Vogel, M. Pre-therapy training for adolescents in group psychotherapy: Contracts, guidelines, and pre-therapy preparation. *Adolescence*, 1980, 15, 699–706. (a)

Corder, B. F., Whiteside, R., & Haizlip, T. A study of curative factors in group psychotherapy with adolescents. *International Journal of Group Psychotherapy*, 1981, 31(3), 345–354 (a).

Corder, B. F., Whiteside, R., McNeill, M., & Brown, T. Structuring feedback in adolescent groups: Videotape use and group participation in group assessment forms. *North Carolina Journal of Mental Health*, 1980, *13*, 5–9. (b)

Corder, B. F., Whiteside, R., & Vogel, M. A therapeutic game for structuring and facilitating group psychotherapy with adolescents. *Adolescence*, 1977, *12*, 261–268.

Corder, B. F., Whiteside, R., & Wall, S. *A structured social skills learning program for adolescents designed for administration by inexperienced therapists.* Chapel Hill: University of North Carolina Press, 1981. (b)

Frye, R., & Rockness, P. *Life skills for health.* Raleigh, N.C.: North Carolina Department of Public Instruction, 1974.

Gardner, R. *The talking, feeling and doing game.* Cresskill, N.J.: Creative Therapeutics, 1973.

Gauron, E. F., & Rawlings, E. I. A procedure for orienting new members to group psychotherapy. *Small Group Behavior*, 1975, *6*(3), 293–307.

James, M., & Jongeward, D. *Winning with people: Group exercises in transactional analysis.* Reading, Mass.: Addison-Wesley, 1973.

Masterson, J. F., Jr. Psychotherapy of the adolescent: A comparison with psychotherapy of the adult. *Journal of Nervous and Mental Diseases*, 1958, *127*, 511–517.

Simon, S. B., Howel, L. W., & Kirschenbaum, H. *Values clarification.* New York: Hart, 1972.

Spivack, G., Spotts, J., & Haimes, P. *Devereux adolescent behavior rating scale.* Devon, Pa.: Devereux Foundation, 1967.

Sugar, M. (Ed.). *The adolescent in group and family therapy.* New York: Brunner/Mazel, 1975.

Yalom, I. D. *The theory and practice of group psychotherapy.* New York: Basic Books, 1970.

6

A Therapy Group for Female Adolescent Victims of Sexual Abuse

Lucy Berliner, M.S.W., and
Karen MacQuivey, M.S.W.

LUCY BERLINER is a social worker on the staff of the Sexual Assault Center, Harborview Medical Center, Seattle, Washington, and a member of the clinical faculty of the University of Washington Graduate School of Social Work. KAREN MACQUIVEY is an adolescent/family therapist at Highline Youth Service Bureau in Seattle.

Group treatment for adolescent incest victims has had clinical success in sexual-abuse treatment programs. It is an important component of the treatment response in many well-known programs, and in some it is the primary treatment modality. The National Center on Child Abuse and Neglect in the U.S. Department of Health and Human Services has funded five regional treatment-training institutes for child sexual abuse; victim groups are the primary treatment modality in four of these, including the Sexual Assault Center in Seattle, Washington. In many treatment programs, a group approach is also used for offenders, mothers, and couples. Yet the field of sexual-abuse treatment is relatively new. Only in the past decade has the magnitude of the problem of incest been recognized. Specialization and the creation of specific sexual-abuse programs are recent developments. Much of what is known comes from recent clinical experience and the work of the few sexual-abuse researchers.

The Incest Problem

Authorities still differ on the etiology of incest and the proper treatment for families in which sexual abuse has occurred. The field has yet to produce comparison and outcome studies on the various treatment philosophies, and there is no generally agreed-upon treatment approach that has been demonstrated to be effective in all cases. Nevertheless, there is substantial information about the general characteristics and clinical presentations in sexual-abuse situations.

Patterns of Incest

Incest is clinically defined as sexual activity between family members where the perpetrator is an adult or is significantly older than the child victim or where force is used. Unforced sexual experimentation between two children of similar age would not be considered assaultive or abusive unless one party was disturbed by it.

The incidence of incest cannot be accurately determined because, as is true about sexual abuse in general, most cases are not reported at the time of the assault, and the only data are thus retrospective. Studies of a nonclinical population revealed that as many as one-fifth of the girls and one-eleventh of the boys had been sexually victimized. But over two-thirds of the girls and three-fourths of the boys did not report it at the time (Finkelhor, 1979). Retrospective information as well as interviews with clinical populations show that most victims are abused by people they know, often a relative, and therefore to speak of sexual abuse is usually to speak of incest.

At the Harborview Sexual Assault Center in Seattle, where one author works, more than half of the 730 child victims seen in 1980 were assaulted by relatives, and the largest single category of offenders (43 percent) were parents or parent figures. Nonparent offenders were mainly older brothers, uncles, or cousins. Offending fathers and stepfathers were roughly equal in number, and live-in partners comprised a smaller group. Victims of intrafamily sexual abuse are likely to be girls; boys more often are victims of nonfamily offenders. In about a third of the cases, a younger sibling is subsequently abused. It is common for the oldest girl to be the initial victim and for younger sisters to be successively involved. The abuse generally occurs over a period of years, usually beginning before adolescence (Conte & Berliner, 1981).

The offender may use different ways of involving the child in the activity, from forceful, violent coercion to more indirect means, such as deception or exploitation of the child's youth or dependence. Sometimes violence toward other family members is present in the form of spouse abuse or child battering. The offender is likely to continue the abuse if he has access to the child, the abuse is not discovered, and the victim does not tell anyone.

There is a range of types of sexual contact, from touching offenses to intercourse, often occurring in a progressive pattern. There is also a range of age of onset and of duration. There may be other problems in the family, such as alcoholism, psychiatric or physical disability, unemployment or financial stress, or severe marital discord, although in some cases the family is apparently well functioning. Many instances of incest occur in working-class or middle-class families where the offender has no previous criminal history and is generally prosocial in that he is employed, supports the family, and may participate in community or church activities.

Although there is a range of types of abuse and family characteristics in incest situations, there are some clinically common patterns (Burgess et al., 1978; Butler, 1978; Herman & Hirschman, 1977; Summit & Kryso, 1978). Usually the natural authority of the adult offender and the child's dependence, as well as developmental limitations in the child's ability to understand deviant behavior in an adult, lead to acquiescence by the child victim. She believes that she cannot tell anyone because of the consequences of telling, such as disbelief, blame, breakup of the family, or imprisonment of the offender. The offender generally reinforces or suggests that the victim is to blame for what is happening.

Responses to Incest

Since children have different personalities and their situations are different, a range of responses to incest is found among teenage victims. Teenage victims often develop some form of coping mechanism in order to survive in the family context. The adaptive response of the victim has been called a conditioning continuum (Zaphiris, 1979) or an accommodation response (Summit, 1980). It has been likened to the concept of learned helplessness, where an individual, unable to extricate himself or herself from a situation, ceases attempting to leave and adapts to the hostile environment (Seligman & Maier, 1967).

In some cases adaptive responses to intolerable situations may become symptoms of dysfunction or disturbance in the victims—for example, mental dissociation or running away. A history of incest has been associated with trauma syndrome, a transient, traumatic reaction to abuse or to disclosure; an acting-out response, which includes running away, truancy, prostitution, or delinquency; and an internalized withdrawal response with physical symptoms, psychiatric hospitalization, hysterical reactions, and other somatic complaints. Suicidal ideation and attempts and substance abuse are also common responses.

Some victims present evidence of disturbance before disclosure, some experience a delayed response, and others show an exacerbated response to normal adolescent adjustment problems. The dysfunction can range from mild to severe.

Disclosure and Intervention

Some of the most important factors for successful intervention seem to be the point at which the adolescent comes to the attention of the authorities or treatment agencies and the response of the family to disclosure. Obviously, the prognosis is best when the family believes and supports the victim, and when the offender admits his problem and agrees to seek help and cooperate with whatever is in the best interest of the child victim. Offenders and families have different capacities for responding supportively to the child because there may be perceived conflicts between what is best for the child and what is best for the family—for example, separation of the offender from the family may result in loss of the breadwinner. The treatment needs of the child and legal outcomes are influenced by the degree to which the natural support system can act on behalf of the best interests of the victim.

The circumstances of disclosure are varied. In some cases the incest is discovered by someone who actually observes the abuse or who notices something wrong with the victim or with the relationship between the victim and the offender. Sometimes teenagers report abuse directly because they have gotten old enough or desperate enough to feel that they can no longer tolerate it. The conflict between normal adolescent needs and the exigencies of the sexual-abuse situation become increasingly intense. Some developmental or growth experience may trigger the report, like starting to menstruate, acquiring a boyfriend, or realizing that the abuse is abnormal behavior or a crime. The report may be made in retaliation for unreasonable restrictions on normal adolescent activities such as dating or for inappropriate expectations by the offender for role performance in the household. Although most children tell the nonoffending parent first, some tell a peer, who tells someone on behalf of the victim. In other cases, the victim tells a counselor, who reports the case to a social agency.

A significant number of adolescent victims of sexual abuse are identified after the teenager has come to the attention of social or legal agencies for problem behavior. Sensitive and skilled interviewing by trained professionals is resulting in increased diagnoses of cases of sexual abuse where the child has become identified as the patient or the acting-out party. Some teenagers will already be separated from the family at identification, and others will require temporary placement or long-term foster or residential care. Although it is best for the child to remain at home and for the offender to leave at least temporarily, this is not always possible.

The community where the authors work, Seattle-King County, provides a comprehensive community response to sexual abuse. The established legal agencies, like the criminal-justice system and the Children's Protective Service of the state's Department of Social Services, maintain specially trained individuals or special units for handling sexual-abuse cases. The intervention of the criminal-justice system is designed to minimize further trauma to the child. The offender is encouraged to plead guilty and in most cases is referred for court-monitored treatment while on probation. Some cases are not handled in the criminal-justice system because the victim is not willing or able to participate, because the statute of limitations has passed, or because the abuse occurred in another jurisdiction. In these cases, the Children's Protective Service has legal jurisdiction. Teenagers who have gotten into trouble with the law as a consequence of behavior associated with sexual abuse may also be dealt with by the juvenile court. There are, moreover, various other public and private agencies with an interest in this problem: the Sexual Assault Center, the youth services bureaus, and private family-service agencies.

Treatment Modalities

The various treatment models for incest victims generally reflect different underlying assumptions about the etiology of sexual abuse. Traditional psychoanalytic explanations focus on the abuse as an acting out of unresolved developmental issues (Greenberg, 1979). Structural family therapists see incest as a symptom of dysfunctional family interactions. Other therapists believe that incest is caused by inadequate, socially isolated individuals acting in misguided, inappropriate ways and distorting family roles (Giaretto, 1976). The authors' community describes sexual offenders as having a cognitive behavior disorder that causes dysfunction in families.

Treatment approaches include individual treatment for all members of the family, self-help groups, confrontive group therapy, behavior modification, structural family treatment, victims' groups, mothers' groups, parent-child or couple counseling, family counseling, or a combination of two or more of these modalities. Some programs provide treatment for all family members while others separate the treatment functions among different community agencies.

The Rationale for Group Therapy

Group therapy is only one of a number of possible treatment modalities for the victim of sexual abuse and her family. There are needs and concerns that are best addressed in individual therapy. In many cases some kind of parent-child or family therapy is desirable. The therapy group, however, offers one place where the victim and her personal concerns are central. It is uniquely her resource.

A review of the literature reveals little documentation of the use of groups with this clinical population. The authors could find only three articles describing clinical groups with teenage victims of sexual abuse. One was conducted in an institution where girls had been committed for various criminal and status offenses (James, 1977). Another was for adolescent male victims in a community treatment program (Nasjleti, 1980). The third article describes a self-help group of the large, unstructured kind encouraged by the Child Abuse Treatment Program. in California, the largest program in the country dealing with this problem (Knittle & Tuana, 1980).

Nevertheless, from a clinical developmental standpoint, group therapy is particularly appropriate as a treatment modality for teenagers. Normal adolescence involves a shift from reliance on family to self-reliance and increased peer orientation. Many tasks of adolescence are worked on in a peer group. Since sexual abuse by a parent is an abnormal event, it separates the adolescent victim from normal support systems and exacerbates the adolescent preoccupation with fear of rejection and the need for acceptance by the peer group. The group provides a forum in which to address the sexual-abuse situation and normal adolescent concerns with supportive peers and so to reduce feelings of isolation and guilt.

Sexual abuse is a particularly difficult experience for the adolescent to integrate because it involves two of the central themes of adolescence: sexual relationships and control over decision making. Sexual abuse by a parent is a violation of the normal pattern of sexual development for a young person and a premature exposure to adult sexual behavior. The abuse of parental authority causes a major deprivation for a growing teenager. The normal struggles of adolescence are made much more difficult in the absence of a safe and supportive family environment that models appropriate adult behavior and roles.

At the same time that she loses family support, the adolescent sexual-assault victim feels isolated from her normal peer group because she is different in exactly the experience areas that are most at issue during adolescence, even though she has the same needs for belonging and acceptance. To share her problems might lead to further rejection, or her behavioral reactions to the abuse situation might already have caused rejection by her peers—for example, because she appears too sophisticated or "fast." Victim groups guarantee acceptance on the sole basis of having been a victim. Girls who belong to different subgroups at school and might never socialize outside the groups—for example, "stoners" and "straights"—are able to interact relatively easily. The group provides a predictable and regular social context away from the home setting. It offers the opportunity for making new friends, getting support for feelings and actions, having access to information, sharing experiences, practicing new behaviors, and asking for help. The victim may have feelings about family members or the family situation that cannot be expressed at home because such expression causes conflict or is not supported. The group offers a safe outlet for sharing any feelings or opinions.

Purpose of the Group

In the context of this supportive environment, adolescents may explore feelings about the offenders, the offenses, their mothers, the system, and themselves. Clarification about the adult responsibility for the incest and all subsequent disruptions and explanations to the victims about their roles help to alleviate self-blame. Information about what to expect and what will happen in the intervention and legal processes can take place here. The group can address normal issues of adolescence that are affected by the sexual-abuse situation, like having flashbacks while with boyfriends or being afraid of contact with boys. Sometimes there are specific issues related to the sexual-abuse situation that the group can help the victim with, for example, preparing for a court appearance or helping her to know if she is ready to have her father return home.

In many cases the group affords the victim a source of information and education, not only about the experience she has had but about normal adolescent concerns such as human sexuality, birth control and pregnancy, boyfriends, family conflicts, school problems, and planning for the future. Group leaders can teach problem solving and skills development in a peer setting. This means that the group also focuses on behavior problems exhibited by adolescents that, although caused by the abuse, still represent dysfunction. Social approval and peer-group pressure can be used to support desired behavior change in victim participants.

In all incest situations, the parents or other adults have compromised their roles with the victims. Without a model for responsible adult behavior within the family, other models become very important. Group leaders are in a position to model responsible yet supportive behavior in adults. The adolescent has the opportunity to interact with and observe adults who recognize and respect the needs of children.

The Group Model

The model of a therapy group for adolescent victims of sexual abuse presented here is a composite of groups conducted by the authors at the Sexual Assault Center in the Harborview Medical Center and at a youth services bureau, both in Seattle.

Group Composition

Over the course of a year, group members represent a wide range of abuse situations, points of intervention and outcomes, and personality types. Each victim responds to and copes with the abuse differently and may therefore present with different symptoms of distress and different behavioral responses, which in turn affect treatment planning. In many cases the coping style of the adolescent determines the victim's current functioning. Some of the most commonly seen clinical patterns relate to the manner in which the victim had adapted to living with a long-term abusive situation.

> T was sexually abused by her father from age 10. He would come into her room at night and touch her genitals. She would pretend to be asleep. The contacts increased and became acts of attempted intercourse. T and her father never had a conversation about the abuse and acted as if everything were normal, with only a hint of tension developing two years later. A summer trip to relatives for two weeks made her realize that she didn't have to go to sleep at night afraid, so when she returned home she started blocking her door at night with a bureau. Her mother discovered this and, upon questioning, T finally told about the sexual assaults.

Other group members had been defiant toward the offender and resisted the contact. When there is resistance, the offender may use physical violence, threats, or verbal abuse. In these situations, the victim may end up being rebellious and hostile, breaking rules, running away, skipping school, or actually getting involved in delinquent activity. Cooperation with sexual demands may be rewarded with extra privileges or money. The family usually identifies the victim as the cause of the problem by this point, and there is a great deal of conflict and alienation between the victim and her family.

> L was sexually molested by her stepfather beginning at age 3. As she became a teenager, she began to rebel and be defiant at home. Family fights were frequent. She started skipping school, drinking, being sexually active. Finally she turned to running away. In desperation, her family placed her in residential treatment. After several months a trusted counselor explored the possibility of sexual abuse and discovered the incest.

Some girls had accommodated to the sexual abuse and participated, however reluctantly, because they believed they were helping the family. The offender may convince the victim that she is the only one who understands and can take care of him and the rest of the family. Her sense of identity and influence is associated with her role in the abuse. She will say she both loves and hates her father. There may be no mother present, or the mother may be disabled by medical or psychiatric illness and unavailable as a parent. There is likely to be a competitive relationship between mother and daughter because of resentment about the "special" relationship between offender and victim.

> Fourteen-year-old W had been sexually abused by her stepfather since age 9. Her mother had been married twice before and had a drinking problem. W would often sleep in bed with her parents, and later she and her mother would alternate spending the night with the stepfather. Then a couple of W's friends also got involved in sexual games with the stepfather. W didn't really like the molesting, but she did like her special position in the family, being an equal to her mother and getting treated like a grown-up. And she didn't have many friends anyway. She finally revealed the abuse to a school counselor.

The responses of the family, the offender, and the system to the group member varied. Postdisclosure reactions are highly influenced by whether the child is believed, especially by the mother. The mother is seen as the critical factor in successful recovery of a family.

> T's mother had had no previous idea about the abuse and responded with immediate belief and support. She confronted her husband and demanded that he seek help. She also cooperated with criminal prosecution and Children's Protective Services requirements. The family was basically functional and had very positive factors: both parents were employed in good jobs, neither had a criminal history, and there were no other major problems. The offender felt guilty and wanted to change.

> By the time L told of the abuse she was already alienated from her family and living away from home. Her father denied it and claimed that L was making it up to avoid facing her problems. Her mother was so frustrated and tired of dealing with L that she was not inclined to be sympathetic. It took several months for her to finally come around to believing L. The offender partially admitted the abuse but minimized its seriousness; he said it had happened long ago and therefore was not important. He denied it had anything to do with L's current problems.

> When W told of the abuse, her father denied it and claimed she made it up because she got into trouble and was mad. Her mother didn't believe it. W was placed in a foster home but immediately threatened suicide if she was not returned home. She never denied that she had been abused, but she refused to press charges, saying it would never happen again. According to her, there was no problem anymore, because disclosure had led to her separation from her only source of support, however deviant.

Obviously, the treatment plan depends on how cooperative the various family members are in working toward a solution that assists the victim in recovery and minimzies the possibility of further offenses by the perpetrator. The best solution is that in which the victim is the central concern and her well-being is the goal of intervention. The available community resources will determine how well individual families can respond to incest victims. Incest is not a problem that can be solved without intervention.

> T's father moved out during the treatment process. T had a temporary period of adjustment reaction and moderate acting out. She participated in a victims' group for about one year. Her mother was in a women's group, and after more than one year of intensive individual and group treatment, the father began gradually to move home. The family is now living together and no longer in treatment.

> L's mother finally came to believe L and divorced the husband because he wouldn't do anything about his problems. She began to realize that the marriage was not working at all. L returned home to live with her mother after receiving parent-child counseling at the treatment center. She was in a victims' group for over a year.

> W's father finally admitted molesting her and agreed to counseling. He was terminated for failure to progress. Her mother believed the sexual abuse but blamed W. After several months in the group, W's increased understanding of what had happened began to influence other family members. Her father returned to counseling, and her mother also began individual counseling.

Group members manifested a range of reactions to the sexual abuse. Some exhibited clinical symptoms such as suicidal thoughts and behavior, nightmares, depression, self-inflicted injury, conversion reaction, abdominal pain, somatic complaints, psychosis, sleep and appetite disturbance. There was drug and alcohol abuse. School failure, truancy, disobedience, family conflict, and getting into trouble were other results. Yet the common experience of sexual abuse and common stage of adolescence bound group members despite individual clinical differences. Even victims with different personalities and coping styles participated in the group successfully. The degree of sophistication or even intellectual functioning did not seem to make much difference. At one point, the following girls participated enthusiastically in the group:

> At 15 S was attractive, vivacious, and very socially conscious—always wearing makeup, dressed like a model. She talked incessantly about her latest boyfriend. She skipped school, got drunk, and regularly wondered if she was pregnant.

> R was 17, pale, dark-haired, always dressed in black, and had scars on her wrists from numerous suicide attempts. She had been hospitalized and was very depressed. She chain-smoked and rarely spoke.

> P was 16, pretty, long-haired, and went to a church school. She would sit quietly, never initiated a conversation, and barely responded when directly questioned. She seemed content but did not assert herself until she had been in the group one year.

M was overweight and lived in a treatment center. She had problems at school, had been in trouble with the law, and used speed. She had a low opinion of herself.

Members stayed in the group varying lengths of time. The girls who had strong, supportive family systems tended to remain for briefer periods. Some girls drifted in and out as their circumstances changed. The most loyal members were usually those who had deficits in their primary support systems and for whom the group helped meet basic needs.

B lived with her stepmother and father. Her stepfather was the offender, and her mother had chosen to stay with him, although he had refused to cooperate with treatment. B's little sister lived with an aunt, and her older sister with a boyfriend. B. felt rejected by her mother and did not get along with her stepmother. Her father worked out of town.

L revealed at age 17 that her father had sexually abused her. She did not feel at all close to her stepmother. Her mother lived in another part of the country and was an alcoholic. When her father and stepmother divorced, L was suddenly forced to live on her own in a community where she had no relatives.

Group Organization

The group meets weekly for two hours late in the afternoon so as to interfere as little as possible with school and other normal activities. At any one time, membership ranges from 15 to 18; attendance averages from 8 to 12. The group is ongoing rather than time-limited because of the value of having girls at different experience and coping levels available for support and education of new members. New members are admitted only during the first meeting of each month so that group time is not continually taken up with introductions and orientations. Girls remain in the group from six months to a year.

The structure is relaxed and informal so as not to provoke challenge and rebellion, but it is directed enough to allow the group to accomplish its goals. The therapist is comfortable both with teenagers and with the subject of sexual assault. Needless to say, the personality and the style of the therapist will always have a lot to do with the way any group operates and how successful a clinical experience it is. Victim groups do not succeed unless the counselors are generally skilled at working with teenagers in group settings.

Confidentiality about topics discussed in the group is assured, unless the member's safety demands that a report be made to appropriate authorities. Group members are encouraged to assume as much responsibility for the group as possible. Together they decide on group values and rules—for example, smoking (one group allows only one smoker at a time) or participation (not required initially). They also volunteer to make presentations to the group on subjects of common interest—for example, self-defense, suicide, chemical dependence. The sharing of food creates an atmosphere of closeness. In one group the leader provides snacks each week paid for by donations from offenders.

Group Goals

The group has two goals, once the immediate safety of the victim has been assured as much as possible: first, to focus on particular consequences of the incest experience and its disclosure—for example, depression, acting-out behaviors, or similar "crises"; second, to develop a treatment plan designed to return the child to normal, positive life experiences and relationships.

Goals are introduced to the group members in this way: "The group is here to provide you with a safe and supportive place, free of blame, to talk about your sexual-assault experiences, to answer questions, to explore options, and to help you get in touch with your own power and strength. It is a place to meet others who have shared your sexual-assault experience, make new friends, and have fun. Our goal is for you to be able to say, 'I'm not feeling so alone, so depressed, suicidal, or guilty. I understand my family and the role I was put in. I can feel my feelings and share them with others.'" The girls are encouraged and helped to develop their own personal goals.

Group Format

There is an agenda for group meetings that the therapist adheres to very flexibly because of the tendency of girls of this age to fight constraints and to resist tasks as well as the likelihood that unexpected events and crises will arise. The agenda is as follows: introductions and reiterations of ground rules if new members are present (10 min.); "brags"—the sharing of one thing each member did or said in the past week that she really enjoyed and/or was proud of (5 min.); business announcements and contracting for personal time in group when members ask for a certain number of minutes (5 min.); education component, a short lecture and discussion covering topics generated by both the leader and the group members—for example, myths and facts about incest, dreams and nightmares, how to talk assertively with boys about sex, rape prevention, guilt, anger, birth control, homosexuality (30–45 min.); time for personal sharing and problem-solving with the group (30–60 min.); evaluation (5 min.); journal writing time (10 min.).

When she enters the group, each member is given a notebook in which to record thoughts, feelings, impressions, questions, and concerns. Time is allotted each week in group to make journal entries, and then the leaders collect the notebooks and add their own written feedback during the week between meetings. This is a tool for giving individual private support, encouragement, and feedback, particularly on issues the girls may not be ready to talk about in a group setting, and the private reading of the journals is a ritual before each session begins. The journals serve also to reflect for each girl the changes she undergoes during the course of her involvement with the group.

Themes and Exercises

The therapist tries to incorporate into each group meeting, at some level, a variety of themes.

Building Rapport and Trust. The commonality of the experience of sexual assault by a family member is established by recognizing that all the girls in the group share this experience. The leader practices self-disclosure where appropriate and models a frank and explicit style in discussing sexual matters. She explains and continually reinforces the importance of confidentiality, as well as other ground rules that are set by everyone present, so the girls will know clearly what to expect from the group. Mutual support is encouraged, and it is clearly communicated that it is okay to come to group and listen if a girl doesn't feel like talking. If the girl has told the story of her incest experience to other workers—the Children's Protective Service or the prosecutor— she is not pressed for details; if she has not, she is encouraged to share the story one time. "Getting to know you" exericises are done—for example, having each girl say, "If we had never met and you were trying to find me in a crowd, you would know me because I am the one who . . . ."

Building Self-Esteem and Self-Confidence. "Brags" are used to encourage self-centered activities and comfort in talking about and being proud of them, and to teach acceptance of compliments with no discounting. An example is this body-image exercise: Each girl looks to the person on her right and says something positive about her appearance—for example, "Your eyes are a beautiful color," "Your muscles are in good shape." The recipient must respond with "Your're right!" Positive self-statements are encouraged, and the power these can have in changing self-perceptions is explained. Each girl can establish an informal hierarchy of tasks to generate accomplishment and self-mastery.

Feeling Exploration. Adolescents appear to act more than they talk about or process feelings, so group members are helped to interpret behavior by looking at cognitive messages they give themselves. The expression of feeling and understanding are encouraged. The girls learn to identify feelings in their bodies (for example, an anxiety knot in the stomach), build a feeling-word vocabulary, and receive validation and support for sharing of feelings. There is special focus on validating expressions and positive outlets for anger and anxiety. Both cognitive and behavioral interventions for coping with depression and guilt are taught—for example, cognitive restructuring, creating self- and environmental reinforcers, social-skills training, modeling and rehearsal. It is important to let the girls know that their feelings are natural and common reactions to the trauma of incest and to tell them over and over that they are not to blame.

Stress Reduction. Group members are taught stress-reduction exercises, such as breathing awareness and relaxation training. They are encouraged to develop these tools, along with a regular program of exercise or body movement, and they often brainstorm ways to help each other relax.

Self-Responsibility. This issue comes up often. Experience has shown that these young victims frequently take (and are expected by their parents to take) responsibility for everyone but themselves. There is frequent discussion of the importance of assertive expression of and self-responsibility for feelings and behavior, especially in terms of regaining power and control in their lives. A sexual-assertiveness training model is helpful.

Action. Talk is of little use unless the girls are given the opportunity to practice new behaviors. The group itself offers a place to try out new ways of acting, and the group members are given behavioral assignments (which they can invent themselves) specific to the several themes discussed above, which they report back on each week. Another way in which the girls are able to decrease their feelings of helplessness and powerlessness is by writing letters to judges, family members, and even the news media, so that they can share their experiences, vent their feelings, and educate the public. Group members have also gone to court together to demystify the legal process as well as support a group member who must appear at a trial.

Personal Time for Sharing and Mutual Problem Solving. It is important that each girl have the opportunity to receive individual attention from the group and to discuss other issues that may or may not relate directly to the incest experience—typical adolescent issues like parents, friends, school, drug and alcohol abuse, or expected crises like upcoming trials, anniversaries, and holidays. Group members are encouraged to ask directly for what they want and need from the group.

Fun. Having fun should be an integral part of the group experience. Throughout the group process, it is important to address the developmental stage of group members and develop activities appropriate to adolescence. It is not unusual to find that the girls are expected at home to carry out responsibilities beyond their years, so this is balanced by encouraging playfulness, even silliness, at times. Noncompetitive games (such as "Ungame" by Parker Brothers) and sharing of food snacks are helpful. The importance of social interaction opportunities cannot be overestimated. Often these girls have few outside peer supports and may be far behind their age group in social and emotional development while far ahead in life experiences. That these girls have a foot in both the adult and the child world is painfully obvious.

Termination

Group members are not officially terminated so that if further problems arise the group continues to be available as a resource. Some girls gradually decrease their attendance or may stop for a while and later return. It is perfectly normal for an adolescent's interest in the group to be influenced by other, competing interests like a job or a boyfriend. It is important to allow group participation even if it is not regular. The girls consider themselves always to be members and may return long after to check in or to share an important life experience like graduation, marriage, or a baby. They frequently continue friendships formed in the group.

Problems

The support of the parent or caretaker of the teenager enhances the likelihood of successful participation in the group. The parent must be convinced that the group is necessary and beneficial to the child's recovery. The practical complications of arranging transportation and sitting and waiting for the child to come out of group sessions may inhibit parental cooperation.

If the group does not seem to have the desired effect on the victim's behavior, the parent may oppose treatment. This happens when victims become assertive and articulate their desires or express their anger. It is particularly disquieting in a previously acquiescent teenager. Since the group is designed to be supportive of the victim, feelings and beliefs that may be in conflict with the parents are reinforced if they are the victim's true feelings. If the mother wants her husband back, she is likely to be unsupportive of a treatment that supports an adolescent who hates her father. In some cases the teenager uses newly learned assertiveness skills in normal parent-child power struggles and seeks to use the group as an ally against the parent.

Another issue is that the girls often enjoy the group time and use it for social as well as therapeutic purposes. It may be difficult for parents to see this as a valid part of treatment.

The group leader can enlist the parents' support by educating them about the ways the group is useful in helping the girls' recovery. If some of the likely reactions or problems can be anticipated, parents can be helped to see the rationale for allowing the girls the time and place to work out all the different feelings that go with being victimized.

Conducting a group made up of teenage girls can be an intense clinical experience. They can be wonderful, funny, enthusiastic, and supportive of each other. They are also frustrating and aggravating. Inevitably the girls interrupt and break into smaller groups and start talking. They can attend to one particular issue for only a short time. There has to be relief from emotional intensity or a teaching context by allowing brief, limited digressions—for example, telling jokes or socializing. But the leader must be able to control the group process without generating defiance.

References

Burgess, A. W., et al. *Sexual assault of children and adolescents.* Lexington, Mass.: Lexington Books, 1978.

Butler, S. *Conspiracy of silence: The trauma of incest.* San Francisco: New Glide, 1978.

Conte, J. R., & Berliner, L. Sexual abuse of children: Implications for practice. *Social Casework,* 1981, *62,* 601–606.

Finkelhor, D. *Sexually victimized children.* New York: Free Press, 1979.

Giaretto, H. Humanistic treatment of father-daughter incest. In R. E. Helfer & C. H. Kempe (Eds), *Child abuse and neglect: The family and the community.* Cambridge, Mass.: Ballinger Publications, 1976.

Greenberg, N. The epidemiology of childhood sexual abuse. *Pediatric Annals,* 1979, *8*(5), 16–28.

Herman, J., & Hirschman, L. Father-daughter incest. *Signs: Journal of Women in Culture and Society,* 1977, *2*(4), 735–756.

James, K. L. Incest: Teenager's perspective. *Psychotherapy: Theory, Research, and Practice,* 1977, *14*(2), 146–155.

Knittle, B. J., & Tuana, S. J. Group therapy as primary treatment for adolescent victims of intrafamilial sexual abuse. *Clinical Social Work Journal,* 1980, *8*(4), 236–242.

Nasjleti, M. Suffering in silence: The male incest victim. *Child Welfare,* 1980, *59*(5), 269–275.

Seligman, M. E. P., & Maier, S. F. Failure to escape traumatic shock. *Journal of Experimental Psychology,* 1967, *74*(1), 1–9.

Summit, R. *Typical characteristics of father-daughter incest: A guide for investigation.* Unpublished manuscript, Harbor-UCLA Medical Center, Torrance, Calif., 1980.

Summit, R., & Kryso, J. Sexual abuse of children: A clinical spectrum. *American Journal of Orthopsychiatry,* 1978, *48*(2), 237–251.

Zaphiris, A. G. *Sexual abuse of children.* Unpublished manuscript, Graduate School of Social Work, University of Denver, Denver, Colo., 1979.

WORKING WITH WOMEN

7

Women's Groups

Teresa Bernardez, M.D.

TERESA BERNARDEZ is professor of psychiatry and director of group psychotherapy training in the department of psychiatry, College of Human Medicine, at Michigan State University, East Lansing.

In the past ten years, women's groups have blossomed among lay and professional counselors. The women's movement supplied the motivation to examine women's lives from a different perspective and with a different set of rules. Consciousness-raising (CR) groups, a grass-roots attempt to share unvalidated female experience, were the operational tool of change. They proved highly successful in bringing about awareness of the social expectations that produce and maintain women's difficulties (Lieberman & Bond, 1976) and of the options available to resolve them. Many psychotherapists took note of the CR experience and found the outcomes sufficiently positive to apply some of the characteristics and purposes of CR groups to therapeutic groups (Bernardez, 1978b; Brodsky, 1973; Kirsh, 1974; Kravetz, 1980).

In the early years of this evolution the primary feature borrowed from the CR groups was the emphasis on the social position of women and its contribution to pathogenic adaptations. The therapeutic groups thus started out with an emphasis on helping women to become more autonomous, to clarify their identities, to increase their competence and skills, and to develop bonds of friendship and support among women. Similarly, assertiveness-training groups were born of the interest in helping women to achieve the tools to overcome helplessness and low self-confidence.

Small groups led by and composed of women were shown to achieve greater growth and empathy and were characterized by supportive affective behaviors (Aries, 1976; Carlock & Martin, 1977; Eskilson & Wiley, 1976; Jakubowski, 1977; Meador et al., 1972; Piliavin & Martin, 1978). In both encounter groups (Meador et al., 1972) and in self-help groups fashioned after CR groups (Whiteley, 1973), emphasis was placed on the corrective emotional experience that occurs when women discover the commonalities in their predicaments and the role of the environment in producing conflict.

The absence of men and male authorities increases the freedom of women to discuss taboo subjects (Brodsky, 1977) and to explore their sexual experiences, needs, and desires. Because same-sex groups are more task-oriented and cooperative (Eskilson & Wiley, 1976) and because women are socialized with a greater ability to show support and emotional understanding (Piliavin & Martin, 1978), the consensus is that women's groups achieve greater change and at a faster rate than mixed groups.

Except for groups of adolescents and pregnant women, my experience with groups before 1971 had been primarily with long-term mixed groups. It had been fairly traditional at that time to use the all-female composition for those groups in which women shared a specific developmental stage or crisis. I had attributed the successful outcomes of these short-term groups to the sharing of an important life stage and had not paid sufficient attention to the contribution of the sex composition. But when I had an opportunity to closely observe CR groups in my community, I realized the common features in these diverse experiences.

In 1971 I decided to apply to therapeutic groups those aspects of CR groups that seemed dramatically effective. I began to conduct short-term groups, lasting an average of nine months, for women who sought psychotherapy for a variety of problems. It was my intention to conduct them in such a manner that the patients could continue to use the groups by themselves after I had ended my therapeutic contract with them. I set for myself the task of recording and studying the process and of following the groups up a year after termination.

During the next ten years, I conducted and followed up nine groups of women. I also experimented with separating the sexes in mixed groups that I co-led with male colleagues. In addition, I conducted an average of two women's groups a year for medical students, psychiatric residents, and graduate students as well as an average of four workshops per year for women professionals. These latter experiences were primarily devoted to helping professional women break their isolation, find group support, and look at their situations from a new perspective. Although in this paper I will be focusing on therapeutic groups, my experience with women in different settings has convinced me that women's groups of all kinds are singularly helpful to contemporary women.

I would like to report on the characteristic conflicts that develop in women's groups (process), the method and approach of conducting them (technique), the achievements they realize (outcome), and the indications and contraindications for their use.

At the outset I would like to describe briefly the common features that make these groups helpful to women. In this I will cite both my own experience and that of others (Brodsky, 1977; Kirsh, 1974; Kravetz, 1980; Rice & Rice, 1973).

Special Features of Women's Groups

If we pose as problematic for women that they have been encouraged to be dependent, to rely excessively on authorities other than themselves, to become discomforted by other women because of the introjection of devalued images of self, it follows that a women's group would necessarily, to be therapeutic, strive to correct these propensities. The growth of autonomous thinking, beginning to rely on one's own experience, acknowledging one's own authority, and learning to identify the ways in which women devalue their own ideas, intuition, and skills should be part of the therapeutic experience. Several women authors have pointed out the characteristics of positive outcomes in the therapy of women (Bernardez, 1978b; Brodsky & Hare-Mustin, 1980). These are development of competence and skills of self-mastery; assertiveness, and freedom from negative feelings; redefinition of goals and "feminine" behavior; achievement of a balance between self-enhancing behavior and service to others; development of positive identification with other women; and resolution of inhibitions in creative and serious work.

A women's group makes possible a number of these goals by virtue of its composition and female leadership, but the factors that I have found highly connected with successful outcomes in these groups deserve specific address.

The Role of the Environment in Women's Disorders

Awareness of the role the environment plays in inducing pathogenic adaptations in women has an important therapeutic potential. It clarifies the origins of common dilemmas of women, removing the element of personal responsibility from conflicts stemming from women's social position. This recognition reduces the guilt women assume for problems not of their making and the loss of self-esteem connected with the sense of being inadequate or dysfunctional. Once the problem is seen in perspective, the patient can choose the best solution for herself. This involves the therapist's confirmation and validation of women's awareness of discrimination and the restrictions that have resulted in accepting sex-role stereotypes.

Shared Leadership Functions and Autonomy

The experience of being a leader—that is, of giving direction or lending resources while sharing as a member in the nurturing contact of the group— is specially valuable for women. Many women have been discouraged from showing initiative and authority by the isolation that results when they do so. As a result, women fear that the price they have to pay for autonomy and for the open exercise of their abilities is the loss of nurturance, support, and affiliation with others.

To encourage contributions from every member and to create an atmosphere of respect for each other's differences, ideas, and preferences, the therapist is well advised not to direct the group's interactions or dictate the content. I tend to regard as my tasks the facilitation of communication, the clarification of issues in which there are commonalities or conflicts, and the attribution of meaning to interpersonal or group dilemmas. I have found it helpful to focus on the here-and-now of the interaction when the group seeks to avoid a difficult issue. The focus on the present and on the group participants makes for lively exchanges and the possibility of directly exploring conflictual themes. Although the past is also explored, it is to understand and modify experiences in the present. The application of a group-centered approach (Ezriel, 1952; Sutherland, 1952), although not exclusive of interpersonal approaches, tends to encourage the development of a "work group" (Bion, 1961). The advantage of such a development is that the participants experience the excitement of a collaborative task with other women and learn to resolve the multiple obstacles that come in the way of working together.

My additional purpose is to furnish the group with the skills required to continue the therapeutic task after I no longer work with them. The women then have the alternative of functioning as a supportive or therapeutic group by themselves. The potential of any women's group to become its own instrument of continuing transformation needs to be emphasized, since one of the contributors to depression in women is their isolation and loss of female affiliations (Bernard, 1976). To encourage thinking of such alternatives and to make it "real," I have found it helpful for the group to hold therapeutic sessions in my absence. The sessions are taped so that I can review them and work on issues that come up in my absence. The patients discover their own skills at those times and have the opportunity to experience their own abilities and deficiencies. Issues of dependency, autonomy, and differentiation are salient in those sessions. They are utilized in the following sessions to train the group in the skills needed for eventual successful functioning without the therapist.

Separation Anxiety in Short-Term Groups

An important therapeutic feature of short-term groups is the heightened awareness of their termination, which can be used to deal with problems of separation, endings, and loss.

Separation anxiety and the defenses erected against the experience are important subjects for women's groups. The reality of separation and ending is approached by my groups through meetings without the therapist. Because separations are often problematic for women, this is an area to pay special attention to. Women place great emphasis on relationships, and seem to invest far more in them than men do. Women are often involved in dependency struggles that have not been clearly identified, and in many cases they have had little opportunity in their development to establish separation and differentiation from maternal objects.

These two aspects of the group—its time-limited nature and the sessions without the therapist—foster initiative, autonomy, and self-reliance among the participants.

The Absence of Men

It is not just the presence of women only but the absence of men that appears to be responsible for the greater achievements of female groups. In mixed groups there is an automatic reliance on sex-role division of labor, with men doing "sex-appropriate" fighting for positions or expressing anger and criticisms and the women nurturing and expressing sadness, longings for dependency, tenderness, and positive emotions. It takes a much longer time in mixed groups for members to acquire the valuable characteristics of the opposite sex and to break away from the constrictions of sex stereotypes. A way to permit increasing awareness of sex-bound conduct in mixed groups is to separate the sexes temporarily (Bernardez & Stein, 1979).

The Female Therapist as Role Model and Transference Figure

The presence of a female in the role of therapist in the group offers several advantages that can be profitably utilized.

Women and Authority. Women have not often been seen in the position of experts, and the availability of such a role makes possible the questioning of traditional assumptions about women and leadership. The therapist can model a benevolent yet assertive and confident authority, one that does not require submission but that encourages open questioning and examination of her role.

Women and Power. Challenging the stereotype, the therapist is shown as having power and dealing with it in spheres other than the home. Since women have been prominent in power only in the lives of children, they have little experience with adult-to-adult relationships with women in power. Viewing and experiencing the therapist dealing with power in the group lifts it from the realm of infantile experience and opens it for examination, challenge, or emulation.

Women and Success. The therapist models yet another role that has been all too scarce for women: that of a competent and successful professional. The presence of that model permits hopeful identifications in the process of evolving one's own identity.

Women and Work. The prohibitions of "world-building work" (Paget, 1981) for women—that is, work in the public and social sphere—have constrained women in the area of creative endeavors. Seldom encouraged to take themselves seriously and to think of doing great works of art, of becoming senators or orchestra directors, women have been greatly inhibited in the use of their talents. The female therapist automatically disconfirms these notions by her respectful attitude toward her own work and toward the abilities of others. Child rearing, a creative and important work choice, is to be regarded in the group as one of the choices open to women but not as a compulsory choice and not as the only one.

Definitions of job, career, and work may be important here. Job is an activity required for economic or social reasons; career is the aspect of one's job or one's work that can be exploited or improved for status or economic gain. I reserve the word work for important activity that involves creativity, originality, or emotional investment. Motherhood, for instance, may be described as a job, a career, or serious work depending on the reasons for doing it and the creativity that is devoted to it. Certain activities, however, can qualify only as jobs or tasks (e.g., washing dishes) because they have no opportunities for growth or creativity inherent in them.

The female therapist in her own person will inevitably portray some options better than others, but she can underline the element of choice in the matter of work, the importance of selecting a desired activity, and the development of talents wherever they are present. The serious investment of energy in the pursuit of life work for women is an important social issue as well. Women have available an average of 25 years—10 of them alone (McMahon, 1980)—after the rearing of children when their talents and interests can be utilized for public purposes, even if they have chosen full-time motherhood for their first career.

Transference Reactions. Transference reactions occur in groups toward the therapist and other participants whether the therapist utilizes them or not. Because these reactions are often obstacles in the way of appropriate adult responses to other women, they merit exploration in the group. Since the group dilutes individual transferences and can be used to check the reality bases of the reactions with the help of other group members, those responses that seem irrational or forbidden, that block the group's progress, or that inhibit the participants are specifically focused upon.

Because the group is of short duration, the primary goal in discussing transference reactions is the practical one of separating realistic from fantasized expectations. The female therapist will frequently be assigned the role of the ideal mother who gives nurturance and has no needs of her own (Chodorow, 1980). Disappointment with the therapist for not fulfilling these unconscious expectations needs to be openly discussed, for it bears a strong relationship to members' own excessive obligations of selfless service to others.

Conflictual Themes

To give some live idea of the process in women's groups, I will describe some of the most common conflictual themes.

Sexual Experience and Sexual Function

Women have been inundated with misinformation about their sexual experience and behavior. In attempting to adapt to male expectations, many women have developed inauthentic sexual standards more in accord with men's desires than with their own. This handicaps the search for self-definition and is often responsible for heterosexual conflicts. In addition, women tend to assume the blame for this confounding state of affairs, which leads them to further adaptation to standards not of their own making.

In a women's group, the discussion of sexual experiences is franker and freer than in mixed groups. The presence of other females who can validate similarities helps to debunk myths and expectations that do not conform with one's experience. Contrasting views among the women break the stereotypes and help everyone discover the richness and diversity of erotic experiences. This exploration is not limited to experiences with others but encompasses the awareness of one's own bodily needs, functions, and pleasures that predate sexual attachments.

When concerns about sexual adequacy and the fears accompanying comparisons with other women come up in the group, the all-women context makes it an ideal arena for exploration and resolution. The absence of men is an important factor in the degree of openness that can be achieved, since the presence of men tends to place women in competitive relationships and causes them to hide their true experiences. An example is this discussion of the subject in the sixth session of one of my groups. The session had started with an intense discussion of a member's unhappy marriage and her extramarital relations. The sexual theme had surfaced timidly, and I had commented on how gingerly the issue was being approached.

KAREN. But it seems like the whole thing about everybody—I don't know everybody—the people that have talked, that I have heard talk and myself too, have all got one thing, whatever that is, that keeps you from being completely sexual. Yours is that you still feel married, yours is you are married and you can't leave your kids, you can't be out on your own. Mine is the hang-ups I have about my body and the way it looks. Everybody I am sure has got one. And it all seems to be the thing I'm not doing is . . . I know as long as I hang onto that thing about body hang-ups that I'm never going to be as sexual as I can be, and I'm an incredibly sexual woman and I know that.

DIANE. Are you saying that we get rid of our hang-ups?

KAREN. What I'm saying is for me. (She laughs. The group breaks into loud laughter.)

APRIL. Oh, my God! (Laughter.)

KAREN. Anyhow, for me what it boils down to is that fear that if I was as sexual as I would allow myself to be I'd screw 24 hours a day, 24 different guys. And I know it.

EVE. What it really is is one giant great fear. I think that has something to say for it, yeah, what would happen if I really cut loose.

BARBARA. I was just sitting here just envying the hell out of you. I wish I felt tremendously sexual. I don't feel myself that way at all. I really envy you that you should feel that way. Every time I've had a friend who has talked like that I just sit there . . . and my jaw drops and I think, what the hell must it be like to be that way? I can't imagine!

APRIL. Inconvenient?

DIANE. I think though . . . just to analyze it a little bit, I think part of it is—ah . . . I don't know, but I have a feeling Karen . . . and maybe recently with me I have been more satisfied sexually.

BARBARA. That certainly would do it, wouldn't it?

KAREN. I don't think that is it at all, because I have always been satisfied sexually.

EVE. Oh, God! I haven't.

KAREN. I always have, from the time I've been 16 years old when I first started petting with guys. And I've always had one orgasm after another for years and years and years.

EVE. Jesus Christ!

KAREN. And when I let myself go and I allow myself to do it, I will have orgasms without being touched.

EVE. Jesus Christ!

KAREN. So I know I'm a sexual woman.

EVE. You sure do have a good basis for that statement.

DIANE. Well, I think that . . . okay, that's sort of what I'm saying.

KAREN. You mean the more satisfied I am the more I want it? Is that what you are saying?

DIANE. Yeah . . .

BRENDA. Or maybe that your orientation changes from being oriented toward some things is just really being oriented toward a certain kind of feeling. You are now coming into it and your rebirth.

DIANE. Yeah, oh yeah. But it is hard to—I mean I sympathize with Barbara's statement that someone else talks like they have had such a great feeling.

EVE. (Sadly.) It makes me feel very mad because I used to be real sexy and I've lost almost all of it, and it's really bad to have felt that way and not any more. I'd almost say that it's better not to ever have been. When you say one thing, I think I must have twenty things that are hanging me up!

APRIL. I haven't had an orgasm in months and months, and I didn't have one with Bob. I enjoyed him tremendously, and I still didn't have one. And I don't know . . . to never have enjoyed it? I can't say that.

EVE. You couldn't?

APRIL. No. It softens me like nothing else has. Didn't you—

EVE. What softens you?

APRIL. Becoming a woman softened me and taught me, God, appreciation for a million things.

EVE. Becoming a woman . . . what do you mean?

APRIL. Having orgasms.

EVE. I don't know, I've never had one.

APRIL. No, you just said you did. Jesus! How am I misreading everything? You just said something about enjoying and you wish you hadn't enjoyed because—(Several people talk at once.)

EVE. Enjoyment doesn't mean that you have had orgasms. I said I have felt sexual before. Can you see a distinction?

THERAPIST. Do you see how we tend to assume that everybody has the same experience? (Several people speak at once excitedly.)

EVE. I tend to assume that nobody else in the whole world has ever had my experience and I'm really . . . I thought that's what you meant and that's why I asked. That's why I pursued it. I said Jesus Christ because to hear what she's saying is like, I know—oh, yes, it's phenomenal.

DIANE. To me, too. Very upsetting and very . . .

BRENDA. I'm just glad she's here. We're glad she's here because, because that experience is basic, and the more I can learn about it . . .

EVE. What?

BRENDA. Hers.

EVE. Having an orgasm is basic?

BRENDA. Yeah, sexually. Yeah, having an orgasm is basic. And the more I can learn about it, the more . . .

EVE. But I think when you don't have it you really want it.

BRENDA. Yeah, but it's a lot more complicated than that. For me, anyhow. I mean, there are all kinds of things going on inside me that have to do with why I said I'm glad Karen is here. The recognition that we have among us all the experiences we need to grow.

EVE.   Is Karen going to give me an orgasm?

DIANE.   She may be able to say something.

THERAPIST.   It sounds like the concern is that if we talk freely, you know, somebody will be up here like Karen who is going to be 100 percent all right. If she has 100 orgasms she is at the top.

EVE.   She's at the top now.

THERAPIST.   And there is obviously some envy about somebody who speaks like Karen speaks. On the other hand, I think the concern is that those attempts at putting people in categories will prevent us from knowing what our experience is like.

KAREN.   Yeah, because the way I felt as soon as I said that and other people started to talk was just really weird. And it was like, oh my God, I should have kept my mouth shut. Because I've had that response from other people. Because I blurt things out without finding out what other people's experience is and then I just feel real alienated. People push me away.

EVE.   I felt very put off by your saying it.

BRENDA.   You were putting her off while she was talking.

EVE.   Well, I felt put off. I felt we jumped only from talking about a relationship with one kind of person or another, and I felt like you were getting into some things.

KAREN.   Part of what goes on with me is that sex is very easy for me to talk about. I have talked to a lot of people about very intimate sexual kinds of things. Not just men I've been involved with. Other women, my children— I'm incredibly open with my children—and it's not difficult for me. A lot of times I just end up blurting stuff out without realizing another person's never even said any of that stuff.

EVE.   I think when you made that statement that you are a very sexual woman, that's pretty upsetting to me because I used to think I was a very sexual woman . . . and (cries) I'm not now and it really bothers me a lot, you know. When you see something like that gone, then maybe you don't have everything you want in life. You say, where do things come from and where do they go to? There's somebody up there who pulls the strings or something?

KAREN.   (Warmly.) When you talk it sounds like what you are saying is it's gone for good.

EVE.   Well, when something's gone it really feels like it's a long ways away, doesn't it?

Sexual Identity, Mother-Daughter Relationships, and Relations with Other Women

The composition of a women's group makes it ideal for the exploration of early identification patterns, conflicts about separation and autonomy (often strongly connected with improperly resolved early conflicts with mothers), and feelings of alienation from or competition with other women.

Mothers are discussed incessantly in my women's groups, often with disappointment and reproach. Many women blame their mothers for their secondary place in the world and for their low self-esteem. The view of mothers often presented is identical to the societal myth of the self-sacrificing nurturing person with no needs of her own that a mother is expected to conform to. It is difficult to reconcile such a view of one's own mother with a personal destiny of autonomy and self-realization. The contradictions, grievances, and rivalries in this relationship and the primitive love and hate that mothers evoke have to be heard and clarified. Often women need to evolve from the tendency to blame mother and yet identify with her as a devalued object in order to move beyond mother's fate and strive for their own self-realization. In the process, a positive bond with mother and other women is acquired. The resolution of a woman's feelings toward her mother and other women has great impact on her self-esteem and on her chance of achieving a well-anchored and positive sense of femaleness. These issues have to be resolved prior to conflicts in the heterosexual or homosexual sphere. For, regardless of sexual preference, early attachments that are conflictual and cannot be resolved tend to be displaced onto later sexual attachments.

The maternal figure is thus always at the origin of the female's struggles to define later relationships and her own sexual identity. Sexual prohibitions are often identified with her and explained via the fantasies of mother's own sexual orientation and activity. Many women assign to their mothers most of the prohibitions that ruled their sexual awakenings. This is very likely the case. Mothers were supposed to raise chaste daughters who would not be in danger of being sexually exploited and who could satisfy the social requirements of a wife. Change in the standards for women, requiring more and more responsiveness on the wife's part, and change in the availability of contraceptives, making sexual relations less risky for the female, have placed women in a paradoxical position: raised to be chaste, they are expected to be capable of sexual responsiveness but limited to relations with their husbands. This new set of contradictory expectations and prohibitions, defined in relation to masculine requirements, produces conflicts in women. The frustration engendered is channeled to mother, perceived as bitter about her situation or envious of her daughter's potential freedom. Patients are seldom aware that the social conditioning of women made most mothers incapable of having fully satisfying sexual lives and programmed them to rear restrained and compliant daughters. The therapist in a female group is alternatively seen as the "bad" and restricting mother and as the ideal, permissive, and encouraging mother women wish they had.

The connection between sexual experience and relationships with mothers is exemplified in the following exchange from the seventh session of the same group reported above. The discussion reveals the ambivalent bonds between mothers and daughters and the way they are examined in the group from both vantage points (as daughters, as mothers) and in relation to the female therapist.

EVE. And maybe you felt that hostility and like, boy, if *I* can't have it, you can't. Does that remind you of mother? That reminds me of *my* mother.

KAREN. It reminds me very much of my mother. Because I have just gotten in touch with the fact that all my life . . . therapists have told me before, "Your mother could never have enjoyed sex, and the way you talked about what your mother was like she couldn't have done it." And I have never accepted that. I won't—I have not, up until . . . tonight. I'm feeling different about that. I don't know. But I have always felt . . .

DIANE. You think she did enjoy it?

KAREN. I think she did never, ever enjoy it, ever.

EVE. Have you always thought before that she did?

KAREN. Yeah.

EVE. Where did that put you in relationship to her? Better than her if you enjoyed it and she didn't?

KAREN. Something wrong with me because I was and she wasn't.

EVE. Boy!

DIANE. That's an interesting thing to bring up. I wonder if I didn't enjoy it because I knew my mother was. Which I know she was.

EVE. I think I never enjoyed it because I knew my mother didn't. Me and mom were kinda joined together. You know, like mom never did and so I'm certain I unconsciously allied myself with my mother. It's the only way I ever did ally myself with her. You know, my mother was down here about a year ago and she said something about my daughter. She said, "Boy, in a little while you are really going to have some competition from her." And I said, "Zap!" I really reacted, and my mother went "Eeeeh!" When she revealed herself she was really scared, you know. But I'm sure that was a very revealing comment.

APRIL. I get a soft spot in my heart when I think about my mother raising three daughters. Believe me, I really do. My heart just kinda feels like I'm bleeding for her. Christ, if I had to raise three daughters I would flip! The competition hit me right away when I had kids. I was so thankful I had boys you wouldn't believe it! I absolutely wanted no competition.

EVE. I know what you mean. I'm feeling like that's really a terrible feeling, and yet I know—I've gone through myself with my daughter. Especially at preadolescence.

KAREN. Right. I have an eleven-year-old daughter who is beautiful. Beautiful little body.

DIANE. I had a man come see me and I've got four lovely daughters. (Much laughter.)

CARLA. I never could compete with my mother. She's always been skinny. I've never been as little as her. (Group laughter.)

APRIL. But you know, you think about how nice to be so confident, to get to a point in your life that you are so confident and content and secure with yourself that then you can begin to enjoy that daughter. And what a beautiful relationship you can have. In that sense I regret not having daughters. Not that I think I'll change this at all. But, I really do—there's a warm feeling there that I'm missing out on. Especially when she comes back now and says how beautiful a relationship she has with me in particular—how she had none before I was married and how nice it is now. How she enjoys it so much.

DIANE. Who is that, your mother?

APRIL. Yeah.

BARBARA. I really visualize myself having a relationship like that with my oldest boy. I think that he and I will always be very close. We have a very good relationship, and I can only see it as something that will grow. I don't think his sex has a whole lot to do with it. It's just the kind of person he is.

THERAPIST. Yet I do think that the sex may make a difference in as much as you are reminded of what your mother did to you as a daughter, you see. And what you all were talking about: "This is what I felt in regard to my mother—how I assume she felt toward me and now I have a replay with my own daughter."

APRIL. Yeah, instant replay. My mother was extremely cold. Extremely cold woman. Very, very critical. Very little warmth. If I wanted a good hug and, you know, ten minutes of warmth, it was my father. Or an older sister. It was never my mother. Never. I felt she rejected me, and in turn I could never, you know, relax.

THERAPIST. Okay. I think I hear now a feeling that this is also happening in the group. That the issue of mother rejecting our growing, budding sexuality is happening right here.

GROUP. Yeah.

KAREN. Yeah, for me it was like—I want to say more about that because it felt like, there I go, blurting it out again, and I always blurted things out all my life and one of the things I always got slapped down for when I was growing up was because I was a spontaneous little kid and I got stepped on all the time for it. And so I very much had the feeling of "you don't ever do that at home, you do that with other people." So my family has no idea what I'm like, and they're missing a whole lot (sadly). I'm missing a lot, too. But that was what the feeling was. Don't do it here, do it someplace else where they can't see you.

EVE. I wonder if you felt that way about Teresa's response to your comment?

KAREN. I don't remember what your response was.

EVE. Well, I don't exactly remember what it was either, but I wonder if it sort of came on as . . . well, she went on to say we can't talk about our sexuality as how many orgasms you can have or whether you have a man or whether you do it by yourself or . . . but more like your sexuality as a female.

KAREN.   No, I didn't feel slapped down by that because I had been thinking the thing I said earlier tonight. Thinking about that for a couple of months in terms of knowing that I am doing that and seeing . . .

EVE.   See, I guess I am saying that a woman like Teresa—I am always looking for mother, and if you are not going to do it, I'm going to imagine it, you know. If I can find a good mother, that is neat! If it's a bad mother—here we go again.

THERAPIST.   You hang onto that?

EVE.   You bet! I've got a good mother going now.

DIANE.   I don't understand that. I'm really lost. Everybody else seems to understand what you are saying.

EVE.   Well, like if you go to a male therapist, he is going to be a good father for you. If you go to a female therapist, hopefully one who is very supportive and permissive, you can have a good mother. This goes through friendships and all kinds of relationships.

APRIL.   I had one for two years and it was a pain. I didn't even grow in that kind of therapy. He kind of calmed me down.

EVE.   Why did you stay in a relationship like that for two years?

APRIL.   I thought that's what I needed. More coping, more therapy. When I look back at it now it was devastating, like neutrality. There was not a . . .

EVE.   I don't know. For me it was liberating because I never had any female figure in my life say, "Do it, do it, say whatever you know." I just had always experienced limitations and unspoken restrictions.

Conflicts with Assertiveness, Anger, and Negative Affects

There is consensus that women are affected by strong prohibitions surrounding aggressive behavior (Bernardez, 1978a; Brodsky, 1978; Cline-Naffziger, 1974; Meador et al., 1972; Wycoff, 1977). Their socialization tends to lead them to question their "femaleness" when they are openly angry or when they assert their own needs rather than consider first those of others. In a therapy group with men, these prohibitions tend to be naturally enforced, for the male members inadvertently take up the role of discharging the aggression or expressing dissatisfaction for the female members since they are socialized in the opposite direction.

In a women's group there is less chance of such inhibition, and there is no opportunity for vicarious expression of criticism and negative feelings through men. Although the tendency of women to nurture and support is sometimes an obstacle to expressing negative feelings, it is ultimately a helpful characteristic since it leads to a better integration of positive and negative feelings, permitting caring for others but not at the expense of the self. This is one of the distinctive differences between CR and self-help groups and therapeutic groups. Not infrequently leaderless groups tend to veer away from the acknowledgment of anger in the group, and they are disrupted when such avoidance is no longer possible.

The presence of a leader is very helpful in providing the minimum of safety and guidance required to examine feelings that are potentially destructive to the group and whose destructiveness members so often exaggerate. Much depends on the therapist's own comfort with these feelings and her tolerance of the tension and fear that they may bring with them. She must be capable of permitting members to express their anger while encouraging reflection and the search for its causes. The therapist's belief system, her own socialization, and her conviction that the discussion and exploration of such experiences within the group are crucial to the resolution of many dilemmas in which conflicts with aggression paralyze women tend to determine how thoroughly and successfully these feelings are explored.

It is my conviction, based on my own group experiences and my observations of other women's groups, that it is relatively easy to have a supportive and caring group of women and that members and therapists may collude in maintaining a nurturing group for fear of their own and the group's aggressive tendencies. The exploration of negative feelings does not need to do away with the caring expressed by the members toward one another. It does move beyond the safety of such context, however, to clarify and resolve conflicts in that area. The decision to open up the group's awareness and tolerance to criticism and negative feelings from within is what is crucial. Often the women are able to discuss among themselves feelings of anger about others, but they avoid similar experiences in the here-and-now of the group and thus they miss the opportunity to learn directly what the difficulties consist of.

This task is handled differently by different therapists. Some structure the sessions so that a feeling of safety is maintained. The members can then experiment within clear boundaries with voicing negative feelings toward one another in a helpful and direct way. I recommend a combination of guidance and freedom. The freedom to express negative feelings depends in great measure on the skills and experience of the therapist and on her conflicts and fears regarding her own angry feelings. Once allowed to emerge and be demystified, anger is found to be a common human experience, sometimes the result of frustration and pain, sometimes the healthy reaction to an injury to one's self-esteem or to the violation of personal boundaries.

Most women experience their anger with guilt, and they seldom find it justifiable. They are, therefore, confused about the varieties of reactions assembled under this term and quite inexperienced in the multifaceted expression of such different feelings. The therapist needs to point out the role of social injunctions in maintaining the prohibitions about angry behavior or protest in women, for they tend to assume responsibility for their thwarted expression or they become frightened when they explore the intensity of their feelings. The group can be helpful in encouraging women to attempt different ways of expressing such feelings openly and directly toward one another and to increase their tolerance of criticism and disapproval from others. This is another sensitive issue for women, because they have been reared to seek approval and acceptance from others, and their well-being and sense of accomplishment often depend on such response. Receptivity to others' feelings and views should be supported when the woman is not expected to disown her own experience and direction to obtain acceptance by others. I agree with Miller (1976) that the affiliative, caring, and receptive characteristics of women are positive aspects of their socialization and should not be devalued. A better balance needs to be achieved between such traits and the appropriate freedom to value, love, and consider oneself. The group offers multiple opportunities to observe the behavior of its members and test the appropriateness and adequacy of less traditional stances.

To exemplify the situation that women have been in and the solution that one member of the group perceives as the most desirable, let me quote Marianne (in another group) describing it in her own way through a parable:

SUSAN. You know what occurs to me. You have mentioned three theories that people have of you. That would be very scary to me, to have people telling me what they think I'm up to. People telling me different things. Because I would tend, in my own insecurities, to believe and not believe and get even more confused.

MARIANNE. That has also happened to me in the last year. That's why I'm at a place now where I can say, "Well, I know you believe that but that may not be the truth, sweetie."

SUSAN. But you have to say "may not."

MARIANNE. That's okay. That's okay with me now. I was so confused last year at this point. At about this time of the season. Everybody was telling me what to do. That's when I remembered the fairy tale about the old man and the boy and the donkey. I don't know if you know that, but an old man, a boy, and a donkey are walking down the road. They are going to the market, and the donkey would carry their things back home. A group of people pass and someone says, "What a lazy donkey, you should use him." So the boy gets on the donkey and they go on. Another group of people pass and say, "Lazy boy, the old man should ride the donkey." So they change places and continue on. Another group of people pass and say, "Lazy old man, look at that poor boy you let walk." (Laughter.) The old man and the boy decide to both get on the donkey. They go along. As they begin to cross a bridge, another group of people come by and say, "Poor donkey." (Laughter.) So, the old man and the boy throw the donkey over the bridge and walk to the market. (Laughter.)

And what I have been trying to do is learn what I want to do with the donkey and tell everyone to "fuck off." (Laughter.) And then after I've learned how to do that, to not have to say "fuck off" but just to be able to smile, knowing where they are coming from, and say, "Yes, I hear you, but I have my own ideas."

Method and Approach

Psychotherapists are not neutral members of their culture. Their work is not value-free (Rawlings & Carter, 1977). The present situation of women makes it imperative for psychotherapists to become aware of their own biases and irrational expectations that stand in the way of enhancing their patients' freedom of choice and ability to grow. Elsewhere (Bernardez, 1976) I have pointed out the irrational beliefs that psychotherapists share with other members of the culture in regard to women's behavior and the way they interfere with the optimal outcome in psychotherapy. Particularly considering the tendency of women patients to be compliant, it is important in a women's group that the therapist encourage members to assess critically the therapist's conduct and feel free to point out prejudicial comments whenever present.

This does not mean that the therapist must assume an apologetic or masochistic stance. She has skills and authority in certain areas, and her knowledge is valuable to the group members. It is in lending these skills to them, and in helping them free themselves from excessive dependence on and compliance to her authority, that the therapist performs her most valuable service.

I set my task as that of keeping the group working at sharing experiences freely, resolving conflicts as they appear, and encouraging more clarity and openness in communications with one another. These functions are gradually taken up by the members themselves. The therapist's function then is to monitor that progress while constantly being aware of external sources of distress, social constraints, and contradictory expectations about women that the members have accepted as their own. This valuable task, far from enabling the members to escape responsibility for their behavior, permits clarification of the choices and alternatives open to women in the midst of social contradictions.

Indications and Outcomes

Since I believe with others (Brodsky & Hare-Mustin, 1980) that women's groups are the modality of choice for most women involved in a variety of contemporary struggles, it may be helpful to consider first the exceptions. Individuals in crisis who require rapid and intense intervention might need to be seen individually until the crisis is resolved. Women whose complaints center on their marriage should have available marital therapy when their partners are interested in working with them. An attempt should be made to encourage the spouse's involvement in the resolution of the conflict, because the chances of transforming the relationship are higher when both partners are involved in treatment (Epstein & Volk, 1981).

In cases of severe depression, the group may be experienced as too demanding by the patient. Depression, however, is a common complaint of women and one that is addressed in the group from the start. The various factors that contribute to depression in women are taken up in the group and dealt with separately and together, from learned helplessness to inappropriate self-blame, from inhibition of anger to self-derogation. But the patient needs to be able to maintain a minimum of functioning to profit from collective examination of what makes so many women depressed.

I have not included psychotic women in my groups. The women who benefit the most are those struggling with conflicts of sexual and personal identity, those searching for integration in family and work roles, and those who struggle with vocational aspirations. But often the women who feel dismayed, depressed, and alienated and yet express no major complaints are the ones who make the most progress. The opportunity to discuss taboo subjects and the permission to share forbidden realizations are invaluable to women who have not been permitted conscious awareness of their complaints and of the reasons for their unhappiness.

Although I have attempted to compose my groups with women from different occupational, educational, and racial backgrounds and of different marital status and ages, the realities of making short-term groups available conspire against waiting for the ideal composition. I have therefore placed upon the members of the group some of the burden for making the group "work," doing the best with the restrictions imposed at times by homogeneity, at times by heterogeneity. My main task is to exclude those few individuals who would not profit from the group.

I have experimented with different approaches to evaluating candidates for my groups. I have attempted collective, group-centered selection of members as well as the more traditional route of from one to four individual evaluation interviews. I have found that the short-term evaluative interviews permit me a better knowledge of the person and a more individualized relationship with each patient and are thus valuable in this regard. They have not made me any more able to predict the group's ideal composition.

Sharing decision making with the group about new members tends to create "safe" groups. The patients who are too shy or afraid of rejection and competition withdraw early in the proceedings. The group thus formed is more homogeneous although more likely to work well together.

One- or two-session interviews appear to me sufficient in most cases to decide on the advisability of the group for the particular patient. They have the advantage of not fostering special bonds with the therapist that may conflict with attachment to the group. Much of the task of evaluating conflicts and strengths is done within the group context.

The most conspicuous outcomes in the members of these groups are the disappearance of the depressive state that so many women live in and the gains in work and educational goals. These changes appear related to the gain in knowledge of the social traps and expectations they are then able to move away from, and to the experiencing of themselves as capable, trustworthy, and strong people that occurs within the group. A good number of patients have remarked on their capacity to permit themselves new freedoms, explore new paths, and entertain new ideas and plans with hope and the support of others. An important element for patients has been the group as an arena for exploration of new behaviors. Women become more able to speak confidently, to take risks in communicating openly, and to rehearse the expression of hitherto forbidden negative feelings. Although much remains to be done at the end of the group, the patients are furnished with the tools of change and have opened doors toward promising paths. If patients are interested in further therapy, the group has made them exceedingly aware of what they need and how to find it. If they are willing to continue with the group (an alternative chosen by three of the nine groups I followed up), the members become a supportive network for future explorations and growth.

References

Aries, E. Interaction patterns and themes of male, female, and mixed groups. *Small Group Behavior,* 1976, 7(1), 7–18.

Bernard, J. Homosociality and female depression. *Journal of Social Issues,* 1976, 32(4), 213–238.

Bernardez, T. Unconscious beliefs about women affecting psychotherapy. *North Carolina Journal of Mental Health,* 1976, 7(5), 63–66.

Bernardez, T. Women and anger: Conflicts with aggression in contemporary women. *Journal of the American Medical Women's Association,* 1978, 33(5), 215–219. (a)

Bernardez, T. Women's groups: A feminist perspective on the treatment of women. In H. Grayson & C. Loew (Eds.), *Changing approaches to the psychotherapies.* New York: Halsted Press, 1978. (b)

Bernardez, T., & Stein, T. Separating the sexes in group therapy: An experiment with men's and women's groups. *International Journal of Group Psychotherapy,* 1979, 29(4), 493–502.

Bion, W. R. *Experiences in groups.* New York: Basic Books, 1961.

Brodsky, A. The consciousness-raising group as a model for therapy with women. *Psychotherapy: Theory, Research and Practice,* 1973, 10(1), 24–29.

Brodsky, A. Therapeutic aspects of consciousness-raising groups. In E. I. Rawlings & D. K. Carter (Eds.), *Psychotherapy for women: Treatment toward equality.* Springfield, Ill.: Charles C Thomas, 1977.

Brodsky, A., & Hare-Mustin, R. Psychotherapy and women: Priorities for research. In A. Brodsky & R. Hare-Mustin (Eds.), *Women and psychotherapy*. New York: Guilford Press, 1980.

Broverman, I. K., Broverman, D. M., & Clarkson, F. E. Sex role stereotypes and clinical judgments of mental health. *Journal of Consulting and Clinical Psychology*, 1970, *34*(1), 1–7.

Carlock, C. J., & Martin, P. Y. Sex composition and the intensive group experience. *Social Work*, 1977, *22*(1), 27–32.

Chodorow, N. *The fantasy of the perfect mother*. Paper presented at Michigan State University, Apr. 18, 1980.

Cline-Naffzifer, C. Women's lives and frustration, oppression, and anger. *Journal of Counseling Psychology*, 1974, *21*(1), 51–56.

Epstein, N. B., & Volk, L. A. Research on the results of psychotherapy: A summary of evidence. *American Journal of Psychiatry*, 1981, *138*(8), 1027–1035.

Eskilson, A., & Wiley, M.G. Sex composition and leadership in small groups. *Sociometry*, 1976, *39*(3), 183–194.

Ezriel, H. Notes on psychoanalytic group therapy: II, Interpretations and research. *Psychiatry*, 1952, *15*(2), 119–126.

Jakubowski, P. Self assertion training procedures for women. In E. I. Rawlings & D. K. Carter (Eds.), *Psychotherapy for women: Treatment toward equality*. Springfield, Ill.: Charles C Thomas, 1977.

Kirsh, B. Consciousness-raising groups as therapy for women. In V. Franks & V. Burtle (Eds.), *Women in therapy*. New York: Brunner/Mazel, 1974.

Kravetz, D. Consciousness-raising and self-help. In A. Brodsky & R. Hare-Mustin (Eds.), *Women and psychotherapy*. New York: Guilford Press, 1980.

Lieberman, M. A., & Bond, G. R. The problem of being a woman: A survey of 1,700 women in consciousness-raising groups. *Journal of Applied Behavioral Science*, 1976, *12*(3), 363–379.

McMahon, S. L. Women in marital transition. In A. Brodsky & R. Hare-Mustin (Eds.), *Women and psychotherapy*. New York: Guilford Press, 1980.

Meador, B., Solomon, E., & Bowen, M. Encounter groups for women only. In L. N. Solomon & B. Berzon (Eds.), *New perspectives on encounter groups*. San Francisco: Jossey-Bass, 1972.

Miller, J. B. *Toward a new psychology of women*. Boston: Beacon Press, 1976.

Paget, M. A. The ontological anguish of women artists. *New England Sociologist*, Spring/Summer, 1981.

Piliavin, J. A., & Martin, R. R. The effects of the sex composition of groups on style of social interaction. *Sex Roles*, 1978, *4*(2), 281–296.

Rawlings, E. I., & Carter, D. K. Values and value change in psychotherapy. In E. I. Rawlings & D. K. Carter (Eds.), *Psychotherapy for women: Treatment toward equality*. Springfield, Ill.: Charles C Thomas, 1977.

Rice, J. D., & Rice, D. G. Implications of the women's liberation movement for psychotherapy. *American Journal of Psychiatry*, 1973, *130*(2), 191–196.

Sutherland, J. D. Notes on psychoanalytic group therapy: I, Therapy and training. *Psychiatry*, 1952, *15*(2), 111–117.

Whiteley, R. M. Women in groups. *Counseling Psychologist*, 1973, *4*(1), 27–43.

Wycoff, H. Radical psychiatry for women: Politics and women's problem-solving groups. In E. I. Rawlings & D. K. Carter (Eds.), *Psychotherapy for women: Treatment toward equality* Springfield, Ill.: Charles C Thomas, 1977.

A Self-Control Therapy Group
for Depressed Women

*Esther D. Rothblum, Ph.D., Leon Green, Ph.D.,
and R. Lorraine Collins, Ph.D.*

ESTHER D. ROTHBLUM is a postdoctoral fellow at the Yale University Depression
Research Unit, New Haven, Connecticut. LEON GREEN is assistant professor at
the Graduate School of Applied and Professional Psychology at Rutgers University, New Brunswick, New Jersey. R. LORRAINE COLLINS is assistant professor
of psychology at the State University of New York, Stony Brook.

Depression is the most widespread psychiatric disorder existing today, not only
among patients involved in therapy but also among nonpatient populations
randomly drawn from the community.

The present chapter presents an approach to group therapy for one subset
of this large population—depressed women. Since depression has been found
to occur in women at twice the rate it occurs in men (Weissman & Klerman,
1977), women represent a high-risk group for depression. This chapter begins
with a discussion of diagnostic criteria and prevalence rates for depression,
along with a brief review of possible etiological factors specific to depression

Research for this chapter was supported in part by NIMH Training Grant MH 14235. The
authors would like to thank Myrna M. Weissman, Ph.D., for her helpful comments.

in women. The remainder of the chapter focuses on a description of two behavioral treatment groups for depressed women: their rationale, implementation, results, and implications for future treatment. By outlining both the methods and the critical issues related to the delivery of therapeutic services for depressed women, we can further enhance the efficacy of group treatment for this population.

Diagnosis of Depression and Prevalence Rates

Diagnostic Criteria

Depression can be considered a mood, a series of symptoms, or a syndrome. The third edition of the American Psychiatric Association's *Diagnostic and Statistical Manual of Mental Disorders (DSM-III)* (American Psychiatric Association, 1980) provides three criteria for identifying a major depressive episode: (1) a dysphoric mood or loss of interest and pleasure is present and relatively persistent; (2) at least four of the following eight symptoms are present nearly every day for at least two weeks: poor appetite or weight loss, insomnia or increased sleep, psychomotor agitation or retardation, loss of interest in usual activities, loss of energy or fatigue, feelings of worthlessness, diminished concentration, and suicidal ideation; and (3) there is no evidence of mania, psychosis, organic mental disorder, or normal bereavement.

One of the problems in research on depression is that many of the diagnostic criteria, including the dysphoric mood, are difficult to assess directly; thus the diagnosis of depression is made primarily on the basis of self-report. To overcome this problem, researchers have developed self-report symptom scales that define and clarify specific behaviors, affects, and cognitions related to depressive episodes. Inventories commonly used for assessing depression include the Minnesota Multiphasic Personality Inventory (MMPI) Depression (D) Scale (Dahlstrom et al., 1972), the Beck Depression Inventory (Beck & Beamesdorfer, 1974), and the Lewinsohn Pleasant Events Schedule (Lewinsohn & Shaw, 1969).

The MMPI D-Scale, traditionally used to assess depression, consists of several dozen true/false items such as "No one seems to understand me." The Beck Depression Inventory provides 27 groups of statements from which the patient is asked to select the one statement in each group that best describes the way he or she felt during the preceding week. The Lewinsohn Pleasant Events Schedule provides a list of 49 activities; patients are asked to indicate how often they engaged in each activity during the preceding 30 days. Patients are also asked to state the perceived "enjoyability" (reinforcement potential) of each activity on a 1-to-3-point scale.

Prevalence Rates

In epidemiological research, the point prevalence rate is defined as the proportion of the population exhibiting the specific disorder at a particular point in time. Boyd and Weissman (in press) have reported point prevalence rates, based on symptom scales, for depression ranging from 9 percent to 22 percent of the general population. When analyzed in terms of sex, point prevalence rates for men range from 6 percent to 19 percent; for women they range from 11 percent to 34 percent. These findings support an earlier finding that women may experience depression twice as often as men (Weissman & Klerman, 1977).

The 2 to 1 sex ratio of depressed women to depressed men is found in different regions of the United States as well as in other Western countries. As with depression in general, this ratio seems to occur in both patient and nonpatient groups selected randomly from community surveys of the general population. Exceptions to this sex ratio are provided by studies of populations in developing countries and studies that focus on manic depression, where the sex ratio is fairly well balanced (Weissman & Klerman, 1977).

Research on Women and Depression

Several theories have been advanced to account for the sex difference in depression rates. First, it has been postulated that biological factors might account for the sex difference. In the most complete review to date, Weissman and Klerman (1977) summarize the evidence for possible genetic transmission of susceptibility to depression and for female endocrine physiological processes in depression. The evidence they cite concerning the relationship between depression and genetic factors is inconsistent: good evidence supports a genetic factor in depression, but studies on cross-linkage are conflicting. There exists very good evidence that depression increases during the postpartum period. The evidence for premenstrual tension and for depression as the result of oral contraceptives is inconsistent. Finally, there is very good evidence that menopause does not result in higher rates of depression. Thus further research is needed to clarify the influence of biological factors in depression.

Several environmental factors have been postulated to account for the high rates of depression among women. First, women's roles may be more restricted than men's and allow less financial, social, or occupational gratification. Second, women may be socialized to be unassertive, dependent, and passive; these qualities lead to depression rather than action during stressful situations. Third, as the media increasingly present exceptional women who have "made it" in high-level careers, many women may feel depressed with their own inability to meet these rising expectations. Finally, women may be taught to be helpless and to experience a lack of control over their environment, so that the perception of no relationship between their efforts and any significant results would lead to depression.

Much recent research has focused on specific factors relating to women's roles that could account for high depression rates. The following factors are some of the research conclusions discussed in a recent review by Rothblum (1983).

Social/interpersonal deficiencies are a major risk factor for depression. Women who lack a social network of family and friends or who are not involved in an intimate relationship are more depressed than women who have meaningful interpersonal relationships (Brown et al., 1975; Pearlin & Johnson, 1977). Women are more likely than men to report depression in response to rejection or distance in a relationship and after experiencing a loss of self-esteem (Parker, 1980).

Marriage serves a protective role for men but not for women. Married men are less depressed than never-married men, whereas married women are more depressed than those who were never married (Gove, 1972; Radloff, 1975). Not only are married women more depressed than married men, but depressed married women also have more marital problems (Bullock et al., 1972). Housewives experience more marital friction and are less satisfied with their work than employed married women (Gove, 1972; Brown & Harris, 1978). However, employed married women carry a dual load of work when they combine housework with their jobs (Radloff, 1975).

Separated and divorced women constitute the largest category of depressed individuals (Hirschfeld & Cross, 1982). A study of marital disruption (Briscoe & Smith, 1973) indicates that depressed divorced men and women constitute different samples. Women are likely to become depressed in a disrupted marriage, often as the result of specific events contributing to the marital friction. Few demographic variables distinguish depressed women from their nondepressed counterparts, suggesting that it is the events leading to divorce that result also in depression. Depressed divorced men, on the other hand, have histories of precipitating interpersonal and sexual factors that are not present among nondepressed divorced men. This suggests that, among men, the incapacitating symptoms of depression may result in divorce.

Women constitute the majority of *single parents*, with accompanying financial problems, loneliness, and difficulties in maintaining meaningful social contacts. Ilgenfritz (1961) identified fear of loneliness, loss of self-esteem, practical problems of living, and specific concerns for children as the major stressors facing single mothers. Divorced mothers experience little respect and negative social attitudes. In fact, single mothers often are blamed for a variety of social problems, such as the need for welfare (Brandwein et al., 1974).

The presence of young children in the home is a major factor contributing to depression among women (Shapiro et al., 1979). Additionally, depressed women have difficulty with child rearing. They have less involvement in their children's lives, experience difficulty communicating with their children, show a loss of affection for them, and report considerable friction between themselves and their children (Weissman et al., 1972). The effect of the mother's depression on children, notably adolescents, is negative (Weissman et al., 1971). Conversely, women become less depressed when grown children leave home (Radloff, 1980).

Employment has generally beneficial effects for women (Hall & Gordon, 1973). A study focusing on employed women and housewives in treatment for depression (Mostow & Newberry, 1975) found that employed women displayed significantly more depressed symptoms before treatment but recovered faster than housewives. Housewives were more impaired in social adjustment, had more economic problems, and displayed more boredom after treatment. One may argue that women in the labor market occupy jobs with lower salaries and status, and fewer opportunities for upward mobility, than men.

There has been little research on women in *nontraditional roles*, such as professional or executive women. Welner et al. (1979) investigated psychiatric illness among women physicians and Ph.D.s in the community. Their results indicated that 51 percent of women physicians and 32 percent of women Ph.D.s had primary affective disorders. Their study found little evidence of other forms of psychiatric illness. The women physicians were not only significantly more depressed than the Ph.D. sample, but they were also more severely depressed and had had more depressive episodes. Sixty-seven percent of depressed women M.D.s and 70 percent of depressed women Ph.D.s reported prejudice against them in their training or employment; the figures for nondepressed M.D.s and Ph.D.s were 50 percent and 48 percent, respectively. Thus prejudice was reported significantly more often by depressed women. Similarly, Pitts et al. (1979) examined American Medical Association records of deaths of physicians. They found the suicide rate for women M.D.s to be 6.56 percent higher than that of male M.D.s and four times higher than the suicide rate for white American females of the same age. Although additional research is warranted to corroborate these findings, it appears that professional women are at significantly more risk for depression and suicide than other women.

In our society, it is more acceptable for women than men to *express depression*. Hammen and Peters (1978) used both male and female college students to rate male and female confederates who played a standardized depressed or nondepressed role over the telephone. Results showed that depressed persons of the opposite sex were most strongly rejected. Female raters made little distinction between depressed males and females on role impairment. Male raters, however, considered the depressed females more impaired. Raters became significantly more depressed following an interaction with depressed actors.

What are the effects of long-term interactions with depressed individuals? Kreitman et al. (1970) and Nelson et al. (1970) investigated the effects of long-term interactions on women who were living with neurotic husbands. Sixty male outpatients and their wives were interviewed and compared with 60 control couples (Kreitman et al., 1970). Patients' wives were five times more likely to be incapacitated than control wives in household roles, social activities, health, and child rearing activities.

Finally, there is some evidence that men make better use of *coping strategies* in the face of stressful life events (Pearlin & Schooler, 1978). Thus women are not only at higher risk for depression but they seem to receive less preparation to cope with disruptive life events.

Rothblum (1983) concludes: "Basically, the woman who hopes for marriage, a family, and a providing husband who will be the sole wage-earner is dramatically increasing her chances of depression. On the other hand, the woman who enters graduate or medical school to pursue an advanced degree traditionally reserved for men is not immune from stress and depression" as a result of the prejudice and sexism in these professions. Thus rates of depression and suicide among professional women are extremely high. It is evident that depression among women is significantly affected by women's sex roles in relation to work, the marital relationship, and motherhood. In general, traditional sex-role stereotypes about women place them at greater risk for depression.

Starting the Depression Groups

The Rationale

In 1977 staff members of the outpatient psychological clinic at the Graduate School of Applied and Professional Psychology at Rutgers University in New Brunswick, New Jersey, established a depression treatment program that consisted initially of two short-term therapy groups for depressed women based on behavioral techniques. This initiative seemed indicated for the following reasons:

1. Since depression is a high-frequency clinical diagnosis and women are depressed at about twice the prevalence rates of men, group therapy is a more cost-effective method of treating comparatively large numbers of women than individual therapy.
2. It is evident from the preceding sections that the environment plays a

major role in precipitating depression. A group setting allows individual members to share their experiences related to risk factors for depression, such as marital and interpersonal difficulties, childcare, housework, and employment-related stressors. Clients can also self-disclose more readily if they realize that others share their problems.

3. The group setting enables women to recognize that their emotions and experiences are not unique or unusual, thus validating these experiences. Clients who attribute the causes of their depression to their husbands, their bosses, or to themselves will instead realize commonalities with other patients.

4. Support and advice from group members provide more broad-based and varied feedback than that from one therapist. Furthermore, group members may also provide more practical advice concerning details of coping with domestic and job-related problems than the therapist, who may have less in common with the clients' lifestyles.

5. Since depression often results in lack of energy to engage in activities and thus in social isolation, the group serves a social function by increasing client social involvement and activities.

6. Finally, women have limited financial resources and can afford the relatively low cost of group therapy more readily than the cost of individual therapy.

The staff of the depression treatment program had several goals in forming the group-therapy project:

1. To provide a program for women who were clinically depressed and who wished to enter treatment for depression.

2. To offer a short-term (six week) treatment program that focused on active intervention strategies and that required daily activities to change the concomitants of depression.

3. To investigate the outcome of treatment over a three-month follow-up period after the last treatment session, during which the clients practiced intervention strategies on their own.

The remainder of the chapter will focus on these components of the group-therapy program.

Group Members

To publicize the depression treatment program, advertisements were placed in three local newspapers describing the program and soliciting applications for group membership. A total of 69 applicants telephoned to express their interest. They were given more information about the treatment program and told the fee. They were also told that they would be required to complete a series of assessment procedures in order to be accepted into the program.

Forty-two applicants attended the pretesting session. Of these, 20 women fit the acceptance criteria, which included: (1) not receiving other psychotherapy at the time; (2) scoring at or above the level of clinical depression (T $\geq$ 70) on the MMPI D-Scale; and (3) not scoring above the depression score on any other clinical scale of the MMPI.

These 20 women were accepted into the program and organized into two groups of 10 each. However, two women in each group failed to attend the initial group meetings. Thus each of the treatment groups started with eight women. One woman dropped out of each group during the course of the treatment program: one after two sessions for unspecified personal reasons and the other after all six sessions because of disagreement with the philosophy of the group. There was no attrition during the maintenance phase of either group. The results of the program were tabulated for the 14 women who completed it.

Of the clients who participated in the treatment program, the majority (58 percent) were 40 or over; 21 percent were in their thirties; and another 21 percent were in their twenties. Fifty percent of the clients were married, 29 percent divorced or separated, and the remainder were either single (14 percent) or widowed (7 percent). The majority of the women (78 percent) were employed in secretarial/assistant positions, two were housewives, and one was unemployed.

Before entering treatment, clients were asked about the nature of their depression. Durations of the current depressive episodes ranged from one month to "all my life." In general, durations were divided into three categories: less than one year (21 percent), one to five years (29 percent), and over five years (46 percent). Thus most clients reported long-standing depressed moods.

There was a large range of perceived precipitating events for the depression. Three clients (21 percent) listed the breakup of their marriage, five (37 percent) did not know a specific event, and the rest (42 percent) listed such events or factors as job stress, being overweight, and death of a significant other.

Most clients (86 percent) reported past episodes of depression preceding the current episode. However, fewer than half (36 percent) reported previous therapy for depression.

Conducting the Therapy Groups

The Therapists

Two female therapists led all sessions of the depression treatment program. Both were advanced graduate students in clinical psychology and had experience in group therapy and in self-control behavior therapy.

The general aims of the treatment program were to provide (1) a structured, cumulative method of intervening in the depressed mood and behaviors; (2) a supportive environment; and (3) skills for coping independently after the termination of treatment. The guidelines for the treatment program were taken from Rehm's (1977) *Self-Control Therapy Manual,* which had been used for the self-control of depression (Fuchs & Rehm, 1977).

Structured Intervention

The first session began with an introduction to the treatment program. Information sheets were distributed that stressed self-help based on strategies developed by Rehm, such as the following:

Depression can be looked at in various ways. Traditionally therapists have attempted to deal with depressed feelings by uncovering personality variables which, they believed, lay behind the symptoms of depression. More recently psychologists have been focusing directly on the actual here-and-now functioning of the person, believing that if current behavior changes in a meaningful way then the person's feelings will improve accordingly. In this program our goal will be to help you to change your own pattern of activity, in order to feel better (Rehm, 1977).

The goal of the treatment program was described on the information sheets as follows:

To control your own behavior effectively, you will be teaching yourself to do three things:

1. Monitor behavior—checking to see which activities have been performed.
2. Evaluate behavior—comparing each activity against standards you have set for yourself.
3. Rewarding behavior which has met the standards you set for yourself.

As we hope you will soon see for yourself, these three things are a means of increasing your rate of satisfying activity, which in turn influences your positive feelings (Rehm, 1977).

Thus clients were informed that mood was the function of one's own behavior and that they could gain greater control by learning skills that would help them work toward goals of their own choice.

The first and second treatment sessions focused on *self-monitoring.* Clients were instructed that depressed individuals selectively attend to negative events and to immediate rather than delayed outcomes of behavior. Thus a woman might focus on the one criticism that her boss made that day rather than the eight compliments that preceded it. Similarly, this woman might dwell on the rejecting nature of the criticism instead of receiving it as feedback to incorporate into her next project. Clients were trained to orient toward positive activities as target behaviors—that is, to work toward participating in those activities that commonly result in pleasurable outcomes, though not necessarily immediately. Clients were urged to seek out opportunities to participate in these activities, and continually to discover potential pleasurable events in their environment. Most of the first two sessions was allotted to group members' suggestions and discussion of self-monitoring.

The third and fourth sessions continued discussion of self-monitoring, but focused now on *self-evaluation.* Depressed individuals tend to set overly harsh criteria for their behavior and to attribute failure to the wrong sources. Thus a woman who spent 15 years at home raising a child might be devastated if she does not immediately succeed in obtaining an interesting, highly demanding job. She is setting her immediate goal too high, even though it is a plausible one for her in the future. The group sessions focused on attainable goals. Clients were instructed to develop lists of subgoals, realistic components of larger goals. A client who wanted to lose 50 pounds included a detailed exercise and caloric-intake program that called for three hours of exercise a week and eating no more than 1,000 calories a day. A divorced woman planned to engage in two social events a week and to invite a close friend to go shopping or to a movie whenever she felt lonely. Clients were instructed to evaluate their performances in these subgoals rather than to overgeneralize by focusing on the long-range goals.

The last two group sessions focused on *self-reinforcement* in addition to self-monitoring and self-evaluation. Depressed individuals frequently blame themselves for failures rather than feel good about their accomplishments. This pattern of "punishment" lessens persistence and increases depression. Clients were instructed that "self-reward" or reinforcement makes efforts more pleasurable and increases motivation. Thus clients were instructed to self-administer rewards in the form of pleasurable activities. These rewards were given for engaging in the difficult and time-consuming subgoals described in the previous sessions. Furthermore, rewards were to be administered *contingently*—that is, only if the activity had been completed. Thus the weight-loss client decided to set aside one dollar for each completed hour of exercise and for each day she ate within her 1,000-calorie limit. This money was then applied to the purchase of a new wardrobe. A client who had difficulty asserting herself to coworkers rewarded herself by telephoning a friend long-distance each time she asserted herself at work. Self-reinforcement is particularly important as subgoals become routine and tedious.

Homework Assignments

It is evident from the description of the treatment program that homework assignments played a major role. Particularly in short-term group programs, in which direct client contact with therapists may not be extensive, it is important that clients engage in treatment-related activities between sessions. To illustrate the role of homework assignments, we will describe the assignments of a specific client. Ms. T was a 44-year-old secretary who recently had been divorced. She attributed her depression to the social isolation she felt as a newly single woman. She had relied extensively on her husband to initiate social activities during her marriage, and now she felt that she had no friends.

Homework assignments for the self-monitoring phase included:

1. Engage in positive activities.
2. Record positive activities in a Daily Activities Log provided by the therapists. Records should be made as soon as possible after a positive activity occurs. Daily logs should be kept at hand (e.g., in purse) and brought to group sessions.
3. Do not record failures or negative activities.
4. Monitor every positive activity/event, no matter how trivial (e.g., relaxing nap, warm shower, admiring beautiful scenery).
5. Record subsequent *mood* experienced during the positive activity on a scale from 0 (miserable) to 10 (euphoric).
6. Compute average number of activities per day and average daily mood rating each week. Graph these ratings (optional) on graphs provided by the therapists.

After the first session, Ms. T's daily activities log looked as follows:

Positive Activities	Mood Rating
Enjoyed brisk weather	8
Looking at attractive scenery	8
Thinking about something good/personal achievement	8

Clearly, this client was not engaging in much active behavior. After receiving feedback on this along with encouragement to engage in more pleasurable activities, she recorded in her next log:

Positive Activities	Mood Rating
Expressing myself to another person	10
Learning how to crochet	5
Working on my knitting	8
Caring for myself	8
Getting a good meal	10
Looking forward to a social event	10
Making time for myself	10

Homework assignments for the self-evaluation phase consisted of pursuing subgoals, recording subgoals, and administering points according to their importance or usefulness. Specifically, directions included (Rehm, 1977):

1. Prompt clients to maximize points by doing the following:
   a. Do each positive activity more often.
   b. Do more different positive activities.
   c. Set more reasonable, achievable subgoals.
   d. Work at a few higher, more significant subgoals.
   e. Break down new or significant behaviors into components.
2. Even though stress is on significant or difficult activities, clients should not neglect to accumulate points in easier ways. Suggest that these subgoals be arranged hierarchically according to difficulty or order in which they must be enacted.
3. Direct clients to continue monitoring and graphing as before, but now to record each engagement in a subgoal/component behavior. They should briefly describe what they did, note what it is a subgroup of, and rate their subsequent mood.
4. Encourage clients to deliberately engage in subgoal behaviors.

Since Ms. T was working on becoming more socially active, she chose subgoals relating to initiating friendships and participating in social and interpersonal activities. An entry in her log reads:

Positive Activities	Mood Rating	Points
Took care of myself	8	
Talked to someone on elevator	10	10
Made something for party on Thursday	10	3
Went shopping	10	5

Finally, in the last phase, self-reinforcement, clients "rewarded" themselves by engaging in a pleasurable activity each time they accomplished one of their subgoals. Thus clients were asked to: (1) reward positive activities, (2) be generous with rewards initially, (3) reward activities contingently.

Supportive Environment

Throughout the treatment program, the therapists encouraged ideas and discussion by the clients. Clients were supported in their efforts to initiate activities and solutions for their own depression-related behavior and affect. Clients were also encouraged to assist others with example, feedback, and support. The group became increasingly cohesive and the atmosphere was one of camaraderie.

Cost of Treatment

The financial costs of psychotherapy are often prohibitive for women. To encourage attendance in the depression treatment program, clients were asked to deposit $50 at the first group session and then received a refund of $5 at the end of each session they attended (including the first). If clients came to all nine sessions (six weekly and three follow-up monthly sessions), the cost of the entire program was only $5, which was used to cover advertising and secretarial expenses. (Clients who wished to drop out of the program received a refund of their entire fee.) Thus treatment costs were used to motivate clients for therapy; in effect, clients were paid for coming with their own money. This method has been used successfully in the area of weight reduction by Collins et al. (1980).

Maintaining Treatment Effects

A major goal of therapy is to ensure maintenance of treatment effects. Thus we were concerned that clients continue therapy-related activities on their own after the termination of the six-week therapy period. To provide feedback for clients during this crucial posttherapy stage, three follow-up sessions were scheduled at one-month intervals after treatment was completed. During these "maintenance" sessions no new techniques were presented. Rather, clients were encouraged to discuss their progress and their improvement was assessed.

Results of the Depression Treatment Program

The assessment battery we administered to clients before treatment was re-administered after the last treatment session and at each monthly maintenance session. We were also interested in measuring the degree to which clients had participated in the treatment-related activities.

Our data indicate that clients attended a mean number of 5 sessions out of a total of 6 and completed a mean of 3.36 homework logs out of a total of 5. Clients engaged in a mean of 3.75 pleasant activities daily and gave the accompanying mood an average rating of 6.62 out of a possible 10 (highest mood).

The same symptom-assessment scales given before treatment were administered after treatment and at the one-, two-, and three-month maintenance sessions. Because the full-scale MMPI takes several hours to complete, it was administered in its entirety only before treatment and during the last maintenance session. At all other maintenance sessions, only the MMPI D-Scale items were administered.

Significant assessment-period main effects were thus apparent for the global

MMPI D-Scale and for the cognitive scale (Beck Depression Inventory), as well as for other MMPI subscales, such as K, Psychopathic Deviance, Male-Female, Paranoia, Psychasthenia, Mania, and Social Introversion. One explanation for the improvement, in the direction of lessened psychopathology, of the above MMPI scales during a depression-treatment program could be the number of items that are considered part of the D-Scale at the same time that they are also part of other scales. Rush et al. (1977) studied the typical MMPI profile of clients whom they had admitted to a depression-treatment program. They found clients to score at a T of 70 or above on F, Hypochondria, Psychopathic Deviance, Paranoia, Psychasthenia, Schizophrenia, and Social Introversion, as well as Depression. Another explanation could be the tendency of depressed clients to answer items in the direction of pathology as a result of their low self-esteem and self-devaluation, both frequent symptoms of depression. Improvement in self-esteem as a result of treatment would be likely to reverse this tendency, thus producing improvement on the other clinical scales of the MMPI. Finally, it is also possible that these scales show general improvement. It is not certain why the Lewinsohn Pleasant Events Schedule did not show any improvement on depression, except that it seems to be only the more global measures mentioned earlier that indicate significant differences in the present program.

Conclusion and Recommendations

This chapter makes the following points concerning group therapy for depressed women:

1. Depression is twice as prevalent among women than among men. Recent research on women's roles indicates that marriage, divorce and separation, the presence of young children in the home, the dual stress of housework and job, and employment in nontraditional jobs for women are all risk factors for depression. This consideration of these factors should be incorporated into treatment programs.
2. There is a high attrition rate among both applicants for a depression-treatment program and accepted clients. Future programs might loosen admission criteria and offer increased motivational incentives for attending group sessions. Furthermore, our data indicate that the majority of clients did not seek treatment for past episodes of depression. Efforts might be directed at targeting such populations through the news media or through general practitioners.
3. Clients both adhered to the group treatment program and improved on depression symptoms. The program was cost-effective in that it was group-administered and short-term (six weeks). Homework assignments

assured continued participation in treatment-related activities between sessions.

4. Clients maintained improvement at three months follow-up and reported continued adherence to treatment activities.

Feminists have claimed (e.g., Chesler, 1972) that sex-role biases of mental-health professionals contribute to women's emotional distress by readily allocating clinical diagnoses and treating women in the context of the "sick role." Mental health professionls, on the other hand, may argue that "consciousness raising" alone without regard to psychopathology could prove harmful as women are urged to become "liberated" without regard to their own readiness or emotional independence to assume new roles. The group-treatment format, we believe, can constitute an ideal compromise: a structured therapeutic model within a setting that exposes clients to other women in similar situations, with the potential for receiving feedback and providing mutual support.

References

American Psychiatric Association, Task Force on Nomenclature and Statistics. *Diagnostic and statistical manual of mental disorders* (3rd ed.) [*DSM-III*]. Washington, D.C.: American Psychiatric Association, 1980.

Beck, A. T., & Beamesdorfer, A. Assessment of depression: The depression inventory. *Modern Problems of Pharmacopsychiatry*, 1974, 7, 151–169.

Boyd, J. H., & Weissman, M. M. The epidemiology of affective disorders. *Archives of General Psychiatry*, in press.

Brandwein, R. A., Brown, C. A., & Fox, E. M. Women and children last: The social situation of divorced mothers and their families. *Journal of Marriage and the Family*, 1974, 36(3), 498–514.

Briscoe, C. W., & Smith, J. B. Depression and marital turmoil. *Archives of General Psychiatry*, 1973, 29(6), 811–817.

Brown, G. W., Bhrolchain, M. N., & Harris, T. O. Social class and psychiatric disturbance among women in an urban population. *Sociology*, 1975, 9(2), 225–254.

Brown, G. W., & Harris, T. O. *Social origins of depression*. London: Tavistock, 1978.

Bullock, R. C., Siegel, R., Weissman, M., & Paykel, E. S. The weeping wife: Marital relations of depressed women. *Journal of Marriage and the Family*, 1972, 34(3), 488–495.

Chesler, P. *Women and madness*. Garden City, N.Y.: Doubleday, 1972.

Collins, R. L., Wilson, G. T., & Rothblum, E. D. *The comparative efficacy of cognitive behavioral approaches in weight reduction*. Paper presented at the annual convention of the Association for the Advancement of Behavior Therapy, New York, November 1980.

Dahlstrom, W. G., Welsh, G. S., & Dahlstrom, L. E. *An MMPI handbook*. Vol. 1, *Clinical interpretation*. Minneapolis: University of Minnesota Press, 1972.

Fuchs, C. Z., & Rehm, L. P. A self-control behavior therapy program for depression. *Journal of Consulting and Clinical Psychology*, 1977, 45(2), 206–215.

Gove, W. R. The relationship between sex roles, marital status, and mental illness, *Social Forces*, 1972, 51(1), 34–44.

Hall, D. T., & Gordon, F. E. Career choices of married women: Effects on conflict, role behavior, and satisfaction. *Journal of Applied Psychology*, 1973, 58(1), 42–48.

Hammen, C. L., & Peters, S. D. Interpersonal consequences of depression: Responses to men and women enacting a depressed role. *Journal of Abnormal Psychology*, 1978, 87(3), 322–332.

Hirschfeld, R. M. A., & Cross, C. H. *The epidemiology of affective disorders: Psychosocial risk factors.* Manuscript submitted for publication, 1982.

Ilgenfritz, M. P. Mothers and their own: Widows and divorcees. *Marriage and Family Living*, 1961, 23, 38–41.

Kreitman, N., Collins, J., Nelson, B., & Troop, J. Neurosis and marital interaction: I. Personality and symptoms. *British Journal of Psychiatry*, 1970, 117, 33–46.

Lewinsohn, P. M., & Shaw, D. A. Feedback about interpersonal behavior as an agent of behavior change: A case study in the treatment of depression. *Psychotherapy and Psychosomatics*, 1969, 17, 82–88.

Mostow, E., & Newberry, P. Work role and depression in women: A comparison of workers and housewives in treatment. *American Journal of Orthopsychiatry*, 1975, 45(4), 538–548.

Nelson, B., Collins J., Kreitman, N., & Troop, J. Neurosis and marital interaction: II. Time sharing and social activity. *British Journal of Psychiatry*, 1970, 117, 47–58.

Parker, G. Vulnerability factors in normal depression. *Journal of Psychosomatic Research*, 1980, 24, 67–74.

Pearlin, L. I., & Johnson, J. S. Marital status, life-strains, and depression. *American Sociological Review*, 1977, 42(5), 704–715.

Pearlin, L. I., & Schooler, C. The structure of coping. *Journal of Health and Social Behavior*, 1978, 19(1), 2–21.

Pitts, F. N., Jr., Schuller, A. B., Rich, C. L., & Pitts, A. F. Suicide among U.S. women physicians, 1967–1972. *American Journal of Psychiatry*, 1979, 136(5), 694–696.

Radloff, L. Sex differences in depression: The effects of occupation and marital status. *Sex Roles*, 1975, 1(3), 249–265.

Radloff, L. S. Depression and the empty nest. *Sex Roles*, 1980, 6(6), 775–781.

Rehm, L. P. *Self-control therapy manual.* Unpublished manuscript, 1977.

Rothblum, E. D. Sex role stereotypes and depression in women. In E. D. Rothblum & V. Franks (Eds.), *The ailing feminine stereotype: Sex roles and women's mental health.* New York: Springer Publishing, 1983.

Rush, A. A., Beck, A. T., Kovacs, M., & Hollon, S. Comparative efficacy of cognitive therapy and pharmacotherapy in the treatment of depressed outpatients. *Cognitive Therapy and Research*, 1977, 1, 17–37.

Shapiro, D. A., Parry, G., & Brewin, C. Stress, coping and psychotherapy: The foundations of a clincial approach. In T. Cox & C. Mackay (Eds.), *Psychophysiological response to occupational stress.* New York: International Publishing, 1979.

Weissman, M. M., & Klerman, G. L. Sex differences and the epidemiology of depression. *Archives of General Psychiatry*, 1977, 34(1), 98–111.

Weissman, M. M., Paykel, E. S., & Klerman, G. L. The depressed woman as a mother. *Social Psychiatry*, 1972, 7(2), 98–108.

Weissman, M. M., Paykel, E. S., Siegel, R., & Klerman, G. L. The social role performance of depressed women: Comparisons with a normal group. *American Journal of Orthopsychiatry*, 1971, 41(3), 390–405.

Welner, A., Martin, S., Wochnick, E., Davis, M. A., Fishman, R., & Clayton, P. J. Psychiatric disorders among professional women. *Archives of General Psychiatry*, 1979, 36(2), 169–173.

9

A Therapy Group for Battered Women

Bruce Rounsaville, M.D.,
and Norman Lifton, M.A.

BRUCE ROUNSAVILLE is assistant professor of psychiatry at the Yale University School of Medicine, New Haven, Connecticut. NORMAN LIFTON is supervisor of group psychotherapy at the Connecticut Mental Health Center and lecturer in psychiatry at the Yale Medical School.

Although there is growing evidence (Gelles, 1974; Straus et al., 1980) that the victims of wife abuse are numerous, little attention has been given in the psychiatric literature to treatment strategies directed to them (Hilberman, 1980). In this paper, we present our experience evaluating and treating a group of battered women and assess the implications of this work. We attempt to show that battered women are a large group of patients who need and can use treatment but, because of dynamic and social features of their problem, are frequently inadequately helped by current treatment methods. We point out how treatment plans can be developed to meet the special needs of battered women while avoiding the common pitfalls.

Background of the Project

During his psychiatric training, the first author was struck by the number of women in his evaluation and couples-therapy caseload who were repeatedly physically abused. To get some preliminary idea of the frequency of this problem, he reviewed the charts of 180 patients who participated in a study testing the differential effects of Triavil and psychotherapy on depression and found ten cases where physical abuse was mentioned and eight where it was strongly implied. In no case, however, was any mention made of an attempt by the therapist to deal specifically with this issue. These findings led to the decision to organize a therapy group for battered women.

Identification of Patients

For this purpose, battered women were defined as married or unmarried women over 16 who had been physically abused to any degree by male intimate partners within three months of the referral. Subjects were identified from two settings in New Haven, Connecticut: the Connecticut Mental Health Center and the Yale New Haven Hospital emergency room (only women presenting to surgery or psychiatric services were identified). Evaluating clinicians— mental health professionals at the Connecticut Mental Health Center and surgery and psychiatric personnel at the hospital emergency room—were informed of the project by written and verbal communication. They were requested to identify battered women by asking their patients specifically if they had been beaten by a male partner. They were further requested to inform patients who had been beaten of the availability of counseling and possible group treatment around the issue of abuse.

For the staff at the Mental Health Center and for mental health professionals in the hospital emergency room, the referral process was straightforward. Patients who expressed a desire for treatment were told they would be contacted, and their names were given to the first author. For patients presenting to surgery, the referral process involved two steps. First, they were offered immediate psychiatric counseling while in the emergency room. In most cases, this was provided by the first author, and a follow-up appointment was made at that time. In other cases, the psychiatrist on call saw the patient and then referred her to the first author for follow-up care. Seventy-five women were identified in the two settings.

At the follow-up interview, the first author discussed with the patients their histories and their legal, social, and treatment options. They were then asked to complete a number of questionnaires, including a coded history form prepared for this study. In addition, current depressive status was evaluated using the Center for Epidemiological Studies Depression Scale (CES-D), a 20-item patient self-report scale. Thirty-one women were interviewed in this fashion,

14 referred from the Connecticut Mental Health Center and 17 from the hospital emergency room. Henceforth, this group of 31 who were interviewed will be referred to as the "screened" or "evaluated" group. Except where otherwise specified, all data pertaining to the history and characteristics of our sample are derived from this group.

Among the treatment options offered to the women were individual psychotherapy, couples treatment, and group psychotherapy designed especially to deal with the problems of battered women. Couples therapy was presented as the treatment of choice if the women were interested in reconciliation and if they could gain the cooperation of their partners. Of those interviewed, 4 said they wanted no further contact, 18 expressed interest in joining the "battered women's group" (10 from the emergency room, 8 from the Mental Health Center), 2 chose couples treatment, and 4 chose to join other groups. The battered women's group was started after 17 women had been screened and 9 had agreed to join. Screening continued over three months until the number of 31 was reached, and during the course of the group new members were added to replace dropouts.

Patients' Characteristics

The 31 patients who showed up for the screening interview represented a wide range of religious, social, racial, and ethnic groups. Younger women predominated, with 64 percent being under 30; two women, however, were in their 50s. Abuse took place in the context of marriage in 68 percent of the cases and in extramarital relationships in 32 percent. Because the patients tended to reflect the socioeconomic characteristics of the clients of the Mental Health Center and the hospital emergency room, there was a preponderance of patients in classes IV and V (Hollingshead, 1957) and more blacks (35 percent) and Catholics (52 percent) than in the population at large. Other characteristics of the sample are described elsewhere (Rounsaville, 1978a, 1978b).

Most of the women had been repeatedly abused over extended periods. The average period of abuse was 6.7 years, and all had been abused more than five times. In 80 percent of the cases, the abuse had begun in the first year of the relationship and in 48 percent it had occurred regularly at a rate of more than once a month. Eighty-four percent of the women had been injured severely enough to seek medical treatment at least once, and 81 percent had at a minimum been beaten with fists. Given the severity and frequency of the abuse, it seemed remarkable that the relationships had endured for such long periods of time. Many battered women report that fear keeps them with their partners; in our sample, 71 percent stated that their men had threatened to kill them if they left. We will discuss other reasons for the relationships' durability in a later section.

Treatment Problems

From the interviews, corroborated by reports in the literature, it became clear that battered women face a number of problems that are specific to them and others that they share with other prospective psychiatric patients. These include both practical and intrapsychic barriers to reducing their victimization.

Practical Issues. Most writers (Gayford, 1975; Martin, 1976; Nichols, 1976; Pizzey, 1974) who have discussed the battered-women problem have emphasized the practical difficulties in preventing further abuse. These are considerable and numerous. The principal difficulty is the danger represented by the abusing partner. Many battered women, including 71 percent of our screened group, are threatened with death by their partners if they consider leaving them or calling the police. Several writers have pointed to the inadequacy of currently available protection. Women who seek aid from the police quickly find out that the police are not ready or able to respond quickly or often enough to ensure their safety. Those who seek legal solutions encounter expensive and time-consuming civil remedies or mild and slow-acting criminal sanctions for abusive partners (Martin, 1976; Truninger, 1971).

A battered woman must be very active in taking matters into her own hands to protect herself or to get away from an abusive partner. Given the well-documented failure of divorced men to support their ex-wives, the majority of battered women face having to support themselves financially if they leave. This is particularly difficult for women who have minimal personal or financial resources and children to support. Those with few job skills face a tight job market and low-paying jobs under the best of circumstances. Welfare rules frequently require that women be divorced before payments can be made, although obtaining a divorce may take months, particularly for those who must rely on public-assistance legal advice. In this connection, Nichols (1976) sees counseling for battered women largely as practical advice-giving designed to guide these women through the legal and welfare systems and to direct them to private shelters where they can obtain safety. She advises against the use of traditional psychoanalytic concepts in thinking about battered women.

Psychological Issues. Although reality-focused counseling may suffice for those who clearly and decisively want to leave their partners, there are many features of the abusive situation that require the therapist to address psychological issues. Like rape victims, these women have sustained violent mistreatment at the hands of men, but unlike rape victims, their persecutors are their husbands or boyfriends with whom they have sustained intimate involvement as well as abusive maltreatment. As noted from the sample, abuse from the partner is not a once-in-a-lifetime event but a frequent occurrence. Battered women are not those who have been able to take effective action to prevent abuse such as leaving their partners, calling the police, or pressuring their partners to take the problem seriously by genuinely threatening to leave. These are women who feel helpless, indecisive, and unable to use what resources are available to them.

Perhaps the most important clue to the women's failure to act is the intermittent, episodic nature of the abuse. After the abuse has taken place, reconciliation usually follows. In hope of maintaining the relationship, the women try to see the abusive behavior as exceptional. Many in our sample spoke of a "Dr. Jekyll/Mr. Hyde" aspect of their husbands. Others saw their partners' responsibility as impaired and their blame diminished by alcohol, social and financial pressures, or overwhelming emotion. Sixty-one percent reported that their husbands had been drinking at least half the times that they abused them, and 77 percent said that their partners tried to keep themselves from abusing them, implying that the abuse resulted from loss of control rather than from intentional action.

Battered women are frequently unable to act because they suffer from clinically significant depressive illness. Of those screened in our project, 80 percent rated themselves significantly depressed on CES-D self-reports. Improvement in mood is usually required before depressed patients can take steps to improve their social adjustments (Weissman et al., 1974), and this may require treatment. Symonds (1975) points out that victims of violence feel like those who have lost loved ones. What they, in fact, have lost is the sense of security and trust in society at large and in those whom they have previously relied upon to protect them. This sense of loss must be much greater in women who have sustained violence at the hands of partners on whom they relied not only for protection but for love and support. Paradoxically, this sense of the precariousness of the partner's love may contribute to an increased sense of need for him.

Battered women are frequently socially isolated. Some writers (Martin, 1976; Pizzey, 1974) have remarked on the controlling, possessive, jealous nature of many battering husbands who abusively try to restrict their wives' social contacts. Many battered women restrict themselves from involvements outside the home to prevent suspicion and further abuse from their partners. In our sample, 24 of the women (77 percent) described their husbands as excessively controlling.

The social stigmatization of victims of violence (Symonds, 1975) is anticipated or experienced by these women. Many do not leave home for fear that their injuries will be noticed. They do not discuss their plight with others for fear of being blamed and rejected—a common experience for those who do admit their situation to friends or professionals. This sense of stigmatization is a crucial issue for treatment because it heightens both the depression and the unwillingness to seek help. The women are particularly ashamed of wanting to remain in the relationship, a desire that puzzles both themselves and those with whom they share their stories.

The women frequently see their victimization as shameful and deserved.

Most underestimate the pervasiveness of the problem in society at large and associate it exclusively with lower classes. Those who are working class see it as further proof of their degraded social status. Many feel responsible for the problem, thinking that they have caused their men to become violent and hoping that by "being better wives" they can make their husbands more content and hence less abusive. This idea is usually false. In fact, the majority of the men had given evidence of having been repeatedly violent or socially deviant before becoming involved in their current relationships. Although the women were slightly more likely to have had histories of psychiatric contact (65 percent versus 51 percent), the partners were significantly more likely to have had histories of arrest, drug or alcohol abuse, or violence outside of the home. An intercorrelation of factors in this sample revealed a .40 (p less than .05) correlation between the women's psychiatric histories and the partners' tendency to alcoholism and a .54 (p less than .01) correlation between the women's psychiatric histories and the men's having been arrested. It appears, then, that to a significant degree women in the sample with psychiatric histories had paired with men who were either alcoholic or deviant from the law. The fact that 65 percent of the women had had previous psychiatric contact is notable in that, despite the treatment having taken place in most cases during the period of abuse, there was little reduction in violence.

A particularly striking phenomenon is that abusive relationships in which no intervention takes place are frequently long-lasting despite severe injuries to the women. As noted before, the average length of time during which the women in our sample were significantly abused was 6.7 years. This feature of the battering relationship has been interpreted to imply that the women are masochists who invite abusive treatment and would be abused by nearly any partner. In addition to the evidence that the partners were violent men in many settings, there is evidence from our group that the women were victims in this setting only. Only a few of the women had had lifelong, repeated patterns of being physically abused. Only 26 percent had been beaten as children, and only 17 percent had been beaten by previous male partners. Moreover, once the women had left their abusive partners, most did not become involved in a second abusive relationship. Of ten women interviewed by the first author who were able to leave abusive partners, none had entered another abusive relationship.

Planning the Group

The Rationale

From the foregoing, we decided that a treatment plan for the battered women in our sample had to consider a number of points: (1) the women would perceive themselves to be socially stigmatized and therefore of low status and worth; (2) they were likely to see psychiatric treatment as further evidence of their stigmatization; (3) most would be depressed and consequently feel shamefully hopeless and helpless; (4) they were likely to see themselves as personally responsible for situations that had complex causes not related to them; (5) they would have a sense of uniqueness due to their social isolation; (6) they would tend to use the defense of denial and would be likely to attend intermittently at first, thinking that their problems had been solved; (7) they were likely to underestimate their strength and resources and were consequently likely to be highly dependent; (8) they would feel threatened by premature pressure to leave their partners despite their initial strong statements that this was their intention; (9) they would be fearful of retaliation by their partners; (10) they would need practical advice concerning police, legal assistance, welfare services, jobs, and shelter; (11) they were likely to have limited financial resources and to consider payment of even a small amount burdensome, especially if they wanted to keep the therapy secret from their partners.

Given the social isolation and feeling of stigmatization of the women and our desire to foster a sense of competence and independence in them, we decided that group therapy was the preferred modality. We hoped that exposure to others with similar problems would be supportive, relieving of guilt, and reducing of fear. A reality-oriented, matter-of-fact focus on the single topic of how to manage the violence would provide practical information, present the problem as manageable, and reduce the women's fears that they were "crazy" and hence in need of major psychological change. We decided to make use of consciousness-raising techniques to mitigate self-castigation and increase self-reliance and mutual interdependence. The exploration of individual dynamics was to be played down in order to avoid self-blame. It was felt that an all-women group would be especially important in reducing the stigma of discussing victimization by men.

A decision to limit the involvement of individuals to 12 group sessions was made to foster the women's view that their problem was solvable and to allow turnover so that women in early stages of thinking about their abusive relationships could benefit from the examples of those who had made more progress. We recognized that the women frequently had more than this one problem. Many had extensive psychiatric histories of depression, alcoholism, suicide attempts, and hospitalization. However, we felt that the repeated severe abuse was such a serious issue that improvement in this area was essential for dealing with other difficulties.

Orientation

In briefing prospective group members, care was taken to be welcoming and to avoid pejorative labeling. To reduce the association of therapy with mental illness, the group was presented as an opportunity to obtain information about members' problems, share their difficulties with others, and think clearly about the choices available to them rather than to seek a "cure." They were specifically told that this was not to be a group of mentally ill people but rather a group of women facing a common, terribly difficult problem requiring careful decision making. To further minimize the tendency to see the treatment as implying long-standing mental defects, the limitation of group involvement to 12 sessions was emphasized. For most of the women, the treatment was free of charge. They were also carefully informed of the confidential nature of the involvement. To allay their fearful expectations that the therapists would be judgmental of them or would pressure them to leave their partners, the goals of the group were defined as simply to allow them a chance to articulate their choices without being directed or persuaded by the therapists to make any particular choice.

The initial focus on practical issues was felt to be vital for several reasons. Many of the women were simply deficient in information, having had no prior knowledge of community resources available to them. Presenting this information implied that action was possible. It was also felt that an initial matter-of-fact emphasis might prevent premature disclosure of shameful, affect-laden aspects of the abusive relationship.

The problem of guilt and self-blame was to be met by presenting the women with alternative ways of thinking about their situations. Surprisingly, the women tended to be highly "psychologically minded" in a self-castigating, destructive sense. They saw their involvements with abusive partners as related to permanent defects in their individual characters resulting from traumatic childhood histories. They felt that they had to be "crazy" to remain with their partners. This psychological explanation of abuse was to be countered by a more sociological one. The reformulation of concepts here was in a direction opposite to that taken in traditional psychotherapy, which directs patients to see as internal conflicts that they tend to externalize. It was modeled on the analyzing and abstracting process described by Kirsh (1974) as taking place in consciousness-raising groups. For example, in our group the therapists planned to emphasize the contractual, legal, and political aspects of marriage as a social institution. Women who were ashamed of their lingering involvements in abusive marriages would be informed of the bias in American society toward evaluating women primarily in terms of success in marriage and hence of the social pressures that they were responding to.

Many battered women feel that they bring the abuse on themselves because of their discontent with the limitations that their controlling, possessive partners impose on them. They feel that they should be more accepting and appreciative of the relationship. In our group, the traditional hierarchal, "institutional" model of marriage in which the husband is "instrumental" and the wife "expressive" (Laws, 1975; Parsons & Bales, 1954) would be contrasted with a more equitable "companionship" model (Laws, 1975) in which the partners share roles according to their capabilities and interests. Their frustrations would be explained as reasonable reactions to the thwarting of positive strivings. Those who have on some occasion started a physical fight frequently feel that the massive abuse they received in return was justified as a punishment. To these women a "resources" view of family power would be explained, indicating that physical force was among a number of potential factors in a couple's balance of power (Goode, 1971; Safilios-Rothschild, 1970). The women's decision to escalate an argument to a physical fight would be seen as strategically unwise—moving the conflict to a plane where the partner has superior strength—rather than as deviant or immoral.

Finally, it was noted that the women tended to see the problem of being abused as a crisis that had no continuity with other aspects of the relationship. This view fostered inactivity and prevented them from taking the problem seriously. We felt it was important to point out where appropriate that the abuse was simply a more extreme manifestation of general patterns of domination and exploitation by their partners. In addition to pointing out needless passivity, the therapists planned to be active in emphasizing examples of the women's unrecognized competent behavior. Their failure to recognize their own power and competence was especially remarkable in view of the highly successful past behavior of many of the women, who, although they had achieved educational and occupational goals superior to those of their partners, felt that they would be lost without their partners. A confronting, active, exhortative stance was to be the means by which the therapists would attempt to induce "insight."

In general there would also be an emphasis on raising the consciousness of the women in such dimensions as sharing of experiences, socialization of women, roles and status, labeling and stigmatization, social awareness, personal growth, and strivings for autonomy. The highly structured format of consciousness-raising groups would not be followed, but sharing of experiences and discussion would emerge in a natural, spontaneous manner from the content of the sessions and the implications of themes that were developed. To this extent there would be a similarity to the format of consciousness-raising groups and to the four processes that have been reported as occurring in these groups: opening up, sharing, analyzing, and abstracting (Lifton & Karr, 1977). In addition, our group would have designated leaders, whereas most consciousness-raising groups are leaderless. (As Lifton and Karr noted, consciousness-raising groups sometimes individualize and vary their structures, including leadership, to meet specific needs.)

Therapist Roles

The stance and interventions of the therapists were to resemble in part those of "focused criterion" groups described by Singer et al. (1975). In these groups, such as alcoholic and drug groups, one undesirable behavior is focused on to be given up. In the battered women's group, the behavior to be eliminated was to be helpless inactivity. In focused-criterion groups, the target behavior is addictive in nature and the task is to rid the client of dependence on a cherished substance. The battered-women's group has as its goal for members to give up the self-destructive dependence on an abusive partner. To promote their task, leaders in drug and alcohol groups use techniques that promote identification with the program and allow members a substitute dependency on the group, thus meeting their needs while changing the maladaptive behavior. In the battered-women's group, techniques that fostered substitute dependency were to include initiation through confession and use of uninterpreted group pressures and uninterpreted dependent transference to the leader.

With the development of substitute temporary dependence as a rationale, but not the heavy confrontation and encounter that occur in focused-criterion groups—with accompanying methods that demean and humiliate—the therapists planned to use techniques that would make the group inviting and nonthreatening. Recognizing that interpretations of group process and transference are often experienced as criticism or as deprivation of support, there was an effort to develop positive member-to-member and member-to-leader transference that would be left alone. The interventions of the therapists were to be addressed to individual members or to informational topics, with group issues addressed only when serious group resistances prevented the group from functioning. Relationships developed in the group were to be seen at face value rather than as manifestations of resistance. There would be no attempt to discourage extragroup contact among members. The therapists would offer themselves as authentically helpful individuals, different from other group members primarily because of greater resources and expert knowledge. While attempting to be nonjudgmental toward group members, the therapists would be self-disclosing, offering examples from their own lives and expressing personal opinions. They would provide information, advice, and encouragement in addition to fostering efforts by group members to make their own decisions. They would be active in eliciting participation in the group by silent members.

A male and female co-therapy team was to lead the group. We felt that such a co-therapy team, whose members shared responsibility equally and functioned effectively, would be a useful model to help the women correct distorted images of the roles of both men and women.

The Course of Treatment

The group met for a total of 20 weekly 90-minute sessions from August to December, 1976, at the Connecticut Mental Health Center. In this section we will describe the group's experience around the following topics: membership problems; members' interaction; results; and therapists' interventions.

Membership Problems

A serious and persistent problem for the group was membership size. Although battered women are numerous, those who were interviewed by the first author represented a minority of those identified, and those who followed through in treatment were a minority of those interviewed. Of 18 women who agreed to join the group, only four attended throughout its entire course. At the first group meeting, there were six members and three no-shows. Of the six, four attended the next week and two dropped out. During sessions 8, 9, and 10, four new members were introduced, of whom only two returned for more than one session, and these attended irregularly over a six-week period. During the final six sessions, the group consisted again of the original four members. Because of difficulties in maintaining group size, the limitation to 12 sessions for members was dropped. In reviewing the records of those who became involved in the group and those who did not, we noted that all who became involved showed up for the first appointment, had significant levels of depression (CES-D greater than 25), and, except in one case, had had more than three months of previous psychotherapy.

Members' Interaction

The group became insight-oriented as time progressed. During the initial two sessions, the women discussed only their abusive relationships and they did so quite dramatically, emphasizing the shocking, overwhelming nature of the problem and the total blame of their partners. Each woman spoke in turn, addressing the therapists primarily. Member interaction consisted largely of advice and information-sharing.

In the next four sessions, members began to take a good deal of interest in one another and became very active in mutual exploration of problems and confrontation with inconsistencies. For instance, Myrtle, who early in the group had left her abusive boyfriend, appeared in session 7 to be cheerful and joking after returning to him, and maintained a pugnacious jocularity as she described an overwhelming burden of financial and interpersonal difficulties. After several minutes of this, two other members commented on the contrast between her proclaimed mood and the content of her discussion, and she was then able to speak more openly of her initial disappointment and despair at returning. The group quickly became highly cohesive and supportive.

Safety was a major issue productive of member interaction. At the start of the group, two of the women had recently left their partners and two had not. All had been threatened with death if they left, and the two who had left described their fear of encountering their estranged partners. In response to this, other members offered them shelter and several members communicated by phone between sessions.

Results

During the first eight sessions, the group members initiated a good deal of active personal experimentation and underwent a rapid succession of significant life events. Ellen, a 19-year-old woman who had been in an abusive relationship after being forced to leave her parents' home due to her intransigent rebelliousness, was able to reconcile with her parents and make plans to continue her education. Margaret, who had been married to an abusive, exploitative, compulsive gambler, contacted a lawyer and began divorce proceedings. Mildred, who had been limiting her interests entirely to those of her boyfriend, undertook activities of interest to herself alone.

As well as steps toward self-direction, there were a number of perceived setbacks experienced by some members. Myrtle, who had left a possessive, paranoid, alcoholic boyfriend after being beaten for two years, returned after a 1½-month separation when her mother died after a lingering illness. This was experienced by other group members as a regression, especially because Margaret announced that she had seen a lawyer on the same day that Myrtle announced her move back with James. There was an expectation by group members that "getting better" meant leaving. In Myrtle's case, this was not so. Her relationship resumed on a new footing. Although the boyfriend was still exploitative, they had both recognized his need for her and she assumed a good deal more status in the relationship when she returned. In particular, the beatings, which had been twice-weekly occurrences, ceased when she informed him that her return was contingent on his abstaining from hitting her.

All members of the group experienced a good deal of vacillation about their decisions regarding their abusive partners. This had been anticipated, and the therapists felt that it was a crucial function of the group to be supportive of the women as they moved forward and back, particularly in light of the fact that they were quick to condemn themselves and each other for "being weak" and having mixed feelings about their partners.

The changes that the members had made became apparent when new members were introduced in sessions 8 to 10. These sessions were more like the first two, in which members shared stories of their victimization. However, while the new members tearfully portrayed themselves as passive victims, the older members spoke of their progress and became very active in attempting to engage new members in the group. Several expressed disappointment when two new members did not return after the first session.

One of the new members, Barbara, was the focus of much attention when she was introduced to the group. Young, attractive, highly depressed, and tearful, she described affectingly how her husband had brutally beaten her, threatened her with a gun, and kept her homebound and terrorized through the seven years of her marriage. Two group members offered her places to stay, and the leaders were active in offering her practical advice and reassurance. She responded warmly to the interest of others but declined the offers. Before the next session, she called up and angrily demanded to be transferred to some other sort of treatment, stating that she had immediately hated the female co-therapist and could not conceive of returning to a group in which someone who was so condescending would hear her discuss sensitive material. She remembered the therapist saying, "What can our group do for you right now?" and felt that this represented an attempt to humiliate her.

The two who did return quickly made moves to mitigate the abuse they received. After one session, Joanie was able to evict an alcoholic partner who had lived with her for two years, telling him that she was in treatment and threatening to call the police. After two sessions, Lois, who had been abused for 18 years by an extremely violent husband with a long criminal record, called the police for the first time, an act that frightened the husband and changed the family balance of power somewhat.

By the fifteenth session, all the women had consolidated impressive gains and their lives had begun to stabilize. Three had left their partners and three had stayed but had become more active and self-protective in their relationships. In all six the abuse had stopped. During the final five sessions, attendance, particularly by those no longer with partners, fell off. Although the leaders screened a number of new referrals and several agreed to join the group, none attended even a single session. It was decided to terminate the group after the twentieth session, and members were informed of this in the seventeenth session.

Therapists' Interventions

The nature of the therapists' interventions evolved parallel with the nature of members' participation. At first informative and supportive, the therapists became more confrontational and interpretative. For example, Margaret, who began the group by portraying her husband, Pete, as an unmitigated villain, was able to understand her own participation in the abusive interaction after a number of group members and a therapist confronted her with her "infuriating" habit of giving mixed messages. She had repeatedly portrayed herself as helpless and needy, but she rebuffed those who offered help.

The therapists had no systematic plan to change the nature of their interventions as the group progressed, but they had a sense that, by changing techniques, they were following the lead of the group members themselves in exploring their own difficulties. The members were, in fact, highly curious about their behavior with the battering partners and with others in general. Those who had been able to leave their abusive partners wanted to prevent a recurrence by looking at how they had become involved in the first place. Ellen, for example, became interested in her fear of men and feelings of inadequacy about sexuality. She had never had a satisfying sexual relationship and felt that the abuse she received was in part deserved because of her inability to satisfy her partner. During the course of the group she began to date a former boyfriend, who, as the battering one had done, promised her a permanent, stable relationship in which he would take care of her. As she discussed this offer in the group, she began to realize both her attraction to the promised security and her desire to pursue her own goals at school without prematurely closing off her own life plans.

When new members were introduced, the therapists briefly returned to their supportive, nonconfrontational stance, reestablishing the original battered-women's group concept. Despite the changes in type of intervention, the therapists maintained their openness and efforts to act as models. The members were particularly impressed when, at a session at which there had been a problem with double scheduling of the meeting room, the female therapist competently and firmly handled the angry physician who was demanding that the group go elsewhere. The women took a good deal of interest in the female co-therapist as a professional, but also saw her as more approachable and tended to call her for between-sessions advice.

Group Themes

Dependency and Helplessness

Dependency and defenses against it were the principal themes of the group. The most striking dynamic of group members was the combination of overwhelming feelings of helpless neediness and fiercely guarded counterdependence. This mixture of needs pervaded their dealings with others and may be a clue to the dynamics of the battering relationship.

Themes of helplessness were the first to surface. For example, the members frequently confessed giving in to their partners because they were "swept away" by their "uncontrollable" feelings while trying to be strong. Several described "melting when he smiles at me" or being "unable to control myself when he tells me he's sorry." They portrayed themselves as having fallen into the abusive relationships with no prior knowledge of their partners' violent tendencies. This head-over-heels quality allowed them a sense of diminished responsibility for their own desires.

The women felt ashamed and uneasy, perceiving their strong desires for intimacy with men who abused them as abnormal. This discomfort became evident in comments about the male therapist. He was seen as tolerant and odd, interested in their difficulties but also liable to reject them. After discussing her sexual interest in her abusive partner despite the violence, one member asked him, "How can you keep from walking out when you hear all these women talking about these things? You must think we're really crazy!" When members saw the two therapists conferring after a meeting, they speculated at the next session that the therapists were planning to hospitalize the entire group or otherwise send them away.

Despite these hesitations, the women became quickly and strongly involved with one another and with the therapists. They were very apprehensive when a member or a therapist was absent and would sometimes insist that the person be telephoned immediately to be reassured of her safety and continued interest in the group. On several occasions, members stayed at the Mental Health Center for up to an hour after the session, chatting. Most were in contact with one another between sessions, and near the end of the group the three younger members had an evening out together at a singles bar.

Given this sense of interdependency in the group, the problems of absenteeism and low group membership were painfully felt. In fact, one member who attended only the first session was discussed almost weekly for the next six sessions. Another member telephoned her and reported back that she had run into a good deal of difficulty after separating from a highly possessive and vindictive partner. As new aspects of her problem became known, members lamented her nonattendance and their inability to be more helpful to her and also affirmed their own sense of the group's value.

Relationships with Men

Ashamed of their dependency, the women attempted to externalize their intense attraction to their abusive partners by emphasizing the men's menacing coerciveness. A major topic was the partners' attempts to control the women's actions so that their complete attention and interest would be focused on the men. This feature of the partners' behavior was, in fact, extreme, approaching delusional jealousy. Margaret's partner called her every half hour from work to ensure that she had not gone out. He did not allow her to shop or run errands alone and even accused her of having an affair when she took 15 extra minutes at a hairdresser's appointment. Myrtle's partner revealed to her that, even in early courtship, he had followed her around in his car to check on her alleged involvements with other men. All the women complained that their partners had restricted their friendships even with other women, and many had reduced their social lives to visiting relatives accompanied by their partners. Two of the women were working while involved in the group, but others described their partners' abusive efforts to keep them from holding jobs for fear that they would meet other men at work. The women's reactions to their partners' possessiveness were mixed. Some believed that the extreme jealousy was an indication of their partners' love and concern for them, but anger and resentment were also expressed.

A second way that the women saw themselves as externally forced to remain in abusive relationships was out of concern for "sick" and helpless partners. The tenderest moments of the group occurred when the women discussed their partners' need for them, such as when they were suffering from minor physical ailments or hangovers. The men were then seen as helpless babies, and this behavior was knowingly contrasted with their brutal forcefulness at other times. Myrtle related how her partner complained of losing weight and sleep and becoming despondent during the time she was separated from him. Margaret, whose partner was frequently fearful of violent retaliation for failing to pay gambling debts, tearfully described her desire to protect him when he alternately pleaded with her on his knees and beat her to obtain money. The women saw themselves as most competent and most fulfilled in the roles of nurses and protectors of their men. Several revealed that a major interest in the abusive partner was the desire to save him from himself, and as the group progressed several began to see that they had recognized their partners' impulsiveness and exploitativeness early in the relationship but had chosen to ignore it. Some had hoped to "make a man" of their partners through their nurturant ministrations.

The members became well aware of the similarity between the ways they discussed their partners and their children. Indeed, caring for children was a frequent theme in the group. The women saw both their partners and their children as demanding, potentially overwhelming, and the major focus of their lives. Two of the women who left their partners discussed never becoming involved with other men again but instead devoting their lives to their children.

In the service of others, several of the women were in fact ingeniously resourceful and powerful. One striking fact about the group was the number of members who were oldest siblings. Of the ten women who attended at least one session, eight were the oldest children in their families, and many of them had had a large amount of early responsibility as substitute mothers for their younger siblings. They continued to function in a financial and otherwise caretaking role with their partners. Of the same ten women, five were the major or sole sources of income for the couple and three were equal contributors. In several cases, most of the couples' incomes, including the women's earnings, was devoted to the husbands' leisure-time activities—drinking, gambling, or using drugs. In contrast, the women were relatively abstinent and spoke proudly of their ability to scrape along on very little while their partners wasted money. Margaret, in particular, was at her strongest and most resourceful in defense of her husband. She not only gave him money for his debts but also confronted his racketeer creditors and bargained with them on several occasions.

The women's protection of their partners was in marked contrast to their failure to protect themselves. Prior to their involvement in the group, only five of the women had had their partners arrested following their partners' abuse of them and none had pressed charges. This pattern of unwillingness and inability to act as skillfully for themselves as they did for others was pervasive, reminiscent of the discussion of "altruistic surrender" by Anna Freud (1946). She described the avoidance of conflict through abdicating strivings for the benefit of self and deriving gratification instead through the pleasure of others.

Dynamics of the Abusive Relationship

In the screening interviews and in the course of group treatment, patterns emerged from the women's divergent life histories. Extreme discomfort at accepting either their dependency needs or their autonomous strivings characterized the majority of battered women screened and may be a key cause of their becoming involved in abusive relationships and being unable to separate once involved. The pairing of depressed women with alcoholic men probably brings together two people who manifest frustrated dependency needs in different fashions. Weissman and Klerman (1977) suggest that alcoholism in men may mask underlying depression.

In 24 of the 31 screened women, the involvement with their partner was either their first with any male or it took place rapidly and under severe duress. At these times, the women lost their usual control and saw their partners, however flawed, as the answer to their problems. Ellen, for example, became involved with Bob while seven months pregnant after having been abandoned by her fiancé, the father of her child, and disowned by her parents. During the completion of the pregnancy, Bob was gentle and caring despite his frequent abuse of drugs and alcohol. Margaret had just separated from her second husband, a gangster with an extremely violent temper, when she met Pete. She feared for her life, and when Pete showed an interest in her and promised to protect her, she felt that her prayers had been answered. Myrtle had nursed her mother through the terminal phase of a long illness after splitting up with her first husband. Exhausted and depressed, she felt relieved when James started to take control of her life, spending his time with her and watching her every move.

The women's initial relief at having their lives organized by controlling, demanding, and seemingly powerful partners was replaced by frustration and resentment when they began to feel more comfortable in the new relationships. In the process of becoming hastily and incautiously involved with their partners, and perhaps as a factor in selecting them, the majority of women had chosen men who were in many ways less skillful or powerful than themselves. As long as the women were in crises and the partners were the rescuers and protectors, the relative weakness of the partners was not apparent. As the women began to recover from their crises and to take on more responsibility for themselves and more power in the relationships, they challenged their partners' control over them. The partners generally responded with more controlling behavior backed up with the threat of violence.

A good deal of evidence gathered in the screening process suggests the women's greater emotional strength and higher social status than their partners'. The partners were likely to be deviant in society. Fifty-two percent of the women rated their partners as unreliable workers and poor providers, 45 percent were reported to be alcoholics and 35 percent excessive drug users. Fifty-eight percent of the partners had some sort of criminal record. In contrast to the usual "mating gradient" (Gelles, 1974; Leslie, 1976) in which men generally marry women younger, less educated, and of lower social status than themselves, the majority of battered women were superior to their partners in one or more of these respects.

Within the relationships, there was evidence of "role reversal." The evaluated women were asked to rate their own and their partners' performances on eight groups of joint tasks. Forty-eight percent reported that their earnings were equal to or greater than their partners', 68 percent said that they handled the couple's finances, and 79 percent said that they made the decisions about major purchases and major family actions. Of the tasks, only car repairs were more likely to be performed by the partner. Moreover, 93 percent of the women saw themselves as equal or superior to their partners in general abilities. Perhaps more significantly, the women saw themselves as being more verbally skillful than their partners. Seventy-five percent stated that they won verbal arguments at least half the time, and 55 percent said that they usually bested their partners in verbal encounters. This "status inconsistency" (O'Brien, 1971) in the relationship may play an important part in leading to abuse.

A common rationale for the men's controlling behavior was sexual jealousy, which was frequently reported by the women to reach delusional proportions. We see the partners' preoccupation with the women's possible infidelity as a manifestation of their overall insecurity in intimate relationships and their despair at being able to control the women. Jealousy was the most frequently reported cause of violent arguments, with 52 percent of the women citing it as the most common topic leading to abuse and 94 percent naming it as a major incitement of violent arguments. Since 45 percent of the men were reported to be alcoholics, there may be a relationship between alcohol abuse and delusional jealousy (Hanks & Rosenbaum, 1977).

Even when the woman is not in fact of higher social status than her partner, she may be perceived as being more powerful and threatening by a man who is especially sensitive to domination by women. Toby (1974) suggests that men who were raised in mother-dominated or father-absent households may be especially sensitive to feeling overwhelmed by their marital partners and willing to use whatever means are available to avoid this. Of the women screened, 45 percent reported that their partners had been permanently separated from their fathers before age 15 because of death or divorce. Beating their wives seemed to be a partially successful means of controlling them, as evidenced by the sense of helplessness and inability to act described by the women in the group. However, as previously noted, the women were not able to accept submission and continued to try to assert themselves, which in turn led to further abuse. This cycle of the women's being abused, submitting, and then reasserting themselves to be abused again can continue indefinitely. One 55-year-old interviewee said that she had been beaten for 35 years.

The partnership of an ambivalently dependent woman with an impulsive, compulsively masculine, needy, controlling, and paranoid partner, besides leading to recurrent high tension and violent explosiveness, may be "stably unstable" because it satisfies deep needs in both partners. Storr (1968) suggests that extremely narcissistic, dependent relationships are likely to be most violent because each partner feels threatened with the loss of a vital part of himself if the other tries to leave. For the woman, the relationship provides constant companionship and a highly organized life in the service of another while avoiding the recognition of her own needs. The man, in turn, avoids feelings of loss of control, failure, and dependency by exercising excessively strict dominance over his partner. The hypothesis that violence can act as a defense against intimacy (Kardiner & Fuller, 1970) may be pertinent here in that, by keeping the relationship in a state of intermittent chaos, both partners manage to avoid ambivalently desired closeness with each other.

Discussion

Our evaluation of the battered-women's group is that it was successful in a limited way. For those who were able to use it, it was very helpful, but it did not appeal to most of the women screened and to an even larger majority of the battered women initially identified. Of the many questions raised by our experience, these will be discussed: (1) What caused the high dropout rate? (2) Why was the group successful at all? (3) How does this group compare with other types of therapy groups? (4) How representative was our group of the population of battered women? (5) What are the implications for the development of further services for battered women?

Membership Recruitment and Maintenance

Many of the dynamics and realistic features of abusive relationships combined to reduce the women's desire to participate in treatment. First, fear of the partner's retaliation or coercion by the partner were important factors. The therapists could offer no protection for the women other than the advice to seek help from the police or at a women's shelter. Several of the women who told their partners about their involvement in the group reported that their partners were angry and demanded that they drop out. It is noteworthy, however, that the partners quickly became less abusive when they knew that their actions would be discussed.

Second, in contrast to our intention for the group, the stigma attached to being in therapy and being abused may have seemed compounded in a battered women's therapy group. It was noted that those who did not show up were less likely to have had previous psychotherapy and were thrust into the role of psychiatric patient after initially presenting with physical complaints. The sense of stigmatization may have been exacerbated by the presence of a male co-therapist since women who have had painful relationships with men may have anticipated that the male therapist would be as scornful of them as other men had been. This anticipation in fact was stated by several members in the course of the group.

Third, given the women's sense of helplessness and hopelessness, some may have seen the group as simply another hollow promise of help that was sure to fail.

Fourth, for reasons previously discussed, many of the women were strongly locked into the abusive relationship and did not want to take their problem seriously. In addition, there was usually a highly gratifying period of reconciliation between abusive episodes, so the motivation for treatment was minimal at that time. Serious consideration of breaking off the relationship was highly threatening to these ambivalently dependent women, who feared that they could not survive without their partners. Group members tended to see leaving the abusive partner as the best solution, and this expectation may have inadequately allowed for exploration of the possibilities for change if the relationship was maintained.

Finally, the offer of help in what was often the most conflicted aspect of their lives may have been highly premature. Battered women frequently present with numerous symptoms and only secondarily mention the battering relationship, even though their difficulties may be closely related to this. Perhaps only as the women begin to obtain symptom relief and gain confidence can they fruitfully engage in serious thought about their basic predicament.

It should be noted that our membership problems were not unique to us. Similar difficulties of enlisting and maintaining members were described to us by local feminists who had begun offering peer counseling to battered wives.

How the Group Was Helpful

There is a remarkable contrast between the stability and duration of abusive relationships when no intervention takes place and the ability of some of the women to change or end their abusive relationships when they are able to obtain and accept outside help. One might expect them to make no progress at all since, although the abusive relationship is particularly destructive to the women, it does fulfill deep needs of both partners. Nevertheless, when group members were given the opportunity to gain some distance from their ambivalent involvements, they were surprisingly able to recognize the self-destructive quality of their involvement with the men. Of particular importance in the treatment was the women's gaining a sense of their own competence and learning that, in a different, nonhierarchical relationship, they could be both giving and receiving of care and love. It seemed especially vital that the women recognize that they, too, had needs that they had a right to have met.

Comparison with Other Groups

Many aspects of this group were typical of "situation/transition" groups described by Schwartz (1975). He describes the tendency of topic-focused groups to change in scope and in the nature of therapist intervention: "Much of the work of the group leader involves a continuous process of re-definition and re-negotiation with the group about two issues that arise from the weak and flexible nature of the initial contract: the role of the leader and the substance of the meetings." Our movement from "support" to "therapy" group and back was an example of this.

There are many marked similarities between the process and dynamics of this group and those of a group of women with severe dependency problems described by Scheidlinger and Pyrke (1961). The attendance problems, the surprising openness of the women, the quick development of high cohesiveness, and the preoccupation with caretaking activities for demanding husbands and children were common to the two groups. The empathic, supportive approach of the therapists was also similar but with different results in that Scheidlinger and Pyrke's group had fewer dropouts.

The difference between the two groups may be that the battered women in our group were highly defended against their dependency needs and threatened by a high degree of intimacy. For this reason it might have been better for the therapists to have been less supporting and inviting for some of the patients. In particular, Barbara was seen as manifesting both sides of her ambivalent desires and thereby being unable to make use of the group. At first needy and gratefully accepting of the quickly offered support from the group, she rapidly became angry and suspicious and avoided further meetings. Such contradictory behavior was hurtful and infuriating to group members, and it can be imagined that it provoked similar reactions in Barbara's abusive partner.

Representativeness of the Group

Due to the nature of the sampling, it seems likely that our group may not have been representative of all battered women in several obvious ways. The members were predominantly in classes IV and V, which was representative of the treatment settings but probably not of battered women in general. They admitted to being abused, an admission that more severely abused, less severely abused, or more frightened women might not make. They were interested in treatment, seeing the battering relationship as undesirable and seeing psychiatric intervention as potentially helpful. In this respect, it is significant that 65 percent of the women screened and 83 percent of those who expressed interest in the group had had some prior psychiatric contact. Moreover, most of the women evaluated complained of significant symptoms of depression and were probably motivated for treatment by these painful affects.

The women in our group were in some ways similar and in others quite different from those described by Snell et al. (1964). He saw the typical woman in his sample as "aggressive, efficient, masculine, and sexually frigid" as well as domineering of her passive, "castrated," ineffectual, alcoholic husband. Although we were impressed by the strength of the women in our group in the service of others, we were also impressed that their husbands were quite dominating, exploitative, and compulsively masculine rather than passive and "castrated." This difference between the two groups may be related to sampling methods. While Snell's group was middle class, the men alcoholic, and the referrals obtained from courts in which the men had actually been convicted of assaulting their wives, our sample was working class, with some nonalcoholic men, and none of the 31 women had successfully pressed charges against their partners. One similarity between the two groups that may be of importance is the stability of the abusive relationships until intervention from outside the dyad took place. In Snell's group, the women took legal action against their husbands when teenage children began to become involved in the couple's argument. In our screened group, no women left their partners without some sort of outside pressure or intervention.

In describing the behavior of the partners, we recognize that we are reporting secondhand information. However, the picture we received of the partners from the women was quite similar to that described by Faulk (1973), who studied English men who had been charged with serious assault on their wives. He describes five personality types: (1) dependent-passive; (2) dependent-suspicious; (3) violent and bullying; (4) dominating; and (5) stable and affectionate. The partners described by our patients tended to fall in categories 2 to 4. It is interesting that none of the women evaluated described their partners as either dependent and passive or stable and affectionate. One might expect that wives of "dependent-passive" or "affectionate" men might be less discontented with their partners and less likely to seek treatment.

Implications for Treatment

Membership seems to be the key problem in offering group therapy to battered women. The low follow-through rate might lead one to conclude that battered women are content with their lot and that special treatment should not be offered to them. However, given the severity of the suffering that many endure and given the eagerness of women in England to seek refuge in shelters when they are made available (Pizzey, 1974), this is probably an erroneous conclusion. The conclusion suggested by our experience is that psychiatric counseling or focused short-term treatment does not appeal to most battered women.

Treatment by psychotherapists may be unappealing because it does nothing about the many practical problems the women face. Offering treatment once a week is not adequate for a woman who is terrorized 24 hours a day. Shelters that offer adequate protection should be made more widely available. When therapy is indicated, treatmemt within the context of a safe shelter may be more appropriate. Legal changes and modifications of welfare regulations, such as those proposed by Martin (1976), may facilitate a battered woman's ability to deal with her problem.

It may be advisable to allow the women to make small steps toward treatment, possibly as part of a more comprehensive program modeled after open meetings of Alcoholics Anonymous in which prospective members can attend lectures and talks without being identified and can participate in the programs at a level that is comfortable to them.

Two modifications in the therapy plan are suggested. A brief individual treatment preceding entry into the group may prevent too rapid confrontation with overwhelming issues in the group. In addition, adding women who have different sorts of problems to the group may maintain the openness of discussions of battering but keep the women from feeling that they are members of an outcast class of patients.

In summary, the experiences reported in this paper suggest the following points regarding the psychiatric treatment of battered women:

1. Psychotherapy with battered women can be useful to those who stay in treatment. However, it should be recognized that the majority of those presenting for help with problems resulting from recent abuse will not be interested in psychiatric care and are more likely to accept help in a nonpsychiatric setting (Rounsaville, 1978a).

2. Group therapy may be a preferred treatment modality for battered women in that it reduces the isolation, allows for a manageable substitute dependency, and fosters specific concentration on the problem. However, individual therapy should be considered as an alternative to or in preparation for the group, as the amount of self-disclosure involved in group treatment may be prohibitive for many who might still be able to use treatment. Studies of the comparative effectiveness of different treatment modalities for battered women are needed.

3. The therapist can expect the patients to be highly ambivalent about the

battering relationship and to express this inside treatment by irregular attendance and outside treatment by repetitive attempts at reconciliation and separation. It should be recognized that many of the women will not want to leave an abusive partner, even if the abuse continues and despite vociferous protestations that they want to leave. Care must be taken not to accept only one side of the women's ambivalence.

4. In the course of group therapy the therapist can expect dependency issues to be of central importance and must be careful both to allow the patients' reliance on the group and to prevent the involvement from becoming threateningly close, which may cause some of the patients to drop out.

5. Although the setting of limited and practical goals is advisable, the patients may be able to tolerate and, indeed, may demand more exploratory psychotherapy as they become comfortable with the group.

References

Faulk, M. Men who assault their wives. *Medicine, Science and the Law*, 1973, *14*(4), 180–183.

Freud, A. *The ego and the mechanisms of defence*. New York: International Universities Press, 1946.

Gayford, J. J. Wife battering: A preliminary survey of 100 cases. *British Medical Journal*, 1975, *1*, 194–197.

Gelles, R. J. *The violent home: A study of physical aggression between husbands and wives*. Beverly Hills, Calif.: Sage, 1974.

Goode, W. J. Force and violence in the family. *Journal of Marriage and the Family*, 1971, *33*(4), 624–636.

Hanks, S. E., & Rosenbaum, C. P. Battered women: A study of women who live with violent alcohol-abusing men. *American Journal of Orthopsychiatry*, 1977, *47*(2), 291–306.

Hilberman, E. Overview: The "wife-beater's wife" reconsidered. *American Journal of Psychiatry*, 1980, *137*(11), 1336–1347.

Hollingshead, A. *Two-factor index of social position*. New Haven, Conn.: Yale University, 1957.

Kardiner, S. H., & Fuller, M. Violence as a defense against intimacy. *Mental Hygiene*, 1970, *54*(2), 310–315.

Kirsh, B. Consciousness-raising groups as therapy for women. In V. Franks & V. Burtle (Eds.), *Women in therapy*. New York: Brunner/Mazel, 1974.

Laws, J. L. A feminist view of marital adjustment. In A. S. Gurman & D. G. Rice (Eds.), *Couples in conflict*. New York: Jason Aronson, 1975.

Leslie, G. R. *The family in social context* (3rd ed). New York: Oxford University Press, 1976.

Lifton, N., & Karr, A. *Consciousness-raising groups as alternatives to traditional therapy*. Paper presented at the First Regional Congress of Social Psychiatry, Santa Barbara, Calif., Sept. 6–9, 1977.

Martin, D. *Battered wives*. San Francisco: Glide Publications, 1976.

Nichols, B. B. The abused wife problem. *Social Casework*, 1976, *57*(1), 27–32.

O'Brien, J. Violence in divorce prone families. *Journal of Marriage and the Family*, 1971, *33*(4), 692–698.

Parsons, T., & Bales, R. F. *Family socialization and interaction process*. Glencoe, Ill.: Free Press, 1954.

Pizzey, E. *Scream quietly or the neighbours will hear*. Harmondsworth, Middlesex: Penguin Books, 1974.

Rounsaville, B. J. Battered wives: Barriers to identification and treatment. *American Journal of Orthopsychiatry*, 1978, *48*(3), 487–494. (a)

Rounsaville, B. J. Theories of marital violence: Evidence from a study of battered women. *Victimology*, 1978, *3*, 11–31. (b)

Safilios-Rothschild, C. The study of family power structure: A review 1960–69. *Journal of Marriage and the Family*, 1970, *32*(4), 539–552.

Scheidlinger, S., & Pyrke, M. Group therapy of women with severe dependency problems. *American Journal of Orthopsychiatry*, 1961, *31*(4), 776–785.

Schwartz, M. D. Situation/transition groups: A conceptualization and review. *American Journal of Orthopsychiatry*, 1975, *45*(5), 744-755.

Singer, D. L., Astrachan, B. M., Gould, L. J., & Klein, E. B. Boundary management in psychological work with groups. *Journal of Applied Behavioral Science*, 1975, *11*(2), 137–176.

Snell, J. E., Rosenwald, R. J., & Robey, A. The wife-beater's wife: A study of family interaction. *Archives of General Psychiatry*, 1964, *11*(2), 107–112.

Storr, A. *Human aggression*. New York: Atheneum, 1968.

Straus, M. A., Gelles, R. J., & Steinmetz, S. K. *Behind closed doors: Violence in the American family*. Garden City, N.Y.: Anchor Press/Doubleday, 1980.

Symonds, M. Victims of violence: Psychological effects and aftereffects. *American Journal of Psychoanalysis*, 1975, *35*(1), 19–26.

Toby, J. Violence and the masculine ideal: Some qualitative data. In S. K. Steinmetz & M. A. Straus (Eds.), *Violence in the Family*. New York: Harper & Row, 1974.

Truninger, E. Marital violence: The legal solution. *Hastings Law Journal*, 1971, *23*, 259–276.

Weissman, M., & Klerman, G. Sex differences and the epidemiology of depression. *Archives of General Psychiatry*, 1977, *34*(1), 98–111.

Weissman, M. K., Klerman, G., Paykel, E., Prusoff, B., & Hanson, B. Treatment effects on the social adjustment of depressed patients. *Archives of General Psychiatry*, 1974, *30*(6), 771–778.

10

A Therapy Group for Low-Income Hispanic Women in an Outpatient Psychiatric Clinic

Alan Menikoff, M.S.W.

ALAN MENIKOFF is director of Hotline Victims Services Agency in New York City and is a psychotherapist in private practice.

For approximately 18 months—from February 1978 to September 1980—the author conducted a psychotherapy group for Spanish-speaking women (mostly Puerto Rican) suffering acute psychological-social dysfunctions caused by environmental or life-stage crises. The goal of the group was limited to assisting these women to return to their levels of prior functioning. The group was open-ended, its membership changing several times over its course.

The Institutional Setting

The group met in an outpatient clinic of South Beach Psychiatric Center in Brooklyn, New York. As a unit of the New York State Department of Mental Health, the hospital had a commitment to both the aftercare population and the nonhospitalized outpatient population within its catchment area.

This particular clinic served an area of diverse neighborhoods, ranging from a large public-housing project on its western boundary to an affluent professional community on its eastern edge. The population of this area was similarly diverse: blacks, Hispanics, ethnic whites. The location of the clinic encouraged its use by the Hispanic community. This use was further encouraged by the presence on the staff of a bilingual clinician—myself—who had served as liaison/consultant to the major ambulatory medical facility in the public-housing project and so was recognized by many of the patients of both the psychiatric clinic and the medical facility.

Because of the setting of the clinic, a variety of patients presented: those discharged promptly from the county admitting hospital; those discharged after months or years of state-hospital confinement; and those patients whose internists could offer them nothing for their insomnia, anxiety, or depression. The group was intended to address one subgroup of these patients: those with acute psychological and social dysfunctions. Many of the patients ultimately selected for the group had long-standing psychological dysfunctions, but the group deliberately did not target these chronic disorders.

Organizing the Group

The Rationale for Group Therapy

The choice of group as a treatment modality was dictated by several considerations. First, many of the patients did not speak English sufficiently well to engage in verbal psychotherapy in that language, and the clinic's bilingual staff was limited. I had had previous experience conducting a long-term group with this population (Menikoff, 1979) and had become convinced of the effectiveness of the identifications that could be established even in a group with a brief therapeutic focus.

Most important was the sociocultural homogeneity of this population. The social roles occupied by the women who attended the clinic could uniformly be described as traditional-conservative (Canino & Canino, 1980; Torres-Matrullo, 1976). They posed their problems as adjusting to a given life situation rather than as seeking to remedy the context of their dysfunctions. One saw this in their infrequent challenges of social assumptions and more specifically in the frequent focus on their roles as caretakers for their children, even when the children were already adults. Whatever political commentaries such conservative positions might prompt, those shared values could serve to support the individuals in the group and enhance their functioning within their defined roles.

Selection of Patients

In the clinic, each psychiatrist was responsible for all the patients of nonmedical clinicians under his direction. Selection of group members was made in consultation with this psychiatrist, so I had the benefit of his thinking and also the opportunity to scrutinize the patients' medical records. This was important, since many of the patients suffered from moderate to severe physical disabilities, often masked or confused with psychogenic symptoms.

The formation of the group began with the interviewing of prospective members. This was possible only after the staff of the clinic had been informed of the purpose of the group and of the type of members desired. Because the clinic had a large census with a broad mix of patient characteristics, I had a wide range of choices.

Basic Criteria. Initially and through the life of the group, the selection criteria were broad. We were less concerned about psychotic symptomatology than about interpersonal skills. We looked for people who were able to listen and empathize, to communicate, and most important to actively reflect on their situations. We felt that people who attributed their plights to metaphysical forces lacked the motivation to change.

The ability to listen was considered essential for entering the group as well as indicating some motivation for change. Although a major exclusionary criterion was the presence of severe paranoia, we considered and tried several patients who were obviously paranoid to the clinical eye but whose characteristic vigilance the layperson frequently mistakes for attentiveness. There were other patients who, though not paranoid, had such constricted affect or spoke so softly that we were not sure if they would make any empathic connection to other patients. Some of them turned out to be significant contributors, proving capable of listening and responding empathically to other group members once a measure of trust had been established.

The second quality we looked for in the patients was the capacity to talk about what they had heard and to share their own experiences. This ability suggests a development beyond the extreme narcissism that we frequently found an obstacle to the effective mutual use of the group. Patients' capacities to share information about themselves are, of course, closely correlated to the index of paranoia. There were some patients who, while not paranoid, failed to comprehend intuitively the benefits to be derived from sharing their experiences with others.

Because of the planned short-term nature of the group, the patient's capacity to communicate with someone other than the therapist was particularly significant. This was difficult to measure before the group began. But the goal of the group was to reestablish pretraumatic functioning of the individual patients, including reestablishment of supportive peer relationships that had suffered so much disruption. There were some patients who, for a number of reasons, were unable to share of themselves with anyone other than the therapist. In retrospect, this last item deserved more weight as a selection criterion than we gave it.

The ability actively to reflect on their situations was noticeably absent in many of the patients screened for the group. With the establishment of trust among group members over a period of months, a number of patients were able to lower their defenses sufficiently to examine their problems and feelings in the group and thereby became open to change.

Marginal Selections. As mentioned above, we did not exclude patients because of their psychotic manifestations. In fact, we tried several patients about whom we had doubts for just this reason. Some were readily accepted by the group, but others never made an adequate adaptation to the group culture. We found in the end that the presence of psychosis did not in itself predict functioning in the group.

One patient, tried in another group with no success, is representative of the type of patient we learned to avoid. This woman of 38 years had a fixed delusion that she was being filmed in the nude when she entered the bathroom of her apartment. As she had refused to expand on any aspect of her life beyond this delusion, we suggested to her that she join the group. (She had reluctantly agreed to accept medication and was by then on a regular regimen of a major tranquilizer.) But in the first group session it was obvious that her rigidity, almost more than the bizarreness of her delusions, kept her from making any affective connection with others.

One patient who never made even a minimal joining to the group was telling in the pregroup interview. She was almost unintelligible in her speech, talking inaudibly and with no focus in the content. We erred in assuming that we understood what she was saying without having her be explicit. She attended only one or two group meetings, then stopped coming, although she continued to see the physician for medication.

Another patient showed a more promising interpersonal picture in the individual interview but became taciturn in group meetings. Despite this withdrawn behavior, she continued to attend meetings and showed herself to be benefiting from the group primarily because of the support she derived from the other members. She seemed to be more active in explaining her needs to the staff psychiatrist, reserving these complaints for her sessions with him. Yet she made a point of informing the group when she was going to miss a session and made numerous sacrifices to attend.

As many of the patients we considered were severely or moderately depressed, the level of depression and its effects on their interpersonal functioning was also a selection consideration. Here there were some surprises. One of the most severely depressed women we saw, who was herself hospitalized for depression later in the course of the group, became a central figure around whom the patients could rally their nurturing impulses. She herself spoke about getting a great deal from the members. Her interpersonal style is best described as withdrawn and lethargic; her verbalizations were most frequently monosyllabic. Despite her subdued interpersonal profile, she apparently bene-fited in some measure from the group. And so retarded psychomotor activity alone was not a good prognostic indicator.

Another highly depressed woman was one who had recently learned of a serious cardiac condition that forced her to limit her activities. She was inau-dible and uncommunicative with the professional staff. Yet she had been mar-ried for more than 20 years, and we took this as evidence of stronger interpersonal skills than had been observed in the intake process. We decided to try her in the group in an attempt to address the depression she presented. From the start she felt intensely uncomfortable in the group and did not attend after her first meeting. This was another example of the difficulty of predicting who would adjust to the group.

Losses and Stresses. As can be seen, the group consisted of women with a wide range of psychic integrations. All of them were burdened with cumulative environmental stresses, and many of them had in common a recent loss (Brown et al., 1975). Ana had a daughter who had attempted suicide. Carmen had adopted two children of her sister's after the murder of the sister by the sister's husband. Delia had recently moved from another section of the borough and found herself without any support in the new community (in addition, she had numerous physical complaints, a frequent symptom in this population). Elis-abeth suffered life-threatening illness in her husband. Felicita had a second unsuccessful marriage on top of years of struggling to care for a severely re-tarded daughter.

The patients were more or less able to attach their symptoms to a particular precipitant in their lives. (We assumed that those patients who identified one significant loss would be more responsive to brief interventions than those who presented less clearly identified stressors, but this assumption was challenged.) They also demonstrated numerous characterological pictures underlying these symptoms. One woman presented, by history, conversion symptoms; another presented severe psychotic ruminations, unassailable to verbal interventions, yet showed some improvement in symptoms while these ruminations per-sisted.

Carmen, who was suddenly caring for twice the number of children on the death of her sister, presented several hysterical symptoms. She had voluntary-muscle paralysis, which took her to the emergency room regularly (Rothen-berg, 1964). (Because of the debilitating nature of these symptoms and hyper-tensive episodes, we carefully followed her medically.) She was frequently depressed and tearful at these times and she did not take solace from sharing her burden with the group. While a precipitant was clearly defined in her eyes and ours, she had other chronic problems.

Ana, whose daughter had attempted suicide, had a year earlier been tempted to have an affair with a younger man. In the group she assumed a narcissistic role, stressing the fear and anxiety she felt and minimizing the fears of others. She was persuaded that she had a terminal illness—with little or no medical consultation—and was dreadfully afraid of any suffering. She said she did not fear death if it was not painful; she feared only pain or serious discomfort.

Group Format

The building that housed the clinic had years before been a medical health station to which these same patients had brought their children for their inoculations. Now, what had been a cold and uninviting public facility had been converted into an attractive clinic, complete with carpeting, sofa chairs in the waiting room, and a warm beige decor. The staff, from receptionist to chief of service, was remarkably considerate of the serious anxieties that brought these people to seek psychiatric help. Given such an inviting environment, it was not uncommon to see a patient arrive an hour (or two!) early to visit with others in the waiting room.

The group met weekly for 1½ hours in my clinic office, which was just large enough to accommodate 6 or 7 members, the maximum size on any given day. Thirteen patients participated over the course of 18 months. Attendance ranged from two to seven, with the average about four or five. The group met in the morning while children were in school. No refreshments were served because I felt they would divert members from the serious purpose of the group. Before they joined the group, I tried to impress on members the usefulness of sharing life experiences with others and made clear that the work to be done in the group was their work, although I would be present to monitor and make suggestions. Group meetings were unstructured. If nobody began a session— a rare event—I would ask members who had been troubled in recent weeks if the same problems obtained.

Early Phase

Because of the stated focus on the group—short-term resolution of situational dysfunctions—and the constantly changing membership, the sequential phases of group process were not easily identifiable as in a more orthodox group of long duration. The tasks of the early phase of group process were, in fact, present throughout the group's life. These included defining the goals of the group and of individual members; establishing a group culture with both stated and unstated norms; mutual assessment of each individual by the others in establishing inclusion criteria, acceptance, subgroups, leadership roles, and the like.

Inclusion and Acceptance

As new members were regularly added to the group, questions of inclusion were frequently in the forefront of the group's attention. New members were subjected to not-very-subtle interrogations as to why they were coming to the group and whether or not they "belonged," a quality idiosyncratically defined by each questioner.

Questions of inclusion were frequently measures of the degree of stresses and losses that the new members had suffered. Felicita, whose daughter was in a facility for the retarded, was deemed deserving of membership and was not challenged. Members accepted her readily despite her erratic attendance and aloof stance when present. On the other hand, Juana, whose main complaint seemed to be a daughter whose adolescence was slightly tumultuous for that age group, was "inquired out of the group." She was regularly asked why she was attending the group when she seemed to have everything under control.

As mentioned above, psychosis was not a criterion for exclusion from the group. The patients' tolerance for this was considerable. A florid psychosis was casually ignored, while hysterical symptoms, equally dramatic although not as intractable, were experienced as threatening and worthy of emotional distance by the members.

Child Rearing

A common subject of the group was child rearing, particularly educating adolescents. Because of the ages of the patients, most either had lived through their children's adolescence or were currently going through such a stage with all the tumult characteristic of this period. Because of their shared historical and cultural backgrounds, the women occupied conservative, traditional positions in the community and in their families. By role they were primarily caretakers. The result was that they were given to experiencing their anxieties through the lives of their children. Questions of curfew, good and bad peer groups, sexual activity, and the like were readily available as topics. They were more or less able to shift from these vicarious concerns to their egocentric concerns, addressing the latter in constructive ways.

Juana was a good example of this dual focus. Her daughter was 14, growing into independence more quickly than Juana had anticipated. One of Juana's chief concerns was her "inability" to talk to this daughter frankly, feeling that she was doing her harm in forcing her own conservative views on her. As Juana was at the same time thinking about going to work outside the home, questions of social role and cultural definition of those roles became prominent. Her ability to see the relativity of such roles permitted her to confront this daughter while concurrently pursuing employment for herself.

Talking about children, like any other subject, can serve several functions. It provides a common focus in the group. It can also serve to defend against depression as one derives self-esteem through the accomplishments of one's children. Delia is a case in point.

Delia was a bright, intelligent woman, free of psychosis. Her depression was clearly related to marital separation, a move from her old neighborhood, and declining health. As Delia was older than the other members, her children were also older. They were old enough to have accomplished something in life from which their mother could derive satisfaction: one was a teacher, another a nurse, a third was in the armed forces. When other members described the ordeal of having an adolescent in the apartment, Delia would talk with pride about her children. I did not challenge this. The goals of short-term treatment are less ambitious than those of long-term treatment, and they do not necessarily include addressing this rivalrous behavior, which can serve to divide the group.

Delia was obviously trying to buttress her failing self-esteem, which had been assailed by her losses. In long-term treatment one might have inquired why she needed to distance herself from the others, why she needed to stand apart. The answer was clear: she wanted to be defined by her children's accomplishments and not only by her losses. As this vicarious pleasure served to restore her self-esteem and was not overly divisive of the group, it was not challenged.

The Middle Phase

The so-called middle phase of groups, where among other changes one sees an increased cohesiveness and possibly a challenge to the leader's authority, did appear. These developments were surprising precisely because of the turnover in membership and the erratic pattern of attendance.

Cohesiveness

One of the signs of cohesiveness is the presence of peer communications. After three or four months, this group became more group-centered and less leader-focused.

Maria, who spoke in the most hushed tones and was out of the group for several months—for a psychiatric hospitalization for her depression and because of family illnesses (her husband's and mother's)—returned to the group to warm, spontaneous inquiries about her well-being and her mother's and husband's health. Maria continued to be one of the members who would elicit these comments and questions each time she appeared.

Ana was another member who elicited expressions of interest and concern whenever she appeared. Despite good verbal interaction between her and the intake staff, Ana showed little capacity to listen empathically to others. In addition, she was firmly fixed in her self-preoccupations, punishing herself for fantasized infidelities a year earlier. Despite these poor signs, she was able to surrender this self-centered stance over the course of several months. The group was obviously instrumental in this progress as they alternately listened respectfully and with amusement to her "carryings on" with so few "real problems" to concern herself about. It was our impression that some of the movement of this woman was due to her thorough acceptance by the group. Even her frivolities and anxieties about her "imagined" problems were attended to by the group the way one listens to the obvious fantasies of a child, not denying them yet communicating that one does not share them. Ana was finally able to take herself to the feared doctors for a realistic assessment of her medical condition. She later became regular in attendance and loyal in her attachment to several members.

Delia had recently moved from her old neighborhood to the area of the clinic when her application for public housing was approved. In addition, she had a cardiac condition and required major dental work. The first loss alone removed her from a neighborhood where she had lived for many years and raised her children. Now that she was uprooted from that community, she did not have the network of friends she knew formerly. She identified this as a source of her depression. She was an outgoing woman who probably had made friends easily in the past, but the combination of her new setting and her deteriorated health proved too much of a burden. She did not have the strength to cultivate the friendships she earlier enjoyed. Now finding herself among new acquaintances in the group, she perked up and eagerly became socially involved.

Scapegoating and Splitting

A paradoxical illustration of the group's cohesion was witnessed when the group actively ignored one member. This example demonstrates several issues: patient selection, group norms, and subgrouping.

Ninfa came to the group when she had an increase in paranoid anxiety. She was a woman of 50 with two grown children, one of whom shared her apartment. In many respects, she was the least representative of the group: she was actively involved with religion, carrying a Bible to the group and quoting passages to comfort the others. She had been hospitalized several years earlier for paranoid ideation, whereas most of the others had avoided hospitalization. And she was violent in a way that none of the others were, having killed a dog that was disrupting her neighborhood.

When Ninfa began in the group her blunted affect did not disturb any of the other members and they spoke to her with the inquiring attitude they used for others. But when they were met with answers that did not reveal her to be emotionally available to them, they became less interested in learning about her. Clearly, she was difficult to "warm up" to, and the members quickly gave up attempts to do so. While other patients were uncommunicative verbally, they were able to elicit members' interest; Ninfa could not convey this mutuality. In selecting her for the group, we underestimated her paranoid history and current paranoid ideations and overestimated her capacity for mutuality.

Despite this woman's isolated position, splitting did not appear to be a serious form of resistance. This was perhaps not surprising, given the limited contacts the members had with each other over the course of the group. And yet, because several members remained on the edges of the group, this scapegoating deserves some attention.

Ninfa came to the group with complaints of chronic insomnia. She cited a current precipitant, yet she clearly had strong depressive and paranoid tendencies as evidenced by her previous psychiatric hospitalizations. What alienated her from the group was her attitude toward violence. Despite her obsession with religion, she portrayed herself as a tough woman who would take no abuse from anyone. The example she gave early in the group was her intentionally killing a dog whose owner had been unwilling or unable to keep it quiet. This deed, remembered by the others and communicated to subsequent members, served to label her as strange and different from the other members. It was this label, plus her flat affect, that positioned her outside the mainstream of the group. The result was seen in the lack of spontaneity in the members' questions to her. Ninfa was not obviously missed by the others, and her absences were far more frequently met with relief than regret. When she did return after an absence, she was not questioned with interest about her whereabouts in the interim.

Because the patients' contacts with the psychiatrist were routinely little more than brief interviews, these contacts became a focus of the group in several respects: transferential, rivalry among members, splitting between the group leader and the psychiatrist. At least one case split the treatment and threatened the effectiveness of the group.

Carmen came to the clinic after adopting her nieces. She had quickly found that caring for these girls, on top of her own children and the shallow support from her husband, was too much. She became tearful, anxious, insomniac. She attended the group erratically and divided information between the group and the psychiatrist.

Carmen was an attractive woman whose youthful dress and carefully coiffured blond hair hid her 45 years. She attracted attention by her air of self-respect, best evidenced by her appearance and her erect posture. Despite this, she spoke sparingly to other members of the group and reluctantly to the group therapist. Yet her attendance improved, and she reported a lessening of depression. In her contact with the psychiatrist she would reveal relevant information, thus securing his support, while gently refusing to continue on the antidepressants he prescribed, claiming that they had no effect. The psychiatrist and I maintained close communication and permitted her to parcel out her anxieties this way as we had no good understanding of why these divisions were maintained. Yet her situation was sympathetically received by the others, and she obviously felt less alone in her status as heroine to her nieces.

Confrontations

While group members occasionally avoided the confrontations that I thought would be beneficial, they were challenging at times. Consistent with the climate of support and protection that prevailed in many of the sessions, these challenges frequently took the form of defenses of the weaker members.

Ana was frequently confronted by others for her lack of sensitivity. When another woman described her past work in a garment factory and the terrible effect the noise had had on her nerves, Ana suggested that she seek employment in the local sweatshop. Several of the others attacked Ana's suggestion as typically insensitive. As she was given to these unrelated comments—ignoring the object of her comments—and also demonstrated a strong narcissistic streak, these challenges were productive for her. She was taken aback and given pause to think about her behavior.

Perhaps because of her role in the above incident, Ana was listened to seriously when she talked frequently about her paralyzing fear of illness and the accompanying pain. Just as frequently, Maria compared her own suffering to everyone else's. She concluded, "Ana doesn't have this fear of death that I have, so hers can't be so bad." The members finally began telling Maria firmly that someone else was in worse straits than she and that she was unsympathetic and self-centered.

This was the kind of situation that this group seemed particularly able to help with. Maria had one of the more stable lives of the group members. She had been married for 20 years to a man with a secure income from his restaurant. While she insisted that there was no passion between them, they were together with no talk of separation. She came to the clinic with complaints of insomnia and was obviously troubled: she spoke quickly, jumping from one subject to another, unable or unprepared to stay with any gainful topic. She agreed to join the group reluctantly, suggesting strongly that she could see no benefit to be derived from talking with other patients. And initially she was right. She showed little interest in others' problems except as they showed her to be suffering more than they. She made this very clear, repeatedly minimizing others' suffering and maximizing her own. The group members tired of this and made it clear that they thought she was insensitive and did not have any serious problems in comparison to others. I could hear her refrain become weaker as she simultaneously sought the medical care she had postponed for months.

Terminations

Frequently more difficult to negotiate than individual beginnings were individual terminations.

A strong factor discouraging terminations was the emotional support the group provided. Most of the patients were experiencing losses of family, lifestyle, or health, and they had few resources in the natural community to draw upon. Their financial resources were extremely limited, most of them being supported entirely on public funds. The stigma attached to leading marginal lives, socially and financially, frequently aggravated already poor self-images and self-critical responses. When in the group they experienced acceptance and understanding from others, they responded with sudden vitality.

The strongest and most resilient patients, those who showed the most gains in the group and appeared to have reached premorbid levels of functioning, were the very ones who did not easily move out. Juana, for example, by her own assessment and ours, had reached her prior level of functioning. She was not on medication, so there was no need for regular visits to the clinic on that account. But she was reluctant to separate herself from the supportive network of the group. When ultimately she did leave, her departure was unplanned and we considered her termination only de facto.

Delia was another member who gained dramatically in the group and then proved reluctant to depart. Initially anxious and self-absorbed, she became a woman who could speak confidently of caring for herself and others. This healthy altruism was met with genuine gratitude from the other group members, which in turn bolstered Delia's self-esteem. In the face of this circle of mutual support, my efforts to have Delia terminate treatment were not successful. She remained in the group several months beyond the date indicated by the symptom picture.

Reviewing the gains of these more resilient members and their reluctance to leave the group, I am inclined to support the idea of a peer group to "catch" psychotherapy-group members when they leave short-term treatment. Such a natural support group, conducted by the members themselves, perhaps with periodic professional consultation, could satisfy the normal desire of these women to socialize with their peers and might well serve to avoid recurrence of the dysfunctional behavior that first brought them to the clinic.

References

Brown, G. W., Bhrolchain, M. N., & Harris, T. Social class and psychiatric disturbance among women in an urban population. *Sociology*, 1975, *9*(2), 225–254.

Canino, I. A., & Canino, G. Impact of stress on the Puerto Rican family. *American Journal of Orthopsychiatry*, 1980, *50*(3), 535–541.

Menikoff, A. Long-term group psychotherapy of Puerto Rican women: Ethnicity as a clinical support. *Group*, 1979, *3*(3), 172–180.

Rothenberg, A. Puerto Rico and aggression. *American Journal of Psychiatry*, 1964, *120*(10), 962–970.

Torres-Matrullo, C. Acculturation and psychopathology among Puerto Rican women in mainland United States. *American Journal of Orthopsychiatry*, 1976, *46*(4), 710–719.

IV

WORKING WITH COUPLES

VII

WORKING WITH COUPLES

11

A Psychodynamic Couples' Group
Led by Married Co-Therapists

Hylene S. Dublin, M.S.W., A.C.S.W.

A clinical social worker in private practice in Winnetka, Illinois, HYLENE S. DUBLIN is also a consultant in group and milieu psychotherapy at the Northwestern University Institute of Psychiatry in Chicago. Her husband/co-therapist Richard A. Dublin, M.S.W., A.C.S.W., is Director of Professional Services, Jewish Family & Community Services of Chicago.

Often, in my clinical-social-work practice with a client seen individually or in group therapy, I would find us progressing to a point where the spouse reacted to the changes being made by the client or the pressures on the spouse to change. Typically, the client had been dealing with long-repressed feelings toward parents and, consequently, toward the spouse, and had begun to be more expressive of his or her feelings—more overtly angry, demanding, or self-protective. The spouse, feeling pressured to respond to this "new" behavior, felt challenged, and frequently the marriage was threatened.

In other instances, where couples had been seen together, a focus on the interaction between the two had resulted in heightened resistance by one partner when certain defensive patterns were being examined.

This led to a growing recognition on my part that a group setting would offer a unique opportunity to examine couple as well as individual dynamics. It would provide the possibility for a dilution of the mutual-projection system in marriages through the presence of others, as well as an opportunity for couples to get some distance from the ongoing assaults and counterassaults in their relationships.

In addition, the opportunity of working with my husband (also a clinical social worker) as co-therapist intrigued us both—for it appeared to offer still additional clinical advantages and to provide a challenging new personal-growth-promoting experience for us. Since 1971, when our first couples' group was formed, we have worked with 21 couples, some in time-limited groups, others in long-term, open-ended groups, beginning in a private hospital's outpatient psychiatric clinic and moving later to a private-practice setting.

To introduce the reader to a time-limited model of psychodynamically oriented couples' group psychotherapy, let me first provide a theoretical rationale for couples' group work, to be followed by a consideration of selection critiera, a description of the preparation of prospective couples, technical considerations regarding the co-therapy team, phases and processes of the group, techniques to be utilized, particular problems and pitfalls, as well as specific examples of work with couples.

Theoretical Considerations

Individuals tend to carry unresolved conflicts from childhood into their choices of mates and to act out these conflicts in the marital relationship. These choices, as Meissner (1978) explains, have to do with the need for gratification of "usually unconscious and predominantly narcissistic needs." Kohut (1971) discusses the manner in which persons with narcissistic character disorders choose involvement with others in order to complete inner narcissistic defects—that is, to complete what Meissner (1978, p. 39) calls the "inadequately differentiated self." There is involvement with and dependency on an object choice, but the relationship is not one of independent, adequate, relatively autonomous individuals; rather, this personality defect tends "to permeate and contaminate the attachment in an uncontrolled, undisciplined, unorganized, and relatively primary process manner. Thus, the object relationships of such individuals tend to be perfused in varying degrees with this kind of primitive psychic energy which is communicated in subtle and predominantly unconscious ways within the object relationship and comes to affect the functioning and responsiveness of the object, as well as the operations of the subject" (Meissner, 1978, p. 39).

The choice of mate reflects this underlying need for fulfillment or completion so that a complementarity of behaviors or roles is sought—particularly around such issues as "dominance–submission, sadism–masochism, superiority–inferiority" (Meissner, 1978, p. 42). Partners, although often having complementary or opposite but intermeshing behavior patterns, are seen by many clinicians as having attained similar levels of development or maturity but often as acting out opposite sides of a developmental conflict or issue—the opposite sides of the coin, so to speak.

What is often idealized and experienced as fulfilling or satisfying in the other during courtship may later become the source of irritation or frustration. The responsible, dominant, patriarchal husband who provides all can later be experienced as controlling and demeaning by the same "underadequate" wife who once needed this response. On the other hand, the all-providing husband can tire of caretaking and responsible behavior, which is never quite right or enough. But still the two may persevere in this unsatisfying way of expressing their mutual needs. "The conspiracy to maintain the marital neurosis is often based on its mutually gratifying nature in spite of complaints to the contrary" (Flint & MacLennan, 1962, p. 357).

Boas (1962), in his work with married couples in Holland, coined the term "zipper relationships" to refer to the mutual, neurotic interactions in particularly difficult-to-treat marriages. Ultimately, he also concluded that couples' group psychotherapy was the treatment of choice for such couples.

Let us turn for a moment to a consideration of other advantages offered by group psychotherapy for couples. Yalom (1970) has listed several curative factors in group psychotherapy that are particularly beneficial to the population I have been describing.

"Universality" is especially significant. Despite the many possible social involvements of marital couples, there are few arenas where the "real" aspects of marital interactions can be viewed and understood. In a therapy group, the shame and guilt about one's own marital difficulties can be relieved through recognition that others have similar or more far-reaching difficulties. One is not alone.

In addition to reducing guilt and anxiety about one's own inadequacies, the group provides couples with an opportunity to see neurotic patterns of interaction in others that may replicate their own neurotic interactions. It is, of course, much easier to see in others what we avoid seeing in ourselves. This factor makes group therapy a particularly effective vehicle for interpersonal learning, in that all dyads have something to learn about themselves and from each other.

Since the marital interaction is the reciprocal or complementary interaction of two individuals struggling with similar developmental issues, the group offers an opportunity for both individuals within the couple to learn something about their own intrapsychic processes as well as about the nature of their interpersonal, reciprocal relationship. This facilitates the goal of greater development and differentiation of self. Through providing the opportunity for involved interaction with other individuals and dyads, the group permits in-

199

dividuals to see and experience themselves outside the dyadic relationship and to accept greater responsibility for recognizing and acknowledging their own feelings, needs, and behaviors.

"Interpersonal learning" is enhanced through feedback from other group members on the here-and-now interactions of the couple in the group. The group is able to break into the struggle between the two individuals locked in transferential interactions (the mutual-projection system) and point out the projections and distortions expressed by each. At this point, because of the consensual viewpoints as well as the support of other group members, the individual is encouraged to examine and consider the nature of his or her distorted behaviors within the marriage and within the group setting. Also, with the focus on the here-and-now interactions, more affect is available, leading to a greater propensity for change.

Noteworthy also is the fact that, with this couples' group model, each individual is encouraged to take responsibility for his or her own feelings and behaviors, fostering individuation and personal growth. As individuals make changes, they are supported and encouraged by other group members, who have less stake in the projected image maintained by the spouse.

Selecting Couples' Group Members

In considering the intertwined processes of selecting and preparing new group members, emphasis should be placed on the latter aspect. Pregroup interviews can be useful predictors of the effectiveness of a time-limited couples' group experience, particularly if emphasis is placed on teaching prospective couples how group therapy works and developing a good working relationship with the co-therapists. I share Yalom's impressionistic view that "the more often a patient is seen pretherapy, the less likely he is to terminate prematurely from the group" (Yalom, 1970, p. 218). This is particularly necessary in establishing bonds with the co-therapy team, especially if one or the other therapist has seen the couple jointly or individually prior to consideration for group. It follows axiomatically that both co-therapists should be present at pregroup screening sessions. Otherwise, the kind of "splitting" described by Yalom as attempting "in a variety of ways to undermine the therapists' interrelationship and to intrude between them" (Yalom, 1970, p. 319) is even more likely to occur.

There are a number of pertinent guidelines regarding selection of potential couples' group members that I wish to bring to the reader's attention. One must remember, however, that even the most cogent theoretical considerations must be discarded in favor of attending to individual needs, motivation, and the availability of "workable couples."

The kind of setting in which the couples' group is located has had, in my experience, a significant effect on issues of selection. Family-service agencies, for example, may have more access to suitable couples than outpatient psychiatric clinics, where patients as well as staff tend to define problems and services in individual rather than in couple or family terms. Private practice also tends to attract fewer couple clients until the practitioner has become known for this work.

Like many group therapists, and as recommended by the group-therapy literature in general, we try to select couples' group members with a view to balancing the needs for homogeneity and heterogeneity (Yalom, 1970). In a short-term group, extensive interaction is necessary. Interaction is intensified and cohesiveness is heightened when group members are more homogeneous (Neighbor, 1963). For these reasons, in short-term groups of three-to-six months' duration, we have stressed homogeneity in our selections—especially in the areas of age, intellectual ability, capacity for self-awareness, level of ego function, and similarity of the life task or phase within the marriages ("recently married couples, groups of new parents, groups of couples with teenaged children, and groups who are facing the problems of retirement": Alger, 1976, p. 368).

As the duration and goals of the group are altered (by the decision to continue a previously planned short-term group or by initiating a longer-term group), the advantages of homogeneity are outweighed by the gains in perspective, understanding, and feedback available with a more diversified population.

Even in short-term groups, there is a need for heterogeneous elements (Hastings & Runkle, 1963, p. 88) or the group will stagnate or flounder. Too many similarities in marital patterns or interactions (e.g., a group including only passive males with hostile, controlling females) will result in reinforcing these patterns rather than in presenting other ways of interacting within the group and within the marriage. Therefore, a balance of behaviors and reactions needs to be represented in the group, particularly around the issues of intimacy versus distance, dominance versus submission, aggressivity versus passivity, and superiority versus inferiority. Levels of verbalization as well as specific problem issues or areas need to be dissimilar. If the group is too homogeneous, there is no impetus to change what is experienced by all as comfortable and familiar, particularly some of the complementary marital patterns previously described.

An often-overlooked consideration in the selection of group members is the fact that the selection of the first couple or couples determines a good deal about future selections. Once a couple of a particular age range or life phase has been included, the therapist (or co-therapists) must recognize that a certain parameter has been established that affects future choices. This is also true when considering other personality, interactional, or marital-conflict issues, since a couple with one interactional pattern would benefit most by being balanced by a couple with a very different pattern so as to stimulate self-examination and change.

We have found it harmful to the group to include couples on the verge of an immediate decision to divorce. Indeed, we ask prospective group members to agree not to terminate their relationship precipitously during the life of the group—even though divorce is not precluded as an eventual possibility. Instead, they are asked to delay acting on such feelings until those feelings have been recognized and explored within the group. This is necessary both to guarantee a real opportunity for couples to work on usually avoided issues and because precipitous departures are destructive of the group itself.

We also exclude couples with no commitment to examine and work on their relationship and couples in which one spouse is coming merely to "keep the other happy." These couples or individuals tend to act contrary to the intended self-revelation and work focus of the group and to establish antitherapeutic norms.

Finally, it is important that group members have at least some awareness of the mutuality of their differences. This issue is dealt with, very specifically, during the screening sessions, as will subsequently be described. Without some awareness of the reciprocal or complementary nature of their marital difficulties, couples might enter the group without the expectation that both need to take responsibility for participation, self-revelation, and change. They must be made to realize that one cannot hope to change the "bad" spouse but can look at and ultimately change only his or her own feelings and behavior.

Preparatory Interviews

Usually two or three interviews are necessary for each couple before they are included in a group. Occasionally, if there is a delay in getting together a sufficient number of suitable couples to begin a short-term group (minimally three couples and maximally five), additional interviews are advisable so that the sense of alliance or connection with the therapists can be sustained and the couples can begin working on their issues without perceiving this period as wasted time. The dilemma here is to provide a sustaining work-oriented relationship without stimulating a too-intensive transference, making transition to a time-limited group more difficult, since there is not much time available for resolving this issue.

While preparation, we believe, is important to develop the capacity of any individual to utilize psychotherapy, it is essential for a time-limited group where it is necessary to provide "patients with some cognitive structure which will enable them to participate more effectively in the group." Also heightened is the need to more rapidly "recognize and work through misconceptions and unrealistic fears and expectations of group therapy" (Yalom, 1970, p. 218).

There is a specific format that my co-therapist and I have found useful in our evaluative-preparatory sessions with prospective group members. Naturally, one has to adapt it to particular couples and situations, but it has been helpful in assuring some consideration of relevant individual, couple, and group issues.

We begin by focusing on the problems that brought the couple to see us. This is necessary to demonstrate that we are interested in assessing their concerns and needs and in eventually choosing, in a collaborative effort with them, an appropriate treatment modality. This is also the area of immediate interest and concern to the couple, and some attempt to respond to this need must be made—particularly if there is a crisis that requires immediate attention so the couple can stabilize and be maintained until the group convenes. Naturally, this examination involves an historical consideration of the problem, including precipitating factors in their current situation. Usually, the couple begins by describing specific, concrete issues. Some immediate "problem solving" may be necessary, but we attempt to move the couple to the recognition that the specific issue may be symbolic of other, larger conflicts within their relationship. In other words, emphasis is placed less on solving the immediate problem than on the process through which the couple deals with each other around this and other issues.

Given our premise about unresolved developmental issues contributing to current difficulties within a marriage in a reciprocal, complementary way, and given the fact that "the relationship of all couples is influenced by the places from which they have come, the ways in which they grew up feeling about themselves" (Fontane, 1979, p. 529), it is desirable to include some exploration of family-of-origin material. Although there are many conscious determinants of marital choice, there is also a strong unconscious aspect (Blanck & Blanck, 1968, p. 148) that has been affected by one's earlier familial experiences. "Gaining awareness through discussion of family history brings to light some separation–individuation material and thus enables couples to work through a portion of this material" (Fontane, 1979, p. 532). Exploring these familial issues during the preparatory sessions with both members of a couple lays the groundwork for future understanding of some of the causes of their difficulties and provides a framework for revealing the different feelings, needs, and wishes that each has regarding the relationship. The reciprocal or interactional nature of these can subsequently be examined.

A secondary value of this technique is that it can help to defuse the mutual antagonisms (and projections) by making the nature of their origin clearer, more ego-syntonic (acceptable in relation to one's idealized image), and less threatening to examine. Another gain is that it presents the co-therapists with an opportunity to test prospective members' capacity to consider their behaviors in these terms, and to estimate the degree of their psychological mindedness and ability to develop insights into their own and others' behavior.

At this juncture (when appropriate, based on evaluating the foregoing material), my co-therapist and I move to helping the couple consider how group psychotherapy might be useful to them. Using a specific concern they have expressed, we help them to understand how the problems they describe can be explored, understood, and worked through in a group context. We consider it essential in motivating a patient to consider entering a group that some notion of the relevance of this modality to his or her personal problems be recognized.

The couple's previous experiences in groups must now be considered. The amount and nature of their current social interaction outside the marital relationship should be explored, including current interactions with family-of-origin members. How social are they? How comfortable are they in being open and direct with others? Do they tend to feel self-conscious and anxious in groups? What is the nature of interactions with significant others—bosses, parents, teachers, siblings, co-workers, other peers? What is the nature of their interactions with their own children?

In addition to current relationship issues, the co-therapists need to determine something about past group involvements, beginning with sibling relationships. How did each marital partner deal with siblings, friends, schools, clubs, other group activities? What might be predicted about their comfort in or capacity to utilize a short-term couples' group based on these earlier experiences? Can specific problem issues in group-centered relationships be delineated, and can concern with these be part of the working contract with the therapy group?

Having spent considerable time learning about the couple's problems, their individual needs and concerns, and the nature of their involvement with groups, the co-therapists must now do some teaching about group therapy. Content should include how the group works, what the couple might expect, and how they can most effectively operate to make the group experience useful to them. This approach includes many of the aspects stressed in Yalom's views on preparation (Yalom, 1970, pp. 222–223), although we refrain from the more didactic approach. We focus initially on the couple's expectations, wishes, fantasies, and fears concerning the group experience, explore those, and ultimately clarify misconceptions about the nature and dangers of the group's procedures and process.

Specifically, we share some notions about the "social microcosm" interactional emphasis in the group, which includes examining here-and-now interactions between the couple and other group members. This includes confronting individuals with how they operate with each other, exploring feelings toward the spouse, other members, and co-therapists. What is particularly highlighted is the need for as much honesty and directness as possible and the expectation that this will increase as they and other members develop more comfort with and trust in each other (Yalom, 1970, p. 222).

Other factors are stressed in the establishment of a mutually accepted contract. Couples are encouraged to spell out their unique goals in terms of areas of understanding as well as changed behavior. In addition to these personal expectations, prospective members are informed of the necessity for regular and punctual attendance—of the fact that members grow to count on dealing with each other and that irregularities complicate the development of necessary trust and affect the consistency of dealing with issues. Prospective members are warned to anticipate some feelings of frustration and confusion during early sessions. They can expect that these will dissipate as they learn to use other group members more effectively and to concentrate less on securing direct help from the co-therapists.

Social interaction outside the group is explained as something that may cause complications within the therapeutic situation. Members are encouraged to bring back to the group any outside interactions, since these may impinge directly on feelings or behavior within the group. It is our experience that expressly forbidding such outside socializing only tends to stimulate those who need to act out rebelliously against authority figures and might force these issues underground.

Following consideration of these varied individual, couple, and group issues, my co-therapist and I (through open sharing of our respective opinions) reach a conclusion concerning the suitability of the particular couple for the short-term couples' group. The reader must recognize, however, that this conclusion is the result of an ongoing process that has involved the prospective couple from the very beginning so that their level of motivation, anxieties, and reservations have been examined for some time and worked with accordingly. In particular, we feel it is crucial for a successful group involvement to explore both sides of the couple's inevitable ambivalent feelings about joining the group. Couples who are aware only of their positive feelings tend to make superficial connections and are unable to withstand the initial disappointments they experience in the group. The co-therapists, too, have been forming opinions, sharing impressions, and keeping the couple informed of any issues or concerns that they might have. If they agree, the couple is invited to participate in the group, share whatever doubts or reservations might still remain, reflect upon their reactions to the co-therapists during this process (which is important for assessing the nature of the beginning transferences), and complete a specific plan regarding their formal starting date within the group.

The Co-Therapy Team

Co-therapy as an issue in group psychotherapy tends to stimulate intense reactions among clinicians. There are those who strongly advocate this approach, and others who argue that "often the second professional person is there because the primary therapist is reluctant to take full responsibility" (Berne, 1966, p. 23). Then there is the view that "the co-therapy approach may have some specific advantages but many potential hazards as well" (Yalom, 1970, p. 318). Markowitz states that his decision to join with a female co-therapist in a couples' group was based on his recognition that "in the group each patient re-creates his own childhood family configuration—which resulted in his pathological development—and projects it onto the co-therapists via transference. Our hope has been to effect corrective change through interaction with substitute parental figures" (Markowitz, 1968, p. 273). My suspicion is that attitudes about co-therapy often reflect personality differences among therapists.

In contemplating the formation of a time-limited couples' psychotherapy group in an outpatient psychiatric clinic of a large private general hospital, I considered the opposing arguments. In general, I felt that the advantages of a co-therapy team, particularly since there was the opportunity of having my husband as the co-therapist, far outweighed the disadvantages. Marital therapy should provide an experience through which two people learn to differentiate themselves as individuals without this being experienced as destructive of their relationship—through which they learn that individuals can be separate and unique, can recognize and respect this in themselves and their spouses, and still be able to share in the pursuit of life tasks, goals, and pleasures. The constructive interaction of a married co-therapy team provides the clearest evidence that this is possible.

The presence of a male-female co-therapy team (especially when the members are married) rapidly induces the parental transferences that need to be visible for a significant aspect of the group's work. This creates the possibility, also, for a balance between the fatherly and motherly support available to group members (Levine, 1979, p. 298) as well as the opportunity for an examination of the complex oedipal issues that may impinge on the marriages.

One incident in a six-month, time-limited group may illustrate this. Ralph, a 34-year-old passively angry man, had failed to recognize his need to dominate his wife as a reaction to his anxiety about the power his mother had had over him. Whenever I attempted to explore this with him, denial and anger would surface. It was only after my husband commented on the same behavior, got a more positive response, and pointed this out to him that Ralph was able to begin to explore the long-repressed anger he had felt toward his critical but depriving mother—which he had been reexperiencing with me.

Writers have stressed the necessity for equality of status of co-therapists (Berne, 1966, p. 24; Levine, 1979, p. 297; Yalom, 1970, p. 318). Particularly in the context of representing the idea of equal and shared responsibility and privilege within a marriage is this significant! Because my co-therapist and I have had similar training and experience (having met in graduate school) as well as opportunities to develop ourselves professionally in different ways, we were secure in our professional identities and relatively comfortable with the give-and-take necessary for effective shared therapeutic responsibility. Before beginning, however, we were somewhat anxious about the effect of this undertaking on our marriage. If anything, however, our professional collaboration has clarified and enhanced other aspects of our relationship. We have learned about ourselves from our groups.

We share the view expressed by Occhetti and Occhetti (1981, p. 76) that co-therapy teams should meet regularly to discuss "the group's interaction during the last group meeting, the meaning of members' behavior, the co-therapists' responses to specific group members, the diagnostic significance of any family history that was revealed, and the determination of significant issues for future exploration." To this list we would add the need to explore and discuss the differing perceptions of the two co-therapists, to express our pleasure or dissatisfaction with each other's participation as well as our own, and to gain some comfort with and respect for unresolvable differences in such a way as to utilize these in a complementary manner within the group.

It has been suggested that co-therapist disagreement expressed during the first few sessions is alarming and confusing to a new group (Yalom, 1970, p. 318). I agree. I believe, however, that during a time-limited couples' group it is important for co-therapists to reveal differing opinions and conflicts so members can perceive that disagreements are not demeaning, threatening, or destructive and that they do not indicate unresolvable conflict that must lead to a dissolution of the relationship.

It is also noteworthy that my co-therapist and I have somewhat different theoretical orientations. Although eclectic, both of us have had training and experience based on psychoanalytic concepts and ego psychology. My co-therapist has moved more definitively into the area of family psychotherapy from a systems-theory perspective, while I have focused more intensively on a psychodynamically based view of family and marital therapy. These differences appear to have enhanced rather than diminished our effectiveness in the group—resulting in a complementarity that adds significantly to our understanding of the issues and the process. Thus the understandings and sensitivities of one therapist can be augmented by the different theoretical and personal perspective of the other—the old "two heads are better than one" cliché.

Another advantage of the co-therapy relationship is that it frees the co-therapists to function differently within the group. If, in an interaction, one co-therapist can remain supportive, the other can confront more freely, knowing that the necessary balance will be maintained. At another time, one co-therapist may be more involved with dynamic exploration or interaction with a particular group member while the other is free to maintain a group-focused perspective. It is important that these differing roles be exchanged freely so

207

that neither member of the co-therapy team feels locked into one set of behaviors. This flexibility will demonstrate to couples in the group that they too are not locked into one way of behaving in their marriages.

Perhaps the most significant advantage of co-therapists leading a couples group has to do with the possibility of balancing one co-therapist's countertransference or neurotic response to an individual with the presence of the other, thereby reducing the possibility of an impasse (Rosenbaum, 1978, p. 154). The co-therapists' "own identifications and countertransferences are likely to be particularly hard to control in this type of group" (Flint & MacLennan, 1962, p. 360). These countertransferences on the part of either co-therapist can be identified and explored in postmeeting discussions. This provides an opportunity for the co-therapists to deliver and receive useful feedback on their group participation. It appears to work most effectively, however, with co-therapists who are relatively comfortable and secure with their capacity to function individually as group therapists as well as in a collaborative relationship (and for married co-therapists, this applies to the marriage as well).

The co-therapy relationship within the couples' group is so important, particularly in a time-limited context, that problematic, untested, or unequal cotherapy relationships are highly inadvisable. The availability of supervision and/or consultation is another significant aspect to be considered, for these provide a neutral arena where issues or stalemates in the co-therapy relationship can be examined.

Group Phases

The Initial Phase

There is no structure, format, or exercise with which we begin the group. Usually we start by reminding people of the reason for their being there: the desire to understand and improve their marriages by seeing themselves more clearly as individuals. We encourage them to begin talking freely and interacting with each other around this common task.

Couples begin by focusing on the concrete areas of disagreement or controversy in their marriages—issues of money, child rearing, uses of time, sexual needs, etc. They appear to deal with other group members superficially at first, testing the responses to their early attempts at communication and self-disclosure. Despite the tendency to keep things superficial, there is often much anger at and blaming of spouses. Members and therapists are encouraged to take sides. Individuals appear to want other group participants to solve problems through advice giving, although the advice itself is rarely experienced as helpful. The members talk only in terms of the marital dyad and experiment little with interacting with others except through solicitous, advice-giving responses. What seems different here from other beginning groups is that the marital relationship is an already formed subgroup, and this appears to make for "a heightened emotional group climate in the early period" (Leichter, 1962, p. 154). It also accelerates the tendency to deal with conflict and negative affect, although this behavior tends to operate more as a defense against getting involved with other group members and with more personal issues.

There is much turning to the co-therapists for structure, direction, and simple answers. The dilemma for the co-therapists at this point is to respond sufficiently to demonstrate concern and support but to avoid the urge to solve problems. Their true goal is to encourage the group in its process of interacting and evolving into a source of significant closeness, caring, and mutual understanding. This is needed so that members can risk interacting freely, learning more about themselves and experimenting with change.

As the group continues in this vilification of marital partners, it takes on an intensely competitive quality. Who has got the worst marriage? Who is most in need of sympathy and understanding? This parallels more clearly the "second stage" of the beginning phase of group psychotherapy as outlined by Yalom (1975, p. 306).

As this stage continues, members become increasingly frustrated by "the lack of progress in the group." An earlier honeymoon reaction—feeling relieved at beginning the process, joining the group, and gaining some initial support—is dissipated. The co-therapists are attacked for their lack of effectiveness and their inability to provide easy solutions. The task for the co-therapists at this time is to encourage and tolerate such expression of anger and disappointment (based on the unfulfilled wish for an omnipotent parent who satisfies all needs). The leaders must ultimately encourage the group to examine the basis of these feelings and to recognize the power and responsibility that group members have for looking at and resolving their own difficulties in a process in which help is available.

There follows a period of group closeness and good feeling. Couples begin to accept the notion that their difficulties are mutual and therefore somewhat under the control of each of them as individuals. A new sense of power prevails. Hastings and Runkle (1963, p. 86) describe this stage in their couples' group this way: "By the sixteenth meeting the group had begun to be aware of the operation of their marital neuroses within the group as resistance and were then able to formulate an immediate group goal of controlling their defensive behavior enough so that free communication could take place." It is at approximately this point that a three-month, time-limited successful couples' group terminates. Couples are feeling closer to each other and other members and have reached a plateau of clearer understanding about mutual responsibility and power within their relationships. It is a period of hopefulness and increased intimacy.

Boas describes this phase of his couples' group as follows:

Improvement usually occurred during an early stage of treatment, sometimes after an acute flare-up in marital tensions. Such improvement was only symptomatic and not yet based on real structural changes, for these can occur only after the couple has worked through the specific mechanisms controlling their zipper relationship. However, initial improvement did lead to a manifest relaxation in the relationship, which in itself created the necessary atmosphere for tackling the causes of the underlying conflicts. (Boas, 1962, p. 150)

Other family therapists may take issue with Boas's view of the nature of the changes within the couples' relationships. Many would argue that this plateau is a reasonable one at which to terminate treatment—with lasting change resulting. There does remain, however, the option of continuing the work by negotiating a new contract or by establishing a more ambitious time frame. In this regard, the obligations, philosophy, and monetary constraints of the treatment agency as well as the motivation and capacities of the couples must be considered.

The Middle Phase

In groups committed to continuing in a six-month, one-year, or open-ended time frame, the transition to a middle or "working phase" of group therapy is possible. Perelman (1960, p. 142) states that "after the initial phase the group operates as any therapy group."

This transition to a working phase involves a necessary move from the all-positive, totally supportive third segment of the first phase that operated "in the service of cohesion" (Yalom, 1975, p. 312). Otherwise the group remains stultified in dealing only with similarities and the need for mutual support, and very little work toward actual change can take place. The co-therapists must facilitate this shift by pointing out what has been happening in the group and questioning the lack of disagreements, etc.

In the working phase, members talk less about what "he did" or "she did" and more about themselves—their wishes, reactions, behaviors. Group members become more comfortable (with co-therapist modeling and encouragement) in challenging and confronting each other without experiencing this as endangering the basic group stability. The here-and-now focus, with special emphasis on giving and receiving feedback, becomes the primary group mode. In fact, one unusual advantage of this couples' group format is that defensive members can finally accept confrontations from others that they have been unable to hear when coming from spouses or therapists. Peer feedback and support become significant modes leading to self-awareness and change.

There is much less focus on the marital relationship during this phase, except to connect up with some notions about reciprocal interactions. Members are struggling with their own developmental issues and dilemmas, an aspect of the differentiation of self we view as necessary to the development of a more satisfying marital interaction. There is opportunity for experimenting with new ways of being and for learning more about oneself through the behaviors and self-revelations of others.

Family-relationship issues that have left members with complex emotional residues are examined in relation to the transferences that develop toward group members and co-therapists. There are frequent attempts to relate here-and-now interactions to previous life experiences so that insight can be gained into the earlier determinants of current attitudes and reactions. Hastings and Runkle (1963, p. 87) describe this during the middle phase of their couples' group: "The group has lately become increasingly active in bringing out childhood material and in relating hostile and distrustful feelings toward members of the opposite sex to experiences with parents and siblings." This also provides opportunities for "corrective emotional experiences" within the group—for example, reexperiencing an old dilemma but resolving it in a new way with another perspective, different people, and more positive circumstances.

Flint and MacLennan (1962, p. 359) highlight this aspect: "A relationship similar to that which a patient has with the spouse may be developed with another group member or the therapist, thus calling attention to the marital transference and providing a crucial focus for therapeutic investigation."

Termination

There are many styles of disengaging from the group. In using the term here, I refer to the termination planned at the beginning of a time-limited group or to the final phase, decided upon in process between group members and co-therapists, experienced in an open-ended group. In both these situations, there is a planned disengagement based either on a predetermined time span or on the consensus that previously discussed goals have been accomplished; there is some sense of appropriate completion, and there is the opportunity for the entire group to work together on this process.

Having come to understand something of their neurotic complementarity in terms of their own intrapsychic dilemmas (more or less, depending on time frame and readiness), individual members are now able to refocus on their marital relationship and on changes taking place in both of them. They can begin forming a new level of trust, intimacy, etc., based on recognition of the differing needs of two separate, adequate people—not the overadequate-underadequate, dominant-submissive, sadistic-masochistic stances that had previously characterized their relationships. This phase evolves naturally during an open-ended psychotherapy group, although couples differ in their timing. In the three-month and six-month time-limited groups, it is necessary for the co-therapists to stress the need to reconsider relationships in new terms once couples have begun to understand their complementarity. The co-therapists must keep the termination focus clearly in mind and bring this before the group so that feelings can be dealt with directly.

In the process of terminating, it appears useful to encourage couples to describe what they have learned about themselves and each other, what remains unfinished business, and their ambivalent feelings about their relationships with other members and co-therapists. It is also important that they be encouraged to describe the negative as well as the positive feelings about the group experience and to place it in perspective in their lives. This provides an opportunity for reworking some of the unfinished aspects of previous separation experiences, particularly those related to leaving behind parents and others in the process of growing up.

Co-therapists, too, have strong feelings about the group ending, and it is particularly at the end of a group that co-therapists should be free to be transparent in their reactions. This will help members further acknowledge their own competency and adequacy in relation to therapists with feelings and foibles of their own.

Occasionally (two out of 21 couples in our groups), as they approach termination, couples have recognized fundamental differences in their personalities or needs and have concluded that they have too little that is nonconflictual on which to continue their relationship. The group has been useful at these times in helping these couples determine and evaluate their feelings. In these situations, separation or divorce has been regarded as a positive outcome because the groups felt that the issues had been examined and that no one had acted precipitously. In one situation, the abandoned spouse was able to derive support from the group during this process.

Problems in Couples' Groups

In our work with couples, the issue of marital dissolution is of concern from the outset. To include couples where one or the other (or both) is totally committed to divorce would hamper the group's functioning. The co-therapists' stance is that our task is not to save marriages. It is to enable individuals to learn as much as possible about the complex nature of their emotional needs so they can make realistic, satisfying decisions about the course of their lives. During pregroup screening sessions, marital dissolution can be discussed as a possible outcome, but we establish that this decision should be deferred until considered in the treatment process.

Of considerable difficulty in a couples' group is the task of moving away from the concrete issues of the marital dyad. Generally in group-therapy situations, group members are less interested in the concrete problem-solving efforts of other participants. In the couples' group, the presence of the spouse reinforces this preoccupation with external events and effects a collusion to "mask deeper conflicts which remain unstated and unexamined" (Flint & MacLennan, 1962, p. 358). This is further reinforced by the fact that "there is considerable investment in maintaining the status quo in marriage" (Flint & MacLennan, 1962, p. 359) so that repetitive attempts at avoidance tend to be supported by both spouses (and the other couples as well). The desire for change is often overwhelmed by the fear of change.

One key aspect of dealing with couples seeking marital therapy is that "their motivation in beginning therapy . . . has not been . . . primarily that of recognition of and desire to overcome individual problems but of changing the spouse" (Hastings & Runkle, 1963, p. 88). This is symptomatic of the mutual-projection system and must be dealt with during pregroup screening as well as during early group sessions. It is the pivotal issue upon whose resolution any real growth or change for the couple depends. The resolution of this issue signifies completion of an important piece of the work and heralds the movement of the group into a more active working phase.

One of the dangers in a couples' group is that spouses may learn something about the feelings or motivations of the other that they use later in a hostile or retaliatory way. The group must establish at the outset the norm that individuals are not to be punished for self-revelation or acknowledgement of weakness, and attempts should be made to monitor this norm.

An example of the difficulties presented by subgrouping in couples' groups occurred in an early group. Two of the four participating couples consisted of critical and complaining wives who were constantly lambasting passive, withholding husbands. Other group members began to challenge this behavior—to question the nature of these laments and to suggest how hostile they seemed. The two couples, similar in age and ethnic background, began to socialize together rather consistently. Finally, at the wives' behest, they split off from the group without warning. Hindsight suggests that these two similar couples were threatened by the group's challenge to their marital projective systems. The women used each other to complain and ventilate their feelings and to reinforce their views of these unsatisfactory men. They were able to avoid examining their own roles and behaviors. Avoidance or flight became the solution, facilitated by the fact that their subgrouping behavior was not sufficiently recognized or challenged by other group members or the co-therapists.

On occasion, one member of a couple has felt ready to terminate from a group and the other has not. After attempting to help the couple evaluate their readiness to terminate and arrive at a mutually agreeable decision, we have resolved this dilemma by allowing the motivated spouse to continue. Sometimes this reflects the concern of one spouse who feels challenged by the group to make changes and is a sign of flight; at other times, it is a reflection of differing individual needs in regard to the process. Our solution reflects a significant principle underlying much of our work with groups: the importance of participants as individuals as well as members of a dyad.

Finally, we have not restricted our work in couples' groups to married couples. On two occasions we have had living-together couples who decided to marry during the course of their groups. For each of these, the issues around making a formal commitment were crucial, and a time-limited format with married couples proved useful. One of the couples subsequently continued work in an open-ended group.

A couples' psychotherapy group provides unique opportunities for separation/individuation work unavailable through conjoint couples work. Particularly in highly conflictual complementary relationships, the presence of other individuals is crucial to the ability of partners to acknowledge the mutual-projection system under which they operate and to recognize their own roles in their marital difficulties.

References

Alger, I. A. Multiple couple therapy. In P. J. Guerin, Jr. (Ed.), *Family therapy: Theory and practice*. New York: Gardner Press, 1976.

Berne, E. *Principles of group treatment*. New York: Oxford University Press, 1966.

Blanck, R., & Blanck, G. B. *Marriage and personal development*. New York: Columbia University Press, 1968.

Boas, C. van E. Intensive group psychotherapy with married couples. *International Journal of Group Psychotherapy*, 1962, *12*(2), 142–153.

Flint, A. A., & MacLennan, B. W. Some dynamic factors in marital group psychotherapy. *International Journal of Group Psychotherapy*, 1962, *12*(3), 335–361.

Fontane, A. S. Using family of origin material in short-term marriage counseling. *Social Casework*, 1979, *60*(9), 529–537.

Hastings, P. R., & Runkle, R. L., Jr. An experimental group of married couples with severe problems. *International Journal of Group Psychotherapy*, 1963, *13*(1), 84–92.

Kohut, H. *The analysis of the self*. New York: International Universities Press, 1971.

Leichter, E. Group psychotherapy of married couples' groups: Some characteristic treatment dynamics. *International Journal of Group Psychotherapy*, 1962, *12*(2), 154–163.

Levine, B. *Group psychotherapy: Practice and development*. Englewood Cliffs, N.J.: Prentice-Hall, 1979.

Markowitz, M. Analytic group psychotherapy of married couples by a therapist couple. In S. Rosenbaum & I. Alger (Eds.), *The Marriage relationship: Psychoanalytic perspectives*. New York: Basic Books, 1968.

Meissner, W. W. The conceptualization of marriage and family dynamics from a psychoanalytic perspective. In T. J. Paolino & B. S. McCrady (Eds.), *Marriage and marital therapy*. New York: Brunner/Mazel, 1978.

Neighbor, J. E., et al. An approach to the selection of patients for group psychotherapy. In M. Rosenbaum & M. M. Berger (Eds.), *Group psychotherapy and group function*. New York: Basic Books, 1963.

Occhetti, A. E., & Occhetti, D. R. Group therapy with married couples. *Social Casework*, 1981, *62*(2), 74–79.

Perelman, J. S. Problems encountered in group psychotherapy of married couples. *International Journal of Group Psychotherapy*, 1960, *10*(2), 136–142.

Rosenbaum, M. The co-therapeutic method in the psychoanalytic group. In H. Mullan & M. Rosenbaum (Eds.), *Group psychotherapy: Theory and practice* (2nd ed.). New York: Free Press, 1978.

Yalom, I. D. *The theory and practice of group psychotherapy.* New York: Basic Books, 1970; 2nd ed., 1975.

12

A Workshop Approach to Couples' Therapy

*Rae Dezettel Perls, Ph.D.,
and Stephen R. Perls, D.Ed.*

A clinical psychologist in private practice in Albuquerque, New Mexico, RAE DEZETTEL PERLS is also clinical associate professor in the department of psychiatry, University of New Mexico School of Medicine. STEPHEN R. PERLS is associate professor in the department of psychiatry and coordinator of group psychotherapy in the psychiatric residency program at the University of New Mexico School of Medicine.

The weekend workshop for couples experiencing marital distress is an extension and intensification of the basic couples' group experience. For several years we conducted a weekly, 1½-hour couples' group for clients already in conjoint therapy. Our experience with the weekend workshop, however, proved so much more productive that we have abandoned our regular couples' group, preferring now to hold extended weekend workshops every four to six months.

Rationale of the Workshop Approach

Advantages and Limitations of Couples' Groups

Couples' group psychotherapy can be an important adjunct to conjoint therapy. Couples gain heightened understanding of their own marital interaction patterns when they receive feedback from other married couples. The opportunity to share concerns and observe the processes and resolutions of other couples' conflicts is extraordinarily useful for couples caught up in their own concerns and conflicts.

When the therapy takes place in a group rather than in the more typical conjoint session with one psychotherapist, there is increased awareness of the couple's nonverbal as well as verbal communications. In the typical conjoint triad, the therapist learns the "language" of the couple and, over time, joins their communication system. While a case can be made for the usefulness of this connection between the couple and their therapist, this joining can also desensitize the therapist to double meanings and veiled messages. When the therapist becomes dulled to shifts in tone, eye contact, or body positioning, he or she loses effectiveness as a facilitator of change and becomes a party to the status quo. A couples' group brings the fresh eyes and ears that are so necessary for new discoveries.

Couples' groups seem to have built-in life spans. After several years of conducting couples groups on a weekly basis, more and more often closed and time-limited, we realized that the most powerful new awarenesses were derived from the initial reactions to encountering other couples. Early sessions seemed to be filled with discoveries, excited sharing, and a very high level of interest not only in one's partner but in other couples. As the months passed, however, the couples all too frequently interacted in patterned ways that supported the status quo in the individual marriages. While there certainly continued to be opportunities to see one's own position reflected in the processes of other couples in the group, there also appeared to be a growing comfort with and acceptance of what was experienced.

Development of the Workshop Approach

Out of a desire to provide a more powerful intervention, we began experimenting with a short weekend format for couples already being seen in conjoint therapy. Marital therapy, by definition, is short-term. The clients' message is: "We've felt badly together long enough. This has to feel better or we'll split. We'll tolerate the discomfort just so long." Some couples endure the pain a long time, but they won't continue to experience that pain plus the pain of spending money on it for very long! The wear and tear on the therapist is also costly, so all parties to the therapy are generally eager for methods that produce results more quickly. Our short weekend format proved so productive that we expanded it to a full two days and eventually dropped our once-a-week couples' group in favor of conducting weekend workshops several times a year.

The one or two days of uninterrupted focus allows the co-therapists to introduce exercises in self-awareness, compromising, risking, and sharing that require more time than the usual 1½ hours. In the workshop, it is more difficult for an individual to hide and wait. The atmosphere encourages and supports the experiencing and sharing of feelings, allowing the couples greater self-disclosure and more intensive interpersonal confrontation. The extended time affords opportunities to create safety and support as well as data (feelings, thoughts, ideas) that the couples can work through in future conjoint sessions.

Using an existential approach, we structure exercises in which all couples participate. We also focus on "here and now" issues between couples as well as between individual group members. There is time for confrontation, negotiation, and resolution in this type of extended communication experience.

Organizing the Workshop

Selection of Couples

Couples are screened for the weekend workshop by either of the co-therapists. Unless we are doing a training workshop for professionals, these couples will have had some conjoint therapy experience prior to the workshop. In general, we select couples whose marriages are not in crisis. That is, we want to be clear with ourselves and with the couple that their marriage is "on." Therefore, all the couples will have had a number of conjoint couple-therapy sessions with one of the co-therapists or with a referring therapist known to us. They will have had opportunities to share histories, clarify issues, and define some behavioral goals. They will already have learned the language of ownership and given up, to some extent, the habit of speaking for the other and reporting from a "we" position. They are willing and ready to further explore I-Thou boundaries.

The weekend experience is much more productive when we know that all the couples are working at their marriages in a serious and committed way and that we are not dealing with an unusual or intense focus on making or breaking a marriage on this particular weekend. We prefer the focus to be on new discoveries, clearer communication, and positive enhancing opportunities between the couples. So we make our best efforts to choose couples whose energies are already directed toward healing and growth and away from basic crisis resolution. We prefer a minimum of three couples and we generally work with a maximum of six.

It must be remembered that short-term therapy with couples can really focus only on the relationship or marital unit. If either member of the couple has intense personal problems, he or she is not a good candidate for short-term couples' therapy. Thus we assume—on the basis of previous therapeutic encounters, initial interview, or referral source—that the individuals selected for the workshop are reasonably intact and able to focus on their relationships and the external environment.

The Co-Therapist Team

On the basis of our experiences as co-therapists with other opposite-sex partners, as well as our work together co-leading couples' groups, we are convinced of the value of a male-female co-therapy team in marital psychotherapy groups. A co-therapy team does not, of course, automatically lead to more effective treatment. It is essential for the co-therapists to engage in "authentic mutualism." This does not mean that the co-therapists work on their unresolved status needs and sibling rivalries in the group, but it does acknowledge that some of these issues might exist between them and that co-therapists must not "play games" with each other while in the therapeutic encounter. We also have become aware of the added positive dynamics of bringing to the psychotherapy experience with couples our own real-life coupledom. Our clients appear to enjoy and benefit from the opportunity to interface with co-therapists who are indeed co-leaders, equals, and full partners.

The opportunity for client modeling is obvious. While our own personal marital issues are never agenda items for the group, we continue to give each other permission to draw on our experiences as a couple just as we would use ourselves if the focus was individual. The way in which we interact, cooperate, communicate, and resolve issues in the group as partners certainly is observed and commented upon by the participant group members. The fact of our own long-term, ongoing partnership communicates our respect for and commitment to the goals of the marriage contract.

Schedule, Setting, and Fees

The workshop is held in the office group room of one of the co-therapists. Typically, we begin our weekend schedule at 9 A.M. on Saturday and work together through a sack lunch and a casual dinner hour until 9 or 10 in the evening. We reconvene at 9 or 10 on Sunday morning, once again going through the lunch hour together and adjourning between 3 and 5 on Sunday afternoon. This format provides as much as 18 hours of group work time.

A modified schedule has us begin at 10 A.M. on Saturday and work until 4 that afternoon, reconvening again at 10 A.M. on Sunday and going until 4 P.M. with a short break for lunch together. For training purposes, we have used a six-hour day effectively.

Physical arrangements that are comfortable and airy are particularly important when working for such an extended period of time. Chairs that are not too hard but give support are most useful. Pillows are used by many group therapists, but there must be enough of them to give the cushioning and support needed for many continuous hours of use. Ample opportunities to get up and move about and take short breaks seem necessary. In any extended therapy experience, it is useful to have available a variety of beverages and snacks so participants can replenish themselves after particularly difficult interpersonal situations. Eating together adds to the sense of cohesiveness and focus.

We are very aware that the economics of a weekend group experience can be troublesome. Since two therapists are involved over an extended period of time, it is obvious that the fee structure could present problems for some of our clients. We base our fee on what we feel is a reasonable rate per therapist and divide that by the number of couples involved. A two-day extended couples' session may cost $350 per couple, while a one-day, six-hour session may cost $125. In a clinic setting there can be more flexibility regarding these fees than there is for those of us in private practice.

Group Process in the Workshop

In general in our weekend workshops we experience the basic three phases usually observed in psychotherapy groups. In the first phase there is an interest in discovering, making connections to assure inclusion, and general goal setting. "Business" arrangements allow for a superficial "checking out" of each other. The second or middle part of the experience is characterized by focus and therapeutic work. This occupies the largest part of our time together. The third and final phase is concerned with resolution and closure.

The First Phase

Typically, we begin the workshop with introductions and a review of the ground rules. The ground rules are simple. First, all that goes on is confidential. That means no discussing this experience in public places or with people not in the group. Second, each one of us is responsible for himself or herself during our time together; each participant speaks for himself or herself only, not for the partner or for the world in general. Last, we review the time schedule, making it clear that all are expected to participate full-time. Smoking, meal breaks, and other issues related to procedures are negotiated. The expectations of the therapists and members are shared. This initial arranging of ourselves is the beginning of the group. From the time we say "Hello" the group has begun.

Our preference is for one or two structured exercises before we inquire about issues the members want to work with. We want to create the opportunity early in the process for members to meet each other within defined boundaries but not as "presenting problems." We also want the couples to see immediately that they will be interacting with each other in ways not typical for them. Therefore, we may do some guided fantasy work, pair drawings, or introductory exercises, or we may set up a couple task.

A typical introductory activity is for participants to describe themselves at that moment using three adjectives—for example, "I am sensitive, apprehensive, and excited" or "I am scared, anxious, and cold." This gives the couples and the co-therapists a quick sense of each person without focusing on problems or conflict. Another introductory exercise that is not particularly threatening and is sometimes humorous is the "If I were a . . ." game. The therapist suggests a category such as type of soup, famous person, place, flower, etc. Each person responds with a specific example. Typical responses for soup are "beef barley" or "cream of tomato"; for place, "the mountains," "San Francisco," or "a deserted island"; for flower, "daisy," "rose," and the occasional off-beat "cactus flower."

Nonverbal drawing exercises encourage communication experimentation. Drawings may be made by couples as well as individuals, and group members interpret their own drawings. The feedback between couples relating to their drawings, and the observations of the process made by other group members, quickly reveal the power concerns at issue between a couple.

As the couples begin to spontaneously question and react to one another, we structure less and facilitate with more probing inquiries. We offer support and reassurance when someone is afraid. When the group can be therapeutic without our intervention, we back off from leading to participating or simply observing. The eating breaks provide some time to be quiet and reflect as well as opportunities for all of us to get to know each other's "social face."

The Middle Phase

As we move away from early structuring and group cohering toward sharper focus on particular couple issues, we are aware that we have left the first phase of our time together. This shift into the middle or "work" phase is often heralded by one couple pressing to clarify and personalize their time together in the group. Typically, one of the partners will "tell on" the other: "She always runs out when I confront her with my displeasure," or "He never *says* anything at home; that's why we're here—to get *him* to talk." This point also brings demonstrations of couple protectiveness: "We're really doing fine; we just came to have a new experience together," or "We're here because Rae told us to come!" or "I really love George, he's just overworked." Someone is sure to complain that "so far what we're doing is too superficial." When this occurs, the individual is ready to "encounter." In this middle phase, hostilities and heightened levels of emotional reaction are generated and responded to in more confrontational ways.

We expect that some genuine therapeutic work on an important issue will be done by almost every couple during the weekend. Couples let us know when they are ready for that focus. They tend to bring up such concerns as disagreements about child raising, dissatisfaction with their sex lives, fears and jealousies related to people outside their partnership, and problems of money management.

The partners may speak psychologically different languages and need assistance in interpreting each other. It's not unusual to hear a husband say to his wife, "You won't initiate anything." She says, "What do you mean?" and he replies, "You see, you just won't *say* anything," to which she responds, "I don't know what you want me to talk about." Another example: A man says, "I don't know what your feelings really are about that argument the other night." His wife responds, "I told you at the time I didn't understand why you were so upset about leaving the party early." He says, "And I still have no idea how you felt when I shook you!" She replies, "None of it made any sense."

Often we see couples who do not communicate in the same mode—for example, one member may verbalize while the other uses touching or actions. It is not uncommon to find the male partner unable to understand what his spouse is talking about when she says that he is insensitive to her needs. He does not tell her what he is experiencing when he is with her, and this lack of verbalizing on his part is taken by her to indicate that he is uncaring or unsharing. He, on the other hand, feels that he lets her know what he wants and needs by touch and other nonverbal signals and does not see the necessity to "talk."

The task of the co-therapists, with the aid of other group members, is to help such a couple to clarify confusions and expectations and then to experience each other in a different way. One device is to have the couple exaggerate in the group what they usually do at home and thereby to become more fully aware of what they do with each other and how it is received by the other. The emotional and cognitive data obtained in this way can be examined by other group members for similarities in their own lives.

Closure

There are several cues, aside from the clock, that we are entering the final phase of the workshop. Some couples who have a sense of personal completion will begin to ask theoretical questions, seeking more didactic information. There will be observations about the group process. Withdrawn participants will be confronted by more involved members and urged to share more. Individuals will spontaneously give feedback to participants other than the spouse concerning "hidden agenda" and wishes regarding that person's behavior. Thus a husband will share with another man's wife his initial reaction, hope, or fantasy about her. He wants some connection and now it's safer to acknowledge this and accept whatever her reality of him is at present. A wife will project her hostility toward her husband onto some other man in the group with a "wish" like "I wish you would listen more carefully to your wife" that really expresses what she wants from her own spouse.

Toward the end of the session we ask everyone to draw themselves with colored markers and give the drawings to their partners. Each partner is asked if he or she can accept the self-portrait of the spouse. We use this method to confront issues of acceptance, criticism, judgment, wishes for change, etc. In a recent workshop one of the husbands drew a side view of himself that he thought was rather good. When he shared this with his wife, she expressed disappointment that he had not portrayed himself strongly enough. She felt that he negated his true strength and utilized only part of his skills and abilities. We asked the wife if she could accept his drawing of himself or wanted to change it to reflect the way she saw him. In the discussion that followed, the husband explored his feelings of self-worth and the wife her need to control and manipulate her husband rather than accept him as he saw himself.

As a final task, we ask for feedback around the circle regarding how participants experienced their time together. We want to know what had meaning or surprise for them. We encourage sharing of appreciations with each other. We usually feel pleased with our own efforts as co-therapists as we work through intimacy and withdrawal issues for them as well as for ourselves. We know that we have put out a lot of energy in a short time. We have never yet regretted the time and effort spent.

Issues and Problems

Comparison with Other Groups

There are some similarities between the workshop format and more traditional couples' group approaches. Like other groups, our workshop explores expectations, assesses difficulties that couples have with each other, and assists couples in setting goals for the time that the group is together. A major difference from other groups is the more active role of the therapists in structuring the workshop's activities so that the participants can develop a sense of cohesion rapidly, learn to think of self separate from—yet affiliated with—spouse, and perceive options in confronting or avoiding each other.

Little, if anything, has been written on the use of arts and crafts materials in couples' therapy. We have developed a variety of tasks that require drawings to be done by individuals, couples, and the group as a whole. Modeling clay is used to explore proximity needs and fears through the building of model living quarters. Games and other structured activities are employed. By opening couples up to a variety of responses, we encourage them to be more playful with each other and not to focus exclusively on the "problem" aspects of their relationship.

Dropouts are a problem for most therapy groups. In the workshop experience, the dropout rate is virtually nil. Most couples see the commitment to the weekend as a commitment to the partnership. Those who "change their minds" give notice ahead of time.

Role Stereotyping

Many of the couples who participate in the workshop appear to have limited views of the role and function of a spouse in the marital relationship. Through one of the structured tasks on role stereotyping, participants are able to obtain a much clearer idea of their own and their spouses' attitudes, expectations, and prejudices toward typical roles that men and women play. The information derived from this task can lead to closer identification with other participants and reinforcement of constructive approaches.

It becomes clear to all participants during the role-stereotyping activity that a great deal of support is available from members of one's own sex. It is only when an individual is unreasonably out of step with societal expectations of sex-role behavior that support may not be available. In such cases, further exploration can assist the person to understand how having this particular bias might create some difficulties in the marriage.

Over the years, we have found that there are few behaviors/attitudes that group members consider uniquely "male" or "female" and that most behavior depends on situational learning. For example, in the past, role stereotyping suggested that most women are "catty," "overly emotional," and "soft" and that men are "withholding," "distant," and "aggressive." Lately, group members have been saying that "it depends" or that "nothing is true for all men or all women." This indicates that we can't make assumptions about how our mates are feeling or how they will behave based on general societal expectations. This awareness places more pressure on individuals to attend to each other and can ultimately lead to closer feelings with increased understanding of the unique qualities that each person brings to the partnership.

Sexual Issues

Can sexual issues be brought up when the group has been in existence only a relatively short time and when trust for each other has barely developed? The answer will vary from group to group. Some couples feel comfortable discussing their sexual concerns and quickly establish the norm that it is okay to talk about intimacy, orgasms, affairs, etc. We do not insist that sexual issues be discussed during the workshop when participants do not bring up the topic on their own. We assume that it is the prerogative of the clients to raise issues as they are ready to deal with them, and we will work with them at their pace.

Conclusion

Our couples' workshops have been successful in a number of ways. When couples experience each other in new and creative ways, it is difficult if not impossible to continue seeing each other in the same light.

When a couple see each other for several hours in a variety of circumstances that are different from the usual ways in which they encounter each other, they have a choice of responding in two basic ways. First, they can respond in their traditional mode, which becomes obvious in a short time because it appears not useful in the new situation. Therefore, the couple is asked to look at what it does for them to continue their traditional and apparently inadequate responses. Second, they can respond in different and creative ways, which then allows them to see that the other is capable of seeing and experiencing alternative approaches, responses, and feelings.

This does not necessarily mean that couples will easily alter their system. It does mean that they can see that there are options available. If they don't choose alternative methods of dealing with each other, they then become aware that it is their mutual choice not to change, and it is more difficult to blame the other or the institution of marriage for their current frustrated condition. At the very least, the weekend group gives them a new shared experience to draw on in their continuing conjoint therapy.

V

WORKING WITH THE AGED

13

A "Staying Well" Group at a Senior-Citizen Center

Esther Siegel, R.N., M.S., and Anna Leifer, Ph.D.

ESTHER SIEGEL is consultant to Dept. of Nursing at New York University Medical Center and a psychotherapist in private practice. ANNA LEIFER, a practicing psychoanalyst, is a psychotherapy supervisor at the Institute for Advanced Psychological Studies at Adelphi University.

The striking growth of the aged segment of our society—both in absolute numbers and as a percentage of the total population—has called attention to our lack of basic knowledge regarding the physiological and psychological processes of aging. There has been little investigation into the enduring effects of time on the functions of living organisms. Still less is known regarding the impact of time on the character, personality structure, defensive system, coping style, etc., of the individual. Researchers have generally been less than eager to plumb the vagaries of old age, traditionally subsuming persons in the later phases of life under the rubrics "65 and older," "the aged," and "senior citizens," as if those who have grown old have, in the process, lost their individuality.

We wish to thank Barbara Reiss, M.S.W., director of the Senior Center in Great Neck, New York; Elaine Goldman-Jacks, R.N., M.S., director of the Center on Aging, Adelphi University; and most of all the group members themselves who allowed it to happen.

229

This avoidance of the phenomenon of aging on the part of the scientific establishment is shared to a large extent by psychotherapists and related mental health counselors. It is often difficult to find a therapist willing to accept an older person for treatment based on insightful integration. Wilensky and Barmack (1966) reported that the bulk of social work and psychology graduates entering the helping professions were reluctant to work with senior citizens. These students reflected a universal value system that automatically imbues the young with such qualities as flexibility, conscientiousness, and hopefulness, while the old are equally unrealistically endowed with qualities of rigidity, closed-mindedness, and pessimism. Those preferring to work with the young believe that all that is new, novel, and fresh is also pliable and self-motivated. They cling to the notion that only a young client can achieve positive therapeutic results and thereby reinforce the therapist's sense of effectiveness. In other words, they assume that the older individual is unable to provide the interpersonal validation they need in their work.

With limited interest in the elderly from virtually every quarter, health care practitioners have been hard pressed to implement strategies based on sound theoretical speculation. Weiner et al. (1978) note how few procedures in working with the aged have been adequately replicated to provide satisfactory validity coefficients. Nevertheless, a handful of enterprising clinicians have attempted to forge a theoretical base leading to a set of replicable procedures. Among them, Ebersole (1980) and Butler and Lewis (1973) have designed life-review and reminiscing techniques in group psychotherapy for the institutionalized aged. Remnet (1975) has developed programs to alleviate the loneliness and anxiety of newly admitted patients in nursing homes. Goldman and Woog (1975) reported the results of an interdisciplinary, continuing-education curriculum designed to create a therapeutic environment for both patients and staff in a long-term residential setting.

Weiner and her colleagues (1978) have put together the first comprehensive handbook giving a variety of approaches for the delivery of mental health services to the elderly. They offer step-by-step guidelines for instituting group-based activities designed to foster reality orientation, remotivation, sensory and memory training, self- and environment awareness, etc. Their book also provides an excellent review of the literature, giving gerontological findings from a variety of disciplines as well as philosophical viewpoints underlying group-counseling approaches.

The Preventive Health Care Needs of the "Young Old"

All these reports, however, are concerned with alleviating the plight of the elderly in hospital or health care settings. The investigators have been interested primarily in the rehabilitation of the nonfunctioning or regressed patient or with the restoration of self-help skills in the frail elderly. Their main focus has been on reconstruction or repair of prior faculties and capabilities.

But the vast majority of the aged in this country do not live in institutions. Ninety-five percent of the 22 million elderly are well, active, and reasonably self-sufficient. They live in their own communities, where they have roots in family, friends, and neighborhoods and where they enjoy recreational and sometimes occupational outlets. While their needs, problems, and strengths vary, they comprise a substantially healthy and fairly mobile conglomerate. These have been called the "young old" and they are expected, as a group, to become more educated and to look for more meaningful uses for their additional years. Those who work with the elderly will be dealing increasingly with this sort of individual.

Within this group of elderly there are the so-called "passive aged," comprising approximately 5 percent of those living in communities, who are in poorer health and are less ambulatory but are capable and desirous of living on their own. The passive aged are more intact and function better than the institutionalized aged, but they become increasingly dependent, with time, on supportive social and rehabilitative services close to home.

Despite the overwhelming numbers of senior citizens living in communities, there are virtually no reports in the literature of any systematic approaches to help the active young old remain in good mental and physical health, or to assist the passive aged to maintain their ability to function outside a residential health care facility. This lack of interest in a primary prevention model is especially significant in view of the susceptibility of this age group to both mental and physical illness.

Old age brings accelerating changes in the body's biological processes and general declines in physical endurance and psychosocial functioning. There are decreases in visual, tactile, and hearing acuity as well as changes in physical appearance. The older person confronts graying hair, loss of teeth, wrinkles, and a loosening of skin and muscle tone. Not only are there bodily changes from within that call for reintegration into the self-concept, there are also changes from without, which are sometimes sudden and traumatic.

The senior citizen is particularly vulnerable to stress related to his particular stage in life when events like the death of a spouse, loss of a job, retirement, death of a close family member, change in financial status, change of residence, and so on, are highly likely. On the Holmes and Rahe Social Readjustment Scale (1967), which predicts the possibility of illness based on the amount of pressure coming from such external events, any older individual can readily score in the danger zone. Holmes and Rahe demonstrated that disease often follows a succession of traumatic changes within a given period of time.

Hans Selye (1976) first called attention to the physiological processes by which responses to stress create susceptibility to disease. Chronic stress—the kind that is not released but retained by the body—results in damage to the body's immune system. The activity of coping, of trying to absorb the shock of a devastating event, lowers resistance to disease. During and shortly after these periods of heightened stress the person is more likely to develop not only the diseases commonly associated with stress such as ulcers, high blood pressure, and heart disease but also infectious diseases, backaches, and even accident proneness.

Simonton and his associates (1978), who are oncology specialists interested in the link between stress and cancer, have demonstrated a relationship between the way certain individuals handle stress and the incidence and recurrence of cancer. They argue that emotional stress, mediated by the limbic system via the hypothalmus, suppresses the immune system, leaving the body vulnerable to cancer and other diseases. Simonton's groups developed an extended treatment program for advanced cancer patients using techniques for learning a positive attitude, relaxation, visualization, goal setting, managing pain, exercising, and building an emotional support system which has brought about substantial remissions in various forms of cancer.

Cousins (1979) described his own experience with serious illness and the ways he participated in his rehabilitation. He feels that not only is there a direct connection between despair and malignancies, there is an equally direct connection between such positive emotions as love, laughter, joy, and pleasure and getting and staying well.

The value of meditation for relieving tension has been well documented. LeShan (1974), like Selye, Simonton, and Cousins, believes strongly in the mind-body relationship and in the importance of regular periods of deep meditation to enable the individual to summon his or her inner resources to counter life's blows. Meditation, when practiced regularly and conscientiously, produces a physiological state of deep relaxation coupled with an increase in alertness. Tension indicators are reduced and the metabolic rate and heartbeat slow down. This physiological state appears to be the opposite of the state brought about by stress.

Starting the "Staying Well" Project

Subscribing to the relationship between stress and illness, and understanding the particular susceptibility of senior citizens to stress because of their stage in life, we wanted to implement group procedures for identifying and reducing stress with a reasonably well elderly population. Our goal was to develop and test the effectiveness of a series of exercises designed to decrease the incidence of mental and physical illness or, put another way, to increase the feeling of well-being. The exercises, which will be described below, employ imagery and visualization tasks, both of which have been described in the literature as difficult for older persons (Arenberg & Robertson-Tchabo, 1977, p. 430). Our hypothesis was that, if properly adapted within the context of a supportive group structure, the techniques could be effective.

We first contacted the head of a local university-based Center on Aging and asked her to help us get a sample population. This contact activated a series of meetings between the project leaders, the director of the Center on Aging, a university representative, and personnel at a suburban Long Island senior citizen center. The purpose of these meetings was to work out such details as mode of presentation, time, duration, goals, and philosophy of the group as conceived by the leaders. These preliminary meetings were extremely valuable in bringing about a consensus on a number of matters so that senior-center personnel were able to convey to their members confidence and optimism about our project. We also needed to enlist their cooperation in publicizing our venture and in deciding such issues as how we would limit the size of the group and the best time of day for its meetings. We both felt strongly about the value of giving adequate time to this early planning stage if we were to forge a working relationship with center personnel respecting their roles and competencies and defining ours.

Our project was welcomed by senior citizen center personnel, especially the director, who recognized the need for this type of intervention model. They were, however, skeptical about the possibility of substantial outcomes in a cohesive, sustained group. They felt that the main obstacle to regular weekly attendance at our group meetings was that senior citizens came to the center for recreation, not for therapy. They reported that all previous group leaders had been unable to enlist their members in any ongoing, cohesive, goal-directed experience.

In addition to the usual functional arrangements required when establishing a new group—for example, the time, place, and duration of meetings and the number of participants—two less-common issues required resolution. The group needed a name and a method of attracting members. Since what was being offered would represent an unknown quantity to prospective members, the name, it was felt, should convey in an honest way the group's purpose and direction without overtly labeling it a therapy group. The leaders recognized the reality of the age-cohort effect related to a general nonacceptance of psychotherapy modalities. The concern expressed by center personnel regarding failures of past attempts was therefore not dismissed. "Staying Well" emerged as a name both descriptive and sufficiently neutral.

The second issue, that of attracting members, would best be accomplished by an open membership solicitation. Of equal importance to the presentation of the idea of the group would be the presentation of ourselves. A positive "acceptance-recognition" (Linden, 1977, p. 146) toward us as prospective leaders had to be established at the outset.

Announcing the Group

Effective advance publicity filled the small auditorium of the senior center with approximately 200 members. Center records indicate a daily attendance between 20 and 200 depending on the offering. This is a well-elderly population with ages ranging from 60 to 90. Means of transportation to the center included: self-transport—automobile; self-transport—foot; family-member transport; and public conveyance.

Contrary to recommendations made to us in the planning meetings, we risked introducing ourselves as psychotherapists since our primary goal at the outset was to establish authenticity. Our introductory remarks described the group as a vehicle to promote feeling well by learning techniques of stress and tension reduction. The group would meet for ten sessions of 1½ hours. Mostly we just talked with the audience in an informal way. During the question-and-answer period, it became apparent that there did not exist a clear frame of reference for what we were offering; past experiences were of discussion, activity, and socialization groups rather than self-exploration. We unequivocally represented the self-exploratory aspect as the process by which participants could effectively learn to reduce stress. As Zarit (1980) points out, groups should not be billed as being for discussion of objective topics when their real aim is to provide psychotherapy. This, Zarit notes, frequently happens at senior centers, which, in addition to being dishonest, is seldom productive for the leaders or the members.

Some of the questions and comments did, in fact, express the concern that it not be a "Bob Newhart kind of group" (referring to a then-popular TV series humorously depicting group therapy). Several comments reflected the stigma associated with psychological help as indicative of being "crazy" or too weak to solve one's own problems. The literature anticipated this reaction (Eisdorfer & Stotsky, 1977). Ultimately, more than 20 people committed themselves to attend the first group meeting the following week. They reserved the option to leave the group if it did not meet their expectations.

The First Group Meeting

Since this was neither essentially a psychotherapy group nor a group for which models were available, we recognized the need to view it heuristically. This meant adapting traditional models to accommodate this specific population.

An early example of the heuristic aspect was the inclusion in the group of two young women, CETA workers at the center, in addition to the two leaders. The center's director requested that they be included as trainees with the hope that they would be able to conduct similar groups, thus providing continuity if the project proved successful. Their inclusion contributed an intergenerational mix that had proved beneficial to groups in institutional settings (Butler & Lewis, 1973). However, the goal of training them for future leadership roles was not realized. It became apparent that leaders of a group of this sort need to be emotionally and professionally mature, with a knowledge of both individual and group psychodynamics. Our trainees soon recognized that they would not be able to assume leadership roles, but they chose to remain in the group for the learning experience. Thus the group comprised three cohorts: aged members, middle-aged leaders, and young-adult trainees.

Unlike more traditional methods for selecting participants (Yalom, 1975), the 23 aged members at this first session were self-selected, each arriving with different expectations and apprehensions. The chosen time seemed to conflict with mid-morning coffee and/or lunch. During the first meeting, the preoccupation with passing coffee and cake from one to the other served as a comfortable distraction to some but was detrimental to group development. The first norm-setting action, therefore, was to give participants responsibility for handling the obvious diversion. The consensus decision was to limit refreshments in future sessions to an already-prepared container of coffee. This represented an important first step in the assumption of an active role by the participants in their own behalf.

Following brief introductions and the decision to use first names, the General Well-Being (GWB) Schedule, a test published by the U.S. Department of Health, Education, and Welfare, was distributed. This is a self-report instrument designed to assess selected aspects of self-representation of subjective well-being and distress. Age-related factors in test-taking (Botwinick, 1977, p. 582), which tend to be disadvantageous to the elderly, were taken into account in the explanation of the items in the test and the fixing of the time allowed for its completion.

The test was followed by a getting-acquainted exercise. Although the members had known one another for long periods of time and had participated in a variety of activities together at the center, we discovered that they knew little about each other. As leaders, we acted as "model-setting participants" (Yalom, 1975, p. 112), initiating responses to the questions presented: (1) Where did you grow up? (2) Who did you relate to at home? (3) Describe the members of your family. These categories are particularly well suited to the older population. Participants related vignettes of other times and other places, wonderful little stories of family members no longer alive but well remembered. The elaboration of memories suffused the room with a warm glow.

The meeting ended on a positive note with comments overheard on leaving that reflected the excitement of interpersonal discovery—the discovery of similarities as well as differences.

Group Members

Mildly concerned about the large size of the group at the first meeting, we expected that some would drop out. We were not, however, prepared for the drop-off rate revealed the following week. Of the 23 seniors at the first meeting, only 10 returned. Possible reason for the almost 60 percent reduction in size are (1) cohort discomfort with sharing experiences within a group context, an issue alluded to earlier; (2) concern with commitment based on realistic issues of health and transportation; (3) depressive symptoms: the GWB scale indicated moderate to severe levels of depression for several who did not return; (4) low self-esteem manifested by some in the first meeting as having "nothing of interest" to tell others; (5) preference for other activities scheduled concurrently with the Staying Well meetings.

The 10 seniors who did return became committed group members. Seven were female, three male; seven were Jewish, three Catholic; two were married, seven were widowed, one was single; four had not finished high school, five had finished high school, and one had attended college. Brief profiles of the members follow.

Evelyn J., 62, a widow. An attractive, well-groomed woman, she appeared younger than her stated age. She lived alone but within 30 miles of her married children. She expressed a yearning to change her life but felt it was "too late for that." Evelyn missed one session.

Gloria M., 65, single. Living alone for Gloria was a "treat" for reasons that will be described below. She had limited family connections. The center, within walking distance of her apartment, served as a source of connectedness for her. In the supportive group atmosphere, Gloria's initial shyness diminished to reveal a dimension to her personality that surprised group members who had known her through center activities. Gloria attended all sessions.

Lucille J., 70, a widow. She lived alone, had limited family connections, and maintained a low profile in the group. Nevertheless, she attended all sessions and expressed genuine regret at the group's termination.

Sally L., 80, a widow. She lived with a son and his family. In both appearance and manner, she seemed considerably younger than her stated age. Her philosophy was to "look for the silver lining." Sally missed three sessions.

Jennie G., 78, a widow. Jennie lived with a daughter and her family. Her expression was generally sad except when talking about her grandchildren, with whom she seemed particularly close. During the course of the group her son died. Jennie missed two sessions but was glad to return.

Rebecca S., 74, a widow. She lived alone but near two married children. Her wish to find another man was openly expressed, and she often focused her attention on the widower in the group. Rebecca missed two sessions.

Gertie R., 68, a widow. She lived alone but within 20 miles of her family. She described herself as having "a lot of good years left" and seemed actively engaged in living them. Gertie attended all sessions.

Milton G., 75, a widower. Milton, who lived with a son and his family, is described in more detail below. He attended all sessions.

Sidney L., 73, married (for the second time). Sidney lived in the community, and both he and his wife came to the center. More detail is provided below about Sidney.

Jack R., 64, married. Jack had recently retired and wanted "to relax more," but he admitted feeling "at loose ends." He left for Florida two weeks before the group's end.

The Structured Exercises

At the second group meeting, after a brief relaxation exercise, we introduced the first of four exercises adapted from the literature of mind-body unity (LeShan, 1974; Pelletier, 1977; Simonton et al., 1978). The exercises provided focus, structure, and an organizing motif for the group experience. Each exercise was framed to elicit connection with an inner core of strength by a return to the past in the service of taking action on one's behalf in the present. Their design in succession was geared toward establishing a locus of control within the individual, that sense of control that has been described as an especially important component of self-image from a life-span perspective (Lowenthal, 1977; p. 119). Lastly, although formulated in an experiential mode, the educational component could serve to accomplish what Maslow (1959) called the malady of deficient knowledge—of literally not knowing what is good for oneself.

Exercise 1: Fantasy Trip to Inner Guide

The leader directs the group in the following words:

1. With eyes closed, imagine yourself traveling along a path, real or imagined. Travel the path slowly and take time to notice everything along the way. Notice the colors, smells, and sounds around you. As you travel along the path, try to imagine coming to a place—a safe, comfortable, accepting place, real or imagined, a place where you feel at home.
2. Upon arriving there, look around you. Make note of what you see, hear, smell. Is it a familiar place or one that you imagine you would like to visit? In this place, try to find a guide—someone you either know or perhaps knew at another time in your life or someone you imagine you would like to have as your guide.
3. Now talk to your guide. Ask him or her a question of importance to yourself. If your guide is an angry, impatient one, ask him to be more patient and accepting of you.
4. Remain so for several minutes.
5. Now look around you once more—at the guide, at the place so you can remember it, for you will be returning there again.

6. Come back to the room and open your eyes.

Discussion. After the exercise, the experience is processed. Each member is given whatever time is needed for elaboration, frame-setting, in-depth description. The leader should be prepared to offer assistance to individuals for whom imagery and visualization present problems. The older person tends to have more difficulty with this kind of exercise (Arenberg & Robertson-Tchabo, 1977), and adaptation is necessary. It is important for the individual member as well as for the group that each person find "a safe place"; the "finding," however, must be accomplished in a way that does not diminish self-esteem. An example is provided below (p. 243).

Exercise 2: Best Decision

Before proceeding, the leader first sets individual scenes established by each member at the previous session. Doing this is both practical and salutary; the details that are so important to the exercise might be abridged by the participant out of fear of being self-indulgent. Having them related by another provides the pleasure of indulgence without guilt.

1. With eyes closed, return to the safe place.
2. From the vantage point of feeling safe, return to a particular good time in the past. Try to remember the happy quality of that episode—the people who shared it with you, everything that made it a happy time for you. Stay in that time. Focus on the different aspects of the memory, on as many details as you can remember.
3. Now try to remember a decision you made at that time, bearing in mind that this was the *best decision possible* at the time.
4. Stay with the memory for five minutes.
5. Return to the present and open your eyes.

Discussion. Following this exercise, each participant describes his or her experience. Processing needs to tease out real or symbolic aspects of the "best" decision. An example of this is presented below (p. 243).

Exercise 3: Pleasurable Activity

The goal of this exercise is to tie the threads of the preceding two into an activity in the present that will afford pleasure. The focus is on the need to find resources within oneself.

1. With eyes closed, return again to the safe place.
2. Again, return to that happy time when you made the best decision

possible. Let your thoughts wander around in that time and in that decision.

3. Now identify an activity you really loved then but have perhaps stopped doing over the years. Try to imagine whether you might still be able to do that activity, perhaps in another form. Or maybe there was an activity that you never allowed yourself but can do now.

4. Stay with the thoughts for five minutes.

5. Return to the present.

Discussion. Each member is encouraged to explore at least one activity that would be pleasurable to do during the course of the day or week. Important to this exercise is the leader's guidance, persistence, and educative explanations preceding the exercise regarding control over oneself in terms of inner resources. An example is presented below (p. 243).

Exercise 4: Relaxation and Meditation

This exercise was adapted from LeShan (1974).

1. Place yourself in a comfortable position: you can sit, lie on the floor, or stand if you feel more relaxed that way. Loosen any tight clothes, open your shirtsleeves, and take off your tie; remove your shoes if you like.

2. In this comfortable position, start the relaxation exercise together. Count silently each time you breathe out. Count "one" for the first breath, "two" for the second, "three" for the third, and "four" for the fourth. When you get to "four," start with "one" again. The goal is to practice doing one simple thing and to do nothing more. If other thoughts come into your head (and they will), simply accept the fact that you are straying from the task and bring yourself gently and firmly back to the counting. No matter what other thoughts, feelings, perceptions come into your head during the relaxation period, your task is simply to keep counting your breaths, so keep trying to do that and only that.

3. Do not expect to succeed for more than a couple of seconds at a time in being aware only of your counting. You can try it for increasingly longer periods at home. Our goal will be to build the at-home relaxation period to one hour a day. You may want to break this up into three periods of twenty minutes each.

4. You may try different time frames until you find one that suits your individual needs. Once you decide on the best time frame for you, set a timer or place a clock where you can see it without moving your head. Muffle the timer with a pillow or place it in a drawer so the ticking does not distract you.

Discussion. This exercise is not elaborated further in this article. It was presented during the seventh session and proved to be very difficult for the participants, both conceptually and in practice. While some managed, in rudimentary form, to work with it during the group meetings, others found it frustrating. Although we feel the exercise has merit, it might be used to better advantage in a group of longer duration where more time exists for practice.

The Group as an Entity

Group Focus

The content and process of each session were focused consistently toward the interplay between the material emerging from the structured exercises and the curative interpersonal factors inherent in positive group experiences. Shifts in focus occurred only insofar as necessary for group-building or maintenance tasks.

Sustaining the focus on staying well was particularly significant in this group for two reasons: (1) departure from the promised course would have been experienced by members as a form of trickery, to which the response would have been flight, either real or symbolic; and (2) it assisted in rapid development of group culture and norms that in turn aided cohesiveness.

Culture and Norms

The development of a group culture with behavioral norms required careful orchestration. Because of members' natural reluctance toward self-exposure, a climate of safety was imperative, coupled with confidence that the leaders would maintain and preserve this safe environment. Therapeutic group norms outlined by Yalom demanded considerable tailoring to the needs and purposes of this group.

Self-monitoring. The orientation of psychotherapy groups is toward promoting interaction in the here and now for a variety of reasons, one being as a means for understanding the impact one has on others. In so doing, an interpersonal process may become confrontational and transferentially exploratory, which, even if only briefly, reduces the safety quotient. Since this was contracted to be a ten-session group, a here-and-now orientation, although not totally abandoned, was used with discretion, as was process commentary and illumination.

An example of a here-and-now interpretation occurred during the sixth session when the group was exhibiting qualities of cohesiveness. Milton, widowed within the last year, was relating his experience with exercise 3 to the group. His mode of presentation was marked by paucity of detail and a general reluctance to elaborate. He began by lowering his head, then raised his eyes and quickly surveyed the group. He professed not to know what to say since his wife had died. This, indeed, was his characteristic stance in the group, although when the leaders or other group members encouraged or coaxed material from him his responses were richly detailed.

A leader now commented on this fact and offered a possible interpretation. Group members were invited to express their own observations. Those who responded to Milton did so with impressive understanding of the dynamics involved, encouraging him to allow himself to be that which they assumed he had been prior to his wife's death. Milton was visibly moved by the interest displayed toward him and acknowledged that he had become increasingly reclusive, even with his family, since his wife had died.

Self-disclosure. The degree of self-disclosure required careful monitoring. An example of premature and inappropriate self-disclosure occurred during the second meeting following the fantasy-trip exercise. Sally, unable to stay within the boundary of the exercise, strayed far afield, tapping affectively laden material which she disclosed to the group. The others were visibly shaken by the outburst. In subsequent sessions, the leaders were vigilant to prevent intense and premature self-disclosure.

For the most part, however, self-disclosure, limited to the context of the exercises, played a prominent role in appropriate sharing, encouragement, and support, assuming greater depth as meetings progressed. For example, during the seventh session, Evelyn, an active and contributing group member, seemed to hesitate in response to exercise 3, in which one is asked to identify a pleasurable activity. Her hesitation appeared related to embarrassment. With encouragement, she described a secret yearning to luxuriate in a fragrant bubble bath but felt foolish talking about it, much less doing it. The laughter that ensued was not the derisive laughter she feared but rather a freeing kind that prompted others to encourage indulgence of the wish. In response to the encouragement, she said, "What would my children say? They'd think I'm in my second childhood." In this way, she was prompted to talk about a restrictive self-concept that determined many of her actions, past and present. In future sessions, the "bubble bath" served as a shorthand device to depict self-expansion.

Procedural Norms. Our established procedural norms were in marked contrast to those described for psychotherapy groups, namely, "unstructured, unrehearsed, freely interacting" (Yalom, 1975, p. 119). The use of specific exercises geared to elicit responses that members were called upon to share placed it in a structured category with limitations on the level and style of interaction. Members of our group, in fact, waited to be called upon before responding. Part of this was related to the presented format, but without it, paradoxically, there would not have been a group.

Importance of the Group. The members' sense of the importance of the group, a key to effective group functioning, was stressed from the beginning.

One of the early methods for establishing the primacy of our meeting times was related to members' casual attitudes toward punctuality and attendance, undoubtedly derived from their past experiences with group activities at the center. By the third meeting, the point was made that each member was an important part of the group whose absence would be felt by all. Members were asked to call and let someone in the group know if they would not be able to attend. Members then exchanged phone numbers. This produced manifold benefits: (1) the importance of the group was enhanced; (2) the importance of each member was affirmed; (3) members accepted responsibility for either getting to the group or informing others if they could not; (4) for some members, the need to make contact with another person proved particularly meaningful.

Another incident served to promote the importance of the group. Past the midway point, the leaders felt it would be counterproductive to admit new members because of the limited number of sessions remaining. The group had become sufficiently cohesive for members to share their experiences. However, excitement about the group—a measure of specialness connected to membership—had filtered through the center's informal communication system. The center's director approached us regarding the possible introduction of new members who had asked to join. The necessary exclusion was explained but to no avail. At our next meeting, four newcomers entered the room carrying chairs and prepared to join us. There was a tense moment for all in the room. The newcomers seemed determined to stay. Group members greeting the newcomers apparently felt some obligation to welcome them. The trainees looked to us for guidance. We recognized that the integrity of the group would be compromised by this kind of invasion. Consequently, one of us explained the situation and why it would not be to anyone's best interest to enter midway. The newcomers left reluctantly, clearly angry with their exclusion..

It was necessary to spend time discussing the incident with the group, who seemed to waver between feeling guilty about their peers and pleased that the matter had been handled for them. Part of the discussion touched upon the importance of learning how and when to say no to others. During our last meeting, this incident was referred to by several members as a significantly unifying factor.

The Roles of Therapists and Trainees

This was clearly a therapist-led group for the reasons specified earlier. One leader assumed greater responsibility for the exercises while the other focused on the culture and norms of the group and acted as a social facilitator. In spite of the leadership focus, we were alert to the importance of not falling into a pedantic, pontifical role, a role readily accepted by the older person because of cohort differences in education and the authority attributed to those who are educated. We consistently stressed or deferred to members' diverse backgrounds and achievements. During our last session, Sidney summed up what he considered an important ingredient in the group's success: "You never acted like you were above us or talked to us like children the way they do with seniors."

The trainees, as mentioned earlier, provided an important dimension to the group process. The two young women, in their early twenties, both interested in further education in the helping professions, had been with the center long enough to be known by the members. In the group, they assumed responsibility for functional aspects while at the same time actively participating in the format. Initially the older members responded to them as they might to grandchildren—with warm interest and acceptance while at the same time discounting their experiences, even if painful, with comments wistfully reflecting the wonders and joys of youth. With time, the sharing of experiences once again demonstrated the well-known statement by H. S. Sullivan that we are all more simply human than otherwise. When Sherrie, a 23-year-old trainee, described with affect the difficult decision she had made when she took a step toward individuation by leaving a comfortable home and a loving mother, her story apparently resonated within the other members and erased generational boundaries.

Therapist Interventions

The leaders' interventions were consistently geared toward the stated purpose of the group, that is, to provide individual participants with methods for experiencing a sense of well-being with past experiences serving as sources of inner strength in the present. Thus memory was used to direct activity in current life rather than as a means of reminiscence characteristic of a life-review approach. The following two vignettes illustrate how the leaders used the exercises to draw group members into new initiatives.

Gloria was unable to find a "safe place" and an accepting person in actual memory. She was a rather isolated woman, lived alone, had never married, and had sparse family connections. A leader worked with her to find an imagined place with an accepting figure as a guide. The place she was finally able to envision was an open green field with an abundance of wild flowers. With the second exercise, she again expressed inability to remember a really important decision, implying that all her decisions had been made for her by domineering parents with whom she had lived until recent years.

Finally Gloria described an incident that did not initially seem significant to her but that became so in the process of telling it. When her mother died several years earlier, her father, a tyrannical man of European background, no longer wanted to remain in the family apartment with Gloria. He demanded that she go with him to live with his elderly sister. Uncharacteristically, Gloria

243

refused, choosing instead to find a small apartment for herself. This decision was obviously a major one for her but also a conflicted one. After hearing her story, the entire group applauded her decision and the courage it must have taken to make it. What also became clear was that living alone for Gloria meant emancipation rather than isolation.

In the third exercise, Gloria was able to draw upon the first—the field of wild flowers—to formulate an interest she wished to pursue, namely, to learn more about flowers in general and wild flowers in particular. Her assignment was to go to the community library and borrow books on the subject, two of which she brought to the next meeting. Following this, she asked another woman in the group to join her on a trip to a nearby botanical garden. This isolated, frightened woman had become absorbed in a newfound or newly admitted-to interest and had reached out to another person to share it with her.

Sidney chose the early years of his first marriage as the safe, comfortable place to which he returned with the guide, a composite memory of his first wife. In describing an important decision, he spoke touchingly of the difficult decision he and his wife had made with regard to having their only child. The difficulty of the decision derived from his wife's frailty combined with the depression years. In affirming the "rightness" of their joint decision in terms of the pleasure they both derived from raising their son, Sidney spoke warmly and had a powerful impact on the other members.

When Sidney spoke further of his son in the present, he became saddened as he described being estranged from him in his adult years. His son lived with his family in California, and when they spoke on the phone they seemed to have little to say to each other. At the third exercise, Sidney decided he would like to begin corresponding with his son in an attempt to express some of the warm feelings for him that he had shared with the group. By the last meeting, Sidney had begun this assignment and said he felt wonderful about his son's rapid response to him.

In the preceding examples, the therapists acted as guides—encouraging, supporting, and teasing out significant memories. Interpretations were carefully timed and aimed primarily at manifest content.

Results

The General Well-Being Schedule was administered again after ten group sessions. Because only eight of the ten group members completed both the pretest and the posttest, it was not possible to derive an objective measurement of significant change in the direction of increased well-being. Although improvement in well-being did not show statistically significant results, overall gains were demonstrable for these eight on the basis of subjective response and manifest behavior. These achievements included:

1. Steady attendance by a group of elderly people who at times had difficulty in arranging transportation.
2. Requests for continuation of the group, first to the leaders, then by a formal request to the center director. Two years later, the authors have been told, several members persistently question possibilities for a sequel.
3. Friendships were initiated between members during the course of the group as evidenced by people looking for each other, telephoning each other, and spending time together between meetings.
4. The interest of group members in the world around them was stimulated. Things that had been put aside were retrieved and enjoyed again.

The most impressive result by far was the group's evolution into a bona fide therapy experience for a group of senior citizens who were not representative of a clinical population—that is, they had not come to the center looking for therapy. In other words, we accomplished exactly what many experienced clinicians (as well as center personnel) said could not be done. We were able to convert a well-functioning, more-or-less-intact group of elderly people into a committed, conscientious, goal-directed therapy group.

In view of the need for intervention models based on prevention, models that have as their goal the maintenance of good physical and mental health rather than its reestablishment after illness, this group experience is both noteworthy and timely.

References

Arenberg, D., & Robertson-Tchabo, E. A. Learning and aging. In J. E. Birren & K. W. Schaie (Eds.), *Handbook of the psychology of aging.* New York: Van Nostrand Reinhold, 1977.

Botwinick, J. Intellectual abilities. In J. E. Birren & K. W. Schaie (Eds.), *Handbook of the psychology of aging.* New York: Van Nostrand Reinhold, 1977.

Butler, R. N., & Lewis, M. I. *Aging and mental health.* St. Louis: C. V. Mosby, 1973.

Cousins, N. *Anatomy of an illness.* New York: Norton, 1979.

Ebersole, P. P. Group work with the aged: A survey of the literature. In I. M. Burnside (Ed.), *Nursing and the aged* (2nd ed.). New York: McGraw-Hill, 1980.

Eisdorfer, C., & Stotsky, B. A. Intervention, treatment, and rehabilitation of psychiatric disorders. In J. E. Birren & K. W. Schaie (Eds.), *Handbook of the psychology of aging.* New York: Van Nostrand Reinhold, 1977.

General Well-Being Schedule. Washington, D.C.: Department of Health, Education and Welfare, Health Services and Mental Health Administration.

Goldman, E., & Woog, P. Mental health in nursing homes training project, 1972–1973. *Gerontologist*, 1975, *15*(2), 119–124.

Holmes, T. H., & Rahe, R. H. The social readjustment scale. *Journal of Psychosomatic Research*, 1967, *11*, 213–218.

LeShan, L. *How to meditate*. Boston: Little, Brown, 1974.

Linden, M. E. Transferences in gerontologic group psychotherapy: Studies in gerontologic human relations. In S. Steury & M. L. Blank (Eds.), *Readings in psychotherapy with older people*. Rockville, Md.: National Institute of Mental Health, 1977.

Lowenthal, M. F. Toward a sociological theory of change in adulthood and old age. In J. E. Birren & K. W. Schaie (Eds.), *Handbook of the psychology of aging*. New York: Van Nostrand Reinhold, 1977.

Maslow, A. The need to know and the fear of knowing. *Journal of General Psychology*, 1959, *66*, 297–333.

Pelletier, K. *Mind as healer, mind as slayer*. New York: Delacorte, 1977.

Remnet, V. *Psychosocial care of the aged for nurses aides*. Class taught at Clearview Sanitorium, Gardenia, Calif., September 1975.

Selye, H. C. *The stress of life* (Rev. ed.). New York: McGraw-Hill, 1976.

Simonton, O. C., Mathews-Simonton, S., & Creighton, J. *Getting well again*. New York: St. Martin's Press, 1978.

Weiner, M. B., Brok, A. J., & Snodowsky, A. N. *Working with the aged*. Englewood Cliffs, N.J.: Prentice-Hall, 1978.

Wilensky, H., & Barmack, J. Interests of doctoral students in clinical psychology in work with older adults. *Journal of Gerontology*, 1966, *21*(3), 410–414.

Yalom, I. D. *The theory and practice of group psychotherapy* (2nd ed.). New York: Basic Books, 1975.

Zarit, S. H. *Aging and mental disorders: Psychological approaches to assessment and treatment*. New York: Free Press, 1980.

14

A Reminiscence Group for Institutionalized Elderly

*Berit Ingersoll, M.S.W., M.S.,
and Lili Goodman, A.C.S.W.*

Formerly a research associate at the Philadelphia Geriatric Center, BERIT IN-
GERSOLL is now a postdoctoral scholar at the Institute for Social Research at
the University of Michigan. LILI GOODMAN was a resident social worker at the
Philadelphia Geriatric Center and is now a doctoral student in folklore at the
University of Pennsylvania.

Old age is a developmental phase which, like other phases of life, requires
that individuals grapple with fundamental questions. As they approach the
autumn of life, many older people wonder about the significance of their lives.
Their quest for meaning often involves an integration of past selves with present
selves. Thus reminiscence, or the process of recalling past experiences, is
frequently an integral part of the aging process.

Although the reminiscing process emerges from such evaluative tasks, our
society rarely bestows respect upon the memories of the aged. Instead, older

The authors would like to thank Elaine Brody, Fern Ingersoll, Justine Bykowski, Charles Mor-
rissey, Bea Kahn, Stephen Banks, and Jack Rothman for their thoughtful comments on drafts of
this chapter and Judy Emery for her typing.

people's tendency to reminisce is often mistakenly regarded as "symptomatic of maladjustment" (Boylin, 1978, p. 47). Many people view reminiscing as "meaningless wandering of the mind—a sign of deterioration in old age—and. . .react to it with indifference, impatience or at best tolerance" (Pincus, 1970, p. 47). The elderly, who are often acutely aware of this disapproving stance, sometimes attempt to diminish their reminiscing (Boylin, 1978).

Recently, however, considerable empirical and clinical literature has emerged which emphasizes the therapeutic value of reminiscing. Researchers have shown that reminiscing is negatively associated with depression (McMahon & Rhudick, 1967) and positively associated with self-esteem (Lewis, 1971). Butler (1975), a psychiatrist, has found that reminiscing about familiar people and objects from the past helps older adults maintain a sense of equilibrium and security. He has suggested that older people naturally turn to the past as they approach the end of their lives and perceive limited futures ahead. He has called the process of turning back the "life review." This process enables the elderly to "reflect upon their lives with the intent of resolving, reorganizing and reintegrating what is troubling or preoccupying them" (Butler, 1980–81, p. 37). Thus reminiscing can help them find new meaning in life and face death with greater equanimity.

Reminiscing often helps older adults cope with grief and guilt. Recalling those who have died enables individuals to release suppressed emotions and gradually accept the separation (Kaminisky, 1978). Recollections of hurtful or guilt-ridden events can be viewed within a larger perspective—a lifetime that includes joys as well as hurts (Lo Gerfo, 1980–81).

Reminiscing also reinforces the uniqueness of older adults. By bringing alive memories of past selves, the elderly can experience a more complete and full sense of themselves (Kaminsky, 1978). Liton and Olstein (1969, p. 264) noted that by remembering previous situations and roles, older adults with whom they worked "[built] a bridge between the present and the past, and they again [found] their identity." Further, they found that the "stimulating listening" of the therapist helped the older client feel understood and loved.

Indeed, reminiscing frequently facilitates communication between the older person and the listener. Kaminsky (1978, p. 23) viewed the reminiscing of his older clients as a gift, "a sharing of some precious and vital aspect of the person's life, an act of openness and intimacy." In addition, the reminiscences of the elderly can provide a teaching function, enabling the younger listener to gain a better grasp on "the nature of human life with all its successes and problems. . ." (Butler, 1980–81, p. 37). Thus both the older adult and the listener can be enriched by the reminiscence process (Weinberg, 1974).

While clinicians have only recently become aware of the therapeutic value of reminiscing, folklorists, oral historians, and anthropologists have long been interested in the memories of the elderly. Life histories of the elderly have been collected and studied as phenomena in their own right (Holzberg, 1979), used and valued both as a presentational mode (Kramer & Masur, 1976) and as documents of social history (Shiloh, 1972). Many of the techniques developed by these researchers are applicable to the therapeutic process.

Myerhoff (1979), an anthropologist, illustrated the use of reminiscing techniques in her work with Jewish elderly participating in a senior center. She organized a "living history" class to provide participants an opportunity to talk about their past while their thoughts were recorded. Although the class was not intended to be therapeutic, participants found an outlet for self-expression and gained a sense of purpose in the sharing of their memories with other interested peers. This chapter provides a description and discussion of how such reminiscing techniques can be applied to a therapeutic setting. The model described here involves the use of reminiscence therapy with a group of institutionalized elderly.

The Living History Group

Institutional Setting

The Philadelphia Geriatric Center, where we worked, is a large facility that provides a spectrum of residential services for 1,100 elderly people. The center includes two apartment buildings, a nursing home, a hospital, community-based houses for independent living, and services to community residents. The nursing home section, the Home for the Jewish Aged, offers a wide variety of psychosocial and medical services to elderly residents. There are staff physicians, physical rehabilitation professionals, and consulting specialists, including neurologists, psychologists, and psychiatrists. The extensive Human Services Department, comprised of social workers and recreation therapists, maintains a strong commitment to innovative group work. While the Philadelphia Geriatric Center offers excellent supportive services, sometimes residents feel isolated within the large institutional setting. Thus we wanted to form a small, supportive group where such residents could share opinions and personal experiences.

Therapeutic Goals

Inspired by Myerhoff's work with senior citizens in the community, we decided to form what we called a Living History Group for some of the nursing home residents (Ingersoll & Goodman, 1980).

We thought that this kind of group would be particularly appropriate for socially isolated residents at the home who might be reluctant to join a more traditional therapy group. By encouraging participants to discuss historical events and personal memories, as well as to evaluate these experiences, we hoped to provide a therapeutic situation that was affirming and nonthreatening.

Specifically, we developed the following goals for the Living History Group: (1) to facilitate social integration among isolated participants by encouraging the sharing of common experiences; (2) to strengthen these participants' feelings of self-worth by providing them with the attention and concern of others; and (3) to help increase their sense of meaning and identity as they reestablish a connection with previous self-images and transmit their life history to others.

Group Recruitment

Recruitment of participants was a crucial step in developing the Living History Group. In this process, we took special care to recruit group members to maximize the potential for group coherence. We began by asking social workers and recreation therapists throughout the home to identify people who perceived themselves as different and isolated from the mainstream of social activities. We wanted to involve residents who were not overly committed to other activities within the home. We asked the staff to refer residents who were well-oriented and able to converse fairly comfortably. Additionally, we sought participants who enjoyed thinking about the past rather than those for whom the past was extremely painful. We also asked that referrals not include individuals who were extremely depressed, overly domineering, or suffering from profound hearing loss; we felt that such individuals could neither benefit from nor contribute to the group processes.

After receiving a list of potential participants, we visited all of them in their rooms. We described the group and invited them to participate. Rather than speaking of the Living History Group as therapy, we portrayed it as a social/ educational group for sharing memories and listening to others. We attempted to establish a personal rapport with each resident to diminish anxiety about the new experience and to encourage participation. Several residents were immediately taken with the idea of the group. Others were initially reluctant but told us they would try one meeting, while a few stated that they were not interested.

Before the first session and before the subsequent meetings, we reminded each interested participant with a visit and/or a note about the upcoming meeting. These weekly reminders, as well as the fact that we helped bring some of the members to the sessions, helped maintain attendance at group sessions.

Group Characteristics

Membership in the group varied from week to week. Sometimes we had as many as seven members; other times, as few as three. Ten residents (three men and seven women), who were between the ages of 69 and 98, attended at least one of the sessions. Interestingly, this age range represented two generations of elderly. The "young-old," a term coined by Neugarten (1974) referring to people in their sixties and early seventies, viewed the older participants as peers of their parents. When these older members spoke, the others listened carefully and were especially deferential.

All the residents were Jewish; some were born in the United States, but most had emigrated from Europe as children or young adults. Some members of the group were impaired. One member was blind, two had hearing problems, and four were in wheelchairs. Participants were usually sensitive to one another's impairments and often helped each other. One member accompanied her blind friend, and some people in wheelchairs, with staff assistance, actually pushed each other to sessions, thus forming a convoy of wheelchairs.

As social workers in our mid-twenties, we were often regarded as representatives of the younger generation. One of us was Jewish while the other was not. Residents were aware of this difference and were particularly solicitous about explaining customs and rituals so that we would both feel included in conversations.

Group Context

In considering the timing and location of the group, we discussed several possibilities. We decided to hold the group in the early evening immediately after dinner, a time when residents would be awake but without many planned activities available. We agreed that the group would consist of a series of eight hour-long sessions. This series seemed long enough to achieve our goals but brief enough to ensure participants' commitment to the group. Further, we wanted a meeting place that was centrally located, private, and large enough to accommodate everyone comfortably but small enough to provide a sense of intimacy. We decided to meet in a library within the home, a room with which all the residents were familiar and yet which was not much frequented during the evening hours.

Within the room, we tried several different seating arrangements. A sense of cohesiveness and comfort was derived from sitting around a table. The table provided a focus and was a convenient prop for arms and elbows. In addition, it minimized the disparity in physical conditions by concealing medical paraphernalia.

Transportation to and from the group sessions was a concern. While the logistics of organizing a group are generally more complicated in community-based programs for the elderly, some problems may also occur within an institutional setting. Because the nurses and aides were especially busy during our group sessions, we often helped transport some of the participants with motor disabilities to the group. An unforeseen benefit of this arrangement was that the extra time spent with the residents who were especially disabled enhanced our relationship with them.

At each session, as the participants began arriving, they were given name tags. Those who were able wrote their own names, while we helped those who could not. This activity served as an icebreaker as participants laughed at our misspellings and at their difficulties with putting on the name tags. These name tags were particularly important since the group continued to attract new participants throughout the sessions. They helped acquaint and remind us all of one another's names.

Therapeutic Issues

Roles of Therapists

We found that co-leadership was particularly useful when working with a group of elderly participants, many of whom had some kind of visual, auditory, or motor handicap. With two leaders, we could share the responsibility for helping group members interact with one another. For instance, we tried to sit next to those who were hearing-impaired in order to summarize and repeat what others were saying. Thus, while one of us was attending to a specific individual, the other could be more aware of the overall dynamics of the group.

As group leaders and therapists, we held multiple roles. A primary role was to ask questions that would evoke stimulating discussion. Each session was focused on a theme that might generate a number of questions. We formulated some of these questions for ourselves before each session and then decided on one question with which to open the session. The other questions then flowed out of the discussion if this seemed appropriate. We modeled question-asking behavior for others so that, as the sessions progressed, participants became increasingly adept at asking questions of one another.

We also functioned as "students" who were eager to learn from the contributions of the older participants. We emphasized that they had lived a history that we could only read about, hence affirming their memories as meaningful. In recalling various parts of their lives, the participants were sharing information that was important to us.

Another role was that of interpreter, which included the rephrasing of specific comments for the benefit of the group. Sometimes participants made abstract statements, which we would then attempt to concretize by reinterpreting their remarks in terms of the broader discussion. This reinterpretation placed the individual's contribution within the context of the group. We tried to generalize from the experience of one person to the experiences of others.

Additionally, we served as monitors who ensured that all participants had the opportunity to share something meaningful at each session. This role necessitated that, rather than exploring in-depth the comments of a single individual, we set limits on the reminiscing of specific individuals. In the first meetings, a few members often inhibited the contributions of others by verbally dominating group time. When we asked the group members to help us solve this problem, they encouraged us to interrupt those who were overly verbose and they agreed to curtail their own and others' comments. After this discussion, the monopolization of conversations decreased with only occasional reminders from us.

Sad and Painful Memories

Memories that were sad or painful were responded to in a number of ways. Often the most appropriate intervention was a simple acknowledgment that the event which triggered a specific comment was, indeed, a sad one. For example, although a concert of Jewish Klezmer music evoked happy memories for most of the residents, one woman said:

> When I saw the people in that condition listening to the music that they enjoyed years ago when they were young and now they're sitting around in wheelchairs, that hurts me an awful lot. You gotta remind yourself that these people made the world. They made America rich. And now they have to sit listening. Some of them understand; some of them don't. It hurts me an awful lot.

We responded to this comment by acknowledging that, indeed, it is painful to watch those who have led useful lives lose their influence and self-respect.

Other times, we tried to balance sad memories with positive thoughts, thus emphasizing the positive aspects of the members' lives. When, with misted eyes, a male participant was visibly uncomfortable while reminiscing about World War I, one of us commented, "People tend to remember painful things because those are the memories that often stand out. We can also try to remember some of the pleasant things from the past." Given these few moments to regain his composure, the man was able to go on and talk about a more pleasant memory involving his first day in Hebrew School.

Most often participants coped with their sad memories either philosophically or with humor. Several conversations focused on the hard conditions under which many of the group members had grown up. Comments such as "I can remember how we struggled; thank God, we lived it through to tell the tale" were frequent. One woman told a moving tale of how, when she grew up, her family was so poor that she had to share an orange with her five sisters. However, she ended this sad story with a hearty chuckle saying, "But now I can eat all the oranges I want to. That's why I'm so fat." Thus, while we were ready to intervene if necessary, the participants' own philosophical and humorous approaches to life were the most frequent coping mechanisms for the interpretation of their sad and painful memories.

Supportive Nature of the Group

Although initially the conversations occurred predominantly between the group leaders and the participants, the participants soon developed enough comfort and ease to begin relating directly to one another. Within a few sessions, group members showed a high degree of interest in and affirmation of one another. They began to express a greater range of feelings, all of which were received with empathy and support by other group members. As participants became increasingly supportive of one another, we could relax in our efforts to provide affirmation.

This support was evidenced, in part, by the questions group members asked of one another. For example, when one blind participant was unable to think of any memories she could contribute, another asked her, "Were you always blind?" This question evoked a powerful story of when she was a small child, not yet blind, but very lost in a new country. A taciturn man who felt he had little to say was encouraged by participants to talk with questions such as "What kind of work did you do?" and "Were you in business for yourself or a company?"

Equally supportive were the group members' reactions to one another's contributions. "I think that's a beautiful memory" or "That's a wonderful memory" were frequent reactions of one participant to another. When a woman spoke angrily about doctors' insensitivity, one member heartily agreed: "You said a mouthful." To a heartrending testimony from one participant about the difficulties of moving to a nursing home, another answered, "You said it perfectly." The ability of the participants to identify with one another was evidenced by the continually changing mood in the room. Within minutes, the atmosphere could move from tears of compassion as one woman related a sad story to gales of laughter as another woman told of a funny incident she remembered.

Although the focus of the sessions was generally on the positive aspects of their lives, participants also found comfort in sharing their limitations with one another. They were able to express feelings of sadness and grief. Participants often nodded in agreement when another group member spoke. At the end of one session, during which members had shared their accomplishments, a woman remembered sadly that, because of her failing eyesight, she was no longer able to work on the beautiful embroidery that had once been a source of great pride and gratification. Two other participants empathetically turned to her and acknowledged that they, too, were no longer able to sew. As the other members left, the three women sat together commiserating about this loss—one that, previous to this session, each woman thought she alone experienced.

Description of Sessions

Session 1: Introductions

The first session began with general introductions. To emphasize the group's focus on self-affirmation, we asked the participants to introduce themselves to the group by sharing a personal characteristic of which they were proud. Some group members discussed personal traits, such as pride in their ability to be generous and loving, while others mentioned accomplishments and education. Still others spoke of their families or Jewish heritage.

Following these introductions, we distributed a handout highlighting the group's purpose and expectations. We reviewed this handout with the group, stating that we viewed the Living History Group as an opportunity to share our memories and thoughts about things that had happened in our lives. Further, we hoped that we could learn from each other. Each of the expectations (e.g., confidentiality, punctuality, and regular attendance) was discussed and agreed upon by all participants. Leaders also asked participants if they objected to our tape recording the sessions; there were no objections.

To emphasize the focus of the group on memories, we then introduced the group to our timeline. The timeline, drawn with a big colored marker, was on a large piece of poster paper and attached to the wall. On the poster paper was a line to which dates ranging from 1880 to 1980 were affixed at 10-year intervals. Around these dates were a few important historical events with which people in the group were familiar. We suggested that the timeline might help "to recall memories in relation to world events." We asked members to begin by closing their eyes and taking a few moments to think of an event that they remembered between the time they were born and the present.

We found that some members had more difficulty than others relating their personal experiences to larger historical events. When we changed the focus from world events to personal events and emphasized "telling a story" rather than "remembering an incident from history," more memories were related. As members shared their memories, each was added to the timeline.

The timeline assumed increasing importance as the group sessions progressed. It became a symbol that united the new and the old members. A group tradition developed as each new member made an addition to the timeline. One participant commented that having a memory from everyone in the group was nice because "it puts us all together and shows our similarities." Additionally, the timeline helped establish the purpose of the group by visually initiating new members into the group and reorienting the returning group members.

Before closing, we reviewed our ideas for future sessions, soliciting responses and new ideas from the participants. At the end of this session, one participant aptly summarized a purpose of the group when she said, "You feel closer to others when you share memories."

Session 2: Earliest Memories

The first part of the second session focused on earliest memories. The atmosphere of the group was characterized by a special closeness and caring due, perhaps, to the questions discussed, the smallness of the group, and the fact that only women attended this session. We encouraged this intimacy by sharing one of our earliest memories first. In response, one woman warmly remembered her grandmother, who taught her how to braid bread as a child.

The second part of the session moved on to experiences from young adulthood. Memories of courtship evoked feelings of nostalgia mixed with joy and sorrow. These emotions were in contrast to those associated with present-day losses of eyesight, memory, and family members.

In reviewing their varied experiences, one member summarized with a sigh, "We led beautiful lives, didn't we?" Another characterized the group sentiment when she said at the end of the session, "What we shared tonight was love." Members continued to sit together, converse, and express affection for one another even after the conclusion of the session.

Session 3: Early Adulthood

The session, which began as a continuation of the previous week's discussion, encompassed a broad range of subjects from early childhood to early adulthood. One member's narrative sparked another's, resulting in a round of storytelling and discussion about the nature of jobs, salaries, prices, Yiddish theater, and their neighborhoods. While the previous session was characterized by intimacy, this session was more social in nature.

Commonalities as well as differences in participants' experiences emerged. A few members found that they had lived fairly near one another as children. This realization reinforced a sense of solidarity among participants.

As in the first two sessions, repeated stories about the immigrant experience surfaced. Members agreed that "though times were harder back then, they were better." In our interventions, we sought to reinforce members' sense of pride about their ability to overcome obstacles during their youth. We emphasized that this ability was a testament to their strength as survivors.

Before closing, we asked members what they wanted us to do with the stories we had gathered in the group. We explained that we would like to give them a memento of our experience together—either a copy of the timeline or a transcription of a story from each participant. We realized, in retrospect, that this question was problematic in that we asked what they wanted *us* to give *them*. The ambivalence the question engendered was exemplified by such responses as: "What do you mean by give?" and "I know what I want; let me give *you* a scarf." Many participants had been attracted to the group as a means of passing their history on to us as young people. Thus, a more appropriate discussion of the memento would have focused on what they wanted to give us or others of the younger generation such as their children or grandchildren.

Session 4: Greenhorns

Since the topics of immigration and assimilation had repeatedly arisen in previous sessions, we decided to devote an entire meeting to stories about that experience for group members. We began this session by asking, "What was it like to be a greenhorn here?" We used the word "greenhorn" instead of "immigrant" or "newcomer" because it was a term that group members often used to describe themselves. They began by speaking of their attempts to blend into the American culture. They spoke proudly of how they had learned to get along with others who were different from themselves. Several remembered stories about Christian neighbors who had been very helpful. One woman said that she had felt isolated until her children were old enough to attend school and then teach her English. Members spoke about learning how to adjust, moving away from the religious and cultural traditions of their parents and facing the changes and newness in America. We attempted to establish a parallel between participants' coping abilities in the past and present by pointing out how well they had adjusted to a new environment.

We were surprised at the positive nature of memories regarding Jews and Christians. Members did not talk about anti-Semitism in America, possibly because it was less oppressive than in "the old country." Also, as first-generation immigrants, members valued the importance of assimilating into the American culture; thus their stories may have focused on this accomplishment rather than on stories of prejudice and malice. In addition, members may have been responding with sensitivity to the fact that one of us was non-Jewish.

Session 5: Goals, Hopes, and Dreams

In this session, we asked participants to think about their goals, hopes, and dreams as young people. Because we felt that this question might appear somewhat abstract, one of us began the session by sharing a childhood dream—to be President. In contrast, members found they had shared different goals during their youth. For example, most of the women had aspired to be good wives and mothers. Their values were exemplified by comments such as, "We all think, like my mother said, that you should have a nice house, be a good cook, and always find a nice young man who says, 'My wife's cooking is better than my mother's.'"

This discussion provoked us to ask the members whether they would have preferred growing up when they did rather than growing up now. A lively discussion followed. Some thought that, although times were harder when they grew up, life was simpler and the family was more solid than today. Others felt that nowadays younger people have greater opportunity and more freedom to pursue their interests than in the past. Members laughed together as they derided the younger generation, who, despite numerous household conveniences, complained about how hard they worked. One woman spoke with humor and enthusiasm about how well she filled her role as wife and mother:

> When I had children I knew nothing else but to go out and bring home a basket of stuff to eat and bake and cook and make a nice dinner for when the children and husband came home. The table was set and everything was nice. Now, the woman comes home and she hurries and hurries. She doesn't know what to do first. They go out on a Friday night and have a hot dog. A hot dog on a bun on Shabbas [the Jewish Sabbath]!

Participants gained a sense of solidarity by comparing their lives and values to those of their daughters and granddaughters. This session allowed them to reaffirm their values and accomplishments as wives and mothers. They were eager to express their opinions and concerns about the changing morality of the present generation, thus reinforcing their role of maintaining old values and unifying the family.

Session 6: Traditions

Several participants expressed interest in attending a concert featuring traditional Jewish Klezmer music that was scheduled at the same time as the Living History Group. Therefore, members met briefly before attending the concert together. We asked participants to describe what this music was and when it was played. They explained that Jewish Klezmer music was played in Eastern Europe by small bands at festive occasions, combining the folk music of the area with the style of Hebrew sacred music.

The discussion about music evoked memories of times, such as their weddings, when they had heard Klezmer music. The participants, who were all women at this session, told of preparations for their weddings. They found themselves especially involved in the reality of the story world they created when sharing memories of their relationships with their mothers. During this discussion, they perceived themselves as young girls and not old women.

We asked the members what it was like to grow up as women in their time. A few vividly remembered their reactions to their first menstruation and their mothers' admonitions about sex, evoking strong emotions of bitterness, anger, and embarrassment. One member shared, with humor and pathos, her story about the warnings she received from her mother before her wedding night.

Her mother vaguely described what would occur with her husband, and reminded her daughter that it was her duty and obligation to accept her husband's overtures.

The session ended before the concert, which the members attended together. Although they were surrounded by others they knew, they sat together as a group. The concert slowly transformed the audience of residents. The atmosphere of the room changed from lethargy to excitement. As the familiar rhythmic melodies sounded throughout the room, people began smiling and nodding their heads. Soon, many had begun to clap their hands in time with the music, and suddenly a few individuals stood up and began dancing around the room. Others joined the dancers until the room was filled with the excitement of the past. The music served as an auditory link with the past, reminding the participants of joyful events throughout their lives.

Session 7: Turning Points

We introduced the seventh session by reminding members that the following meeting would be our last. Members began discussing their feelings about endings. Remarks such as "the group was like a tonic in my life" demonstrated the importance of this experience for the members. To remind participants of their ongoing capacity to cope with endings, we pointed out that they had successfully negotiated many beginnings and endings throughout their lives.

This interpretation flowed into a question we had wanted to ask: "What was an important turning point in your life?" The discussion that followed was characterized by philosophical thoughts as well as feelings of loneliness, pride, and strength. One member reminisced about coming to the United States while another spoke of the death of a spouse. Pouring out her feelings to the group, a participant spoke of moving to the home as a major turning point in her life:

> I never expected to be in the old age home in my life. All of a sudden in my old age I find myself in the four walls in the old age home with no place to go. When you come into your room from lunch to dinner, you go to your bed and you lay and lay. Or you sit out on the bench with some women who don't want to open their mouths to say hello to you or talk a word to you. And if you say something to them they just stare back at you and you feel, I must be a worm or something and they're so good they can't answer you. The children come to see me on weekends, so they stay two or three hours and they go away and then I'm left with the four walls for the rest of the week. It's a very, very lonely life.

Members reacted strongly to this description. Several were moved to tears. As leaders, we acknowledged that her statement had touched people deeply and that many of the group members felt similarly.

The meeting closed by reviewing the timeline again to ensure that everybody had made a contribution. Participants expressed support and appreciation for one another and sadness about the group's forthcoming termination.

Session 8: Closure

We attempted to create a social ambience in this final session by serving refreshments during the meeting. The closure of the group was recognized by the group members. One woman wore a new dress to the last session. Participants reviewed themes that had been discussed in the previous sessions. They agreed that the memories they had shared were important. They applauded themselves for having "made it through life" while others of their generation had not survived.

To end on a note that would highlight their roles as important elders, we asked the question, "What piece of wisdom can you share—something you've learned that you would like to teach a younger person?" This question evoked responses from members characterized by self-confidence and self-respect. As one woman said, "The public should know that there are old people who have good memories and great intelligence to use. Old people are educated in life and they have ideas to test with the new generations."

The meeting ended with an evaluation of the group experience. Suggestions for future groups were discussed and each member received a copy of the timeline that had been created during the group meetings. In summarizing, we stressed the historical importance of what people had shared, saying that their stories were valuable because they provided us with a personalized view of history. Closing comments were offered specifically to us as representatives of the younger generation: "Your generation has complete freedom. Remember, that can happen only in America. I say you shouldn't violate the law. You can then live and enjoy the life you have."

Discussion

Treatment Outcomes

The sessions ended with a feeling among the participants and ourselves that the Living History Group had been a positive, affirming experience. Together, we had witnessed the meaningful unfolding of our memories. The group members gave us several indications of their attachment to the group and the importance it had assumed in their lives. They looked forward to group meetings from week to week. Consequently, participants attended sessions even when they were tired. One member changed the time of her nightly phone call from her daughter so she could attend group sessions. Another told us that, by looking forward to the group, her week passed more quickly.

Although we did not use any objective measures to determine actual behavioral change that resulted from the group, our observations suggested that the group goals had been successfully attained. Friendships formed spontaneously during the course of the sessions. Alert participants living on the floors where residents were generally disoriented were particularly appreciative of being with residents from other parts of the home with whom they could converse intelligibly. One group member, who was a new resident, lived on a floor that consisted predominantly of confused elderly. In the group, she found two other residents from her floor with whom she could relate meaningfully.

Group participants enjoyed the opportunity to "tell their story." Sometimes they made a conscious attempt during the week to recall stories and relate them to the group during the following sessions. The stories enabled other group members to perceive one another as capable individuals. The reactions of the group members then served to reinforce the self-worth of those who shared their stories.

One participant who brought a special story to the group was Mrs. M. She was initially perceived by many group members as "the poor little old blind lady." She was 93, ambulatory but frail. Mrs. M was self-effacing and referred to her memories as "just a series of dollhouse stories." She had a unique talent, however, for describing past events in vivid detail.

In one session, Mrs. M related an incident that had occurred over 50 years before when her daughter, as a little girl, was hospitalized. The head nurse on her daughter's ward had been very insistent that Mrs. M visit only during the two hours allotted by hospital regulations. Mrs. M described her attempts to sway the stubborn nurse with kind words and small presents. Despite these attempts, the nurse remained rigid about the visiting-hour rules, and Mrs. M's frustration increased.

As group members listened to Mrs. M's story, they became involved with the drama. They empathized with her feelings of helplessness and offered a variety of alternative strategies. Mrs. M's dilemma symbolized the insurmountable obstacles all of them had faced sometime during their lives. As one member told Mrs. M, "That was a beautiful story you brought up, a hard but beautiful story. It could happen to anybody." After hearing this memory, group members perceived Mrs. M as more like themselves and not simply as an object of pity.

The group's emphasis on strengths rather than limitations resulted in members reveling in their personal accomplishments. Several participants relished the role of teacher. They enjoyed advising us, as members of the younger generation, about education and family life. They also liked to explain stories and traditions. Sometimes a member would interrupt the flow of conversation to translate a Yiddish expression and ask with concern, "Do you girls understand?" They viewed us as vessels through which their memories and knowledge might be conveyed beyond their own finitude.

The Living History Group offered participants the opportunity to display personal strengths as well as to talk about them. Some members had excellent skills in drawing people into conversation, while others were wonderful entertainers. Mrs. R, a plump, 78-year-old woman with a hearty laugh and an infectious exuberance, was a natural leader. Having worked in business for many years in partnership with her husband, Mrs. R had developed great facility in social interactions. Now, among other residents on her floor who were disoriented, Mrs. R sometimes lost her composure and verbally attacked her floormates. She was referred to the group so that she might experience herself as a competent and capable woman.

In the group, Mrs. R relished socializing with group members who understood her. She sensitively initiated and directed questions to members and to us, and reinterpreted statements if someone missed the flow of conversation. In speaking of her past, it was evident that, despite many hardships, she had learned to cope aided by her sense of humor. Mrs. R emphasized positive aspects of her own stories as well as those of others. Just as she was able to validate the contributions of others, Mrs. R gained from the group reinforcement for her own warmth and sensitivity.

In addition to our personal observations of the group's impact, various relatives of group members provided us with their reactions. The sister of one quiet and self-deprecating participant said the group had given her sister the opportunity to remember back to times when she was "in charge" of her brothers and sisters and later of her own family. The daughter of a recently admitted resident said that the group had helped her mother adapt to living in the home. The feedback from the relatives served to reinforce our own perceptions regarding the helpfulness of the group for its members.

Meaningfulness of Memory

Memory serves a variety of important functions. Two functions that are particularly meaningful—continuity with the past and connection to the future—were evoked by participants in the Living History Group. Members were able to reminisce about themselves in other contexts and to picture themselves as they had been. Additionally, they expressed their views of the past and opinions about the present, which they hoped to pass on to future generations.

Myerhoff (1980) discusses the importance of "re-membering," a term she borrowed from Victor Turner. She describes re-membering as the reaggregation of one's prior selves and of significant others throughout one's life. The act of re-membering provides a sense of meaning and order as individuals achieve a feeling of oneness with their past. Within the group, members' storytelling frequently provided a vehicle for re-membering. Often they would relate an incident which occurred over fifty years earlier, saying, "I can remember that like it was yesterday." One widow beautifully portrayed for us how her relationship with a significant other kept the past alive. She showed us her wedding ring and explained that the ring was the most important object in the world for her because it provided a connection to her husband. By touching and then talking to her ring, she communicated to her husband all her observations, thoughts, and fears. Thus this symbolic object in the present provided her with a very meaningful link to the past, a link that validated the continuity of her life over time.

Equally as important for some members was having a sense of connection with the future. They wanted their lives to have some significance to future generations. Through their unique experiences and memories, participants could establish this connection. One man metaphorically regarded himself as the key between the older generation and young people today. He derived a special satisfaction in knowing that a few members of the younger generation found meaning in the history he could recall.

Affirmation of Various Expressive Styles

Therapy groups generally focus on feelings. However, since many older people have been socialized not to acknowledge their feelings, therapy groups for the elderly should allow for a broader range of expression. In the Living History Group, different styles were welcomed. There was room for those who enjoyed personalizing their past by anecdotal stories and describing feelings; there was a place for those who liked to philosophize about changes during the past century; and there was an opportunity to state opinions.

Some members represented their memories by bringing their past to light in an emotion-filled story. Kirshenblatt-Gimblett (1974) points out that storytelling is an important form of verbal communication in traditional Eastern European Jewish communities. Storytelling is given most credence when used to make a point. Following this tradition, the Living History Group provided a focus for those who enjoyed telling stories. One particularly good storyteller was Mrs. E. Mrs. E paced her stories so that listeners were kept in suspense. She framed the account of her memory with an introduction and validation of the group members which suggested that her perception of the group activity was a formal one. In response to a question about the turning points in her life, Mrs. E told this story:

> Well I daresay that my story is going to be ever so much different than any one of you ladies, which I am very proud to be here among, and I figure that

every one of you is very intelligent and I'm happy to be in the presence of such nice women. In regards to my own story, you could say I was about eight years old when this took place.

Now, I'll start with my oldest brother. I never knew my oldest brother until I landed to this country. . . . And he brought me over not knowing me. So when I got in where they take off the people at Ellis Island I heard they holler out his name. Well I had his picture, so when I heard the name I knew it must be my brother. But then again, I'd been told that they did so much robbing and stealing of children. You know being as little as I was I couldn't concentrate. So along comes in a little man. We're all little in my family. And I says, "Well he's little, he must be my brother." However, he came over and he started kissing me and the tears came to his eyes cause it was the very first time he had met me as his little sister. And he was so happy, when I saw him crying the tears, I could memorize it as if it was now. He got a hold of me and picked me up. "Oh," he says, "you're my little sister, I find a fortune."

Some of the residents had little interest in sharing their feelings but enjoyed expressing their philosophical thoughts. For instance, the oldest man in the group usually answered questions in an abstract way. The philosophical manner in which he spoke represented the way he conceptualized himself, drawing upon the style of discourse he had learned through years of religious study. He was revered and respected by group members for his age and religious knowledge. He spoke of himself as a "young man" in the following manner:

Well, I tell you. I am what you call *grenets*. That means borders between this and that, between different things in the world, between people and time. Now this young man is in the middle between the very old generation and the younger generation. And I do remember a whole lot of things of the past life and I also know how the new life started.

Still other residents preferred to use the group as a forum for discussing their opinions on certain issues. Mrs. G, a particularly strong-minded and articulate woman, utilized this mode of expression. Her outrage aroused and often stimulated other group members, who agreed with her points but felt unable to express themselves as well. In telling of her interaction with some insensitive medical students and interns who had recently examined her, Mrs. G related her admonishment to them:

An old person comes to you for a checkup. Don't tell him that he's sick because he's old. You wanna take care of the older person? You want him to live long? I say take care of him. Don't push him away and say when he's old he'll get sick. You'll be old someday too and you wouldn't want anyone to do that to you.

Thus each of these expressive modes was accepted by the Living History

Group. This openness and receptivity encouraged the participation of several residents who might have been reluctant to become involved in a group that validated only a limited range of expressive styles.

Treatment Implications

A reminiscence group has applicability to a variety of treatment settings both in and out of institutions. This section offers implications for treatment that we think should be considered when initiating a Living History Group.

This kind of group should deemphasize the contrast between group leaders and members. Leaders can be active participants by sharing personal experiences, memories, and feelings. In so doing, they serve as models for the other participants, assuring them that such sharing is acceptable and safe. Group leaders can also express their own opinions, thus serving as sounding boards off which members can bounce their own ideas. By expressing their own feelings, either in agreement or disagreement with the leaders and other participants, group members validate their own sense of importance. This free interchange between leaders and members encourages participants to reaffirm their own beliefs, thus increasing their sense of identity and meaning.

The Living History Group model is well suited to young group leaders (as well as older leaders) who find the role of "expert" uncomfortable when dealing with people considerably older than themselves. This group provides a context within which the leader can act as student as well as therapist. By assuming the role of student, group leaders enable the participants to be teachers who are passing on their knowledge to members of the younger generation. Young leaders can likewise anticipate their future by gaining a firsthand perspective through the discussions of the elderly participants. This switch from the traditional expert/client role of most therapeutic modalities can be satisfying for both leaders and participants.

It is crucial to appreciate the values of participants when establishing a therapeutic group and attempting to elicit interest from prospective participants. To encourage their involvement, group leaders must consider those values that the participants regard as important. Only in this way can the group experience be a meaningful one. In our situation, since we were aware of the strong emphasis on education among most of the Jewish residents, we stressed the educational value of the group. We also tried to be sensitive to the strong Jewish identification of the participants and encouraged discussion regarding their cultural values.

Finding a common focus among other groups of older people is also possible. While this group emphasized Jewish values, connections other than ethnicity can also provide the framework for a group. In attempting to find this connection, leaders should ask themselves, "What experiences do these people share?" Answers to this question might include historical topics related to the participants' city or state history. Further, groups might be formed among those who share a common work experience or political identity. In group sessions, a series of questions can be developed around these shared topics.

The reminiscence process can be facilitated in many ways. It is most important to frame stimulating questions and to show interest in the participants' answers. It is often helpful if the group leaders establish a theme in advance and then brainstorm about evocative questions that relate to this topic. Generally, only a few questions are needed to stimulate reminiscing and discussions among the participants. Occasionally, however, a question that the leaders find interesting provokes minimal response from group members. In these situations, asking the question in another way can prove fruitful; if not, switching to another question may be desirable.

In addition to questions, other triggers can also provoke long-forgotten memories. Material objects associated with the past such as photos, pictures from old magazines, traditional food, and old gadgets or utensils may prove extremely useful. The vivid reactions to the Klezmer concert demonstrated the role of music in evoking memories. Even people who were not able to express themselves well appeared to enjoy the feelings that the music brought forth. A technique that requires participant initiative but can result in a meaningful sharing involves asking the group members to bring an object with personal significance to a group session. The combination of visual and auditory stimulation can facilitate the reminiscence process.

When recruiting group members, consideration must be given to the emotional characteristics of potential participants. Since the emphasis of this model is on providing a positive experience, groups should be comprised of those for whom reminiscing is enjoyable. There are, however, times when reminiscing can evoke painful, unresolved memories (Butler, 1963). If the group experience does not assist in the resolution of these conflicts, follow-up should be available. Group leaders have a responsibility to provide follow-up counseling or to refer members to appropriate resources for such assistance. Other personal characteristics must also be taken into account. Obviously, participants should be fairly alert and articulate because of the discussion orientation of the Living History Group. Additionally, since many aged people experience problems with recent memory, reminders of forthcoming sessions via personal contact or written notes can be helpful.

While the Living History Group sought people who were well-oriented as participants, a modified use of the method described in this chapter would also be appropriate for confused aged adults. Often their earliest memories are far clearer than recent experiences. Johnston (1978–79) eloquently describes some of her vivid experiences with confused nursing home residents with whom she conducted a group oral history project. She found that these residents responded best to specific questions about objects and places from the past—for example, bedrooms and furniture. In addition, symbolic objects helped her participants relive old memories. A group including both well-oriented and confused older adults may prove problematic as those who are oriented are sometimes uncomfortable relating to the disoriented (Feil, 1967). In using reminiscing with a group of disoriented older adults, it would be best to limit the group size to a small number to ensure quality contact with each member.

Consideration should also be given to group members' physical handicaps. Often visual and hearing impairments lead to frustration and isolation as older adults cannot see or hear to participate in an activity or conversation. Group leaders can ensure that handicapped members' participation is optimal by describing facial expressions to those who are blind and by sitting near participants with hearing difficulties to summarize the comments of others or to ask for repetitions. Similar adjustments must be made for participants with other kinds of impairments.

Maintaining a balance within group process between structure and flexibility is important but often problematic. While structure is needed to set the ground rules, flexibility is crucial for enabling participants to have an influence on the group process. Too much flexibility within the group, however, can lead to confusion. Like Myerhoff and Tufte (1975), we found that during the initial sessions there was a tendency for participants to interrupt one another in an attempt to be heard. To avoid this confusion, the first few sessions should be well structured. Sessions can become increasingly flexible as members understand the purpose of the group and learn that each participant will have an opportunity to share his or her thoughts. Participants can assume more leadership by facilitating discussions and by supporting one another rather than relying completely on the leader(s).

Tape recording of group sessions can prove helpful for both leaders and participants. For the leaders, listening to tapes allows for a detailed review of both the content and process of sessions. In reviewing sessions in this way, we noted many subtleties we had missed when we were intensely involved in the group. For the participants, tapes can be transcribed as a record of their contributions. Information from therapeutic groups is, however, confidential. Therefore the use of any tapes outside the group requires the permission of participants.

Members often enjoy some memento to remind them of their group experience. While we provided members with a group timeline at the end of the last session, many other mementos might be used. Participants could, for example, develop their own personal timelines with several events from various parts of their lives. A story for each participant might be transcribed and combined with those of other participants to produce a small booklet representing their combined efforts. Additionally, a genogram (which is similar to a family tree) can be developed for each participant as they talk about various family members whom they remember (see Ingersoll & Silverman, 1978).

Mementos of this kind represent an important product of the group. Informing potential members of the product before entering the group may provide a reason or incentive for joining. They know they will have a keepsake which they can keep or pass on to other family members.

Although the group described in this chapter was time-limited, living history groups can be open-ended as well. One alternative would be to offer the group on a time-limited basis with an option to continue if members wished. Another possibility would be to organize an ongoing group that members could join or leave at any point, thus enabling a large number of people to benefit from this kind of group experience.

References

Boylin, W. M. *Verbal feedback and oral reminiscing in the aged.* Paper presented at the 25th annual meeting of the Gerontological Society, Dallas, November 1978.

Butler, R. N. The life review: An interpretation of reminiscence in the aged. *Psychiatry,* 1963, *26*(1), 65–76.

Butler, R. N. *Why survive? Being old in America.* New York: Harper & Row, 1975.

Butler, R. N. The life review: An unrecognized bonanza. *International Journal of Aging and Human Development,* 1980–81, *12*(1), 35–38.

Feil, N. W. Group therapy in a home for the aged. *Gerontologist,* 1967, *7*(3), 192–195.

Holzberg, C. S. *Anthropology, life histories and the aged: An exercise in participant intervention.* Paper presented at the 78th annual meeting of the American Anthropological Association, Cincinnati, November-December 1979.

Ingersoll, B., & Goodman, L. History comes alive: Facilitating reminiscence in a group of institutionalized elderly. *Journal of Gerontological Social Work,* 1980, *2*(4), 305–319.

Ingersoll, B., & Silverman, A. Comparative group psychotherapy for the aged. *Gerontologist,* 1978, *18*(2), 201–206.

Johnston, C. Oral history as a group process. In *A common world. Vol. 1: Rural.* Barre, Vt.: Northlight Studio Press, 1978–79.

Kaminsky, M. Pictures from the past: The use of reminiscence in casework with the elderly. *Journal of Gerontological Social Work,* 1978, *1*(1), 19–32.

Kirshenblatt-Gimblett, B. The concept and varieties of narrative performance in Eastern European Jewish culture. In R. Bauman & J. Sherzer (Eds.), *Explorations in the ethnography of speaking.* New York: Cambridge University Press, 1974.

Kramer, S., & Masur, J. (Eds.). *Jewish grandmothers.* Boston: Beacon Press, 1976.

Lewis, C. N. Reminiscing and self-concept in old age. *Journal of Gerontology,* 1971, *26*(2), 240–243.

Liton, J., & Olstein, S. C. Therapeutic aspects of reminiscence. *Social Casework,* 1969, *50*(5), 263–268.

Lo Gerfo, M. Three ways of reminiscence in theory and practice. *International Journal of Aging and Human Development,* 1980–81, *12*(1), 39–48.

McMahon, A. W., & Rhudick, P. J. Reminiscing in the aged. In S. Levin & R. J. Kahana (Eds.), *Psychodynamic studies on aging: Creativity, reminiscing, and dying.* New York: International Universities Press, 1967.

Myerhoff, B. G. *Number our days.* New York: Dutton, 1979.

Myerhoff, B. G. Re-membered lives. *Parabola,* 1980, *5*(1), 74–77.

Myerhoff, B. G., & Tufte, V. Life history as integration: An essay on an experiential model. *Gerontologist*, 1975, *15*(6), 541–543.

Neugarten, B. Age groups in American society and the rise of the young-old. *Annals of the American Academy of Political and Social Science*, 1974, *415*, 187–198.

Pincus, A. Reminiscence in aging and its implications for social work practice. *Social Work*, 1970, *15*(3), 47–53.

Shiloh, A. (Ed.). *By myself I'm a book!* Waltham, Mass.: American Jewish Historical Society, 1972.

Weinberg, J. What do I say to my mother when I have nothing to say? *Geriatrics*, 1974, *29*(11), 155–159.

WORKING WITH PATIENTS
IN A HOSPITAL SETTING

15

A Short-Term Inpatient Psychotherapy Group for Adolescents

By Richard R. Raubolt, Ph.D.,
and Harry L. Piersma, Ph.D.

RICHARD R. RAUBOLT is a treatment team leader at Pine Rest Christian Hospital in Grand Rapids, Michigan. He is also a clinical instructor in the department of psychiatry at Michigan State University. HARRY L. PIERSMA is director of research and psychology training at Pine Rest Christian Hospital and assistant clinical professor at Michigan State University.

Recently, short-term psychotherapeutic interventions have gained critical attention and support from clinicians as well as from insurance payers. The growing expertise in time-limited psychotherapeutic techniques, accompanied by the increasing reluctance of insurance carriers to cover long-term psychiatric hospitalization, has also provided the impetus for the development of short-term therapeutic techniques for inpatient treatment. As is true with many areas of psychotherapy, however, relatively more attention has been devoted to adult populations than to adolescent populations. This is particularly true regarding short-term group psychotherapy with adolescents (Raubolt, 1979).

Relatively little has been written about short-term group psychotherapy with adolescents. Sadock and Gould (1964) reported on short-term group therapy with hospitalized adolescent males. In describing their experiences, these authors suggested that goal-directed activity by the group therapist is essential in creating a positive "group image." There was, however, very little discussion of the specific mechanisms of such therapist activity. More recently, Chiles and Sanger (1977) pointed out that brief group psychotherapy is not the place to engage in significant ego restructuring. They opted for the more limited goals of treating acute crises, teaching social skills, and persuading individuals to seek outpatient psychotherapy upon discharge. Again, the specific interventions necessary to accomplish these goals were not articulated.

This paper will attempt to delineate the special dynamics and techniques of short-term inpatient group therapy with adolescents, and will then describe how these elements were used in a particular therapy group. First, however, we will describe the clinical setting of our particular short-term/crisis psychiatric unit.

The Short-Term/Crisis Unit

Clinical Setting

The Short-Term/Crisis Unit (STCU) is a 13-bed, inpatient psychiatric program that was initiated at Pine Rest Christian Hospital in Grand Rapids, Michigan, in February 1978. Pine Rest is a large private psychiatric hospital offering a full spectrum of inpatient and outpatient mental health services to children, adolescents, and adults. The STCU was developed to deal with two particular patient populations: (1) children and adolescents who were in need of "emergency" hospitalization because of a personal or family crisis, and (2) children and adolescents who it was felt could greatly benefit from "short-term" (i.e., 45 days or less) hospitalization, as opposed to the more long-term, traditional inpatient treatment programs. The treatment program is multidisciplinary in approach. The STCU staff includes two Ph.D. clinical psychologists, two M.S.W. social workers, a psychiatrist, psychology and social-work interns, occupational and recreational therapists, nursing staff, and two full-time special education teachers.

Demographic and Clinical Data

Because the STCU was designed to meet the above needs, the patient population has been quite heterogeneous and has included almost all traditional child and adolescent diagnostic categories. Since the inception of the unit, a data-retrieval system has allowed us to monitor relevant demographic and clinical information for each individual admitted to the STCU. The adolescents admitted to the unit were predominantly (87 percent) middle class or lower. Most (89 percent) were white. More than a third (36 percent) came from intact families. Approximately two-thirds (64 percent) were female. The mean age was approximately 15 years, a figure that may be somewhat misleading since the mean was lowered significantly by the occasional admission of 8- and 9-year-old children on an emergency basis. Most of the adolescents (62 percent) had IQs in the average range. Two-thirds (64 percent) had histories of significant drug and/or alcohol abuse.

Regarding diagnostic categories of patients admitted to the STCU, approximately 15 percent were diagnosed as psychotic, 40 percent as neurotic, 16 percent as personality disorder, and 29 percent as adjustment reactions and behavior disorders (these diagnoses were given according to *DSM-II*). The high percentage of individuals placed in the neurotic category was due to the frequent usage of the diagnosis of "depressive neurosis."

The average length of stay in the ACTU was 34 days. Three-quarters (75 percent) of the adolescents received no psychotropic medication. Parents visited the unit an average of seven times during their adolescent's hospitalization.

Group Therapy in the STCU

The Role of Group Therapy

From the outset, group treatment has been an integral part of the treatment program of the STCU. In addition to group psychotherapy, children and adolescents are involved in such group activities as art therapy, interpersonal skills training, and sex education classes. As might be expected in a program treating such diverse child and adolescent populations, selection factors are critically important to successful therapy groups. Initially, group therapy was conducted with all residents of the unit present. Because of the diversity of developmental levels and clinical diagnoses, we decided to be much more selective in the kinds of patients who were to be involved in group treatment. Procedures were developed to form groups that were relatively homogeneous in terms of developmental level and ego functioning.

Younger preadolescent residents are not included in group therapy. Adolescents who are acutely psychotic are involved only when reality testing is no longer significantly impaired. Severely narcissistic and sociopathic individuals are excluded, because of their inability to empathize and be concerned with others' problems (Brackelman & Berkovitz, 1972). Homosexual adolescents (those who acknowledge and accept their sexual preference) are not included since we have found that such adolescents frequently provoke intense antitherapeutic anxiety in other group members. This can result in angry counterphobic scapegoating and isolation of the homosexual patient by the group in an attempt to control sexual anxiety. Finally, we have found that if we include the above adolescent types in our short-term groups the ability of the group to form positive transference is extremely limited.

Usually there are two groups functioning on the STCU. Each group consists of three to six members and two therapists. Groups typically meet for two 1-hour sessions per week. Thus, because the maximum stay on the STCU is 45 days, each adolescent is usually involved in 10 to 12 therapy sessions.

Perceived Advantages of Short-Term Group Therapy

We believe that short-term group therapy offers treatment advantages for hospitalized adolescents that are not available through other treatment modalities. These include the following:

1. Short-term group therapy provides an opportunity for a more complete diagnostic evaluation of the individual adolescent, primarily by allowing us to observe how the adolescent functions in his or her peer group. This in turn allows a more complete assessment of an individual's developmental level, ego functioning, and object relations. Frequently, an initial evaluation of these factors is made solely on the basis of the adolescent's style of relating to adults, disregarding the capacity to relate to peers.
2. Peer support available in therapy groups helps to foster a working alliance that often cuts through the initial resistance to inpatient treatment commonly present in adolescents. Frequently, adolescents are "tricked" into hospitalization by their parents or guardians, and group therapy provides a vehicle through which individual adolescents can ventilate their frustrations and concerns about hospitalization. Emotional support from peer role models for confronting and working through authority conflicts is provided in short-term group psychotherapy.
3. Short-term group therapy can provide a setting in which an adolescent can quickly rehearse new attitudes and behavior/free role experimentation and psychosocial play (Erikson, 1956). This opportunity to experiment with new behaviors is particularly significant in a time-limited inpatient program, as one of the treatment emphases is rapid alleviation of symptoms so that more adequate problem-solving skills can be quickly developed.
4. The desire to act, which is a crucial part of the adolescent's experience, is encouraged through a short-term approach that synthesizes action techniques with insight development (Rachman, 1975b, 1979).
5. As Blos (1962) noted, adolescence provides a second chance to resolve earlier developmental issues and to crystallize a more autonomous, in-

dependent ego identity. This "second individuation process" is aided by the peer associations that provide for disengagement from childhood dependency. Such associations also assist adolescent attempts at autonomy by providing support and encouragement as well as permitting peer identifications for role tryouts and social experimentations. Short-term inpatient group therapy offers a forum for addressing these separation-individuation issues. Although peer attachments are time-limited in this approach, they are intense. Group members learn to form relationships quickly while recognizing the differing needs of others. They come to recognize varying degrees of personal pathology as well as conflict-resolution strategies. Perhaps most significantly, group members are exposed to a fairly wide range of individuals from different geographical locations, cultural backgrounds, and socioeconomic levels. Such diversity encourages acknowledgment of heterogeneity among individuals and provides opportunities to try on different identities in the search for a consistent autonomous sense of self.

6. Short-term group therapy also serves to dilute the transference with the adult leader. While this is an important function of group therapy in general with adolescents, it becomes particularly important in time-limited groups. In essence, such a format curtails intense dependency attachments on adults while supporting behaviors, thoughts, and feelings that demonstrate independent functioning and self-control.

Intervention and Treatment Strategies

Out of a desire to utilize these advantages of short-term group therapy for adolescents in a clear and forthright manner, we have developed particular intervention and treatment strategies for our adolescent groups. Their goal is the creation of direct, open, emotional sharing and independent action. Every attempt is made to create an authentic I/thou dialogue with each group member. In such a process, the focus becomes one of enhancing growth, activity, and change. Aided by the use of therapeutic contracts, individual members are challenged to use all their resources for self-examination and self-confrontation. Within such a theoretical context, the focus on individuals becomes dominant. This is not to say that group process is negated but rather that "humanistic encounters" (Rachman, 1975a, 1979) between the therapist and a group member provide opportunities for subsequent group interactions.

These "humanistic encounters" involve two stages. In the first, empathy is the hallmark. The new adolescent group member is encouraged to discuss his or her understanding of why hospitalization was warranted. At this point, all reasons are accepted and explored, including blaming parents, the courts, etc. Often this phase ends with the statement by the individual that she has been

277

"forced" into hospitalization. Full expression of anger, betrayal, and fear are accepted and empathetically supported. Our purpose in this phase is to convey understanding in a nonjudgmental, low-key, reflective manner.

Often this response is in direct contrast to the way the adolescent has experienced other adult interactions. As a result, a positive transference can develop. This becomes a crucial ingredient for ongoing self-exploration and change. This phase typically involves the therapist and the individual member. Although other group members are encouraged to join in, they typically do not become involved verbally. It subsequently becomes apparent, however, that they are deeply involved emotionally as each individual adolescent's life history evokes memories, present hurts, and current conflicts. It often appears that the empathy and understanding conveyed by the therapist to individual members is gratefully accepted and internalized by the entire group.

The second stage of humanistic encountering frequently involves direct, emotionally charged, action-oriented techniques. With a working therapeutic alliance established, the therapist extends the range of his activities to foster and heighten emotional experiencing and to provide impetus to behavioral change. Confrontation, role playing, siding with resistances (Marshall, 1972, 1974, 1976), and encounter techniques are presented, each tailored to the individual psychodynamic needs of group members. Group members are offered the opportunity to connect insight with action, to challenge personal fears and limitations, and to develop a greater self-esteem by mastering emotional conflicts. In this stage, the therapist often provokes, guides, challenges, and at times teaches. Throughout this process, the group members and therapists are engaged in an encounter aptly described by Durkin (1964):

> The mode of communication in a genuine I/thou relationship is called dialogue. In dialogue there is a true meeting between man and man, and through it an individual is confirmed in himself and may find his authentic self. Dialogue depends on full acceptance and mutuality between two people. A true meeting is a meeting of souls. Such a genuine meeting is called "encounter."

The individual group members as well as the group as a whole are challenged to confront themselves to examine their fears and own their personal uniqueness. Self-destructive attitudes and behaviors are consistently confronted. With each confrontation, a group member is presented his choice directly and asked to take charge of his life. No excuse for abnegating self-responsibility is accepted; autonomy, assertiveness, emotional growth, and authenticity are emphasized.

Confrontation in this phase of encountering is essentially a validating act. While the group member is challenged directly and intensely, the inherent message is nurturing and optimistic. Based on a positive working relationship that is supportive yet nonpossessive, confrontation underscores individuality and personal resourcefulness. The group members, for perhaps the first time in their lives, are asked to fully and openly assess their uniqueness, their talents, and their strengths. Behavior, attitudes, and feelings that inhibit such self-exploration are closely scrutinized, as are failures to become more responsible and independent.

Group members are typically more verbal and spontaneous in this latter phase of encountering. They become more open in their personal self-disclosures and often interact freely with other group members as well as with the therapist. The end of this phase often coincides with the transfer of individual members to long-term units or to discharge from inpatient treatment. To underscore the themes of this group experience, each member is offered the position of group leader during his or her last group. Group members often use this opportunity to say their good-byes as well as to offer prescriptive recommendations for each remaining member to work on in subsequent groups. This format allows for closure and also underscores the need for positive separation and individuation so crucial in adolescence.

Therapists' Leadership Styles

In our approach to short-term group psychotherapy, the therapist plays an active, vital role. Adopting such a leadership style involves two important functions.

First, the therapist must be willing to engage frequently in intense emotional exchanges with group members. The therapist provides emotional sharing and accepts and channels, in growth-enhancing directions, intense affect. The therapist becomes, in essence, a participant in the action, demonstrating emotional vulnerability while also encouraging cathexis to verbal exchange. This is particularly crucial with hospitalized adolescents, who feel overwhelmed and often powerless to deal with conflicting feelings and thoughts and as a result frequently act out their confused inner lives. Group therapy, however, offers an alternate mode of emotional expression by "turning on" adolescents to the spoken mode. The power of verbal expression to provide emotional catharsis also serves to decathect physical means of emotional expression.

Second, such a leadership style also provides ego identity role modeling (Rachman 1975a). An important element in this process is judicious self-disclosure on the part of the therapist. It is our belief that the group therapist serves as an ego identity role model in expressing and coping with the variety of beliefs, behaviors, and feelings expressed in the group. Such a function recognizes the crucial need in the adolescent for positive, growth-enhancing role models that served to encourage age-appropriate separation and individuation. Therapist self-disclosure offers the adolescent a new view of authority; if sensitively done, it provides an opportunity for resolution of oedipal strife.

A Case Presentation

To illustrate our approach to short-term inpatient group therapy, we will give an encapsulated picture of one of our short-term groups. Included in this discussion will be a description of how the group was selected and prepared for group therapy and descriptions of the phases that we believe many adolescents experience in short-term groups.

Selection of Group Members and Critical Therapeutic Themes

While criteria for selection are important for all therapy groups, they become crucial and complex for inpatient group therapy with adolescents. The most notable issue related to selection is the limited population upon which to draw. Adolescents requiring hospitalization have, by definition, reduced coping strategies, problems in impulse control, and impaired ego functioning. To create from this population a viable therapy group that is supportive and positive is no small task. The group presented for discussion reflects our desire to provide appropriate group balance with regard to age (late adolescence), sex (less than optimal due to high representation of females on our STCU), and distinct styles of interaction (what Redl, 1942, has described as the "toughness-shyness line"). Actual diagnostic category was less significant, the majority being in the category of "depressive neurosis." Rather, the basis for selection was the intrapsychic and interpersonal dynamics involved.

The group's five original members were:

Britt, 18, initially diagnosed as manic depressive, depressive type, and later found to be reacting to an overinvolved, controlling mother. An attractive young woman, Britt was struggling with issues of disengagement and plans for independent living. In group, she was quite depressed, yet was perceptive to the needs and wants of others. Her working agreement in group was to speak for herself and acknowledge her choices regarding feelings and future plans.

Sabrina, 17, a depressed young woman who had been hospitalized after significant episodes of acting out. Her mother was dying of cancer, and her father, a noted surgeon, was emotionally unavailable. In the group, Sabrina was active in exploring her feelings, yet she revealed significant depression and confusion. Her working agreement in group was to more fully acknowledge the imminent death of her mother and develop assertive, direct methods of expressing her thoughts and feelings.

Missy, 16, an angry and bitter young woman given to hostile verbal attacks and drug abuse. She was caught up in intense rage and reactions in an attempt to distance herself from an intrusive, rigid, and domineering mother. In group, Missy was aloof and quiet. While intensely angry about her home situation, she was also consumed with guilt about this anger, which was further complicated by her close relationship with Sabrina. Death appeared to be one of

Missy's wishes for her mother, yet it also represented her greatest fear. Her working agreement in group was to learn to express her anger without guilt and to develop more effective problem-solving skills.

Rod, 16, an intense, anxious young man who often exploded into violent attacks on his family. Rod's father had died, and Rod felt it was his duty to take on parental responsibilities. His mother, who had a history of violence, rebelled against his attempts at dominance, and the two would often physically fight. Rod was anxious in group and often sought to avert discussion of sexuality or depression with jokes and humorous asides. Rod's working agreement in group was to develop stronger peer associations and greater recognition of his feelings.

Claudia, 18, acutely depressed and anxious, presented a number of somatic complaints. She was withdrawn and largely silent on the unit. When she spoke, there was a noticeable quiver in her voice. She dressed in plain, drab clothes that were ill-fitting and out of fashion. Claudia made a great display of her depression, noting that she had seen a number of psychiatrists in the past and stating that she had made the choice to hospitalize herself. This decision was contrary to the recommendation of her outpatient therapist, who had suggested antidepressant medication. Her working agreement in group was to recognize how she used her depression to avoid assuming responsibility for making independent decisions.

This group contained two adolescents (Britt and Sabrina) who had very active and intense struggles with separation, about which they had acute anxiety. Passive-aggressive behavior of an unconscious origin became their method of coping with such internal conflict. These behaviors and dynamics should be contrasted with those of Missy, who was hostile and aggressive in dealing with similar issues. While separation and individuation was a key conflict area for Missy, she dealt with it by rejecting parental standards. Her adoption of a "street lifestyle" included significant drug abuse, shoplifting, and verbal battles with authority figures in her life.

Rod also presented himself as angry and verbal. He, however, had adopted a paternal role in the family with ambivalence that was masked by a domineering, controlling attitude toward those younger or "weaker" than himself.

To this group we added Claudia, who, while separated physically from her family, remained emotionally engaged with her parents. Her somatic complaints kept her parents involved in her life even though she verbally proclaimed her independence. Claudia's continued reliance on her parents was thus justified, in her words, on "medical grounds."

In addition to separation, sexuality was a critical theme in the group. Two members, Missy and Sabrina, had engaged in frequent sexual activity, Missy in an active, challenging fashion with bravado and many stories and Sabrina as a way of showing disrespect and anger for all her mother represented. Britt, on the other hand, had sexual intercourse for the first time just prior to hospitalization. The anxiety provoked by this was a major precipitant to her hospitalization. Claudia had engaged in sexual activity just prior to seeking admission, and her somatic complaints were hypothesized to reveal ambivalence about this behavior. Rod, unlike the other group members, remained parental in his attitude in this area. He revealed both interest and anxiety, evidenced by persistent refrains of warnings to Missy and Sabrina.

The Pregroup Interview

In terms of introducing adolescents into a group, we are guided by Ormont's (1968) idea of a therapeutic contract. Our basic guidelines include the following:

1. It is the responsibility of group members to understand one another and to communicate this understanding verbally within the group sessions.
2. Whatever is discussed in the group stays within the group—that is, individuals will not use information gained within the group to "get back at" or embarrass a group member in another context.
3. As much as possible, group members should put their feelings into words—that is, group members are expected to participate in the group by verbally sharing significant thoughts, feelings, fantasies, and dreams.
4. There will be no acting out of a violent or aggressive character during the group. The only physical activities allowed will be those structured by group leaders.

Within each adolescent's first or second group session an attempt is made to secure an individual "working agreement" concerning specific problem areas to be worked on during group sessions.

It should be noted that these working agreements are quite informal, since rigidity in requesting an "ironclad" contract frequently can intensify initial resistance to treatment. This individual working agreement should also be distinguished from the more general group guidelines given previously, which describe guidelines for *group* interaction. Working agreements focus on *individual* needs and problems.

The group members having been selected for "limited heterogeneity" (Rachman, 1975b), preparation for group therapy commenced. Each prospective member of the group was seen by one or both group therapists. The preparation of each group member was extensive and systematic. The following questions served as guidelines in the pregroup interviews:

- How would you describe yourself?
- How would you describe your family, mother and father, siblings, friends?
- What are your plans for school?

• What are your special interests or activities? What is your favorite rock group?

• What has been the single most important event in your life?

• What is your earliest memory, your latest dream?

• What do you expect group therapy to be like? Any previous group experience?

• Please tell me in story fashion what you expect to happen in your first group session. Where do you sit, who talks first, what do people talk about, how do others act toward you, what kinds of things do you talk about?

• What do leaders say and how do we act?

• How does the group end?

This preparation interview sought to elicit individual perceptions of each person's life story and to provide additional information on each person's interpersonal style. It also provided a projective measure to allay any special concerns or fears that might have interfered with assimilation into group therapy.

The pregroup interview was concluded with the negotiation of an initial individual working agreement. Typically, these agreements focused on problem behaviors related to interpersonal situations—for example, to talk more, to feel more comfortable with others, to control anger, etc. As was mentioned earlier, there was little pressure to be extremely specific for the working agreements, since many adolescents experience this as controlling and judgmental. Our goal is to establish an individual working agreement in order to provide a therapeutic focus, so that individual problems can be discussed openly and individual goals for change can be respected. Such a process also encourages active participation by the adolescent in planning his or her treatment.

Since our therapy groups are of such brief duration, proper preparation is crucial to establish quickly a therapeutic atmosphere for change. A major problem in our setting is the considerable turnover in group membership. At any one time, a group may contain members who have just been admitted as well as those who are soon to be discharged. Though group members come and go, the therapists remain.

Phases of Group Therapy

With the ever-changing membership of our groups, it is difficult to describe group process in the classical sense. We have, however, witnessed a fairly consistent pattern of phases through which individual members move as they participate in short-term group therapy.

Phase 1: Initial Resistance. Individual members are often resistant to group therapy, and their first group sessions are characterized by silence, anger at having to give up some of their unstructured time, and dependence on the group therapist for direction. Despite the pregroup interview, group members often feel ill at ease with each other because they are concerned about how what is said in group will affect relationships on the unit where they live together. Often the result is to attack an "enemy"—frequently the direct-care staff. This attack typically serves two purposes. First, it develops cohesion in the group; since the "enemy" is outside, group members experience a measure of personal safety. Second, it tests the therapists to see if they will become defensive and punitive. Since challenging the therapists directly would jeopardize their reliance on us, attacking the direct-care staff becomes a relatively safe risk. The attack also attempts to split staff and therapists, a maneuver similar to those used with parents (Piersma, in press).

In the group under discussion, Rod spearheaded this process. He bitterly attacked the requirements of locked unit doors and the use of a level system for achieving various unit privileges. He was joined by Missy, who complained about the direct-care staff's urging her to talk about her problems. They were in turn supported by others critical of the control and discipline involved in milieu management.

After listening without comment to these accusations for some time, the therapists pointed out that the group was focusing all its attention on people who were not in the group. We wondered aloud if the members felt this would help them cope with the reasons for their hospitalization. These comments opened the door to a discussion of conflicts with authority figures in general, but particularly with parents who had "unfairly" spirited them off to the hospital.

The group then discussed how they had come to be admitted. The reasons were listened to with empathy and calm. They were not challenged, despite some provocation. Then silence ensued. This silence afforded us an opportunity to review the rules for group sessions and to encourage members to get to know each other in new ways, ways that might be more helpful than their relationships with adults had been. The next few sessions served to encourage this process as members shared problems at home with parents and friends. The leaders adopted an unintrusive role of providing support, clarifying feelings, and encouraging acknowledgment of personal fears.

Throughout these sessions the leaders focused attention on individual members and sought to draw connections between them. Without guidance and support from the leaders, group discussion was halting and uncertain. Members remained unsure of their relationships with each other and hesitated to risk confronting or challenging the behavior of others or initiating discussion of personal difficulties.

Sensing the positive relationships established between individual members and the leaders, and cognizant of the need to focus more intensely on maladaptive behavior and attitudes, we as therapists decided to challenge these behaviors.

During her third group session, Claudia bemoaned her depression, stating that she was not receiving help on her unit since we were not "telling me the causes of my depression." Sensing the resistance inherent in her depression, which rendered others impotent while maintaining their involvement, we decided to side with this resistance. Specifically, we agreed with Claudia when she doubted that she could ever be happy. Further, we exaggerated her statements of hopelessness and suggested that, given her view of life, it was surprising that she was not more depressed. We went so far as to note to Claudia that perhaps she was not yet depressed enough. Surely we had no answers for her.

Claudia exploded in anger, denying our suggestion that she had a choice as well as control of her feelings. She was quite animated. There was no tremor in her voice, and her face grew flushed. The group members commented on these changes and expressed surprise and pleasure at her sense of power. We, as therapists, commented on her courage to actively confront and challenge our statements. To maintain therapeutic leverage, however, we continued to minimize her ability to alter her depression. If Claudia wished to continue to resist us, we suggested, she would have to do so from a healthier, more powerful position, where she could in fact prove to herself, through her behavior, that she was capable of self-control.

Other group members supported Claudia in her attempts to prove us wrong. This provided a corrective emotional experience, in that Missy, Sabrina, and Rod found that they could become angry with adults and translate those feelings into words without losing self-control and without adult retaliation.

This group experience had a significant yet different impact on Britt, who was able to recognize that her depression was the result of attempts to please significant others in her life. She recognized the element of choice in her behavior and feelings. During this session, Britt began to develop greater self-understanding and to disagree with her peers, something she had been unable to do previously on the unit or at home. To encourage generalization of this experience for Britt, we gave her a homework assignment. During the next week, between sessions, she was to initiate discussions with the direct-care staff beginning with "I believe" or "I think" statements.

Phase 2: Engagement. The foregoing group experience caused Claudia to examine her ambivalent feelings about independence and intimacy. It also introduced greater affect into group discussions. Britt, in particular, responded to this change. By focusing on her passivity and dependence, the group challenged her to alter her behavior. As a result, she began to confront others in their attempts to avoid responsibility and became more articulate in expressing her own thoughts and ideas.

At this point a new member was added. Despite preparation and positive assessment by her individual therapist, Bambi did not fit well into this group. She presented herself for her first group session in tight, bright pink slacks and a low-cut chartreuse top. She wore a strong, almost overpowering perfume and considerable jewelry. Despite her outward sophistication, extensive drug experience, and frequent sexual encounters, she was basically a frightened, intellectually limited 15-year-old. The affect now present in the group unsettled her, and she sought to pair off with Sabrina, only to be rebuffed for her intrusiveness. Missy distanced herself from her, perhaps because of their similar backgrounds. Rod was intrigued by Bambi, yet somewhat ill at ease with her descriptions of her sexual experiences.

It was only with a good deal of support from the leaders and the use of some behavioral techniques focusing on loudness of voice and provocative sexual behavior (e.g., touching and interrupting) that Bambi became an active group member. Claudia also provided emotional support, and was in turn encouraged to dress "more stylishly" by Bambi, with positive results.

The engagement phase is usually characterized by heightened activity on the part of the therapists. Focusing on problem areas becomes the goal, and resistances are directly confronted. We attempt to provide a positive emotional experience where the focus is on individual members, with the group providing support. Often this support is provided via assigned roles—for example, a Greek chorus to add greater clarity and emphasize corrective change. Group discussions frequently provide information and assist the therapists in designing humanistic encounters. It should be emphasized that, while members are encouraged to participate in these group experiences, they may decline. Members are not forced to become involved, and the experience is often described in such a way as to offer informed choice.

It should also be noted that discussion is encouraged by group members following such intensive group experiences. The leaders at this point attempt to provide intellectual understanding and a "cognitive map" by which such intense emotional experiences may be synthesized and integrated into daily functioning.

Rod's progress perhaps best illustrates the engagement phase in brief group therapy. In earlier group sessions he had related that he had hit his mother and knocked her down in a fit of rage. Rod felt guilty about this but said he knew no other way to silence her criticisms. This latter statement was challenged in group by one of the leaders. Rod was told very directly and forcefully that his actions justifiably led to criticisms by his mother. His behavior was characterized as impulsive and self-destructive. In response to this confrontation, Rod experienced "becoming angry and frightened of losing control." He was reassured that he did in fact have control over his anger and that what he lacked was experience, based on family modeling, of expressing this anger in words. To demonstrate this idea, a role playing/encounter situation was set up whereby Rod was to talk to an empty chair representing his mother. The therapist, with the assistance of the group, would help him "find words for his anger." Rod began to tell "his mother" of his frustration in a hesitant, halting fashion. With encouragement, he began to express his resentful feelings with power and authority. At no time did he engage in physically threatening behavior, and despite intense affect he remained seated and verbal. Following this "humanistic encounter," Rod was able to accept praise from group members and to examine his adoption of a paternal role with his family and peers on the unit. For Rod, this experience marked entry into the final phase of his group-therapy experience.

Phase 3: Termination. Termination, a crucial issue in group psychotherapy, is seldom addressed in the literature. Yet this phase of group is central to adolescent group psychotherapy because of the range of adolescent developmental issues it raises—feelings of rejection and abandonment, separation anxiety, and ambivalence related to dependence on the therapist. These feelings are often particularly prominent in short-term group therapy on an inpatient unit.

Short-term group therapy has great potential for making termination a positive, growth-enhancing experience. Many adolescents seen on our unit have had very negative "endings" with parents and peers. Some, like Missy and Bambi, have had such destructive and demoralizing relationships with parents that running away becomes a frequent method of escape. To establish individual identities, such adolescents have to act out aggressively to obtain the help they need. Such actions place additional strain on already troubled relationships with adults. In our work in short-term group therapy we feel it is important in the termination phase to underscore options to acting out. Frequently, group members have had such negative experiences with adults that they have never been able to say good-bye in a positive manner. Instead, there has been a lack of closure and great resentment.

Other adolescents, like Britt, have been so overprotected and infantilized by their parents that they lack separate identities. They are so dependent on their parents that independent thought and action are quite foreign to them. A positive termination to group is crucial to these adolescents, who often require encouragement and support to seek age-appropriate emancipation.

To address both patterns of incomplete separation/individuation from parents, we as group therapists focus intently on positive termination to group. Each member's last group session is treated as very special. During this session the departing member is given positive support and feedback from other members and the therapists in a "go-around." This process may be described as a "strength bombardment," because negative feedback and critical remarks are strongly discouraged. It has been our experience that such critical remarks represent anxiety in separation and rob the departing member of closure to the experience of group therapy.

Since approximately 20 percent of our patients are transferred to long-term inpatient units within the hospital, this process of positive feedback is very important. Many adolescents facing the prospect of longer hospitalization are discouraged and often feel defeated. In our short-term groups we emphasize the progress these members made in group. We also underscore the idea that brief hospitalization is only the first step and that long-term hospitalization will offer new possibilities for emotional growth and eventual independence. Such a process is viewed optimistically; members are told that we refer individuals for such treatment only if we believe there is potential for change. A positive termination in group therapy makes it possible for these patients to have a sense of hope in a new therapeutic relationship.

Finally, at each member's last group session he or she is offered the role of "doctor" for the group. The departing adolescent is encouraged to provide honest, direct feedback to the remaining group members and to offer to each a prescription for greater emotional health. Britt's leave-taking provides a good example of this process.

After hearing from the group about the positive changes she had made in becoming more assertive, verbal, and confident, Britt was encouraged to lead the group. In contrast to her first session, when she sat selectively mute and depressed, Britt adopted the role with assurance and pride. She thanked the group for their positive assessment and good-naturedly agreed that her prognosis was excellent. She then focused on individual members, stating that they didn't have to agree with her opinions but hoped they would listen. Claudia was the first, and Britt focused on her depression. She said that she too had once felt powerless to cope with sadness and despair. But she insisted that Claudia could alter this process by "reaching out to people." She encouraged Claudia to talk with others as she had done to Britt. She also encouraged Claudia to recognize the positive effect she could have on people when she was assertive. Finally, with great tact yet directness, she encouraged Claudia to let go of her medical problems and plan her future for herself. Claudia offered no argument to this assessment and said she wished to keep in contact with Britt following discharge. Upon questioning from the leaders, she also agreed that Britt's prescriptions were worth following in future group sessions.

Britt also offered a strong prescription to Rod that served as a beautiful summary for some of the core issues he was facing in therapy. She began by saying that Rod had at first really put her off. His bravado, talk of fights, and demanding tone made it difficult for her to feel comfortable with him. But as she had gotten to know him she had found that he wasn't the "big bear" he presented to the world. Instead, she recognized his sensitivity and compassion, which she liked and appreciated. Britt's prescription for Rod was to use the group as a place to recognize the strength required to be sensitive. She also urged him to be less afraid and guarded with these feelings with others he could trust. These prescriptions were difficult for Rod to hear, and he said he needed time to think about them. This was viewed by the group and the leaders as a positive signal for continued progress in group.

The "doctor's orders" for Rod, Claudia, and the other group members provided a focus for subsequent group discussions. They also offered new options for individual contracts for change to be pursued in both individual and group therapy. Britt's prescriptions, coming from a group member, were apparently heard with less defensiveness and thus provided more impact than if they had come from the adult group leaders. The experience was growth-enhancing both for Britt, who had a chance to "try on" authoritativeness, and for the remaining members of the group, who could examine and explore a peer's perspective of their behavior.

Conclusion

In terms of evaluation of this approach we have no objective supporting data. We are, however, impressed with more subjective changes that have occurred. In the group discussed in this article we felt the following individual problems were addressed through group treatment:

Britt was discharged after five weeks of treatment, began employment as a secretary, and planned to begin college. We believe group provided a forum for her to develop more assertive behavior and to distinguish between her own wishes and goals as separate from those of her mother.

Sabrina was able to deal with her feelings about the imminent death of her mother in a supportive group environment. She was able to acknowledge that some of her acting out was an attempt to cope with feelings of rage and of being abandoned by her mother.

Missy, through her contact with Sabrina in group, was able to see that much of her drug abuse and hostility was related to her relationship with her intrusive mother. Missy since discharge has achieved control over her drug abuse and her hostility is more directly focused on her mother.

Rod, through his group experience, was able to avoid assuming a strictly parental role with peers. As a result he felt more comfortable talking about rather than simply acting on his violent feelings. Rod was also able, because of the above noted changes, to engage in more typical adolescent behavior, including dating.

Claudia, since discharge, is employed as a medical secretary. In group she was able to recognize her ability to make independent decisions. As a result she began to view her depression as under her control and she began to understand that it was an ineffective way of avoiding greater autonomy.

Certainly, we do not mean to imply that the changes in behavior and attitude of the group members was solely the result of group participation. Nor do we mean to imply that short-term group therapy is a panacea for all problems of hospitalized adolescents. But we do believe that this approach is a powerful tool in facilitating growth and changes with adolescents.

References

Blos, P. *On adolescence: A psychoanalytic interpretation.* New York: Free Press, 1962.

Brackelmanns, W. E., & Berkovitz, I. H. Younger adolescents in group psychotherapy: A reparative superego experience. In I. H. Berkovitz (Ed.), *Adolescents grow in groups.* New York: Brunner/Mazel, 1972.

Chiles, J., & Sanger, E. The use of groups in brief impatient treatment of adolescents. *Hospital and Community Psychiatry,* 1977, *28*(6), 443–445.

Durkin, H. *The group in depth.* New York: International Universities Press, 1964.

Erikson, E. The concept of ego identity. *Journal of the American Psychoanalytic Association,* 1956, *4,* 56–121.

Hollingshead, A. *Two-factor index of social position.* New Haven, Conn.: Yale University, 1957.

Marshall, R. J. The treatment of resistances in psychotherapy of children and adolescents. *Psychotherapy: Therapy, Research, and Practice,* 1972, *9*(2), 143–148.

Marshall, R. J. Meeting the resistances of delinquents. *Psychoanalytic Review,* 1974, *61*(2), 295–304.

Marshall, R. J. "Joining techniques" in the treatment of resistant children and adolescents. *American Journal of Psychotherapy,* 1976, *30*(1), 73–84.

Ormont, L. Group resistance and the therapeutic contract. *International Journal of Group Psychotherapy,* 1968, *18*(2), 147–154.

Piersma, H. L. Mom and dad: Views on the relationship between direct care staff and therapists in residential, adolescent facilities. *Adolescence,* in press.

Rachman, A. W. The humanistic encounter. *Psychotherapy: Theory, Research, and Practice,* 1975, *12*(3), 249–254. (a)

Rachman, A. W. *Identity group psychotherapy with adolescents.* Springfield, Ill.: Charles C Thomas, 1975. (b)

Rachman, A. W. Active psychoanalysis and the group encounter. In L. Wolberg & M. Aronson (Eds.), *Group therapy 1979: An overview.* New York: Stratton Intercontinental Medical Books, 1979.

Raubolt, R. *The history and development of adolescent group psychotherapy.* Unpublished doctoral dissertation, The Fielding Institute, 1979.

Redl, F. Group emotion and leadership. *Psychiatry,* 1942, *5*(4), 573–596.

Sadock, B., & Gould, R. A preliminary report on short-term group psychotherapy on an acute adolescent male service. *International Journal of Group Psychotherapy,* 1964, *14*(4), 465–473.

16

A Therapy Group for Adult Inpatients on a Psychiatric Ward

Robert H. Klein, Ph.D.

ROBERT H. KLEIN is director of education and training at the Yale Psychiatric Institute and associate professor of psychology in psychiatry at the Yale University School of Medicine.

The use of inpatient group therapy is steadily increasing. The escalating costs of inpatient care, the mounting reluctance of third-party and government agencies to underwrite these costs, the growing use of the hospital as a transient refuge, the impact of the deinstitutionalization movement, the proliferation of day-care and other transitional clinical facilities, plus changes in the philosophy of inpatient care diverging from long-term custodial-care models—all have contributed to the growing demand for short-term intervention strategies. Indeed, pressure is mounting for professionals to develop short-term group-therapy approaches that are both cost effective and therapeutically efficacious.

I wish to express my appreciation to Serena Lynn Brown, M.D., Ph.D., for her thoughtful and invaluable editorial assistance.

A Brief History of Inpatient Group Therapy

Although short-term or time-limited therapy has been recognized as a valid treatment modality only recently, efforts to treat psychiatric inpatients in groups date back more than 60 years to the work of Lazell (1921), who provided didactic lectures to groups of schizophrenic patients. Increased social contact for severely regressed patients, reduced fear of the analyst, and socialization were recognized as advantages of group methods. Marsh (1931), working with a wide range of clinical problems, including psychosis, neurosis, psychophysiological disorders, and stammering, utilized lectures, homework assignments, and a variety of exercises designed to promote interaction between patients because he concluded that they could also be supportive of one another.

The application of psychoanalytic concepts to inpatient group therapy was initiated shortly thereafter by Wender (1936) in his work with nonpsychotic patients. He conceptualized relationships within the group in terms of transference, and maintained that understanding these relationships would illuminate the dynamics of behavior, lower resistance, and promote partial reorganization of the personality.

Semrad and his colleagues (Mann & Semrad, 1948; Standish & Semrad, 1951) noted the importance of facilitating group interaction, recognizing and accepting patients' underlying emotions, and showing tolerance for their psychotic productions. Working primarily with psychotic patients, they advocated abandonment of the authoritative role of the therapist and emphasized the experiential aspects of the therapist-patient relationship. Similarly, Powdermaker and Frank (1953) reported on the importance of experiential factors in the group, and subsequently (Frank, 1963) noted the value of group cohesiveness as support, the use of group interpretations to stimulate the development of more accurate self-perceptions, and the therapeutic benefits of having role models available in the group for behavior modification. Frank also reported that the benefits of the group would result in improved communication throughout the social structure of the hospital, an observation corroborated by Semrad.

In his recent review, Kibel (1981) notes that the key observations of these early workers—the central role of the therapist, the experiential benefits of the group, and the relationship to the milieu—were not widely applied because of limitations in available conceptual models. While a wide variety of approaches have been developed since then, for the most part they emphasize limited treatment goals, overcoming social isolation, training in social skills, reinforcing reality-centered behavior, modifying maladaptive symptoms, encouraging ventilation and catharsis, and prompt intervention. The range of recommended techniques has included nonverbal exercises (Cory & Page, 1978), psychodrama and related experiential techniques (Farrell, 1976), didactic groups (Druck, 1978), and education regarding symptoms, precipitants, and acceptance of help from others (Maxmen, 1978). The advantages of the group approach are reported to include dilution of transference toward the leader, reality based interaction, and peer support. Sophisticated outcome research documenting the efficacy of these approaches, however, remains sadly lacking. With the exception of only a few well-controlled outcome studies, there is little convincing evidence to indicate the therapeutic value of particular techniques.

Increasing attention, however, is being focused on the importance of examining the nature of any inpatient group in relation to the social context in which patients are undergoing treatment. There is a growing appreciation of the reciprocal influences exerted by the therapy group and the inpatient unit in which it is located. This point of view has been associated primarily with the development of general systems theory (Bertalanffy, 1968; Durkin, 1980; Miller, 1976) and its relevance for understanding inpatient group therapy.

The Ward as Social Milieu

The social system of the ward with its norms, expectations, and values plays a particularly important role in determining patients' behavior in group meetings and has a significant impact on the therapeutic process. Studies of therapeutic communities indicate certain defined ways of thinking, feeling, and behaving that are preferred by the community, and the community's values are effectively communicated through various group methods to new members who enter the community (Astrachan et al., 1967a, 1967b; Astrachan et al., 1968). These overall ward values can be regarded as background factors that influence all types of group meetings. Kibel (1978) points out that it is understandable that patients requiring psychiatric hospitalization are subject to rapid acculturation even on short-term units and in groups with a fluid census. Given the social isolation of the newly admitted patient, the inherent dependency and ambiguity of the patient role, and the process of decompensation associated with significant impairment of self-object differentiation and overdependence on external objects, the patient entering the ward is powerfully influenced by the prevailing norms and cultures.

Although we all might readily acknowledge that the social setting in which a person finds himself or herself has some effect on the way he or she behaves, mental health professionals who treat hospitalized psychiatric patients often appear to operate on the assumption that patients and those who treat them are somehow immune from influence by the world around them (Trick et al., 1974). Quite frequently the disordered behavior of a particular patient is perceived entirely as that patient's response to his or her own internal events, as if treatment is provided for behavioral disorders occurring in a social vacuum (Klein, 1977). In examining the dynamics in a group, for example, inexperienced therapists often search for explanations exclusively on an intrapersonal or intrapsychic level. A failure to take into account the interpersonal and group levels is often apparent. Who is doing what to whom often receives little attention. The mutual cues and responses that shape patients' interactions in the group are frequently overlooked. Furthermore, every group encourages certain exchanges but discourages others. Thereby it controls, shapes, rewards, and punishes the thoughts, feelings, and behaviors provided by its members. What takes place ostensibly within a single individual or between a pair in a group can be viewed from this perspective as an expression of the group as a whole, with certain individuals being called upon, and in some instances essentially being drafted, to take particular roles on behalf of themselves and other group members. It is not unusual, therefore, to find a particular individual in a group somehow appearing larger than life as he or she proceeds to enact a theme that holds universal group interest.

In discussing group psychotherapy for borderline patients, Kibel (1978) notes that the dynamics of the psychiatric unit bear directly on the small-group process. He maintains that a total-treatment approach must consider three dynamic levels of experience: the intrapsychic level of the patient, the process of interaction within the small therapy group, and the corresponding relationships to the dynamics of the total milieu. He views the small therapy group as a subgroup of the larger psychiatric unit. As such, it reflects all the tensions within the total unit system. This follows from the fact that the membership of the small group, both patients and staff, represents the total membership of the entire unit. Selected members from staff and from patients—the two major subgroups within the system—comprise the small-group participants. These participants bring with them into the small group the dynamic and structural problems that exist in the unit as a whole, since, in the case of the patients, they live and work together 24 hours a day. Thus all the interactions involving all the staff and all the patients are mirrored in the transactions of the small group (Klein & Kugel, 1981).

Indeed, Levine (1980) maintains that a study of an inpatient group can serve as a biopsy of the unit milieu in which it is functioning. Borriello (1976) takes such a systems perspective one step further when he cautions that, when one attempts to establish psychotherapy groups in hospital settings, the first task facing the therapist is to appraise the hospital suprasystem. He suggests that the therapist attempt to determine the nature of the hospital's primary task, the methods it uses to accomplish this task, the sources of support for hospital functioning, and whether there is respect and freedom for role-differentiated, discipline-specific activity, innovation, and professional development. He suggests that successful group therapy is unlikely if the system does not respect the dignity of its patients and staff, and if the discharge of patients threatens employees with the loss of jobs or with reports of their behavior to the outside world. The therapist must build collaborative, nonthreatening relationships with other staff, and present his group therapy as supportive of what staff is already doing, not as something that will supersede or replace the staff's efforts.

While it is clear how the larger social system of the ward influences the small group in a variety of ways, it is less immediately obvious how the small group in turn influences the system of which it is a part. To begin with, the small group serves as a vehicle for acculturating patients into the values and mores of the unit—for example, punctuality, mutual responsibility, talking rather than acting, etc. If the small group performs this function effectively, short-term patient management is made considerably easier; patients are enabled to more quickly join the unit and participate in its primary therapeutic task. In addition, the small group is frequently used by the unit as an assessment tool in order to establish and monitor diagnosis, clinical course, and treatment outcome.

The small group can also provide an opportunity for patients to test out their projections, fears, wishes, and expectations regarding the staff and other patients. To the extent that this is not accomplished through verbal communications, such distorted object relationships often are acted out in disruptive ways on the unit. The small group may serve as a forum in which the tensions of the unit can be expressed, explored, and perhaps resolved. Frequently the group functions like the valve on a pressure cooker. In this way, it acts to assure the safety of the unit. Tension and unrestrained impulsive acting out can be effectively reduced and contained so as to preserve a stable holding environment on the unit. The harnessing of emotional conflicts and energy can be accomplished with a small group structure with identifiable boundaries; this factor not only reassures both patients and staff about their fears of losing control, but it also protects the sanctity of other unit boundaries. However, when the small group is charged with these tasks but is unable to implement them, the unit as a whole experiences the reverberations.

Boundary Problems

Several authors (Kernberg, 1973, 1975, 1976; Rice & Rutan, 1981; Singer et al., 1975) have conceptualized the leadership function in groups in terms of boundary maintenance. As noted by Rice and Rutan (1981), certain boundaries are present at all times in psychotherapy groups and demand the leaders' continuing attention. These include boundaries between experience and cognition, between primary and secondary process, between members, between the group and the leader, and between the group and the environment in which it is functioning. Since the boundary tasks facing leaders are so numerous, they must limit their attention to a few interfacing systems that they consider crucial (Rutan & Alonso, 1978).

In the course of providing inpatient treatment to persons who are already anxious, confused, and perhaps psychotic, one must be particularly concerned with the identification of task, membership, leadership, and time boundaries, and with the appropriate regulation of transactions across these boundaries (Klein, 1981; Klein & Kugel, 1981). Clinical experience reveals, however, that when working with patients who are severely disturbed, therapists often demonstrate some of the same dilemmas in adaptive boundary regulation that are manifested by their patients. Kernberg (1973, 1975, 1976) and others have indicated that the entire social system of an inpatient ward is often significantly affected by the nature of the task and the patient population undergoing treatment. Both staff and patients are prone to anxiety, confusion, lapses, and slips in functioning. Working every day in an environment dominated by madness, despair, and irrationality inevitably arouses the anxiety of staff members and provokes a variety of defensive maneuvers, one of which appears to involve the mechanism of splitting, which is used by the staff as well as by patients (Kernberg, 1975; Klein, 1981).

Clearly, however, effective group therapy is predicated on the integrity of group boundaries (Rice & Rutan, 1981). While groups are bounded in many ways—for example, in terms of their task, membership, meeting place—the boundaries demarcating inpatient groups are much less distinct than those of outpatient groups. Given the fundamental importance of adequate boundary maintenance, the blurring of boundaries between the group and a variety of other hospital services is a source of major concern to many inpatient-group therapists.

As noted by others (Rice & Rutan, 1981), the primary goal of short-term hospitalization and inpatient group therapy is to restore rather than to reconstruct the damaged egos of persons in emotional crisis to enable them to return as quickly as possible to their jobs and families and, where appropriate, to enter or to continue reconstructive therapy. However, the very process of hospitalization, which separates the patient from the world of work and family and from the social mores and expectations of society, is conducive to regression. While separation may be necessary and may well provide the patient with a much-needed respite from environmental stresses, it also removes the social structures that reinforce intrapsychic and interpersonal boundaries. When a patient is hospitalized, these structures are replaced by a nurturant atmosphere, a reduction in demands, and the removal of the usual status symbols and social distinctions between patients. This promotes a sense of oneness among patients, creates a united and often supportive community, and provides the comfort of universality.

It also, however, reduces differentiation among patients who are already having difficulty maintaining appropriate boundaries. While the continuing admission of new patients into the hospital reduces social isolation and infuses new blood into the hospital community, inpatient groups are forever beginning as a consequence of this rapid turnover process. Groups are constantly preoccupied with the early stages of their development—that is, with orientation, trust, and dependency at the expense of differentiation and/or autonomy. Furthermore, patients' resources for coping are often so limited that many have difficulty establishing clear distinctions between their inner and outer worlds, between past and present, and between themselves and others. Such limited resources reinforce patients' sense of oneness and dedifferentiation within the hospital. Finally, patients come to the hospital with the wish to be helped, to be taken care of and to be made well again. They often are in need of resources from outside themselves to compensate for their own faulty and extremely limited resources.

Taken together, these factors are highly conducive to the development of a basic assumption dependency group or culture in the hospital (Bion, 1961). In such groups, members are united in the belief that help can come only from the leader, who can, if only he or she will, satisfy all their needs. Members behave in a mindless, passive, and extremely dependent fashion; they act as if the group has met with an omnipotent and omniscient leader whose task is to care for the casualties (Rioch, 1970, 1971).

As noted by several writers (e.g., Kernberg, 1973, 1975, 1976; Klein, 1977, 1981; Klein & Kugel, 1981), this dependency culture often includes staff members as well as patients, since they too are isolated from the outside world, are often vitally concerned with the frustration or gratification of dependency needs, and, in order to defend themselves against their own feelings of helplessness, often collude to maintain such a culture in which they are regarded as all-powerful and all-knowing. Patients, therefore, are constantly exposed to the dangers of dedifferentiation that accompany a dependency culture. Such processes can result in a further loss of interpersonal and intrapsychic boundaries, particularly for persons who are hospitalized for these very sorts of difficulties.

For patients to benefit from the nurturance, support, and universality of inpatient settings, without succumbing to the regressive forces inherent in them, group boundaries must be well maintained to counteract the dedifferentiating and regressive processes:

> The maintenance of strong group boundaries also helps the members re-establish and maintain their own boundaries. It reduces symbioses and the terror of interpersonal relations, differentiates the inner world from the outer world, distinguishes the here and now from the there and then, and begins the restorative process. (Rice & Rutan, 1981, p. 304)

The Inpatient Group: Background and Preparation

Given this social-systems orientation to conducting inpatient group therapy, I will now describe the treatment model and techniques I currently use in my short-term inpatient work. This section begins with a description of the institutional context in which this approach was recently applied and of the patients with whom it was used. This is followed by a discussion of the contract, patient preparation, and the role of the therapist.

Institutional Setting

The 26-bed inpatient unit on which this group was conducted was a locked ward located within a university hospital in a large midwestern city. It was one of four adult inpatient units, each of which was intended to admit patients with specific diagnostic disturbances so as to facilitate ongoing clinical research. The patients treated on this unit ranged in age from 16 to 65 and were diagnosed primarily as having borderline and narcissistic personality disorders. A somewhat smaller proportion of patients presented severe neurotic and antisocial characterological problems with histories of chronic substance abuse, and a minority of patients were diagnosed as having affective neuroses and schizophrenic disturbances.

The average length of stay on the unit was approximately 21 days. The treatment provided was broad-based, including drug therapy as well as individual, group, family, and behavior therapy. The floor staff included three attending psychiatrists with faculty ranks, a clinical psychologist with faculty rank, three social workers, a head nurse, several first-year psychiatric residents, nurses, and nursing assistants. In addition, psychology, medical, and nursing student trainees frequently rotated through the unit as part of their clinical training experience.

The Patients

Most of the patients treated in the group-therapy sessions to be described carried diagnoses of borderline or narcissistic personality disturbance. Consistent with recent reviews of the borderline syndrome (Gunderson & Kolb, 1978; Perry & Klerman, 1978; Soloff & Ulrich, 1981; Spitzer et al., 1979), such patients typically manifested the presence of intense affect, usually hostile or depressed; a history of impulsive behavior; superficial social adaptiveness; brief psychotic experiences; primitive or bizarre associations on unstructured psychological tests; and unstable, stormy interpersonal relationships, often characterized by a profound sense of entitlement, intense dependency, masochism, manipulation, and hostility. Many of these patients sought relationships in which they either took care of others or were involved in highly ambivalent conflicted relationships that pivoted around the giving and receiving of care. Their histories were frequently marked by repeated episodes of self-destructive behavior as well as promiscuity, sexual deviance, and drug abuse. In contrast to schizophrenic patients, who manifest more severe and enduring psychotic symptoms, particularly persistent delusions and drug-free hallucinations, our borderline patients frequently reported transient psychotic episodes accompanied by behavioral regressions. They also reported disabling affective symptoms, including chronic feelings of dysphoria, emptiness, loneliness, and hopelessness. Intense anger was a prominent mood among many of our borderline patients. Disturbances in identity, derealization and depersonalization, and distortions of the sense of reality were also frequently present. In comparison to other patients on the unit, the borderline patients often appeared more demanding and entitled and had considerable difficulties tolerating being alone.

The narcissistic personality-disordered patients frequently demonstrated an unusual degree of self-reference in their interactions with others, intense needs to be loved and admired, and inflated concepts of themselves. Such patients often have limited capacity for empathy, reveal a rather shallow emotional life, apparently derive limited enjoyment from life, and often report feeling restless and bored when there are no new sources available to feed their needs for self-regard. Their relationships with others tend to be marked by intense envy, a tendency to idealize people from whom they expect narcissistic supplies, and profound feelings of depreciation, contempt, and devaluation for those from whom they expect little. Along with a grandiose sense of self-importance or uniqueness and a preoccupation with fantasies of unlimited success or power, these patients are extremely sensitive to criticism or indifference from others and frequently respond with marked feelings of rage, inferiority, shame, and humiliation. Their interpersonal relationships typically involve a deep sense of entitlement, exploitation of others, alternation between extremes of overidealization and devaluation, and a lack of any genuine concern or empathy for others. For both the borderline and narcissistic personality-disordered patients, it is often difficult to establish meaningful treatment goals and tasks because of their shifting levels of functioning, grandiosity, sense of entitlement, self-defeating behavior patterns, and relatively poor judgment.

The patients diagnosed as having antisocial personality disorders were primarily adolescents and young adults referred by the courts. They frequently presented histories of continuous and chronic antisocial behavior that involved violation of the rights of others, erratic and unstable job performance, lying, stealing, fighting, resistance to authority, excessive drinking, and use of illicit drugs. They were often unable to maintain any enduring attachment to a sexual partner and demonstrated irritable, aggressive, and impulsive behavior.

From an object-relations perspective, many of our patients with borderline or narcissistic personality disorders demonstrated defects in the integrative capacities of their egos. Borderline patients in particular demonstrated what Kernberg (1973, 1975, 1976) has described as a primitive division of the ego into libidinal and aggressive components, maintained defensively by the use of splitting to protect a fragile ego built around positive internalizations. Failures to maintain this goal through splitting frequently result in intense anxiety as the ego is threatened by aggressive, uncontrolled components. At a phenomenological level, of course, many of our antisocial patients manifested similar outbursts of impulsive, rageful, and self-destructive reactions.

In their efforts to clarify confusing and contradictory self-images, borderline patients are frequently highly interactive in groups since they need others to act out pathological internalized object relationships. These patients often lack the ability to differentiate and individualize external objects and thus are frequently involved in reenactments in the therapeutic group of internal conflictual relationships. The occasional schizophrenic patients who were admitted to the unit showed similar patterns of relationships in groups. They sought out and clung to objects, but, because of faulty reality testing, their responses were often seriously distorted in a fantastic direction. In the face of intense interpersonal interactions in the group, such patients often revealed an inherent vulnerability to ego disorganization, a lack of autonomy, and an inability to form reliable intrapsychic constructs of reality (Kibel, 1981).

Group Composition

Although group treatment constituted only one of several multimodality therapeutic approaches provided by the unit, every patient was expected to attend some form of group therapy. The implications of this not-so-subtle coercion, some means for dealing with patients' responses, and identification of special problems and practical considerations associated with conducting inpatient group therapy have been discussed in greater detail elsewhere (Klein, 1977).

As is the case for many inpatient units, it was considered an irrelevant luxury to try to apply the selection criteria summarized in recent reviews (e.g., Bond & Lieberman, 1978; Woods & Melnick, 1979), since adherence to such criteria, developed largely for outpatient groups, would result in very few patients being seen for inpatient group therapy. However, some consideration was given to the issue of group composition. Specifically, we considered whether short-term inpatient groups should be heterogeneously or homogeneously composed. In general, the literature (Bond & Lieberman, 1978; Frances et al., 1980; Furst, 1960; Yalom, 1975) suggests that homogeneous groups jell more quickly, provide more immediate support and group identification, have better attendance, are more cohesive, and generally provide increased symptomatic relief. They tend to keep interaction at a somewhat more superficial level and offer fewer opportunities to resolve multiple transferences and to engage in extensive reality testing, since the range of interaction, inquiry, and self-disclosure is more limited. Thus homogeneous group composition may be most appropriate for conducting short-term inpatient groups, especially when time, expense, and patient resources are limited.

One must still ask, however, homogeneous or heterogeneous for what patient characteristics? In this regard, we tried to maximize homogeneity for members' degree of vulnerability, capacity to tolerate anxiety, and overall ego strengths. Here one is especially concerned with what effective resources the members can bring to bear in order to work at the identified group tasks, and at what level and pace the work can proceed. The specific patterns of defense or coping, character traits, or areas of conflict for individual members can remain heterogeneous, in my opinion, whereas their overall degree of impairment or strength, their capacity to tolerate anxiety, and the nature of the resources they have available to do work in the group should be homogeneous.

The Contracts

Just as any system can be thought of as having external and internal boundaries, inpatient group contracts can be thought of as having two major components: the outside contract and the inside contract (Rice & Rutan, 1981). The outside contract refers to the contract established between the group leader and the hospital or unit on which he or she is working. This contract concerns how and where the group interfaces with the rest of the hospital. Specifically, this contract focuses on the expectations that the hospital has for the group, its members, and its leader and vice versa. Rice and Rutan (1981) suggest that such contracts contain agreements that group therapy should be congruent with the overall treatment program of the hospital or unit, that group therapy should be recognized as a primary treatment mode and not merely as an adjunct to another treatment, and that group boundaries should be respected by all staff members and patients. Thus the orientation of the leader and the unit should be compatible, there should be active dialogue among the practitioners of the different modes of therapy, group-therapy time should not be preempted for other treatments, and the membership, space, and time boundaries involving group therapy should be appropriately maintained.

In contrast, the inside contract is that made between the leader and the group members. The establishment of such a mutually defined contract, which is important in any kind of therapy, is particularly important in short-term inpatient group treatment. This contract can be used to define and to maintain group boundaries. It provides a focus for the nature of the work to be done and a vehicle for defining and dealing with resistance; it also grants the therapist the authority to do his or her work with the patient. In my opinion, the contract should include:

1. A summary of the assessment procedure that identifies the patients' major problems.
2. An agreement as to the target problems and goals of the treatment. In the short-term group experience, of course, we are talking about limited, realistic, possible goals.

3. Specification of the practical structural details of the therapy, including such matters as number and length of sessions, time, place, fee, and so on.
4. Discussion of participant roles, which involves an exploration of patients' expectations, misconceptions, and fears about what will be asked of them and what can be expected from the therapist.
5. Discussion of the nature of the treatment process and the focus of therapy—for example, that the group will deal with current life problems, will focus on here-and-now interactions between members, will emphasize honesty and communication between participants, etc. In this context, it is helpful to provide a brief explanation of how therapy works and the most effective contributions that can be made by the patients and the therapist.
6. Identification of the ground rules of the group. Here one can include some discussion of confidentiality, how lateness and absences will be handled, addition of new members, extragroup socializing, whether the group will be recorded and/or observed, discharge from the group, etc.
7. A summary of any discussions held with the patients' primary therapist.
8. An articulation of the nature of the group therapist's responsibility and authority for decisions affecting the patients' care and hospital stays.
9. Discussion designed to encourage a commitment from the patient to attend every session of the group.

Patient Preparation

In the course of formulating an inside contract with a patient, the therapist can initiate the important work of preparing the patient to participate effectively in the group. There is considerable evidence from outpatient group therapy that dropouts tend to occur primarily during the early sessions of the group (Klein, 1982; Klein & Carroll, 1982a, 1982b). Furthermore, there are convincing data regarding the positive effects of various techniques of preparation, most of which focus on reducing patient fears and increasing motivation. Such pretherapy training has been found to reduce latencies for voluntary participation, to increase the amount of time patients spend communicating with others in the group, and to promote self-exploratory behavior (Heitler, 1974). Strupp & Bloxom (1973) found that role-induction interviews and the use of a role-induction film significantly increased patients' motivation to begin group sessions, effected favorable change in patients' understanding of the therapy process and their roles in it, and raised patients' and therapists' expectations of improvement.

Other studies have reported that pretherapy training increases faith in group therapy (Yalom et al., 1966), produces better attendance in treatment sessions (Hoehn-Saric et al., 1964), lowers the attrition rate (Warren & Rice, 1972), facilitates desirable in-group behavior (Sloane et al., 1970; Yalom, 1966), results in significant improvement of a variety of dimensions (Truax & Wargo, 1969; Sloane et al., 1970), leads to higher levels of group cohesion (Bednar & Battersby, 1976), results in more interpersonal openness (Whalen, 1969), and can be effectively used as a means for selecting suitable group-therapy patients (Piper & Marrache, 1981).

It appears to be most crucial, particularly when conducting a short-term inpatient group with participants who are likely to be confused, disorganized, and anxious, to try to appropriately shape patients' attitudes toward and expectations of the treatment situation, and to reduce their fears and misconceptions about what the treatment situation is likely to involve.

The Therapist's Role

Yalom (1975) notes that the basic tasks of the group therapist include: (1) group maintenance, (2) culture building, and (3) process illumination. Certain features of the maintenance task are performed by the therapist prior to the first meeting of the group. Specifically, he or she selects and composes the group, formulates the contract with individual members, establishes the time and place of the meetings, etc. Once the group has begun, the therapist attempts to create an atmosphere in which patients can speak freely and to recognize and resolve any factors that threaten to disrupt the integrity of the group—for example, absences, subgroupings, scapegoating, and so on. He or she also shapes a set of norms in the group that are consistent with the therapeutic goals and tasks. As a process illuminator, he or she may intervene with reflective and empathic statements, clarifications, support, suggestions, interpretations, etc., and may employ a variety of special techniques, such as role playing, psychodrama, marathons, and others.

The literature suggests that, in the short-term group, the therapist's role should be active, directive, managerial, and flexible (Bednar & Kaul, 1978; Bernard & Klein, 1977, 1979; Budman, 1981; Butcher & Koss, 1978; Imber et al., 1979; Waxer, 1977, Wolf, 1965). In the case of the short-term group for inpatients who are fairly disturbed, who have limited capacity to tolerate anxiety, and whose resources for doing psychological work in a group may be rather limited, I believe the therapist should adopt a supportive orientation conforming to most of the following criteria (Klein, 1979):

1. Therapeutic goals are circumscribed in scope, largely focused on symptomatic relief, and do not involve working through neurotic difficulties in the hope of achieving structural changes in personality.
2. The therapist adopts an accepting, supportive, nonintrusive posture that strengthens and encourages focused, realistic, and goal-directed patient posture designed to foster more adaptive, socially accepted strategies for coping and defense.
3. The therapist carefully monitors the level of anxiety among group

members and attempts to prevent it from going beyond a level disruptive of the group's work.

4. The therapist simultaneously attempts to ensure that emotional and impulse expression are accomplished in a controlled fashion, to the extent that that is possible, and that cognitive and emotional balance is maintained with appropriate synthesis and integration of experience.

5. Reinforcement, praise, encouragement, and support are provided largely by the therapist.

6. Relevant content areas tend to be more narrowly focused around symptomatic manifestations; derivative expressions of the most disabling central conflicts; and specific, concrete, practical current life problems.

7. From a topographic point of view, the therapist discourages relaxation of defenses and primary-process explorations in favor of maintaining a closer allegiance to conscious and preconscious phenomena. Virtually no effort is devoted to eliciting and examining unconscious material.

8. From a structural perspective, the group's work is devoted largely to examination of ego and superego personality components. Drive-dominated determinants of behavior receive relatively less attention unless they become disruptive and disabling. Emphasis is placed on ego-building strategies and on helping patients to identify and utilize available social and environmental resources.

9. The group is primarily concerned with examining the immediate here-and-now aspects of experience and the patients' current life situations, with little systematic effort devoted by the therapist to promoting regression for the purpose of eliciting and interpreting unresolved transference issues. Similarly, the there and then, the relevant significant past relationships and events, does not gain extensive and/or intensive examination except insofar as it is spontaneously reenacted in the group.

10. Relatively little attention is focused on examining the group process as an object of study, though sophisticated use is made of various levels of the process through which social influence is exerted.

The Inpatient Group: Process

General Considerations

Before examining the content and process of specific group-therapy sessions, it is important to briefly identify several generic factors that significantly influence the course of inpatient group therapy in this context.

First, the therapist is continually faced with the experience of discontinuity. It is extremely difficult to follow and to develop group themes across sessions because: (1) there are continual changes in the overall patient population and the group membership; (2) group members are exposed to multiple inputs from other staff members outside of the group; (3) patients live together in a confined space, are frequently roommates, and talk extensively to each other between group sessions; (4) external intervening events occur on the unit that often have profound emotional impacts on the patients. The group therapist, therefore, must often work within the framework of a single group session. Larger integrations of therapeutic material over time are difficult to perceive and/or to conceptualize. A here-and-now stance that focuses on subtle changes in the nature of patient concerns and how they are dealt with day by day is often much more effective.

Second, group goals are difficult to identify and they change frequently. While any short-term group requires the establishment and maintenance of a safe holding environment, it also simultaneously necessitates rapid assessment and intervention to promote therapeutic change. Precisely what constitutes such therapeutic change is often difficult to establish, however, since the relevant problems that can be effectively addressed on a particular level utilizing a given set of therapeutic techniques change from one session to the next. Flexibility on the part of the therapist is, therefore, absolutely essential, as is the capacity to continually readjust the therapeutic goals in accord with changing group composition.

Third, since it is not unusual in a single month to see over 30 different patients for various lengths of time in multiple combinations in the group sessions, I have found it useful to try to focus on: (1) what brought the patient into the hospital; (2) what is happening to the patient while he or she is in the hospital; and (3) what the patient will need to deal with more effectively when he or she leaves the hospital.

Group Themes

For purposes of discussion, I have selected 15 consecutive group sessions for review. These represent a cross section of the life of this particular group. Although the group was open-ended and time-unlimited from a structural point of view, it met daily for 1¼ hours and it functioned as a short-term group because of the constantly changing patient population and the fact that patients remained in the group for only brief periods. During this particular 15-session segment, 19 patients—6 males and 13 females—ranging in age from 19 to 45, attended the group. Group size varied from 5 to 11 patients. In 11 of the 15 sessions, at least one patient was discharged and/or one new patient entered the group. Consistent with the patient population admitted for treatment to the unit, the majority of patients seen in the group had borderline or narcissistic personality disorders (11), while the remainder included patients diagnosed as antisocial or mixed personality disorders (5), anxiety disorder (2), and schizophrenic (1).

With this group composition, certain themes regularly recurred: severely conflicted dependency needs; unstable, exploitative, and ungratifying inter-personal relationships; patterns of substance abuse; severe impulse-control problems; self-destructive behavior; difficulties dealing with people in author-ity; resentment at being in the hospital; and perceptions of oneself as a victim, abused and deprived by others.

Dependency. As might be expected in the early phases of any group, and especially in a group with borderline, narcissistic, and other personality-dis-ordered patients, a prominent theme was highly conflicted, intense depend-ency needs. The continual quest for oral supplies and gratification from the therapist as well as the resistance to invitations to work within the group were manifest in virtually every group session. One example can be seen in the opening comments at the start of this 15-session segment. When patients were asked what they would like to talk about, they responded: "Food!" This was followed by much laughter and a series of associations about local restaurants, including "Klein's Restaurant," and what delectable items one might get there. I commented that the patients seemed to be much more interested in going out of the hospital to a good restaurant, where they could be fed, than in remaining in the group to work on their problems. Of course, if they did remain in the group, they would wish to be adequately cared for and nourished. Several patients then revealed plans to leave the hospital against medical ad-vice since they apparently found the experience to be disturbing and ungrat-ifying.

One woman in the group, Ms. A, began to talk about how she felt "better being here than being at home." She noted that there were "too many re-sponsibilities" and that she often felt "overwhelmed." She described her ac-tivities on a recent weekend pass as "sitting on the couch while my husband does the cooking and the washing." Discussion revealed that she seemed to feel guilty about this behavior and fearful of disappointing her husband and children. Her apparent need to protect them and take care of them began to surface as well as her anger at herself for not being able to do so. In fact, during her husband's visit to the hospital the previous evening, she had told him that she thought there was "something seriously wrong with me physi-cally" and that she was fearful she was "having a stroke."

When I asked what she had been thinking about before she expressed these concerns to her husband, she acknowledged that she had been feeling quite tired and actually wanted her husband to leave the hospital. Subsequently, I commented that, like a number of other patients, she did not want demands placed on her and wanted to be alone, but was unable to give herself permis-sion to clearly express such wishes. Her apparent fear of a stroke was inter-preted by the patients as an indirect and disguised expression of her wishes to have her husband leave and to get increased attention from the staff. They agreed with my speculation that this might also represent a way of simulta-neously punishing herself for having such wishes.

In the course of further discussion, this patient's need to feel indispensable to her family was also examined. Other patients noted that her family seemed perfectly capable of managing without her, a fact she seemed reluctant to recognize. They agreed that several other group members also experienced intense needs to feel valued and important. Ms. A's need to feel indispensable to her family was then addressed as a possible coverup for deeper feelings of low self-esteem and her sense that she didn't really deserve much out of life. This in turn was related to her presenting symptoms, which had to do with deepening feelings of depression and despair. Finally, Ms. A began to acknowledge that perhaps her fantasied life-threatening physical illness might represent an expression of her own wishes to be taken care of and to be relieved of responsibility. Group members agreed that these wishes were often regarded as unacceptable by them but were "legitimate" if they were the result of severe illness.

This expression of conflicted dependency needs by our borderline patients incorporated many of the elements described in the literature. Specifically, many of our patients, not just Ms. A, frequently sought to avoid deeper interpersonal commitments and the threat of mutual responsibilities in order to preserve their own precariously limited internal supplies. Exquisitely sensitive to criticism and the prospect of rejection, they withdrew from others but felt quite needy, empty, and unacceptable. Their devalued views of themselves as defective and helpless, however, were often accompanied by overly inflated views of themselves as invaluable and essential to the well-being of others. Similarly, the underlying sense of entitlement manifested by our borderline and narcissistic patients frequently alternated with expressions of rage and guilt they experienced at feeling deprived, exploited, and unloved. Deep feelings of despair and self-contempt appeared to center on a fundamental notion of themselves as bad at the core. Closer examination of their profound anger at themselves and others was often strenuously resisted.

Anger. Thus, in the session described above, Ms. A's anger at her husband and children was not explored initially in any depth. However, in the next session another female patient, Ms. B, began to examine her anger at the demands made upon her by members of her family. Specifically, she talked about having had a tough visit at home in which she too found herself "doing the same old thing." She said, "I felt like a shit. I started getting spacey and wanted to come back to the hospital." After I noted the similarities between her concerns and those expressed by Ms. A in the previous session, she said, "Yeah, I sit around while my husband takes care of the kids. I wouldn't answer him when he asked me questions. I acted crazy." She grudgingly acknowledged not wanting to have to deal with the concerns and demands of others and not wanting to be in a responsible role. She agreed, too, that she was "driving her husband crazy." By ignoring him and acting crazy, she made him believe that she was so sick she couldn't help what she was doing. He was beginning to feel guilty about being angry with her behavior at home. She said her anger was "hard to look at" and labeled it as an unattractive and frightening part of herself because it was linked with her being "selfish." With some support and encouragement, other group members began to confess similar experiences.

A male member of the group, Mr. C, then picked up the issue of anger and began to talk about how, when he was angry, he often found himself experiencing disturbing, obsessional thoughts about "guns, fire power, hurting, and killing." Another group member, Mr. D, an effeminate man who was his roommate on the unit, reminded him that the night before he had punched out the glass in the phone booth on the unit while talking to his girlfriend. In the face of this confrontation, Mr. C noted that he was quite concerned about his relationship with his girlfriend and was worried that he was "making a mistake." He talked about trying "not to let things bother me," but noted that as a child he often went to gun shops where he handled firearms and thought about "the fire power and damage they could cause." He described himself as a youngster as being "a tough kid" who was "out to lunch." Later he said, "What a shame to be so young and so bitter!" After describing his father as "a man of steel," he noted how he himself had gone into the Marines, where he was "able to get out a lot of anger. It was okay there to think about killing people." He agreed, however, that despite his efforts to the contrary, things did bother him and he experienced a constantly rising level of inner tension. The patients agreed that, while some of them, notably the women, expressed their anger and unhappiness by acting crazy or by feeling sick, this young man expressed his anger alternately through disturbing obsessional thoughts and periodic explosive behavior when he felt frustrated by significant others in his life.

Thus the group permitted progressively clearer expression and examination of the underlying rage experienced by the members toward significant others. Sex-linked cultural variations in the particular mode of expression seemed apparent. Nevertheless, via displacement, the objects toward whom these feelings were actually experienced during the group session were discussed in the there-and-then, not the here-and-now. Such affect was not allowed direct expression in group members' interactions with each other or with the therapist, a powerful and frightening object who also represented the demands and potential gratifications that could be obtained from the hospital and its staff.

Victimization. During the next group session, however, a thinly disguised, idealized, but also angry and devalued view of me (and the hospital) began to be expressed in the group. Specifically, Mr. C opened the session with a rendition, à la Ed McMahon on the Johnny Carson television show: "Live from downtown Pittsburgh we have the Bob Klein Show! Bob's special guests today include—" and he proceeded to name all the patients in attendance. "And heeeere's Bobby!" This rendition was provided complete with musical accompaniment. A young woman in the group, Ms. E, who was admitted to the hospital after separation from her husband in the context of a chronically unstable, masochistic, and tumultuous marriage, looked squarely at Mr. C and said, "Maybe this is *your* show." She then mounted a series of provocative attempts to engage him. In a sniping fashion she labeled him "defensive" and "scowling." She tried several maneuvers to wrench further information out of him about his difficulties with his girlfriend. Ms. E exclaimed with obvious glee and trepidation, "Look at the look on his face!" as Mr. C began to emit clear signals of his growing irritation and anger. At this point I noted that Ms. E, who had consistently described herself as a victim, abused and mistreated by others, was currently in the process of provoking Mr. C, a man who had already given ample evidence of his difficulties controlling his temper.

This intervention led to a series of discussions over several sessions centering on provocative masochistic relationships with significant others, feeling vulnerable and victimized, and engaging in physically self-destructive behavior. The reenactment in the group of pathological unresolved object relationships and the roles patients took in creating their own difficulties with others became a focus of the group. Ms. E, for example, recognized that just as she was provoking Mr. C, she did much the same in relation to her husband. Indeed, she said that she was quite upset the previous evening when her husband visited because she wanted to reconcile with him but felt he was tuning her out. Just as she wanted more from Mr. C in the group in the way of information and engagement with her, she also wanted more from her husband, but felt unable to connect with either of these men. Furthermore, Mr. C clearly reminded her of her husband, in part because of his explosive temper.

Several members of the group began to confront Mr. C about his remaining unresponsive to many of them on the unit, although there was no mention of his ambivalent efforts to engage me. He then reiterated: "I don't let things get to me; I just dismiss them." While he agreed with my observation that his barricading himself from others might in fact be perceived as provocative to them and lead them to engage in even more extreme measures to try to engage him, he maintained, "I wasn't going to lose control in here. It takes more than that to get to me. Maybe a threat of violence." At that point he was again confronted by Mr. D, who asked in a condescending, sarcastic manner, "Did your girlfriend threaten violence the other night on the phone when you punched out the glass?" Worthy of note here, too, is that Mr. D was himself in the hospital following a stormy breakup of a homosexual relationship and his engaging in self-mutilating behavior after he had chased his lover with a piece of glass. These two patients then engaged in accusations and counteraccusations, each claiming that it was the other who was really angry and provocative.

After I called attention to this process, group members took up the issue with Mr. C by describing a series of episodes in which other patients had tried to be of some help to him when they saw him becoming upset on the unit. He remained, however, steadfastly reluctant to accept their help or to discuss his concerns. In the context of this discussion he was able to acknowledge his needs to "cover over everything and keep it in watertight compartments." I reminded the group about his comments regarding his father, and another member of the group said that, unlike his father, he was not necessarily a man of steel. When asked by the therapist why he didn't talk to other patients when they extended help, for the first time he admitted that he felt embarrassed at feeling vulnerable and that "I don't want people to see the ugliness inside of me." Group members then turned their attention to Mr. D and noted that he "takes his anger out on all of us," but in a more subtle form in which he disparaged the activities of the group and the therapist by often coming late, reading a newspaper, appearing uninterested, not discussing his concerns, etc. Outside of the group, however, he actively pursued people about issues on which he knew they felt vulnerable.

To a significant extent, Mr. D's behavior appeared to be related to his deep-seated anger and his intense needs for status and recognition. These needs were largely ignored and frustrated in the group. Furthermore, his roommate, Mr. C, seemed to be reaching out successfully to me in the group, while remaining less accessible outside of our sessions. Mr. D's jealousy and re-sentment about these perceived losses, which in part replicated his experiences with his lover prior to his hospitalization, seemed to result in his quest for recognition and supplies taking on a decidedly negativistic and oppositional flavor. Thus he was relating in a manipulative and condescending style certain to antagonize others.

This potentially dangerous provocation of others, along with a wish to es-tablish a special relationship with me, was again enacted when a new patient, Mr. F, entered the group. Mr. F was a very large man with an unkempt, fiery red beard and a loud and domineering manner. The session began with his sitting with his feet up on a chair, making it necessary for one of the other patients to get a chair from the back of the room in order to be a part of the circle. He complained about his unsatisfactory interactions with the nursing staff and said in a swaggering manner that, in contrast to Ms. B, who had been frightened by a lightning storm earlier in the day, he himself was never both-ered by such natural phenomena. He then forcefully presented his views of the authorities on the unit as punitive, irrational, and retaliatory. He expressed his concern that one could not actively confront such people because that would result in seclusion, and concluded by advising others in the group to "be cool" rather than get upset under such circumstances. Ms. B immediately labeled his views "bullshit" and noted that he couldn't possibly have anything valuable to say since he had been in the hospital only three days.

The level of tension rose dramatically, and Mr. C inched his chair toward me as I asked the patients to provide each of the potential combatants with some feedback about their behavior. The new man received relatively little attention from the older group members, but Mr. C was again engaged by others in examining the extent of his rage, his fears of losing control, and his embarrassed wishes for help from others. One group member related Mr. C's current behavior in the group to the fact that he had managed to lose his pass for the previous evening by telling a nurse that he was furious about the fact that his girlfriend, whom he was scheduled to visit, might have been spending time with one of her former boyfriends and that he was experiencing fantasies about shooting the other man. Mr. C needed much encouragement during the session to try to listen to what other patients were telling him and to try not to ward off their comments or put others on the defensive by accusing them of manifesting similar problems. Eventually, he acknowledged that, although he was quite angry with the staff for revoking his pass, perhaps he needed and was indirectly asking for external controls. Again, there was no discussion of the relationships group members wanted but feared with me.

Nonetheless, the notion of feeling used and victimized by significant others outside of the group continued to be examined over the next several sessions. This recurring theme was explored in relation to the female nursing staff and then in relation to parents. Although no group member spoke directly about the therapist, they spoke extensively about abuse from their parents, including physical abuse, and the psychological trauma associated with going through the divorce of one's parents. Patients expressed a deep sense of indignation and outrage about their experiences of feeling deprived by parents preoccupied with their own needs. Adopting a rather rigid, moralistic, and entitled stance, they adamantly maintained that parents and others in positions of authority should be consistently responsible. Despite this general attitude in the group, however, via the use of projection, members individually attacked each other for being too rigid and demanding, and avoided examining their feelings about me.

Low Self-Esteem. Patients' low levels of self-esteem and fragile sense of identity preoccupied the group. A clear enactment of these concerns, coupled with underlying fears of vulnerability and helplessness, took the following form. Mr. G, a 43-year-old black male who presented with a chaotic personal history and persistent drug and alcohol abuse, began attempting to engage Mr. D, who himself was becoming increasingly angry and frightened, and was threatening to leave. At one point he screamed, "Get off my case!" Mr. G turned to the group and confessed that he felt "helpless to do anything to help him."

I noted that his frustration and disappointment might remind him of his deeply disturbing experiences shortly before admission surrounding the death of his father from cancer. He said that, when he visited his father in the hospital, he sensed that his father was slipping away. He said his father "died in my arms," despite the patient's efforts at mouth-to-mouth resuscitation. He spoke in moving fashion about the bond between them, which had been maintained over many years although this man was not his biological father. Subsequently, he said that, despite the intense pain and anguish of this loss, he "could not cry at the funeral."

Ms. H, a younger, white woman, offered considerable support and encouragement to him to begin to look at his deeper feelings, and valiantly tried to reassure him that it was neither weak nor unmanly to cry in the face of such a loss. Later, several patients began to talk about how proud they were of their own children, how much they missed them, and how much they had sacrificed on their behalf. Mr. G was also able to acknowledge what he expected in return for his devotion from each of his children. In particular, he did not want them to run away from life and to use alcohol as a way of fleeing painful experiences as he had done for many years. Nevertheless, despite these apparent insights, the next day he decided to leave the hospital against medical advice.

Wanting help but refusing it, and then engaging in self-destructive behavior, remained a focus of the group. Mr. G reluctantly acknowledged his need for others and his tendency to offer rather than to accept help. In this regard, he was confronted about his decision to leave the hospital. This decision, which group members viewed as not being in his best interest, led into a further discussion of what patients did to themselves that intensified their difficulties. Specifically, Mr. D was asked about his having recently burned his arm with a cigarette. He revealed to the group that he "did it out of spite" because he was angry at himself. His efforts to exercise control in his relationships were failing, he felt a growing sense of anxiety and pain, and he experienced an enormous need to receive some attention and comfort from others. To distract himself from his deepening distress, to relieve the psychological pain, and to gain the supplies he craved while at the same time punishing himself and others for his plight, he began to engage in self-mutilating behavior. In the group he was able to confess his fear of asking for help from others because he felt that no one listened and that his efforts were constantly misinterpreted by both staff and patients.

Several sessions later, after the group had been working at identifying how individual patients set themselves up for hurtful interpersonal experiences and made it extremely difficult for others to successfully engage them, Mr. D began to complain vociferously about his recent experiences with psychological testing. Questioning revealed that he felt that the report about his Rorschach performance was "half right and half off the mark." While he himself had asked to see the Rorschach report, he did not want to know about the various interpretations made regarding his confused gender identity, his view of women as domineering and frightening, and his extreme level of hostility, which threatened to get out of control. A member of the group said that he impressed her as a "time bomb." Others confirmed this view and noted that he continued to pick at their vulnerable spots outside the group. Each additional confrontation seemed to arouse his feelings of being under attack. His extreme sensitivity to anything that could be construed as criticism finally resulted in his leaping to his feet and screaming, "I'm not taking any more of this shit! This group is over!" He stormed out of the room and dramatically slammed the door.

Before the next group session, Mr. C, who was completing the last day of a research protocol, left the hospital precipitously. It was noted in the group that over the past several sessions he had seemed to want to get closer to me and had been asking a variety of personal questions in an awkward attempt to do so. In his absence, several patients, led by Mr. D, began to attack me directly, labeling me "pompous," "arrogant," "someone who forces his opinions on others," and a person who "can tell your life story on the basis of two words!" Several new patients in the group, however, pointed out that I had in fact been rather quiet and "did not say much at all." The level of aggression involved in this attack on me was so profound that three patients later expressed thoughts of having wanted to run out of the room.

By the next day, Mr. C had returned to the hospital and attended the group session. At the beginning of the session he said to me, "Sorry I wasn't here. I heard you got dumped on." This comment was quickly glossed over. The major work of the group then became a review of the events surrounding Mr. C's abrupt departure. This in turn led to a painful but productive discussion of the difficulties patients encountered in separating from others. Mr. D was very helpful to his friend and roommate and provided him with considerable support. He noted that he was able to identify with his feelings of hopelessness and desperation. I chose to underline the importance of his help and contributions to his friend. This seemed to pave the way for further examination of his rage at me. He noted that he himself was getting closer to discharge. As had always been his custom, he tended to "blow things out of proportion" and to "use anger as a way of leaving." He said that he saw in me unacceptable aspects of himself that he did not want to face.

What he did not comment on was the fact that his father had treated him in a sadistic, abusive fashion and that his own sadism was beginning to be sharply identified in the group. Furthermore, there was no discussion about his libidinal wishes toward me, the jealousy and resentment stirred by these reactions, and the fact that these experiences might well be linked with the events preceding his admission. It is also interesting to note here that these two patients, Mr. C and Mr. D, who roomed together and were both diagnosed as borderline, appeared to be relying on a mechanism analogous to splitting: each seemed to express one half of the ambivalence they both felt toward me. To a significant extent both were fused and overly identified with each other. One tended to enact a rigidly stereotyped aggressive, counterdependent, "macho" role, while the other typically adopted a caricatured effeminate, demanding, manipulative role.

Nevertheless, Mr. D was subsequently able to begin to examine his dramatic manipulative interpersonal style, in part as he helped his friend, Mr. C, to examine his tendency to use anger as a means of "leaving with a bang." Mr. D's capacity to work well with his friend by relying on his own personal experiences was underlined in the group. Indeed, at one moment several members, all of whom were college-educated, bright, and verbal, noted, "I guess we behaved like typical borderlines, consistently manipulating and testing the staff and our therapist." As the last of these 15 sessions drew to a close, one of the members gleefully exclaimed that perhaps they could order sweatshirts for the group with a large "B" emblazoned on the front.

Conclusion

Since the group just described was an open group, with patients continually entering and leaving, there was no clear "beginning" for this particular group of patients nor any clear "ending." Therefore, instead of selecting an arbitrary end point of the group to discuss in more detail, I shall conclude by underscoring certain aspects of the therapist's role that, in my view, are particularly important.

To begin with, in my work with the personality-disordered and schizophrenic patients described above, I found that it is crucial for the patients to experience the therapist as accepting and nonjudgmental, as a person able to tolerate the expression of primitive drive content without feeling the urge to retaliate in accord with patients' own self-destructive fantasies. I found that it is important that rules, procedures, and participant roles be clearly explained, yet flexible. When irrational attitudes, expectations, and magical thinking get expressed, the impact of reality can be immediate and continuously asserted in the group. Group members must be consistently cared for, protected from precipitous attack, and assisted in reducing the degree of anxiety and chaos they experience internally by being encouraged to share their thoughts, feelings, and behaviors with the rest of the group and to receive reciprocal feedback. The therapist is often called upon not only to provide a safe holding environment in which the grandiose self-representation of borderline and narcissistic patients can emerge; he or she is also required to examine the vicissitudes of aggression as they are expressed. Such a posture requires clarification, confrontation, and interpretation in the here and now. A fundamental aspect of this role, particularly when working with borderline patients, is that a therapist must encourage the channeling of aggressive drives through verbalization, active problem solving, and especially tolerance and acceptance of projected defenses.

The "clarifying interpretation" (Kibel, 1981) lends itself to use in work with inpatient groups. Such interpretations are designed to elucidate the content of the sessions as reflecting the dynamics of the larger social field, namely, the ward itself. Clarification of these dynamics as reflected in the therapy group can provide an extremely important opportunity for patients, who can be aided to examine their own participation in the process. When the complex determinants of their feelings, attitudes, and behaviors are made understandable, the ego strength of patients, particularly their reality testing, is improved. Such interpretations can begin with the group as a whole, thereby minimizing the anxiety and narcissistic injury of directing such comments to individuals. Furthermore, group-level interpretations permit patients to experience a sense of group cohesion and mutuality, support for the expression of shared conflicts, and some partial drive gratification through member-to-member relationships. For the healthier, better-integrated patients, the group can thus serve as an interpersonal learning experience. For the less integrated, more disturbed patients, such clarification can begin to restore order and to create meaning out of the chaotic verbalizations and behaviors of the other members. In addition, insofar as manifestations of disturbed internal experiences can be understood in part as responses to the environment, the patient can derive comfort from the fact that his or her symptoms may be explainable as reactive, much as the responses of any other individual might be. On the one hand, this interpretive process may in a formal sense involve some deprivation as a consequence of patients no longer being able to disclaim responsibility for their reactions; on the other hand, it is often experienced as supportive and helpful.

In my opinion, another aspect of the interpretive role merits special consideration, namely, the integrative aspect. Specifically, I am referring to the fact that the therapist needs to be alert to the possibilities for assisting patients to integrate their experiences in the here and now with the dilemmas in their current life situations that precipitated admission. This integration across different domains of data is often a crucial element in more insight-oriented therapies (Klein, 1979). Here, however, in work with borderline patients, I believe it is essential to provide this kind of connective tissue for the brighter, more articulate and introspective patients whose primary ego defect lies precisely in their inability to perform this task on their own. Thus the therapist can draw attention to those aspects of the here-and-now process in the group that have direct relevance for the current life problems experienced by individual members. This artful and selective use of the group process requires that the therapist remain well aware of the patients' primary difficulties and that there is a mutual agreement that these issues are to be addressed whenever possible within the group. Because borderline patients have enormous difficulty in differentiating external objects, they are constantly involved in reenacting pathological internalizations and conflicts. There are, however, many opportunities for making these connections in a timely and helpful fashion, provided that a supportive therapeutic alliance has been established. Furthermore, once these disturbed relationships are replicated and identified within the group, additional opportunities are presented for reality testing and interpersonal learning.

Thus, when working with borderline patients, the boundary maintenance and interpretive role of the therapist takes on additional salience. Regulatory, integrative, synthetic, and executive ego functions are precisely the areas in which these patients demonstrate major impairments in functioning. As a short-term group therapist, one is, therefore, concerned with assisting these patients to attribute meaning to their experiences without feeling confused, over-whelmed, and fragmented. This requires the development of a supportive, differentiated, and stable group structure, despite the continuous and rapid turnover in group membership. The therapist must remain alert to clues signaling untoward and potentially disabling disequilibrium; on the intrapersonal, interpersonal, and group levels the therapist is often called upon to exercise a regulatory function wherein he or she focuses on and monitors the level of patient anxiety and affectivity, and the nature and extent of drive-dominated libidinal content. In attempting to promote more open and direct communication, the therapist may need to demonstrate such behavior and to serve as a translator for patients whose communications may be deviant or obscure. The integration of disparate, seemingly disconnected egocentric verbalizations is generally left to the therapist in the early stage of any group, and especially in a group of patients with borderline and narcissistic disturbances. Not only are such patients frequently preoccupied with their own particular concerns, but they often lack the capacity to take appropriate distance to be able to articulate, differentiate, and reintegrate their own experiences. Their synthetic ego skills are likely to be significantly impaired; they tend to rely on the therapist to orchestrate the rhythm and flow of the group and to help them to link their experiences inside the group with those outside. In the absence of active therapist interventions, such patients on their own are constantly struggling with the barnyard noises of an orchestra as it tunes up prior to playing a symphony. Patients feel they have no score to follow in which the individual parts are articulated and orchestrated to form a meaningful whole. The group therapy experience itself can therefore serve as a rehearsal, with the therapist as conductor, in preparation for patients performing in the "real world" outside the protected environment of the hospital. Adequate modeling of this complex conductor role can pave the way for internalization of these functions by individual patients.

References

Astrachan, B. M., Harrow, M., Becker, R. E., Schwartz, A. H., & Miller, J. C. The unled patient group as a therapeutic tool. *International Journal of Group Psychotherapy*, 1967, *17*(2), 178–191. (a)

Astrachan, B. M., Harrow, M., & Flynn, H. R. Influence of the value-system of a psychiatric setting on behavior in group therapy meetings. *Social Psychiatry*, 1968, *3*(4), 165–172.

Astrachan, B. M., Schwartz, A. H., Becker, R., & Harrow, M. The psychiatrist's effect on the behavior and interaction of therapy groups. *American Journal of Psychiatry*, 1967, *123*(11), 1379–1387. (b)

Bednar, R. L., & Battersby, C. P. The effects of specific cognitive structure on early group development. *Journal of Applied Behavioral Science*, 1976, *12*(4), 513–522.

Bednar, R. L., & Kaul, T. J. Experiential group research: Current perspectives. In A. E. Bergin & S. L. Garfield (Eds.), *Handbook of psychotherapy and behavior change*. New York: Wiley, 1978.

Bernard, H. S., & Klein, R. H. Some perspectives on time-limited group psychotherapy. *Comprehensive Psychiatry*, 1977, *18*, 579–584.

Bernard, H. S., & Klein, R. H. Time-limited group psychotherapy: A case report. *Group Psychotherapy, Psychodrama and Sociometry*, 1979, *32*, 31–37.

Bertalanffy, L. von. *General systems theory*. New York: Braziller, 1968.

Bion, W. R. *Experiences in groups*. New York: Basic Books, 1961.

Bond, G. R., & Lieberman, M. A. Selection criteria for group therapy. In J. P. Brady & H. K. H. Brodie (Eds.), *Controversy in psychiatry*. Philadelphia: Saunders, 1978.

Borriello, J. F. Group psychotherapy in hospital systems. In L. R. Wolberg & M. L. Aronson (Eds.), *Group therapy: 1976*. New York: Stratton Intercontinental Medical Books, 1976.

Budman, S. H. (Ed.). *Forms of brief therapy*. New York: Guilford Press, 1981.

Butcher, J. N., & Koss, M. P. Research on brief and crisis-oriented therapies. In A. E. Bergin & S. L. Garfield (Eds.), *Handbook of psychotherapy and behavior change*. New York: Wiley, 1978.

Cory, T. L., & Page, D. Group techniques for effecting change in the more disturbed patient. *Group*, 1978, *2*(3), 149–155.

Druck, A. B. The role of didactic group psychotherapy in short-term psychiatric settings. *Group*, 1978, *2*(2), 98–109.

Durkin, J. E. *Boundarying: The structure of autonomy in living groups*. Seventh Annual Ludwig von Bertalanffy Memorial Lecture, Society for General Systems Research, San Francisco, 1980.

Farrell, D. The use of active experiential group techniques with hospitalized patients. In L. M. Wolberg & M. L. Aronson (Eds.), *Group therapy: 1976*. New York: Stratton Intercontinental Medical Books, 1976.

Frances, A., Clarkin, J. F., & Marachi, J. P. Selection criteria for outpatient group psychotherapy. *Hospital and Community Psychiatry*, 1980, *31*(4), 245–250.

Frank, J. D. Group therapy in a mental hospital. In M. Rosenbaum & M. Berger (Eds.), *Group psychotherapy and group function*. New York: Basic Books, 1963.

Furst, W. Homogeneous versus heterogeneous groups. In B. Stokvis (Ed.), *Topical problems of psychotherapy*, vol. 2. New York: Karger, 1960.

Gunderson, J. G., & Kolb, J. E. Discriminating features of borderline patients. *American Journal of Psychiatry*, 1978, *135*(7), 792–796.

Gunderson, J. G., & Singer, M. T. Defining borderline patients: An overview. *American Journal of Psychiatry*, 1975, *132*(1), 1–10.

Heitler, J. B. Clinical impressions of an experimental attempt to prepare lower-class patients for expressive group psychotherapy. *International Journal of Group Psychotherapy*, 1974, *24*(3), 308–322.

Hoehn-Saric, R., Frank, J. D., Imber, S. D., Nash, E. H., Stone, A. R., & Battle, C. C. Systematic preparation of patients for psychotherapy—I. Effects on therapy behavior and outcome. *Journal of Psychiatric Research*, 1964, *2*(4), 267–281.

Imber, S. D., Lewis, P. M., & Loiselle, R. H. Uses and abuses of the brief intervention group. *International Journal of Group Psychotherapy*, 1979, *29*(1), 39–49.

Kernberg, O. F. Psychoanalytic object-relations theory, group processes, and administration: Toward an integrated theory of hospital treatment. *Annals of Psychoanalysis*, 1973, *1*, 363–388.

Kernberg, O. F. A systems approach to priority setting of interventions in groups. *International Journal of Group Psychotherapy*, 1975, *25*(3), 251–275.

Kernberg, O. F. *Object-relations theory and clinical psychoanalysis.* New York: Jason Aronson, 1976.

Kibel, H. D. The rationale for the use of group psychotherapy for borderline patients on a short-term unit. *International Journal of Group Psychotherapy*, 1978, *28*(3), 339–358.

Kibel, H. D. A conceptual model for short-term inpatient group psychotherapy. *American Journal of Psychiatry*, 1981, *138*(1), 74–80.

Klein, R. H. Inpatient group psychotherapy: Practical considerations and special problems. *International Journal of Group Psychotherapy*, 1977, *27*(2), 201–214.

Klein, R. H. A model for distinguishing supportive from insight-oriented psychotherapy groups. In W. G. Lawrence (Ed.), *Exploring individual and organizational boundaries.* New York: Wiley, 1979.

Klein, R. H. The patient-staff community meeting: A tea party with the Mad Hatter. *International Journal of Group Psychotherapy*, 1981, *31*(2), 205–222.

Klein, R. H. Some problems of patient referral for outpatient group psychotherapy. *International Journal of Group Psychotherapy*, 1982, in press.

Klein, R. H., & Carroll, R. Patient sociodemographic characteristics and attendance patterns in outpatient group therapy: I. An overview. Manuscript submitted for publication, 1982. (a)

Klein, R. H., & Carroll, R. Patient sociodemographic characteristics and attendance patterns in outpatient group therapy: II. Some relationships between these variables. Manuscript submitted for publication, 1982. (b)

Klein, R. H., & Kugel, B. Inpatient group psychotherapy from a systems perspective: Reflections through a glass darkly. *International Journal of Group Psychotherapy*, 1981, *31*(3), 311–328.

Lazell, E. W. The group treatment of dementia praecox. *Psychoanalytic Review*, 1921, *8*(2), 168–179.

Levine, H. B. Milieu biopsy: The place of the therapy group on the inpatient ward. *International Journal of Group Psychotherapy*, 1980, *30*(1), 77–93.

Mann, J., & Semrad, E. V. The use of group therapy in psychoses. *Social Casework*, 1948, *29*(5), 176–181.

Marsh, L. C. Group treatment of the psychoses by the psychological equivalent of the revival. *Mental Hygiene*, 1931, *15*(2), 328–349.

Maxmen, J. S. An educative model for inpatient group therapy. *International Journal of Group Psychotherapy*, 1978, *28*(3), 321–338.

Miller, J. G. The nature of living systems. *Behavioral Science*, 1976, *21*(5), 295–319.

Perry, J. C., & Klerman, G. L. The borderline patient: A comparative analysis of four sets of diagnostic criteria. *Archives of General Psychiatry*, 1978, *35*(2), 141–150.

Piper, W. E., & Marrache, M. Selecting suitable patients: Pretraining for group therapy as a method of patient selection. *Small Group Behavior*, 1981, *12*(4), 459–475.

Powdermaker, F. B., & Frank, J. D. *Group psychotherapy: Studies in methodology of research and therapy.* Cambridge: Harvard University Press, 1953.

Rice, C. A., & Rutan, J. S. Boundary maintenance in inpatient therapy groups. *International Journal of Group Psychotherapy*, 1981, *31*(3), 297–309.

Rioch, M. J. The work of Wilfred Bion on groups. *Psychiatry*, 1970, *33*(1), 56–66.

Rioch, M. J. "All we like sheep—" (Isaiah 53:6): Followers and leaders. *Psychiatry*, 1971, *34*(3), 258–273.

Rutan, J. S., & Alonso, A. Some guidelines for group therapists. *Group*, 1978, *2*(1), 4–13.

Singer, D. L., Astrachan, B. M., Gould, L. J., & Klein, E. B. Boundary management in psychological work with groups. *Journal of Applied Behavioral Science*, 1975, *11*(2), 137–176.

Sloane, R. B., Cristol, A. H., Pepernik, M. C., & Staples, F. R. Role preparation and expectation of improvement in psychotherapy. *Journal of Nervous and Mental Diseases,* 1970, *150*(1), 18–26.

Soloff, P. H., & Ulrich, R. F. Diagnostic interview for borderline patients. *Archives of General Psychiatry,* 1981, *38*(6), 686–692.

Spitzer, R. L., Endicott, J., & Gibbon, M. Crossing the border into borderline personality and borderline schizophrenia: The development of criteria. *Archives of General Psychiatry,* 1979, *36*(1), 17–24.

Standish, C. T., & Semrad, E. V. Group psychotherapy with psychotics. *Journal of Psychiatric Social Work,* 1951, *20*(4), 143–150.

Strupp, H. H., & Bloxom, A. L. Preparing lower-class patients for group psychotherapy: Development and evaluation of a role-induction film. *Journal of Consulting and Clinical Psychology,* 1973, *41*(3), 373–384.

Trick, O. L., Jacobs, M. K., & Spradlin, W. W. An inpatient teaching laboratory as a milieu force. In A. Jacobs & W. W. Spradlin (Eds.), *The group as agent.* New York: Behavioral Publications, 1974.

Truax, C. D., & Wargo, D. G. Effects of vicarious therapy pretraining and alternate sessions on outcome in group psychotherapy with outpatients. *Journal of Consulting and Clinical Psychology,* 1969, *33*(4), 440–447.

Warren, N. C., & Rice, L. N. Structure and stabilizing of psychotherapy for low-prognosis clients. *Journal of Consulting and Clinical Psychology,* 1972, *39*(2), 173–181.

Waxer, P. H. Short-term group psychotherapy: Some principles and techniques. *International Journal of Group Psychotherapy,* 1977, *27*(1), 33–42.

Wender, L. The dynamics of group psychotherapy and its application. *Journal of Nervous and Mental Disease,* 1936, *84*(1), 54–60.

Whalen, C. Effects of a model and instructions on group verbal behaviors. *Journal of Consulting and Clinical Psychology,* 1969, *33*(5), 509–521.

Wolf, A. Short term group psychotherapy. In L. R. Wolberg (Ed.), *Short term psychotherapy.* New York: Grune & Stratton, 1965.

Woods, M., & Melnick, J. A review of group therapy selection criteria. *Small Group Behavior,* 1979, *10*(2), 155–175.

Yalom, I. D. A study of group therapy droputs. *Archives of General Psychiatry,* 1966, *14*(4), 393–414.

Yalom, I. D. *The theory and practice of group psychotherapy* (2nd ed.). New York: Basic Books, 1975.

Yalom, I. D., Houts, P. S., Newell, G., & Rand, K. H. Preparation of patients for group therapy. *Archives of General Psychiatry,* 1967, *17*(4), 416–427.

17

Short-Term Group Therapy for Newly Blind Men

Susan Lavinsky Krausz, D.S.W.

SUSAN LAVINSKY KRAUSZ is an assistant professor in the School of Social Work at New York University and a psychotherapist in private practice in New York City.

> It is superficial, if not naive, to think of blindness as a blow to the eyes only, to sight only. It is a destructive blow to the self-image which man has carefully though unconsciously constructed throughout his lifetime, a blow almost to his being itself (Carroll, 1961).

For the individual who loses his sight, blindness means the end of a way of life. Daily tasks are no longer routine; walking, traveling, reading, writing pose major obstacles. The newly blind person often suffers the loss of career, job opportunities, and financial security, as well as many outlets for recreation and enjoyment. His or her altered relationships with other people—indeed, with the entire social and physical environment—impact on the total personality. The newly blind person must accept an unaccustomed degree of dependency, while at the same time striving to maintain a feeling of personal adequacy and a sense of control over his or her life. This is perhaps the greatest and most difficult challenge to the newly blind.

If we consider the multiple losses experienced by the newly blind, we can begin to understand how blindness almost universally has the power to upset lifelong patterns of adaptive functioning and the total personality organization. Those who work with the newly blind, therefore, must take into account that they are seeing these individuals in an altered state. The crisis is usually accompanied by severe depression, which is appropriate and understandable given the realities of the situation (Sachar, 1975).

The goals of psychotherapy for the newly blind are therefore twofold and must be accomplished concurrently: to help patients mourn their loss and at the same time to provide support and structure so they can continue to feel cared about and a part of the world. During this time of crisis external structure must fill the need that internal function cannot (Peretz, 1970). Structure and consistency in the environment and in the therapeutic situation can enable patients to gather their inner resources for coping and to reestablish control over their lives.

Psychological adjustment to any disability involves recognition of losses and life changes and a restructuring of the ego that will allow for the incorporation of the disability into one's self-image. To accomplish this, the newly blind person must (1) recognize that his survival and positive feeling states are threatened, (2) come to terms with the objective meaning of his loss, and (3) cope with the apprehensions, fears, and anger provoked by the burden of blindness.

This paper relates primarily to the psychological adjustments that the newly blind person must make before he can be restored to his optimal level of functioning, and specifically to the use of group psychotherapy as the primary treatment modality in working with newly blind adults. I will discuss in detail the following issues: establishing a group, group cohesion, transference, countertransference, the mourning process, therapeutic tasks, and treatment interventions. Although the scope of this paper is limited to my experience with blind patients, many of the problems, adjustments, and therapeutic interventions have relevance to work with patients suffering other physical losses.

Background

The Ophthalmology Clinic of the Brooklyn Veterans Administration Hospital sees about 500 outpatients monthly, of whom a small number are legally blind. Most of these are men between the ages of 45 and 70 from lower-middle-class and working-class families. Their religious, racial, and ethnic backgrounds vary widely, and approximately 60 percent are married. By and large, it is an infirm population, the majority suffering from the effects of diabetes, amputations, and strokes in addition to their blindness.

Although their social and psychological functioning varies greatly, the responses of these patients to blindness tend to be similar. Blindness threatens to overwhelm their ego capacities, and to protect themselves they have adopted various defenses. The one most often chosen is to deny that they could suffer such a loss or that it could be permanent (Carroll, 1961). A consequence of this denial is their inability to accept rehabilitation because that would mean resigning themselves to life without vision. There is a magical quality to this denial. The patient seems to say: "If I accept rehabilitation, I will really be blind; however, if I do not learn how to be blind (rehabilitate), I will remain sighted." This massive denial prevents patients from fully experiencing the loss they have suffered and leads to chronic depression and isolation. Even after three to five years, many of these patients remain isolated in their communities and have not received any type of rehabilitation beyond the superficial acceptance of a braille watch or a white cane, which, incidentally, they often have not learned to use properly. Although many of the patients are aware of the comprehensive rehabilitation services offered by the VA and other community agencies, very few make any effort to avail themselves of these services. The thought of being blind is still too frightening to accept.

In 1976, the hospital's Social Work Services Department undertook to help these patients accept their blindness, thereby freeing them to go on toward rehabilitation and achieve their optimal potentials. In view of the social and emotional isolation these patients were experiencing, it was felt that group psychotherapy would be the preferred treatment modality. Yalom (1975) points out that there are several features inherent in group therapy that are not available in individual treatment. The group experience allows patients to discover that they are not alone (universality) and to feel that they are helping others by their participation (altruism). In addition, by observing others coping with the same problems they experience, patients are introduced to the element of hope. All these considerations, coupled with group cohesiveness, were especially relevant to the needs of our blind patients.

During the next two years I conducted four time-limited groups of 12 to 18 weeks' duration for blind outpatients at the VA hospital. The groups, which averaged eight men, met once a week for 1½ hours in my office on the hospital's Ophthalmology Ward. The meeting time was 10 A.M., when the energy levels of these men were perhaps at their highest points of the day. Their other hospital appointments were coordinated with the group meeting time, and the hospital provided transportation.

The criteria for group membership were flexible. Generally, only actively psychotic patients and those with organic brain syndrome were excluded. Although there was no age limit, many patients over 70 chose not to participate. These older patients tended to be uninterested in modifying their lifestyles and were satisfied with dependent relationships within their families. My experience with older patients who did participate proved that age was not a barrier to successful group participation.

Group composition varied depending on the particular clinic population at the time each group was formed. Members' ages ranged from 45 to 79 with most falling between 50 and 62. Members suffered varying degrees of visual loss; nearly all had some residual vision, although all were legally blind.

Despite some variations from group to group, a number of basic issues were salient in all, and these will be the focus of the remainder of this paper.

Engagement

My initial concern was how to engage these patients in a treatment relationship and help them accept the losses brought about by blindness in a way that would not overwhelm the ego. A screening process was developed whereby all legally blind patients known to the clinic were identified and referred for evaluation. At the point of intervention, most patients were depressed and highly defended, actively denying the losses they had experienced. If these patients had been directly confronted with the many problems of blindness at that time, their egos might indeed have been overwhelmed. It was crucial, therefore, that the therapist respect the patients' defenses and resist the tendency to move too quickly into these issues. My activities had to be directed toward strengthening the patients' egos so they could begin to cope with the problems of blindness. Until patients reached that point, I felt, they would be unable to accept the idea of group participation. I found that this process of engagement could be accomplished in two or three individual sessions.

Before the patients could face the crisis of blindness, they had first to experience the therapist as someone who could accept their blindness and reinforce their sense of adequacy at a time when they themselves were questioning it. I conveyed this attitude through my desire to understand the patients' feelings about their total situations as well as their blindness. The meaning of the blindness and the underlying fears and fantasies became gradually more accessible as the patients developed greater trust and security in the treatment relationship and regained self-esteem.

The initial work with the patients involved helping them to share their problems related to performing everyday tasks such as writing, reading, eating, traveling, and so on. Patients' reactions to these daily occurrences were more available because the patients tended to be less defensive about them. The fact that I asked the patient about these problems and was sensitive to them gave the patient a greater sense of security and encouraged the sharing of other areas of difficulty.

Another way that I facilitated this process was to focus on some of the life changes the patients had experienced as a result of blindness. Aside from providing the therapist with valuable historical information, this type of intervention gave the patients an opportunity to slowly begin to share some of the losses they had experienced as well as to portray themselves in normal situations where they had experienced themselves as healthy and adequate. The patients' abilities to see themselves in a more positive light, coupled with the therapist's ability to convey appreciation of the patient in his totality, led to lessening of anxiety and lowering of defenses. Once this had occurred, patients were able to accept the need for treatment and were usually ready to move into a group.

Treatment Issues

Cohesion and Trust

One of the first problems of a newly formed group was the establishment of closeness and trust among group members. In working with blind patients, it was easy to mistakenly assume that, because of their shared problem, they would feel a natural sense of cohesion. Sometimes the group discussion could be quite misleading, and I had to be careful not to take statements of cohesion at face value and thereby avoid the necessary struggles around issues of trust.

Most patients began early in the group process to deny any discomfort or anxiety around the issue of differences. "We're all the same in here no matter what color or religion we are," was the familiar refrain. "We're all blind, and nothing else matters much." At one session, however, one of the patients jokingly stated that Mr. D's people (the Irish) were known to have hated his people (the Italians), but that he felt there was no truth to this. In another group the awareness of differences and the issue of trust centered on the specific group members' having different personal styles and attitudes toward life.

Whatever form the issue took, therapeutic interventions were directed at helping the group to acknowledge existing differences and to verbalize feelings about how this affected their participation in the group. When I encountered massive denial of any discomfort around this issue, I questioned the unanimous response and often pointed out some of the obvious differences among group members. At other times it was sufficient to help group members explore the latent content of some of their remarks, thereby increasing self-awareness and helping them to feel more comfortable expressing their feelings in the group. Ultimately, once the group had gone through this process, the members began to feel less threatened by existing differences, could better identify with each other's similarities, and developed a mutual respect that allowed them to acknowledge and deal with both.

The Female Therapist

Just as there were differences among group members, so too there were differences between the therapist and the group that had to be addressed so a trusting relationship could develop. The two most significant differences were that the members were blind and male while the therapist was sighted and female. Any group process that alluded to this was thoroughly explored. Such comments as "We better not curse in here" or "You can see!" required that I reach for all the underlying feelings, which undoubtedly included anger toward me. The anger may have been related to several of the following issues: the therapist's sight represented the patient's lost object and stimulated feelings of anger related to the loss; the sighted therapist was asking the group to adjust to something that she did not have to adjust to; and because of her sight and gender the therapist was distrusted as unlikely to understand their problems. These unresolved feelings of anger and distrust could have prevented the group from perceiving the therapist as an ego ideal and from aspiring to a higher level of functioning. I had to address these issues early in the treatment process to preclude this possibility.

Through the exploration of process, the group was helped to acknowledge their anger and to begin to discuss their feelings of discomfort related to the existing differences. By reaching for these feelings and supporting the patients' expression of them, I sent out the message that anger was a normal and acceptable reaction to their situation. This lending of the therapist's ego strengths to the group brought about widespread relief. The group members no longer felt they had to hide from the therapist, and they learned that they could bring up threatening issues and trust that the therapist would be able to handle them. The exploration of these issues helped the group to develop greater trust in the therapist and fostered the development of positive transference.

Until now I have addressed myself primarily to the negative transferential feelings evoked by the fact that the therapist was female. However, this fact had many positive effects that facilitated further movement in the group. Group members looking to gain favor with the female therapist (transferential mother) were aware that they would receive support and approval if they shared anxiety-provoking material in the group. This knowledge, coupled with the transference feelings toward the therapist, tended to bring out positive strivings of the group members, allowing them to risk more in the group. Aside from perceiving the therapist as a transferential mother, several other factors related to the therapist's gender also helped patients to progress. Once a positive transference had been established, patients experienced the female therapist as more accepting of their dependency needs, whereas there existed the fantasy that, with a male therapist, they would be expected to handle the situation in a "manly" fashion. Acceptance of their dependency needs as well as their blindness by the female therapist enabled many of the patients to be less fearful of rejection by their wives and helped them to share feelings and deal more openly with them.

Another area in which the female therapist proved particularly helpful to the blind patients was around the issue of sexual anxiety following visual loss. Psychoanalytic investigation has suggested that any physical loss is taken by the unconscious to be an attack on one's physical integrity, particularly one's sexuality. The close unconscious interrelationship between vision and sexuality most often manifested itself in the group through symbolic representation as well as through struggles around dependency and control. The issue was reflected most clearly in the matter of driving a car. (This subject was raised by every member who drove prior to blindness.) To these men, driving a car represented control, status, competence, and manhood; blindness threatened every one of these values. During the initial period of shock following blindness, patients plagued by feelings of impotence and inadequacy regressed to an earlier level of dependency, in which the overwhelming need was to be taken care of. After receiving comfort and support, group members began to experiment and test their ability to do certain tasks for themselves. Patients wavered back and forth, asserting themselves in some situations and retreating in others as they moved toward greater competence.

This struggle between the desire for independence with its risks and for dependence with its protection is perhaps the most crucial struggle for the blind person. It is helpful to accept and universalize the patient's understandable desire to be taken care of, while at the same time pointing out how this may prove to be a problem in the long run. Throughout the groups, this struggle was a major focus of treatment. The therapist's support and positive reinforcement of the patients' courageous efforts to be independent and assertive were of paramount importance. Patients who chose competence and mastery over dependence and passivity were able to find new ways to take control of their lives again. Patients who had not resolved the independence–dependence issue prior to their blindness were less likely to risk losing the secondary gratification and continued to obsess about the power and control they once had. Anything less than complete support of the patients' strivings toward manhood could be destructive and influence them to give up their feelings of control and mastery for gratification on an oral dependent level.

The female therapist's ability to accept the patients' feelings of loss and dependence as well as their independence and virility at appropriate points in the treatment process enabled the patients to move from impotence to potency. In addition, it encouraged the blind men to reestablish themselves as active participants (emotionally and sexually) within their marital and social relationships.

As the sighted therapist, I had another role within the blind group: I was the only one who could actually see what was happening. It was important, therefore, for me to be aware of nonverbal communications and to point out such things as body positions, facial expressions, excessive movements, and so on. However, I had to be cautious to distinguish between those nonverbal cues that were available only to me and those that the blind patients could perceive but might choose to avoid (that is, sounds and audible movements). In the former case, this information served as a valuable source of feedback to group members who needed to know how their communications were being received. In the latter case, the patients were using their blindness as a form of resistance to dealing with feelings, and the intervention had to be directed at uncovering the resistance rather than at providing information. If I had avoided dealing with the resistance, I would have accepted a lower standard of functioning for the patients, reinforcing their lowered self-images.

Throughout each group's life, therapeutic interventions were directed toward facilitating and stimulating emotional communication. Personal resistances were often related to collective group pressure not to open up painful or embarrassing issues. This peer pressure, coupled with the fear of being confronted by painful experiences, supported group resistance. The open exploration of these issues broke through this system and destroyed its effectiveness. Group members could then express themselves more freely and provide valuable feedback to one another. All these techniques were aimed at diminishing resistance and helping group members express their feelings about their loss. The focus on latent rather than manifest content as well as on group process enabled group members to begin sharing their feelings of depression and grief.

Mourning the Loss of Sight

The transition from talking about experiences to sharing feelings of despair was a difficult one. This may have been caused partially by the need to deny such an overwhelming loss and to resist relinquishing the lost object (vision). However, I believe that an additional cause was familial and societal pressure to "adjust" and "accept." Patients feeling that they wanted to be strong or spouses trying prematurely to encourage a positive attitude often prevented the blind person from experiencing the despair and grief that are normal reactions to loss. Unfortunately, this pseudo-acceptance prevented the patient from dealing with the reality of the situation and moving on toward a healthy resolution. Cholden (1958), a psychiatrist noted for his work with the blind, emphasizes that the tragedy of new blindness is only deepened and prolonged by encouraging the patient to escape from facing the reality that is upon him. Cholden argues that it is a false kindness to spare the blind person the shock and grief, that these feelings must be experienced before successful rehabilitation can take place. Essentially, the blind person must touch bottom before he or she can begin the long journey toward a satisfying and productive life.

The patient experiencing depression in reaction to illness may exhibit many or all of the following symptoms: self-recriminations, feelings of hopelessness, self-pity, lack of confidence, suicidal thoughts, and psychomotor retardation (Bellak, 1968; Cholden, 1958). It is crucial that the patient be helped to verbalize the breadth and range of these feelings so that he can begin to mourn the losses he has experienced. Keeping in mind the psychoanalytic understanding of depression as anger turned inward, we must continually encourage the patient to express the feelings of anger and rage experienced as a result of loss. Travis (1976) writes that "the person who channels his anxiety outside of himself through actions, weeping, words of anger and projection of blame is less affected than the person who denies the experience or makes a show of rising above it."

In view of the social and unconscious resistance to expressing grief, I felt it was imperative to encourage and support any expression of feelings in the group related to or set off by the loss of sight. This initially took the form of recounting personal experiences related to medical care, family, or work, without the expression of emotion. Group members were helped gradually to share their affective responses to these experiences and eventually to express their anger about being blind.

Before being able to accept the loss, it was necessary for group members to repeat over and over again their questions about why this had happened to them and their feelings of anger and frustration. For each group member, this was a time of crisis and disorganization in which he tried to make sense out of what had happened yet at the same time struggled to regain the lost object. Topics most often discussed included fear of losing all residual vision, embarrassment at falling or stumbling, reaction to becoming dependent on others, fear of being rejected by loved ones, and countless other issues. During this time of emotional upheaval, the knowledge that others were going through the same thing and reacting similarly was tremendously reassuring. In each group, there was at least one patient who commented that, before speaking to the other group members, he had often wondered if he was going crazy. The reassurance that anger, grief, and sorrow were normal reactions to blindness was constantly reinforced by group members, who shared their frustrations, failures, and feelings of hopelessness.

Group members benefited greatly from sharing the commonness of their experiences and reactions to blindness. However, it is crucial to remember that each individual has unique and personal reactions to blindness that require exploration. These reactions will vary greatly depending on the patient's premorbid level of psychological functioning and previous experiences with loss as well as on the social, cultural, and familial background. For one group member who was extremely artistic and creative, the most painful loss was not being able to sit in the country and see the natural beauty around him. When talking about this, he began to cry for the first time in the group. For another patient, who until one year before had been the family breadwinner, blindness meant that he was no longer the head of the household.

Once group members were able to start this process of sharing the meaning of their loss, the necessary grief and mourning could take place. It was difficult to know, however, when this task had been accomplished. The issue is quite complex, because we do not really know how long it takes an individual to mourn such a monumental loss. Indeed, it may be expected that people will continue to deal with these issues in stages, and will come to terms with different aspects of their loss through the process of ongoing living. My concern in group, however, was whether the members' continuous discussions about their losses and their pasts were an integral part of the mourning process or merely another form of resistance. Once I felt that group members had expressed their affect in response to their losses and appeared to be persevering around this issue, I chose to bring the discussions into the present. Rather than limiting our discussions to the meaning that loss of sight had on their way of life, we moved into dealing with the effect blindness would have on their futures. To allow patients to persevere around this issue would have supported their fears that they could not continue to find new meaning and positive experiences in their lives. After facing the resistance and understanding some of their fears, patients began to look toward the future with less anxiety and greater motivation.

The following patient interaction illustrates this movement. One group member began talking about no longer being able to socialize at a local bar with his old buddies. Appropriately, the question arose as to whether this was a loss brought about by his blindness or if indeed he could go out but for other reasons was afraid to do so. Further exploration revealed that the patient was afraid to find out how his friends would react to his blindness and was ashamed to eat or drink in public for fear of floundering. While group members were able to empathize and provide support, they also helped the patient to face those fears that had effectively isolated him and added to his depression.

Group members helped each other to face the limitations of blindness and to distinguish the necessary limitations from the unnecessary ones. The group norms were such that extreme forms of social isolation were not acceptable. Levine (1979) emphasizes the importance of group norms as a primary determinant of how therapeutic the group can and will be for members. Those group norms that encourage the optimal functioning of the blind group member help to counterbalance influences from his past, giving him the social support to behave differently. Group members helped each other to understand why they behaved the way they did before, and to deal with the feelings that new behavior aroused.

Groups and individuals will vary greatly in their ability to benefit from psychotherapy and will go through the various stages of adjustment at their own pace. It is unlikely, however, that they can make a realistic adjustment to their blindness unless they are able to work through a majority of the phases and conflicts described above. Once patients are able to accept the realities of blindness and progress through the psychological stages of adjustment, they can then address themselves to achieving an optimal level of functioning as individuals and as parts of a family. For any individual, achieving one's maximum potential is a difficult, never-ending task, but for the blind individual the task cannot possibly be accomplished unless some form of rehabilitation is received first.

Despite the fact that acceptance of rehabilitation was one of the original goals for the groups, I deliberately refrained from raising this issue. By allowing the group members to introduce the subject at their own pace, I could be relatively certain that patients had adequately completed the task of mourning and were prepared to move in this direction. Most patients were ready to raise this issue several sessions prior to termination. However, some groups were able to accomplish this task within 12 sessions while others required 18. In my experience, those groups that required more time to reach this point were composed largely of patients who (1) evidenced a greater degree of pathology premorbidly and (2) had been blind for longer than one year at the point of intervention. While these factors should be considered during the planning stages of a group, it remains crucial that the group be allowed to move at its own pace and that the therapist's desire to accomplish certain goals not interfere with this process. Once the issue of rehabilitation was raised, I directed the discussion toward helping group members express their feelings of anxiety and ambivalence around this issue. I avoided providing concrete information regarding specific programs, preferring to use whatever time was available to help group members come to terms with their anxiety concerning rehabilitation.

Evaluation

For these newly blind patients, the group experience had several distinct advantages:

1. It provided a socialization experience that many of our patients had not had for several years, which allowed them to feel less isolated and alone. It also decreased their fear of going out and experiencing new social situations.
2. It helped improve general communication skills and provided members with feedback as to how they were perceived.
3. The positive feelings they had toward the group fostered their own feelings of self-acceptance, allowing them to identify themselves more freely as blind men.
4. Group members established friendships that continued to provide them with networks of support and information. Some patients paired off and went to rehabilitation programs together. This support was especially helpful to those patients who chose to go to Veterans Administration Rehabilitation Centers, which were out of state, but were wary of doing this alone.

When the various groups ended, 70 to 80 percent of the members in each requested information and referral to some form of rehabilitation program. Frequently, two or three follow-up sessions were held with patients and their families to provide concrete information about programs that were available and to discuss concerns regarding the patients' entering into these programs, which often involved a period of separation from the family. Additionally, it was also helpful to connect patients with specific persons at the new agency or rehabilitation center who would continue to help them through the rehabilitation process.

These results were in startling contrast to our previous experience with these and other patients, who, without short-term treatment, were unable to accept rehabilitation. Even those patients who had the least emotional and social resources as well as high levels of dependency premorbidly were able to make excellent use of time-limited group therapy. Regardless of the premorbid level of functioning, those patients who were seen within three to twelve months of the initial visual loss were generally more accessible to treatment and more likely to be restored to their previous state of equilibrium and to go on for comprehensive rehabilitation. Those who had been blind for longer periods of time were increasingly difficult to engage in treatment and tended to benefit less from the short-term group. These results seem to be related to the fact that people in crisis are highly motivated and more available for work than at other times.

In view of these findings, I strongly recommend that every attempt be made to engage the newly blind patient during this period of crisis and that treatment be short-term and time-limited. Rapoport (1965), known for her work in short-term treatment, suggests that in time of crisis "the energy needed to maintain repression may now become available to solve the problem in a more appropriately mature manner." During this time of crisis, the patient's overriding need for help, coupled with his or her high level of anxiety, increases the efficacy of treatment. The time-limited nature of the group provides further focus for the patient and reinforces the constructive aspect of the patient's anxiety.

Aside from the above considerations, there are several other factors that support the use of the time-limited group with the newly blind patient. At a time when the patient is experiencing a drastic loss of self-esteem and confidence, the therapist's expectation that the patient can deal with this problem within a reasonable period of time is itself ego-restorative. It is also quite common for the newly blind patient to suffer a regression and assume an unnecessarily dependent role. While the patient may derive secondary gratification from this behavior, it usually serves to reinforce feelings of inferiority and inadequacy. A long-term treatment situation at this point would merely nourish this unhealthy dependency by providing the patient with a relationship in which he believed he could depend indefinitely on the therapist to help and watch over him. On the other hand, if the initial relationship with a helping person is time-limited, it reinforces the patient's needs to take responsibility for himself and to begin thinking about the future. One patient clearly illustrated this point to me by remarking at a group session that he did not want to begin rehabilitation at X agency while he was still attending the group because it might interfere with our sessions.

Undoubtedly, many of the patients discussed here would have benefited from ongoing treatment in relation to long-standing family or personality problems that had been exacerbated by their blindness. However, it is doubtful that they could have been prepared to deal with these issues until they had successfully resolved the immediate crisis of blindness. Although many of these issues are touched on in short-term treatment, the focus should remain on the immediate crisis. Unnecessary exploration of other issues may also reinforce the patient's resistance to dealing with the anxiety of blindness. Generally, my experience has been that patients who need help with long-standing problems are better prepared to deal with them and more motivated to pursue ongoing therapy after they have successfully resolved the crisis at hand in short-term treatment.

Regardless of the treatment modality, acceptance of blindness—or any other disability—cannot be achieved until several basic tasks are accomplished. These include uncovering basic threats to the ego, acknowledging the losses experienced and mourning them, removing the defenses that stand in the way of facing the major handicaps of blindness, and strengthening the ego so that blindness can be incorporated into the person's self-concept. These tasks can be accomplished only if the therapist is able to encourage and support the patient's expression of feelings and pain without prematurely cutting it off for self-protection. This often involves accepting the patient's expression of overwhelming dependency during the period of crisis and allowing it to run its course. It requires that the therapist be related to his or her own feelings about loss, separation, dependency, and blindness. The therapist's attitude toward blindness will have a profound influence on the newly blinded patient, whose expectations for functioning are minimal. The therapist's conviction that the blinded patient can continue to function and grow will force the patient to reevaluate his own negative expectations. This positive attitude will encourage the patient's strivings toward growth and enhance feelings of self-esteem. Although individuals may continue to feel a sense of sorrow about their visual loss, once fears and resistances are openly discussed, they are better able to feel that they have some control over their situation and can experience it as less hopeless.

References

Bellak, L. Psychiatric aspects of tuberculosis. In F. J. Turner (Ed.), *Differential diagnosis and treatment in social work.* New York: Free Press, 1968.

Carroll, T. J. *Blindness: What it is, what it does, and how to live with it.* Boston: Little, Brown, 1961.

Cholden, L. S. *A psychiatrist works with blindness.* New York: American Foundation for the Blind, 1958.

Levine, B. *Group psychotherapy: practice and development.* Englewood Cliffs, N.J.: Prentice-Hall, 1979.

Peretz, D. Development, object-relationships, and loss. In B. Schoenberg, A. C. Carr, D. Peretz, & A. H. Kutscher (Eds.), *Loss and grief: Psychological management in medical practice.* New York: Columbia University Press, 1970.

Rapoport, L. The state of crisis: Some theoretical considerations. In H. J. Parad (Ed.), *Crisis intervention.* New York: Family Service Association of America, 1965.

Sachar, E. Evaluating depression in the medical patient. In J. J. Strain & S. Grossman (Eds.), *Psychological care of the medically ill.* New York: Appleton-Century-Crofts, 1975.

Travis, G. *Chronic illness in children.* Stanford: Stanford University Press, 1976.

Yalom, I. D. *The theory and practice of group psychotherapy* (2nd ed.). New York: Basic Books, 1975.

VII

WORKING WITH PEOPLE IN CRISIS

18

Short-Term Group Psychotherapy with Suicidal Patients

Norman L. Farberow, Ph.D.,
and Katherina Marmor, Ph.D.

NORMAN L. FARBEROW is co-director of the Institute for Studies of Destructive Behaviors in Los Angeles, California, and clinical professor of psychiatry (psychology) in the School of Medicine of the University of Southern California. KATHERINA MARMOR is therapist in charge at the Institute for Studies of Destructive Behaviors.

Group psychotherapy continues to be a neglected resource in the armamentarium of treatment programs for suicidal people. A review of the literature of the past decade finds group psychotherapy with suicidal persons described in only 22 published articles and chapters (plus an additional ten proceedings articles and four dissertations). The neglect is puzzling, for the group process seems almost perfectly suited for such patients and their problems of loneliness, isolation, detachment, and depression. The group experience counteracts these feelings by providing for the patients a sense of understanding, acceptance, tolerance, and a renewed sense of belonging. The literature supports these views.

The Literature

A selective review of the literature since 1970 indicates that group therapy with suicidal persons in the United States has been conducted primarily in Los Angeles and San Mateo, California. A series of reports from Los Angeles has described programs of both short-term and long-term groups and discussed the dynamics, procedures developed, and results (Alfaro, 1970; Farberow, 1972, 1974, 1976; Frederick & Farberow, 1970; Marmor, 1979, 1980, 1981; Marmor & Farberow, 1974, 1979; Michels et al., 1973; White, 1977; White-book & Farberow, 1974).

In the San Mateo–San Francisco area, Motto and Stein (1973) first described the results of a therapy group with a psychiatrist and a pastoral psychologist as co-therapists. A series of reports followed describing the experiences with various kinds of suicidal groups in the San Mateo Suicide Prevention and Crisis Intervention Center and the Langley Porter Clinic (Asimos, 1979; Asimos & Rosen, 1978; Billings, 1976; Billings et al., 1974; Hackel & Asimos, 1981; Motto, 1977, 1979; Rosen et al., 1974, 1975). The groups included a long-term but open-ended group which was conducted in much the same way as one of the groups reported in this paper, the drop-in group. The experience of the San Francisco–San Mateo clinicians led to a strong endorsement of the group process for suicidal persons. In answer to an assertion by Horwitz (1976) of the superiority of heterogeneous groups, and his belief that depression and suicidal tendencies were contraindications for group therapy, they stated that:

> the "specialized suicide group" was statistically superior to no treatment, individual treatment, and day treatment therapy in terms of suicide prevention. In addition this treatment was substantially superior to traditional group therapy in terms of suicidal outcome. . . . The "specialized suicide groups" have served to foster a healthy identity and feeling of connectedness with a unit of people and to counteract the loneliness and alienation experienced by so many depressed and suicidal persons. (Asimos & Rosen, 1978, p. 516)

Horwitz (1978) accepted their evidence in a subsequent response. Comstock and McDermott (1975) in Houston also confirmed the advantages of group therapy for suicidal patients, stating their opinion that open short-term and closed long-term group programs worked best. Hogarth (1979) reported group discussions conducted by Lifeline, a suicide-prevention program with depressed inmates in a Boston jail, and Weisberg (1973–74) described group meetings of college-dormitory students in which suicidal behavior was discussed and discouraged.

Kibel (1973) pointed out some of the dangers of group work with suicidal patients. If a suicide occurred, the impact on the other patients and on the therapists could be widespread and intense. He described the shock, the feelings of guilt, fears of death and retaliation, fears of accusation from others, and the anger found among the therapists. The patients reacted with shock, panic, feelings of profound loss, anger, guilt, self-blame, and identification with the deceased. Kibel recommended continuing discussion in the group to relieve the feelings of the members. In contrast to the groups reported in this and other papers, Kibel's group was not a "specialized suicide group" and the other group members were not also suicidal, nor were the group leaders specially trained in suicide prevention.

In other parts of the world, Pluzek (1978) in Poland placed adolescents after suicide attempts in five different therapy groups according to needs—e.g., to gain insight, to learn work habits, to organize leisure time, etc. Hadlik (1970) in Czechoslovakia invited adolescents following suicide attempts to attend group meetings which were aimed at boosting initiative and teaching confidence. Wedler and Wedler (1978, 1979) conducted the same kind of open group sessions for suicidal patients in their hospital in the German Democratic Republic. They found a need to guard against "regressive dependence."

Paal (1978) in Israel reported the initiation of a Balint-group for suicidal patients, using the staff of an intensive nursing station. He found the staff effective by being available for help before defensive mechanisms reappeared, making communications between patients and surroundings once more difficult. Požarnik (1975) used analytic group psychotherapy with suicidal patients in Yugoslavia to help the patient regain a failing sense of personal identity. Achté and Rechardt (1972) in Finland and Ott, Geyer, and Schneemann (1972) in the Federal Republic of Germany referred briefly to the use of group therapy among other techniques employed with suicidal patients.

Family therapy as one form of group treatment for suicidal persons has also been discussed by Böcker (1981) in the Federal Republic of Germany; Alanen, Rinne, and Paukkonnen (1981) in Finland; and Braverman (1980) in Canada. In the United States, Richman (1971, 1978, 1979) has probably been most active in conducting family therapy with suicidal patients. Hammer (1972) and Bretz (1975) include family therapy among procedures for working with depressed and suicidal patients.

It is not too difficult to understand why there are so few reports. In general, therapists are not eager to assume the responsibility involved in the treatment of suicidal persons because of the stress, anxiety, insatiable demands, the need to be available at all hours, heavier responsibility (an outcome of possible death or injury), and repeated frustrations. Group psychotherapy is especially useful for the panicky, frightened, anxious patient who is overwhelmed by suicidal impulses and is reaching out for help in getting through the crisis. The patients most often will call each other first, and frequently find that that is as far as they need to go for the desired help. If the therapy is conducted in an agency or a hospital, additional important resources are also immediately available, such as a 24-hour telephone service and a wide range of referral resources.

Also, support for the therapists is usually available through immediate consultation, sharing of the transference, and backup resources. Even when a therapist is in individual practice only and treats several suicidal persons during the same period of time, the therapist is well advised to develop a hierarchy of supports for both himself and his patients, such as consultation, family support, hospitalization privileges, and others.

This paper will describe a program of group psychotherapy in a suicide prevention center, an agency specifically designed to deal with suicide problems. However, the program should be equally suitable for private or public psychiatric agencies or for community mental health centers. While our program includes long-term group therapy, this process will not be discussed in this report. Rather, two short-term modes will be described in detail: a drop-in group and a time-limited intermediary group.

The Agency

The Los Angeles Suicide Prevention Center (SPC) is one of a number of service agencies conducted by the Institute for Studies of Destructive Behaviors. The SPC is known throughout the community, both professional and public, as a telephone emergency service, and receives approximately 15,000 calls annually from suicidal people in a catchment population of about 7.5 million. The calls are answered on a 24-hour basis by selected, trained, and supervised non- and paraprofessionals. In addition, a Life Clinic staffed by professionals, psychology trainees, and psychiatric nurses sees patients on a face-to-face basis on referral from the telephone counselors of the SPC and on direct referral from other mental health professionals in the community. A small proportion are referrals from self or other patients.

The Patient Population

Suicide is a complex phenomenon, its varied determinants including behavior (thinking versus acting), chronology (past, current, or future), motivation (manipulation versus seeking surcease), communication (directed to individuals versus toward society in general), intention (to die versus not to die), and others. There are no "types" of persons who are suicidal; the impulse to self-destruction is found in many kinds of personalities and in many kinds of circumstances. However, characteristics of suicidal subgroups will depend on the nature of the populations from which they are drawn. Many studies of suicide are carried out on particular subgroups, and will have only limited application to other subgroups of suicidal persons. Thus suicidal persons in a neuropsychiatric hospital demonstrate kinds of behavior different from those of suicidal persons calling a suicide prevention center. Despite these differences, there are general features characterizing the phenomenon of suicide which are found in practically all cases, especially when the suicidal feelings are acute.

In general, suicidal people who call a suicide prevention center are anxious, confused, depressed, and desperate, experiencing crises in which an available resolution, ambivalently entertained, is self-destruction. Depression, anger, guilt, anxiety—classic features of many psychiatric syndromes—are present in various mixes and in varying degrees. Evaluations of suicide potential rank the callers to a suicide-prevention center as approximately 40 percent mild, 40 percent moderate, and 20 percent high or serious. However, from a practical clinical approach, every caller is considered serious, and the objective in responding to the call is to reduce or eliminate the suicide potential.

Of major importance from a treatment point of view are two facts: (1) Most of the suicidal callers, and especially those attending the Life Clinic, are borderline cases. They generally are poorly adjusted and barely functioning in the community, and they usually are calling the service because of an exacerbation of their problems which they have not been able to handle and which have overwhelmed them. (2) A large number of the callers are chronically suicidal and need ongoing, continuing care beyond the counseling offered by the phone service.

That the chronically suicidal person is essentially the same as the borderline was recently shown in a study by Marmor (1979). She reviewed the literature on the borderline patient and abstracted the 10 most commonly listed characteristics:

1. Negative or hostile reactions
2. Defective affectional relationships
3. Impaired sense of identity, low self-esteem, feelings of inadequacy, self-hatred
4. Depressive mood disturbance
5. Rigidity of thought and perception
6. Rigidity of behavior, repetitive self-defeating patterns
7. Poor impulse control
8. Polysymptomatic reactions
9. History of previous psychiatric therapy or hospitalization
10. Absence of delusions or hallucinations (except during occasional transitory psychotic reactions)

Of 30 consecutive chronically suicidal patients who had been treated at the SPC between 1972 and 1975, Marmor found that 28 were diagnosed as borderline, the other two as psychotic. She applied the list of characteristics and found that the diagnostic indexes were moderately or markedly present in every instance. The validity of the diagnosis was tested by having four independent clinicians evaluate the diagnoses in 10 subjects selected from the 30 subject sample. A 90-percent concurrence rate between the evaluators and the researcher was obtained along with a 99-percent concordance on the presence or absence of the diagnostic indexes.

The borderline characteristics are found in overwhelming preponderance in the population of our SPC patients and graphically illustrate the difficulty of any therapy program developed for them. It is our contention that the group experience meets their needs to the greatest degree possible, especially when the group formats have been designed specifically for their problems. The drop-in group is one example of such a group program.

The Drop-in Group

Format

The drop-in group was devised specifically to meet the need of SPC telephone workers for an immediate referral resource, a place to which the patients could come on the same day they called. The drop-in group received its name from the format. Group sessions were held daily, always at the same time in the late afternoon for ready access for callers who might be working. Potential members were invited to "drop in" and to use the service as often as they wished. The group was described as a place they could talk to others who might be having the same feelings and to group leaders who were experienced in treating persons who were suicidal. They could talk about their own problems or listen to others as they wished. There were only two major rules they must observe: they could not be violent and they must allow others an opportunity to talk.

Training of the Group Leaders

The group therapists were telephone counselors who had served on the telephones for at least six months and so had achieved experience in working with suicidal persons. Each person served first as a co-therapist with a mental health professional who was highly experienced in group therapy. When deemed ready, the worker was assigned to a group in which the co-therapist was an already-trained telephone counselor, and from that position he/she was eventually assigned to serve as principal therapist in her own group. (Workers were both men and women, of course.) Discussions were held routinely after each session with the program director or other professionals about the events in the meetings, to note changes in the patients, and to instruct about group therapy procedures and principles. In addition to the above, all group leaders attended weekly seminars in which problem patients, significant incidents, and therapy principles were discussed.

Group Process

The group therapists were usually assigned to lead a group once a week, and the patients soon learned that on different days they would meet not only with different group leaders but also with different group members. Consistency in the therapeutic approach was provided by the preparation of capsule notes and recommendations for each patient after every group session. The notes were made available to the group leader before meeting his or her own group that evening.

Patients were asked routinely whether they were in treatment with another therapist. It was not unusual for some patients to call the center rather than their own therapists in the midst of suicidal crises. Frequently, this signified some difficulties in the therapeutic relationships, but it may also have resulted from temporary absence or unavailability of the therapists. If the patient was already in treatment, the therapist was contacted either by the patient or by us with the patient's permission. While the drop-in group was primarily an emergency service, some patients seemed to prefer the format and often wanted to continue to attend without informing their therapists. The patient was firmly informed that his regular therapy was primary and that no continuing treatment could be provided without the approval of his therapist. That many patients liked the drop-in approach and continued to use it is indicated by one year's statistics, which showed that of the 157 patients who attended, 73 (33 percent) attended at least 10 to 14 sessions, and three came over 50 times. Most (55 percent) attended just once, justifying the name drop-in. The ages ranged from 17 to 70, and the sexes were about evenly divided.

Focus in the therapy sessions was on the here-and-now, the primary objective being to help the patient through the immediate emergency. From the wide variety of subjects, complaints, bitter accusations and wistful wishes, the main themes to emerge were feelings of rejection and loss, separation of a loved one, feelings of being unloved and unlovable, feelings of worthlessness, feeling unappreciated and unrecognized, inability to find or keep work, drinking, and deteriorating living conditions, such as no money or place to stay.

Curative Factors

In 1970, Yalom characterized the "curative" factors in group therapy as imparting of information, instilling of hope, universality, altruism, corrective recapitulation of primary family group, development of socializing techniques, imitative behavior, interpersonal learning, group cohesiveness, and catharsis.

The drop-in group provided seven of these factors, deliberately avoided one (group cohesiveness), and disregarded the remaining two (imitative behavior and corrective recapitulation of the primary family group). The adoption of a "no commitment, use-it-if-you-wish" approach, facilitated by the fact of changing membership and leaders, avoided the demand for loyalty or obligation to the group and its members. As a result there was also little or no opportunity for role modeling to be presented except in a general way. Most corrective procedures were offered verbally rather than behaviorally. The family atmosphere was also minimal, with no consistent opposite-sex therapist pair to serve as parental transference figures and no consistent sibling figures attending each meeting.

The drop-in format did focus on imparting information, frequently zeroing in on meeting basic needs, with direct suggestions on how to obtain food, clothing, shelter, and support. Instilling hope was a basic objective of the program, and there were frequent positive expressions of encouragement to solve problems and to plan on a future beyond the next two or 24 hours.

Universality was greatly facilitated by the group experience of sharing the feelings and problems of others and one's own, and finding that they were familiar and experienced by others as well. Suicidal people often feel they are alone and unique in their misery; it is comforting to them to know they have company. It was also very supportive to their own feelings of self-esteem to find that they could altruistically help others, that what they had to offer was often valuable to other group members.

Many borderline patients have had little opportunity to develop any social skills. Negative experiences of social and personal rejection may have increased shyness and reluctance to participate. The highly tolerant and accepting attitude of the group provided a nonthreatening atmosphere for the observation and practice of socializing techniques. Interpersonal learning was encouraged by interaction between the patients. The identification of the group as a suicidal group (feeling suicidal or threatening suicide was the ticket of admission) provided for many, often for the first time, a place where they could finally discuss without embarrassment their self-destructive urges and their prejudged negative personal qualities.

Speculations on Improvements

Reasons for the improvement that occurred unexpectedly among some patients considered incapable of profiting from any therapy are clinical speculations at best. Many of the "hopeless," borderline, poorly functioning persons who seemed to find the format comfortable and who stayed with the group for more than 20 sessions showed changes toward more effective interaction with people, increased socializing, and better jobs and living circumstances. They stated that they liked coming because they were not subjected to the usual demands or expectations, such as to get well, to use mature judgment, or to care for and be responsible for others in the group. The fact that the group membership and leadership changed constantly meant that they could focus on themselves and their own needs without guilt and that they could "use" the group at their own pace relieved of obligations to anyone but themselves. At the same time the role models of the leaders and of the agency exhibited the advantage of being "well" and adapting to society.

Attachment was to the center, not to the group, its leaders, or its members. When crises arose, patients continued to use the emergency telephones and to talk to the anonymous person at the other end of the line. For the therapists, the often regressed, childish, immature behavior was bearable because the reactions were shared by the co-therapists (by many if the patient had appeared on several different days) and because responsibility for the patients' behavior was assumed only while leading the group. When the group session ended, the patients were again the primary responsibility of the center or of their own therapists, if they had any. Thus, for the paraprofessional volunteer therapists, it was an ideal learning situation, one in which they learned by "doing" under close and careful supervision, constant monitoring, and without continuing responsibility. For the telephone workers who were tiring of the anonymous telephone work, it became an opportunity to expand their knowledge, participation, and field of activity. It was new and challenging and extended the length of stay of many of the volunteers who otherwise would have "burned out" or moved on.

Following are a few examples of patients who used the drop-in group:

Ms. V, referred by the crisis lines, was a 24-year-old woman with a long history of disturbed relationships. She was unpredictable, frequently infantile in her behavior, and constantly sought assurance and direction. Unable to resist male advances, she found herself repeatedly being "used" by men who seemed to have little regard for her as a person. She cried in ready sympathy when another group member recounted a difficult experience, but exhibited no understanding of others' needs in the group discussion. She demanded detailed instructions on how to behave in her relations with others. Attendance at eight sessions over a period of several weeks helped her to learn some control in her group interactions, but she still found it difficult to apply what she had learned to her activities outside the Center. A board and care home was found which provided more structure for her, but Ms. V was seen as probably needing close supervision and control for most of her life.

Mr. W was 18 when he first appeared at the center. He was in psychotherapy in a community mental health center but felt it was unable to help him with his depression and suicidal impulses. He had dropped out of school in the past year, the second time in the last three years. He was living with his mother, with whom he was in constant conflict. Several attempts in the past to move out and live independently had resulted in wild threats of suicide on her part if he stayed away. He was angry and bitter toward his mother but was afraid she would take pills if he stayed away. His father had committed suicide six years before and his mother had made him feel guilty by telling him it was problems with him which had so depressed his father. In 14 sessions spread over a period of six months, Mr. W was persuaded to return to school and was given support in establishing his own apartment again. However, follow-up six months later indicated he was living once more with his mother and that he was again having problems with his schoolwork. He was urged to resume attending the drop-in group to provide him with much-needed support when he became suicidal. He did so irregularly until he met a young woman and moved in with her.

Mr. T was a short-order cook who had many problems holding onto his jobs because of drinking. His wife had been in and out of the hospital many times. He was always glad at first when his wife was released from the hospital, but her demands on him would soon begin to weigh heavily and his drinking would increase. On the occasions when his wife returned to the hospital, he would be overwhelmed with conflicting feelings—relief from his wife's unpredictable psychotic behavior and guilt that he had contributed to its reappearance. Mr T's reaction to the pressures resulted in mild overdoses of pills, although on one occasion he used a knife to cut his arm. The group, in two sessions, worked with him to agree to call before he injured himself and to relieve his feelings through talking rather than pain. He learned he was not responsible for his wife's illness and was referred to the hospital social worker to learn how best to interact with his wife when she was home.

The Intermediary Group

A second pioneer short-term dynamic group-therapy program for postcrisis suicidal patients, organized at the same time as the drop-in group, was designated as an "intermediary" therapy group to indicate that it would serve an intermediate function between a crisis-oriented approach and a long-term, insight-oriented approach. The reasons for choosing this type of approach were multiple. Over and above the obvious economic advantage to patients in the form of lower fees and to the clinic in enabling it to serve a greater number of people, time-limited group therapy seemed to possess a number of specific potential advantages for this population of primarily borderline, chronically suicidal patients.

1. The group offered advantages over individual therapy by providing opportunities for interaction with a number of other people and for learning needed socializing skills in the process.
2. For some of the patients the group provided almost the only setting in which they could interact with other people and feel safe.

3. The fact that all the members of the group had attempted suicide as a way out of their problems enabled them to accept one another more easily, to learn from one another by mutual observation, to experiment with new coping techniques, and to provide one another with an important emotional support structure.

4. A time limit that was long enough to provide a new learning experience and some relief of symptoms yet short enough to sustain a high level of interest seemed particularly indicated for borderline personalities, with their characteristic inability to maintain feelings of trust in persons on whom they were dependent.

5. The time-limited process served to reduce the length of the "wait and see" pattern of ambivalence in decision making that characterized these patients.

6. The time limit also served to reduce the extent of avoidance maneuvers, facilitate priority selection, and provide an indirect learning experience in time management.

Format

The group contained a maximum of eight patients who met twice weekly for 1½-hour sessions for an arbitrarily established time period of eight weeks, or 16 sessions. It was an ongoing group, new patients being admitted on referral when vacancies occurred. Patients were accepted on a nondiscriminatory basis and all socioeconomic levels were included. Ages ranged from the mid-twenties to the early fifties. Males and females were about equally represented. Therapists at first were two mental health professionals, certified in group therapy. Later, one of the therapists was an advanced student in mental health.

Diagnostically, the largest group (25 out of 39) fell into the borderline category; some had had transitory psychotic episodes, others were narcissistic hysterical personalities. All had serious difficulties in interpersonal relationships. Scattered among the group were also neurotic personality disorders (9), schizophrenia (3), and manic-depressive reactions (2).

Selection of Patients

Patients were referred from four main sources: (1) the drop-in group; (2) other agencies in the community; (3) private practitioners; and (4) the center's telephone-answering volunteer workers. All patients were interviewed beforehand. All indicated histories of disordered lifestyles, impaired interpersonal relationships, serious suicidal attempts, and prior psychiatric treatment. Suitability was determined by: (1) evidence of some ego strength, either vocationally or educationally; (2) a history of having been able to sustain a meaningful

347

relationship with at least one other person for a period of time; (3) some capacity for self-appraisal; and, above all, (5) a strong motivation to be helped.

In retrospect, however, we found that diagnosis was important, for the manic-depressives did not work well in the group process, tended to solicit and arouse angry responses from the others, and were thus destructive to the group's progress. On the other hand, the schizophrenics in remission who were functioning in jobs proved to be acceptable candidates.

The Intake Interview

Intake interviews were used to evaluate the suitability of patients and to determine the nature of the presenting stresses. They also established trust and began therapeutic alliances that served as transitional bridges for entry into the group. When patients were deemed suitable, the objective of the intermediary group was explained as an effort to resolve difficult life situations by helping them to learn more effective ways of coping with stress. The problems to be focused on were discussed, and mutually agreed-upon goals were decided. These were always short-term, readily attainable goals, chosen to provide an experience of success and of control of their lives. The 16-session, eight-week time limit was stated to be inflexible; this put pressure on both patients and therapists to focus on the therapeutic objectives with a minimum of digression. Patients were assured that the group consisted of people who had shared similar difficulties and that absolute confidentiality would be maintained.

When a patient failed to meet the criteria for entry into the intermediary group, the latter part of the interview was used to discuss an alternative approach that would better serve the person's need, and effort was made to help him or her get placed.

The Group Process

The emphasis in the short-term dynamic group process was on here-and-now problems that were amenable to resolution. Patients were encouraged to present their problems openly to the other members at their first group meeting. They were told that it was just as important to assess one another's strengths as their inadequacies. Empathy was expressed and guilts and hostilities were reevaluated. Patients were encouraged to ventilate their feelings freely, especially their suicidal ones. Although many of the patients continued to use threats of suicide as expressions of their distress, the therapists and other patients responded to such threats without anxiety. Some of the patients stated that it was the first time they were able to ventilate their frustrations, fears, and needs, as well as their omnipotent wishes, and to obtain needed relief.

Adherence to the eight-week time limit emphasized the importance of each session and minimized manipulation and competitive rivalry for special consideration. It also implied the therapists' confidence in the ability of the patients to achieve the therapeutic objectives within the stated time period. The open-ended structure of the group, with patients entering and leaving at different times, did not create difficulties. Rather, it facilitated the integration of newcomers into the group and militated against the development of cliques. At the same time, the constant experience of patients beginning and successfully ending therapy kept the time-limited aspect of the group work constantly in the foreground, and served as a repeated vicarious experience of achievable separation and individuation.

Patients benefited by observing the therapeutic progress of other patients with problems similar to their own. Patients discussed their impaired self-images, their anxieties and their hostilities, and eventually their own strengths as they recognized themselves in the positive behavior of others. They were also able to identify the defensive patterns they had been employing to protect themselves from the humiliation of competitive failure, a recurrent theme in many of their lives.

Despite the fact that during the period they were in the group many sources of conflict could be identified, the therapeutic emphasis was always, insofar as possible, confined to the goals originally agreed upon. Once integrated into the group, patients rarely abused the privilege of contacting the therapists between sessions. When individual sessions were requested, their occurrence was always communicated to the group, but the subject matter of the individual sessions was not revealed without the patients' consent. In fact, however, the patients almost always brought the material into the group session themselves, sooner or later.

The group atmosphere was usually friendly and mutually supportive. At the same time, group members learned to be unsparingly direct with one another. Outward change in the patients usually appeared after the first three weeks. As patients began to improve, increased self-acceptance was revealed in their changing from dark or drab clothes to more colorful outfits. Verbal material began to shift away from expressions of defeat and hopelessness to renewed reality orientation. Behaviorally, this would be reflected in their returning to school, looking for employment, or, for those who had been functioning marginally at their jobs, approaching their work with renewed interest.

The mixed socioeconimic and age makeup of the patients in the group were not problems. The impulse to use suicide as a problem-solving mechanism was the common denominator which leveled all such differences. Thus, a 59-year-old depressed certified public accountant interacted well with two men in their late twenties who were barely sustaining themselves at a marginal economic level. All three exhibited compulsive personality patterns behind which were strong, infantile dependency needs. Both young men had had inadequate fathers who had hurt and angered them. Experiencing the older man's inadequacies in the group brought out the repressed feelings of the younger men and enabled them to understand their own fathers better for the first time. At the same time, the accountant was able, through his interactions with younger men, to realize the kind of feelings that his divorced wife and son must have experienced with him. The interactions resulted in the problem feelings of all three men being faced more rapidly with the empathic support of the total group.

One fascinating observation was that patients were able to discuss their suicidal ideation freely and easily, but found their private fears, phobias, and anxieties much more difficult to talk about. Instead they tended, when discussing their problems, to focus on physical symptoms, sleeplessness, or feelings of depression. However, when a more advanced member of the group took the lead, as when one of them spoke about his phobic fear of entrapment, it led to lively participation by the others and ventilation of their own fears. Some degree of symptom relief occurred in all the patients, reflected in improved self-esteem. Patients learned to face failures more realistically and began to look at each such experience with the question of what their contribution to the problem may have been. They also learned that a major factor in their previous overwhelming feelings of anger was often the existence of unrealistic expectations. They learned to recognize their own manifestations of repressed anger from signs like withdrawal, immobilization, and various forms of acting out. Seeing others in the group come in with tangible results from more adaptive patterns stimulated hope for change in themselves.

Although an effort was made to involve patients in the group process at their very first sessions, patients were permitted to retain control of the degree to which they wished to participate. The other group members were highly sensitive to the needs of newcomers in this regard. The more advanced members recognized the signs of discomfort that they themselves had experienced not too long before. The empathic expression of this shared experience often sped the process of integration of the newcomers. Both emotional and realistic support was readily expressed among the group members. Thus, when an advanced member commented that she had spent the major part of her life protecting her fears, it stimulated a relatively new patient to reveal the enormous extent of her anxieties at finding herself alone after terminating a 15-year marriage. The group's spontaneous reaction was warm and supportive, with offers from several of their telephone numbers for her to use in case of panic.

Transference Reactions

Because of the condensed structure of the treatment program, transference reaction developed rapidly and with great intensity. They were focused in four directions: (1) to the group, (2) to specific individuals within the group, (3) to the therapists, and (4) to the center. While the transference to the group was the most ego-supportive, it also presented the greatest problems in the termination phase. At that point, separation anxiety reactions at leaving the group tended to erupt. These reactions, however, also presented an important therapeutic opportunity; by interpreting and integrating them with the patients' previous reactions to stress, they became valuable elements in the last few weeks in the working through of their problems, particularly of their reactions to loss, their dependency needs, and their fears of change.

Two clinical vignettes illustrate some of the ways in which patients responded to the intermediary group process.

Ms. A, a 32-year-old woman in the process of getting a divorce, came to the center after two suicidal attempts within two months following the breakup of her marriage. In an effort to compensate for her feelings of rejection, she was running around frantically with a succession of different men, and had so neglected her work that she was on the verge of provoking a dismissal from her job.

Ms. A initially presented herself to the group as a compassionate, understanding, and loving partner who blamed herself for her inability to resolve the problems of her marriage. Within a few sessions, she was able for the first time to face her inner rage and jealousy at the woman who had displaced her in her husband's affection, and to recognize her deep narcissistic injury. Her ability to incorporate these previously unacceptable feelings in herself lessened the self-destructive, suicidal impulses with which she had been struggling, and also made her aware of the degree to which she had previously tended to place herself in the role of a victim. As a result, she began to realize the importance of more completely working through her maladaptive patterns. Upon completion of the intermediary group sessions, therefore, she was referred for further work in the long-term group at the center.

Ms. B was a 34-year-old woman with a history of several schizophrenic breakdowns, for one of which she had been hospitalized for more than a year. She was an extremely secretive, highly intelligent person, who had completed all of her requirements for a Ph.D. in science at a prestigious eastern university, but she had decompensated when she was unable to complete her thesis. When she presented herself at the center she had broken with the psychoanalyst who had treated her for 17 years. She was now clinic-hopping to get her phenothiazine medications. She lived alone with three dogs as her companions and security, but nevertheless was holding down a responsible job in an engineering firm. She was, however, on the verge of losing the job because she was having increasing difficulty in showing up for work and in relating to her coworkers.

In the intermediary group work, confrontations dealt primarily with her dependence-independence conflict, with the major emphasis on her strengths, unique qualities, and tenacious struggle for autonomy. After the third week

351

she spontaneously revealed that she had been using a false name, and gave her correct name and address. She also agreed to restrict her source of medication to the center's psychiatrist and to follow the regimen he recommended. During the succeeding weeks she progressively became less distrustful, more communicative and interactive with other members of the group, and less prone to impulsive outbursts of anger or withdrawal. At the end of the eight-week period she had great difficulty in coping with the process of separation. It was necessary to sustain her for a while with brief but structured individual sessions. She continued to see the staff psychiatrist for her medications, and also made liberal use of the center's emergency telephone service during the transition period. At follow-up she was maintaining her emotional equilibrium and functioning effectively on her job, which is the central stable element in her life situation. An important factor in her continued adjustment was her being able to maintain a transference attachment to the center, even though she began to call less and less often. She was helped to reestablish a meaningful therapeutic relationship with a psychiatrist outside of the center.

Treatment Results

The results of the intermediary group treatment program have been most encouraging. Over a period of two years, only three of the 39 patients dropped out of the program without completing the eight-week period. All three individuals, it turned out, were using the center while their regular therapists were away and had concealed their true motivations at intake. Of the remaining 36, 15 were restored to an effective stage of functioning at the end of the eight-week period, having gone back to work or school and no longer feeling suicidal. Sixteen others were motivated to pursue further therapy and were referred for this purpose either to the center's long-term groups or to other agencies or private therapists in the community. The remaining six patients seemed to be limited in their ability to achieve more basic personality change. Nevertheless they reported improvement in terms of their overall adjustment to their life settings. Another indication of the effectiveness of the program might be found in the fact that the 36 patients (out of 39) who completed the program maintained 100 percent attendance throughout the eight-week program. This can, of course, be attributed partly to the short-term nature of the program, but partly also to the degree to which both therapists and patients became mutually engrossed in achieving the limited reality goals they had set for themselves.

Concluding Remarks

Patients from both drop-in and intermediary groups frequently found their way into other portions of the program, which included two long-term groups, a socialization and a creative-expression group. Many of the patients experienced several of the formats, finding that at various points in their progress different formats were effective. For many, the greatest help through their crisis and postcrisis period were the drop-in group and the intermediary group.

References

Achté, A., & Rechardt, E. Brief psychotherapy of the suicidal patient. *Psychiatria Fennica*, 1972, 315–320.

Alanen, Y., Rinne, R., & Paukkonnen, P. On family dynamics and family therapy in suicidal attempts. *Crisis*, 1981, *2*(1), 20–26.

Alfaro, R. R. A group therapy approach to suicide prevention. *Bulletin of Suicidology*, 1970, *6*, 56–59.

Asimos, C. T. Dynamic problem-solving in a group for suicidal persons. *International Journal of Group Psychotherapy*, 1979, *29*(1), 109–114.

Asimos, C. T., & Rosen, D. H. Group treatment of suicidal and depressed persons: Indications for an open-ended group therapy program. *Bulletin of the Menninger Clinic*, 1978, *42*(6), 515–518.

Billings, J. H. The efficacy of group treatment with depressed and suicidal individuals in comparison with other treatment settings as regards the prevention of suicide (Doctoral dissertation, California School of Professional Psychology, Berkeley, 1974). *Dissertation Abstracts International*, 1976, *36*(12-B), 6369.

Billings, J. H., Rosen, D. H., Asimos, C. T., & Motto, J. A. Observations on long-term group therapy with suicidal and depressed persons. *Life-Threatening Behavior*, 1974, *4*(3), 160–170.

Böcker, F. Treatment and follow-up care after suicide attempts. *Crisis*, 1981, *2*(1), 37–40.

Braverman, S. Family therapist: Technician or clinician. *Canadian Journal of Psychiatry*, 1980, *25*(8), 666–670.

Bretz, J: M. Family therapy in treatment of a depressed patient. *Psychiatric Opinion*, 1975, *12*(6), 38–42.

Comstock, B. S., & McDermott, M. Group therapy for patients who attempt suicide. *International Journal of Group Psychotherapy*, 1975, *25*(1), 44–49.

Farberow, N. L. Vital process in suicide prevention: Group psychotherapy as a community of concern. *Life-Threatening Behavior*, 1972, *2*(4), 239–251.

Farberow, N. L. Group psychotherapy in the Los Angeles Suicide Prevention Center. In *Proceedings, 7th International Congress for Suicide Prevention, Amsterdam, 27–30 August 1973*. Amsterdam: Swets & Zeitlinger B.V., 1974.

Farberow, N. L. Group psychotherapy for self-destructive persons. In H. J. Parad, H. L. P. Resnik, & L. G. Parad (Eds.), *Emergency and disaster management: A mental health sourcebook*. Bowie, Md.: Charles Press Publishers, 1976.

Frederick, C. J., & Farberow, N. L. Group psychotherapy with suicidal persons: A comparison with standard group methods. *International Journal of Social Psychiatry*, 1970, *16*, 103–111.

Hackel, J., & Asimos, C. T. Resistances encountered in starting a group therapy program for suicide attempters in varied administrative settings. *Suicide and Life-Threatening Behavior*, 1981, *11*(2), 93–98.

Hadlik, J. Group psychotherapy for adolescents following a suicide attempt. In *Proceedings, 5th International Conference for Suicide Prevention, London, 24–27 September 1969*. Vienna: IASP, 1970.

Hammer, M. Psychotherapy with depressed patients. In M. Hammer (Ed.), *The theory and practice of psychotherapy with specific disorders.* Springfield, Ill.: Charles C Thomas, 1972.

Hogarth, D. J. A model for an in-house program to assist despairing and suicidal inmates/institutional residents. In *Proceedings, 10th International Congress for Suicide Prevention and Crisis Intervention, Ottawa, 17–20 June 1979.* Ottawa: IASP, 1979.

Horwitz, L. Indications and contraindications for group psychotherapy. *Bulletin of the Menninger Clinic,* 1976, *40*(5), 505–507.

Horwitz, L. Groups for suicidal persons: A reply. *Bulletin of the Menninger Clinic,* 1978, *42*(6), 518–519.

Kibel, H. D. A group member's suicide: Treating collective trauma. *International Journal of Group Psychotherapy,* 1973, *23*(1), 42–53.

Marmor, K. Process and termination in group with suicidal borderline patients. In L. R. Wolberg & M. L. Aronson (Eds.), *Group and family therapy.* New York: Brunner/Mazel, 1981.

Marmor, K. The persistently suicidal risk. In H. Davanloo (Ed.), *Short term dynamic psychotherapy* (Vol. 1). New York: Jason Aronson, 1980.

Marmor, K. *An evaluation of the relationship between the chronically suicidal personality and the borderline syndrome.* Unpublished doctoral dissertation, Wright Institute, Los Angeles, 1979.

Marmor, K., & Farberow, N. L. Group process and therapy as aspects of a suicide prevention program. In L. R. Wolberg & M. L. Aronson (Eds.), *Group therapy 1979: An overview.* New York: Stratton Intercontinental Medical Book Corp., 1979.

Marmor, K., & Farberow, N. L. Post-crisis oriented time-limited group therapy of suicidal patients. In *Proceedings, 7th International Congress for Suicide Prevention, Amsterdam, 27–30 August 1973.* Amsterdam: Swets & Zeitlinger B.V., 1974.

Michels, T., Cunningham, J., & Kilpatrick, M. *An exploratory study of group treatment for suicidal people.* Unpublished thesis, University of Southern California, Los Angeles, 1973.

Motto, J. A. Starting a therapy group in a suicide prevention and crisis center. *Suicide and Life-Threatening Behavior,* 1979, *9*(1), 47–56.

Motto, J. A. Starting a therapy group in a suicide prevention and crisis center. In P. C. Cantor (Ed.), *Proceedings, 10th Annual Meeting of the American Association of Suicidology.* Boston, 1977.

Motto, J. A., & Stein, E. V. A group approach to guilt in depressive and suicidal patients. *Journal of Religion and Health,* 1973, *12*(4), 378–385.

Ott, J., Geyer, M., & Schneemann, K. [Multidimensional clinical psychotherapy of a group of children and adolescents after attempted suicide.] *Psychiatrie, Neurologie und medizinische Psychologie,* 1972, *24*(2), 104–110.

Paal, J. Suicide prophylaxis within a Balint-group with the staff of an intensive nursing station in a general hospital. *Israel Annals of Psychiatry and Related Disciplines,* 1978, *16*(1), 46–49.

Pluzek, Z. Efficacy of the treatment program of attempted suicides among youth. In V. Aalberg (Ed.), *Proceedings, 9th International Congress on Suicide Prevention and Crisis Intervention, Helsinki, June 1977.* Helsinki: Finnish Association for Mental Health, 1978.

Požarnik, H. [Some problems of analytic group psychotherapy of suicidal patients in the Department for Urgent Psychiatric Help.] *Anali Zavoda za Mentalno Zdravlje,* 1975, *7*(2–3), 145–150.

Richman, J. Family therapy of attempted suicide. *Family Process,* 1979, *18*(2), 131–142.

Richman, J. Symbiosis, empathy, suicidal behavior, and the family. *Suicide and Life-Threatening Behavior,* 1978, *8*(3), 139–149.

Richman, J. Family determinants of suicide potential. In D. B. Anderson & L. J. McLean (Eds.), *Identifying suicidal potential.* New York: Behavioral Publications, 1971.

Rosen, D., Asimos, C., Motto, J., & Billings, J. Group psychotherapy with a homogeneous group of suicidal patients. In A. Uchtenhagen, R. Battegay, & A. Friedemann (Eds.), *Proceedings, 5th International Congress for Group Psychotherapy, Zurich, 1973.* Bern: Hans Huber, 1975.

Rosen, D. H., Asimos, C., Motto, J. A., & Billings, J. H. Group psychotherapy with a homogeneous group of suicidal persons. In *Proceedings, 7th International Congress for Suicide Prevention, Amsterdam, 27–30 August 1973.* Amsterdam: Swets & Zeitlinger B.V., 1974.

Wedler, M., & Wedler, H. Group therapy with patients after a suicide attempt. *Suicidprophylaxe,* 1979, 6(18), 36–40.

Wedler, M., & Wedler, H. Group work experience with suicide patients. In V. Aalberg (Ed.), *Proceedings, 9th International Congress for Suicide Prevention and Crisis Intervention, Helsinki, June 1977.* Helsinki: Finnish Association for Mental Health, 1978.

Weisberg, P. S. Intensive group therapy with college-age students as suicide prevention. *Groups: A Journal of Group Dynamics and Psychotherapy,* 1973–74, 5(1), 45–48.

White, R. S. The effects of specialized group techniques upon the social isolation and depression of suicidal persons (Doctoral dissertation, California School of Professional Psychology, Los Angeles, 1976). *Dissertation Abstracts International,* 1977 37(9-B), 4714–4715.

Whitebook, D., & Farberow, N. L. Drop-in groups as crisis and post-crisis therapy in suicide prevention centers. In *Proceedings, 7th International Congress for Suicide Prevention, Amsterdam, 27–30 August 1973.* Amsterdam: Swets & Zeitlinger B.V., 1974.

Yalom, I. D. *The theory and practice of group psychotherapy.* New York: Basic Books, 1970.

19

A Group for Relatives and Friends of Patients Hospitalized on an Acute-Care Service

Elaine Cooper Lonergan, L.C.S.W.,
and Gaetana M. Manuele, C.S.W., A.C.S.W.

ELAINE COOPER LONERGAN is currently assistant clinical professor in the department of psychiatry, School of Medicine, University of California at San Francisco and a psychotherapist at Kaiser Permanente Medical Center in South San Francisco. GAETANA M. MANUELE is now a social work supervisor in the department of social work at St. Vincent's Hospital and Medical Center in New York City.

While acknowledging the hospitalized patient as the center of concern, the Department of Social Work at St. Vincent's Hospital and Medical Center in New York recognized the trauma that relatives and friends of patients hospitalized on neurology and neurosurgery services undergo, and in 1975 its staff formed a group for these people in an attempt to meet their emotional and educational needs. Social workers provided the group's primary leadership. Nurses, however, were recruited as co-leaders. Since the group was open-ended, there was continuous turnover of membership. During the course of the group, there were three changes in social-work staff leadership. The supervisor of the group, however, remained the same.[1]

One hundred and four relatives participated in a total of 52 weekly group meetings from December 1975 to April 1978. (A six-week trial group was followed, after a six-month hiatus, by a group that met more or less regularly for a year.) Spouses, children, siblings, and friends of patients attended. Members' ethnicity varied: Hispanic, Anglo-American, black, and Oriental. In age, members ranged from 19 to 72. Although both sexes were invited to the group, members were predominantly female. Each week's membership was somewhat unpredictable, and compositions varied tremendously. It was rare for a patient's relative or friend not to be invited to the group. Only grossly disturbed (delusional or psychotic) people were excluded.

Members attended an average of 1.5 group meetings. As the group progressed, most members attended two or three meetings instead of one. Three members attended 10 or 11 meetings. Attendance at group meetings ranged from one to seven, averaging 3.5 over the 52 meetings. As the group became better known, the average attendance rose from 2.2 to 4.9 members.

The low number of sessions attended by group members is accounted for by the fact that the average hospitalization for patients on the Neurology and Neurosurgery Services was only 18 days. However, some patients remained as long as ten months, and this made possible the development of group norms that were transmitted by long-term members to newcomers.

Patients in the neurology and neurosurgery services suffered from strokes, brain tumors, and brain damage due to severe accidents. A number of patients were in comatose or semiconscious states. Most were totally bedridden and in serious condition. Members of the group at one time, for example, included: Mrs. D, whose son was comatose; Mrs. O and Mrs. G, whose husbands were also comatose; Mrs. M, whose son had been struck by a cab while riding a bicycle and suffered an undetermined degree of brain damage (Mrs. M's daughter had recently been killed in an auto accident); and Mrs. B, whose husband had suffered a massive stroke and might not be able to walk again.

The Literature on Relevant Group Issues

In order to develop a group that would serve the needs of patients' relatives and friends, the literature was examined prior to and concurrent with the formation of the group.

The literature at that time and since then indicates a growing awareness of

---

[1]Social-work leaders were Lorna LeSeuer, Milton Haynes (student), and Gaetana M. Manuele. Nurse leaders were Diane Mancuso and Barbara Roberts. Elaine Cooper Lonergan was the group-work supervisor. Anne L. Boland and Elizabeth A. Healy were director and assistant director, respectively, of the Department of Social Work.

the need to give attention to families of the physically ill (Breu & Dracup, 1978; Epperson, 1977; Gardner & Steward, 1978; Hampe, 1975; Usdin, 1977). Whether the patient lives or dies, family members may confront major life changes. Their companion or loved one may be physically and/or mentally incapacitated, discharged to a nursing facility, require household help, or die. Coping with a hospitalized relative is stressful. Many family members have disrupted their lives dramatically to be involved in the patient's hospital care.

The relationship between physical health and life stress has been well researched and documented (Moos, 1977; Strain & Grossman, 1975; Usdin, 1977). If the emotional needs of the patient are met, his or her chances of recovery increase; if the emotional needs of significant others in the patient's life are met, mental and physical illness in them may be prevented and they will be able to give more support to the patient.

Relatives' anxiety sometimes takes the form of displacing anger onto the hospital staff or seeking information from the staff in a repetitive, intrusive manner. For an overworked and pressured staff, this kind of interruption can be bothersome and irritating. It is a rare staff member who has the time and patience to counsel every relative. Sometimes specific information and direction are all that is needed to alleviate relatives' anxiety.

When staff is harried and does not find time to talk with relatives, an important resource for obtaining vital information about patients is missed. Patients may communicate to their relatives aspects of their physical or mental health status that they do not communicate to staff. Relatives may know of relevant historical information that would be important to share. They may alert staff to discharge problems early in the course of hospitalization.

A number of articles describe the use of relatives' groups to deal with the above-mentioned problems and to help families cope with the stress of illness. A few of these describe treatment groups for relatives of patients in acute-care hospitals (Barmetter & Fields, 1975–76; Bloom & Lynch, 1979; Cahners, 1978; Johnson & Stark, 1980). Most of these treatment groups consisted of members of the patients' immediate families, namely, parents of young children and spouses (Bardach, 1969; Cahners, 1978; Kornfield & Siegel, 1979; La Vorgna, 1979). However, little has been written about the patients' outside support systems, such as extended families and friends.

Of particular interest is that the groups formed in medical settings were open-ended and crisis-oriented. A characteristic of this type of group is that they contained people at various stages of crisis (Bloom & Lynch, 1979). New members stimulated others and provided them with a standard by which they could measure themselves (Bardach, 1969). For example, Cahners (1978) notes that, in his group, the parents of burned children found emotional strength from hearing those who "had been there," and the experienced parents, in turn, felt rewarded by helping the less-experienced parents prepare for the difficult future.

One problem encountered in a hospital-waiting-room group was that its heterogeneity often produced a subtle disharmony and lack of cohesiveness (Bloom & Lynch, 1979). The relatives' group at St. Vincent's did not experience this problem.

In general, the literature demonstrates that a relatives' group assumes the function of a family in a time of need. The group provides a safe place for the expression of strong feelings such as fear, rage, and sadness, ventilation of which is often prohibited by the family and friends (Wellisch et al., 1978). Through the sharing of concerns and emotional pressures, it lessens members' feelings of isolation. It further offers them an opportunity to increase their coping skills, understanding, and perspectives. There is evidence in the literature of the emergence of mutual-support systems that extend beyond the life of the formal group (La Vorgna, 1979).

In addition to having direct therapeutic benefits for families, the groups researched evidenced a benefit to the involved professional health staffs as well. Relatives who viewed the groups as demonstrations of concern for them appeared to communicate more easily with physicians and other professional staff. The groups also provided an educational tool for staff through which they gained a different perspective on the problems faced by relatives (Cahners, 1978; Wellisch et al., 1978).

Although, as mentioned, a number of articles have been written about medical-group programs, it should be noted that such groups are relatively new to the medical setting (Lonergan, 1981). Occasionally, an in- or outpatient service will provide a group for patients or relatives, but these groups are the exceptions, not the rule (Frey, 1966).

The Trial Group

The benefits of a relatives' and friends' group to patients, hospital staff, and the relatives and friends themselves were recognized by the Department of Social Work at St. Vincent's. However, most of the nurses and doctors there had never directly or indirectly participated in any sort of medical group. Only a few of the social workers had experience as group leaders. The group-work supervisor, however, was an experienced group-work practitioner, and she acted as a catalyst for those staff who expressed interest in working with groups.

The decision to start a relatives' and friends' group was made with the understanding that, to survive in the hospital, the group had to have the support of the system, which means that it was crucial for both the group leader and the interdisciplinary staff to feel comfortable with the group (Lonergan, 1980b). To achieve this harmony, the social worker who volunteered to act as the group leader was given the opportunity to choose the medical service with which he felt most comfortable and he received weekly supervision from the group-work supervisor.

The new group leader chose as his medical group the neuro-neurosurgical service because he was most familiar with the patients hospitalized on that floor; they comprised 50 percent of his caseload. Further, visiting hours on the floor were liberal, and relatives and friends were frequently present. Relationships between relatives and staff were sometimes strained. Relatives and friends occasionally interacted spontaneously in the waiting room. A number of relatives came from out of town, were strange to the city, and were quite isolated.

Analyzing the relatives' needs, the group leader formulated the following goals for his group: (1) to provide emotional support to members by stimulating a mutual-support network; (2) to facilitate optimum coping of members by exposing them to an array of coping devices displayed by others; (3) to educate members about disease and resources through staff sharing of knowledge and peer exchange of information.

Preparing the Leader and the Interdisciplinary Staff

Supervision of the new group leader focused initially on his fears about starting the group. His worst fantasies about the group were explored, and concrete solutions to problems of group management were proposed (Cooper, 1976). One of the leader's fantasies was that all the group members would be overwhelmed by grief; that they would turn on him and demand, "Why did you bring us together? For this? We all feel terrible"; and that no matter what he did, he would be unable to alleviate the members' pain.

In a subsequent supervisory session, the leader expressed another worry: "What if only two members show up for the group?" As he developed his fantasy, he felt apologetic and ashamed that his first group meeting was not satisfactory. The members did not like the group and blamed their displeasure on his inexperience. The leader's desire to overprotect group members by providing a perfect experience and his minimizing of his own and the members' strengths were discussed in supervision. The group-work supervisor appreciated that most new group leaders have such fears and that the expression of these fears in the company of a supervisor is of great value.

To elicit the support of the interdisciplinary staff, it was important to solicit staff members' input during the "idea stage" of the group. The group leader met with the head nurse and the medical directors and asked them what they thought about the formation of such a group. The nurses were enthusiastic, but the medical staff was skeptical: "What if they combine against us? What about confidentiality?" The leader was resistant about dealing with the doctors: "They are always in a hurry and can hardly find two minutes to talk to me."

He was encouraged to be more assertive with the doctors, and his efforts were rewarded. One example of this occurred when a meeting place for the group was being discussed. In response to the leader's suggesting the conference room, a doctor said hesitantly, "But what about the encased brains all over the shelves? Would that bother the members?" The leader had not thought of that and appreciated this important observation.

The group was designed to be integrated into the medical care of the patient (Lonergan, 1981). In other words, the relatives' participation in the group was to constitute part of the medical treatment of the patient. It was expected that staff would be able to treat the patient better if relatives were better informed and more content with the attention they received from staff. For this reason, it was important that the group leader communicate with staff members about the results of the group. This communication was to be formal through chart notes and informal through verbal exchange.

Since the group was dependent on interdisciplinary support, it was also important for staff members to help evaluate the group. The group was defined as experimental, with an evaluation to take place after six sessions. A memorandum was written clarifying the goals of the group and distributed to all staff (medical attendings, residents, and nurses) so that more staff members would be aware and participate in the group by referring relatives and by helping to evaluate its effect on relatives and patients. Following is the text of the memo:

> The nature of patients' illnesses on the Neurology and Neurosurgery Services is frequently catastrophic, chronic, or terminal. Family members are often faced with many changes in their emotional and practical way of life. They often feel alone, frightened, and isolated.
>
> I am starting a group for these family members, with the hope that they will share experiences and feelings and be a source of emotional support to one another. They will have the opportunity to explore alternative ways of coping with their situation and exchange practical knowledge regarding the best way of meeting their needs and the patient's. The group will not substitute for my working with patients individually, when indicated.
>
> You may make referrals to the group by calling me or by speaking to the Head Nurse. Once a referral is made, I will keep you informed as to the progress and attendance of the relative through notation on the medical progress sheet. I would also like you to notify me if there is any family member you do not feel should be invited to the group.
>
> The group will be open to all relatives of patients hospitalized on Neurology and Neurosurgery. It will meet for a trial period of six sessions, beginning December 3rd, at 3:00 p.m. in the visitors' lounge. I will be relying on your feedback in order to evaluate the experience and to increase its usefulness to patient, family, and staff.

Attendance

The meeting time for the group was established after the leader took a census of when relatives most visited the floor. This time also proved to be convenient for the nurses. The nurses agreed to help recruit for the group. When patients were hospitalized, relatives were informed of the group and invited to join. The initial invitation was followed by reminders from the patient's nurse and social worker. Nevertheless, attendance was disappointing. The leader's fantasy of only two members attending was, in fact, realized. To enhance attendance, the following steps were taken:

1. Invitations to the group were typed on colored file cards, making them easy to duplicate. The following is an example:

   YOU ARE CORDIALLY INVITED

   TO: A Meeting of Friends and Relatives of Patients Hospitalized on Spellman 4.

   WHEN: Wednesday afternoons 3:00–4:00 p.m.

   PLACE: Lounge

   PLAN: A Chance for Us to Meet and Hear from You and for You to Share Experiences and Information with Other Visitors on Spellman 4.

   Gaetana M. Manuele, Social Worker
   Diane Mancuso, Head Nurse

   These were given to patients, friends, and relatives when the patient was admitted to the floor. Thus the invitation was no longer merely verbal but written as well.

2. A professionally printed sign was posted outside the elevators on the floor. When people came off the elevators to enter the floor, they immediately faced the sign at eye level.

3. Sign and invitations were changed to read "friends and relatives" since a number of significant others were friends and had excluded themselves from attending the group.

4. When relatives and friends expressed reluctance to leave their loved one alone while they attended the group, visiting hours on the floor were changed for group members so they had the same amount of time to visit with the patients.

Despite these efforts, group meetings remained small, with attendance ranging from one to four people.

Composition

The group's composition varied tremendously from week to week. When the group was more homogeneous (in terms of socioeconomic class, intelligence, severity of patients' illness, life situation), the discussion was more in depth (including interpersonal and intrapsychic conflict). When the membership was more heterogeneous, the group still dealt with significant material (coping with hospitalization, exploring resources) but the material was not as personally exposing.

In one instance when a relative with a paranoid personality disorder attended the group, the leader felt the relative "ruined" the session and mentioned the need for participants to be screened. At the next meeting this relative attended, however, she was contained by the group. The comfort with the group process for all the members (it was their second meeting) may have made the difference.

The fifth meeting was particularly hard to manage. The composition of the group presented difficulties. Three women attended, one very disturbed and one quite healthy emotionally. It was Ms. L's third meeting and Ms. C's and Ms. H's first. The leader had not met Ms. H before the group. Ms. H appeared bizarre and not well oriented to reality. She stirred up anger and anxiety in others. Ms. L responded by becoming agitated. The group then attacked the leader. The leader was ready to give up the group after this meeting—it had come quite close to his worst fantasies. In retrospect, however, when one reads a summary of this meeting, one can see that even this problematic session may have produced some positive effect:

> Meeting began with all three women. Ms. L monopolized the meeting. They all said that they had seen each other on the floor and talked informally. Ms. H was tense and angry. She talked about the need for hope and how upset she was. She was angry at the doctors (and everyone else). They all participated in a lively exchange about specialists. Ms. H and Ms. L talked about their children and their despair and their loneliness. They then attacked the leader and the purpose of the group. Ms. H left suddenly and angrily. Ms. L began talking in a fragmented manner and left abruptly soon after. The leader continued to speak with Ms. C about her feelings in regard to the group. Ms. C said it was a relief to be able to talk in a group after being at her daughter's bedside.

The leader went on to have a sixth group meeting and it proved to be a gratifying one.

Accomplishments

The trial group accomplished the goals set for it. Members gained emotional support by finding that they were not alone; others shared similar difficulties and problems. They all felt that their plight was unique and that "outsiders" could not appreciate or understand the nature of their stress. Their involvement with their patients was all-consuming; they could not think of anything or anyone else, including themselves. They all agreed that hope was an essential ingredient to coping.

Members helped one another deal with the realities of hospitalization, particularly with being more assertive with staff. One relative talked to the nurses after a group meeting and succeeded in getting her husband's schedule changed. Another successfully approached her doctor for the first time. Practical information was exchanged, particularly about financial matters and ways to meet the astronomical hospital bills they were receiving.

The group leader continually had to educate the staff as to what were appropriate expectations for the group. Some staff members, he felt, were inclined to see him as a magician who could solve difficult problems. A nurse, for example, wanted him to make a particular relative less troublesome. The leader explained to the nurse that this relative's anger was displaced onto staff and was not a personal attack. This information alleviated the problem.

On the whole, the leader found that the nurses, who were directly involved in the group, felt positively about it. The physicians were not as involved as the leader would have liked. To facilitate better communication and involvement on the part of staff members in the future, the group leader distributed a written evaluation of the trial group:

> The group for relatives of severely ill patients met for six sessions. I want to inform you of some of the results.
>
> Eight relatives attended the group. The changing composition of the group each week influenced the type of interaction that occurred. Stronger members used the group more effectively than emotionally weaker ones. Similarity of feelings was expressed in terms of their being totally consumed by their relative's illness. They expressed not being able to think of anything else. For this reason, they found it especially valuable to talk to one another since they "were the only ones who *really* understood what it was like to have a severely ill relative." It was comforting to each to know that they shared similar feelings and were not alone in their distress. They all expressed a strong need to have hope, no matter how dire the circumstances, and they were able to help provide this for one another. One male patient expressed that he was glad his wife had a place to go where some of her needs were met. It made him feel less guilty about being hospitalized, since this made demands on his wife.
>
> The goals of the group, which included (1) emotional support, (2) exploring alternate ways of coping, and (3) exchange of practical knowledge, were all accomplished. Members got support from each other in articulating their questions and concerns and, after the meetings, were more assertive in communicating these concerns to the medical staff. They also exchanged practical information regarding hospital procedures and financial planning. Their energy was focused on day-to-day, as opposed to post-hospital, planning.

I feel this trial group has demonstrated that this experience can be very helpful. For this reason, I will start a second trial group in the near future. I will inform you as to the date I will begin and all the relevant details. I hope to have closer communication with the physicians so that the group can be viewed as part of hospital treatment and a team approach to patient care can be facilitated. I will screen all new members for the group since I have found that the group is not suitable for all relatives. I will appreciate referrals from all of you.

I take this opportunity to thank all of you for your help with the group. The nursing staff has been especially helpful in selecting and referring relatives for the group and supporting the group with patients, relatives, and staff.

The Long-Term Group

When the relatives' group resumed after six months, it was structured as a long-term, open-ended group. The addition of a nurse as co-leader proved a significant change, although time was required to clarify the roles of the two therapists. Recruitment was facilitated, and the group was better integrated with medical and nursing treatment.

Group Issues

In the long-term group, the following issues were frequently raised: (1) members' appreciation for the opportunity to articulate their plight; (2) revelation and reinforcement of coping mechanisms; (3) rewards and stresses of working with staff; (4) anger toward others; (5) discharge concerns; and (6) financial concerns.

Articulation of Members' Plight. Most participants eagerly took advantage of the opportunity to spell out for themselves and others the details of their particular experience in dealing with a hospitalized loved one. Many group meetings began by each member telling his or her "story." Members usually agreed that "outsiders" who did not share their direct experience could not understand, respect, or appreciate their strains and stresses. This dynamic can partially be explained by the group process of excluding others in order to become a cohesive group (Garland et al., 1973). Following are some examples of members' experiences extracted from process records of the social-work leader:

> Ms. T said that she was constantly anxious and concerned and went home at night and had to keep up a stoical front before the children. She then went to bed and cried herself to what little sleep she got. She dramatized the feeling of anxiety by demonstrating the way she breathed.

Ms. A said she had had several vivid and terrifying nightmares in recent nights. In one, she dreamed that someone was breaking down her door, and that she woke up screaming so loudly that she woke a neighbor, who came to see if she was all right.

Ms. W, a young woman, said she was constantly preoccupied with her mother's illness (stroke) and as a consequence her studies and personal relationships had suffered since she did not have extra time and energy. Up to the time of her mother's illness she had been an easy-going, happy-go-lucky woman. Since the series of strokes her mother had suffered, heavy responsibilities had been placed on her; she had to keep up the home for which she felt unprepared. She was the baby of the family and her mother had always been a reliable, steady anchor.

As relatives ventilated, they revealed struggles with (1) feeling abandoned, (2) guilt, and (3) role changes. Mr. R expressed feelings of abandonment:

Leader asked Mr. R if he came to the hospital every day and he said "yes," except on some very bad days. He said he could not comfortably stay at home—that he felt like an abandoned dog.

Ms. N expressed the double bind she was in which was sure to result in guilt feelings:

Ms. N said she was in conflict over whether to stay here for an uncertain period during her son's recovery (he was in a motorcycle accident and had a severe brain injury) or whether to go back to North Carolina to be with her thirteen-year-old daughter, who also needed her. Leader said that he often saw people going through such conflicts, with two equally important priorities to choose from. He said that it sometimes put people in a position that no matter what they did, they were going to feel guilty and that guilt was an extremely painful emotion. Ms. P said that people shouldn't feel guilty if they did the best they could.

Ms. W in the example above showed that she had to accept a new role in the family after her mother's stroke. Sometimes a man who is a patriarch in the family becomes ill and finds himself totally dependent on others and his wife has to take on his former responsibilities. In a family where sex roles are clearly defined, illness can bring on major readjustments.

Ms. P said she found it difficult being deprived of her husband. This reflected itself sharply when she had tried to fix the plumbing and found this was not her forte.

Reinforcement of Coping Mechanisms. Members seemed to agree that certain methods of coping were valuable and should be encouraged; fusion with the patient and religion were among these.

Members spoke of being totally consumed by the patient's illness. They could think of nothing else or anyone else, including themselves. Their moods went up or down depending on whether the patient felt better or worse. This fusion with the patient was considered adaptive. When questioned by the leader, members would articulate that *after* the patient's fate was determined they would think about their own future. They insisted on being focused on the present.

Members often spoke of religion as their primary source of strength. The following is a report of a meeting in which all but one member, Mr. D, had religion as a support. He apparently felt more despair.

> Leader asked how people were handling the constant worry that accompanied the hospitalization of a relative. From all but one member came a sudden outpouring of religious sentiments, with people saying that they had to rely on God for strength and to rely on the fact that God knows best. Ms. O said that she wore out St. Jude and that she prayed conversationally. Ms. P said church members prayed for and visited her sister. Ms. N said she prayed and wept a lot.

> Leader asked Mr. D how he felt and he said his wife (who had a brain tumor) was very religious but he was not. He often felt very lonely and he didn't have the kind of support others were talking about.

The emphasis on religion is closely allied to coping mechanisms of hope, optimism, and idealization that are known to be of help to people in times of stress (Lonergan, 1981). One's cultural and personality makeup determines the form such coping devices take. Any belief that helps one to feel that one is cared for by a benign force, whether a doctor, mentor, fate, or religion, will help alleviate anxiety.

Working with Staff. The hospital staff members were crucial figures in the relatives' lives. The relatives were dependent on staff, and this reality was bound to elicit intense and ambivalent reactions.

Often staff was praised and feelings of gratitude were expressed. Since members were dependent on those who were caring for and "determining" the fate of their loved one, trust in the staff was comforting to all. As relatives praised staff, they were assuring themselves that the patient had every chance of recovery. For this reason, it was important that the leader not question such praise, even when it appeared excessive.

Staff was unprepared for this praise (they had expected the members to be critical of them) and it resulted in staff's feeling more gratified in providing patient care and in improvement of staff-member relationships.

At the other extreme, anger *was* expressed toward staff in the group meetings. This anger was of two varieties: (1) irrational displacement of anger toward patient or situation onto staff and (2) reality-based anger. Staff had to learn to differentiate between these two kinds of anger and to respond appropriately. The first anger needed to be understood dynamically. It required that staff not take the anger personally but respond to the member in such a way that the underlying frustration be acknowledged. The second type of anger required that staff acknowledge reality problems, encourage member assertiveness (a healthier alternative than the common passive, withdrawn, and depressive mode of dealing with problems [Fried, 1970]), and facilitate effective problem solving. This process is especially helpful in light of the helplessness relatives often feel in coping with the complex and bureaucratic hospital system on top of a catastrophic life event.

Members did become more assertive as a result of participating in the group. Having a nurse and a social worker as group leaders helped members express their valid complaints directly. The leaders followed through on a number of complaints. In one instance a relative complained that the nursing staff had forbidden the patient to drink one of his favorite sodas. The member did not understand the rationale for this prohibition. Others complained about patients having to leave the hospital too quickly and about the shortage of nursing staff in the evenings and at night. Some of these problems were the result of the hospital's budgetary constraints. Staff could acknowledge these real complaints and instruct members as to the correct channels of communication in the hospital; the hospital administration wanted to hear from them. As members became more assertive, their self-esteem was elevated and they felt less helpless (Lonergan, 1980a).

Externalization of Anger. Members' anger over their situation was externalized not only onto staff but onto others (family and friends) as well. Few group members were in touch with their ambivalent feelings toward the patient. When feelings were displaced on other family members, family relationships that were tense before the illness became even more strained.

> Ms. O gave a description of her long and tense relationship with her mother-in-law, who visited her comatose son but who did not speak to her. There had been years in her seventeen years of married life when there was daily, dependent contact. When Mr. O became very ill, the relationship became hateful, with the mother blaming Ms. O for her son's illness. Ms. P said that her family had been divided and quarreled over how to handle her husband's illness (brain damage) and that she had often been upset by angry scenes and blaming sessions.

Discharge Concerns. Relatives were often faced with the difficult choice of whether to care for a limited, handicapped loved one at home—a task that most relatives wanted to assume but that staff doubted they were capable of— or agreeing to the patient's being cared for in an institution. It is at the point of discharge planning that the relative really has to face the severe incapacity of the patient and the fact that his or her life will be changed considerably by a major loss. Even if the patient does not die, he can rarely assume the same role he had in the past.

Financial Concerns. The members' deep concern over finances cannot be overemphasized. Some saw their life savings being drained. They usually did not express anger directly over this, but they did express frustration and anxiety.

> Ms. E's hospital bill for January was exceedingly large and the business office was pressing her to pay the figure and make arrangements for Medicaid. She was having trouble with the Medicaid office in her upstate county. They were insisting she sell some land they owned. There were other money problems and she felt her husband's long illness was ruining her.

For those members whose self-esteem was tied to social class, these pressures were especially threatening. For others, the strain of budgeting at such a stressful period was burdensome.

Challenges for the Group Leaders

Leadership problems that confronted the two therapists included: (1) managing intragroup conflict and competition; (2) facilitating constructive use of group contagion; (3) working out problems of co-leadership; and (4) recognizing their own emotional reactions to the material presented by the group.

Intragroup Conflict and Competition. Beginning groups do not tolerate intragroup conflict well (Garland et al., 1973). Its emergence often interferes with the group's resolving the "trust phase" and becoming cohesive. It is in later stages of the group that conflict is productive.

Relatives attending this group were often very needy and clamored for attention in the group. Some felt envy and jealousy when another member's relative was less ill or progressing well. The leaders had to intervene quickly when such premature intragroup conflict and competition emerged.

> Ms. L's expansive style and appearance (she is a woman in her 60s, quite well dressed and made up, dripping in jewelry) seemed to strike some negative sparks from Ms. M very early on, and much of the remainder of the hour consisted of attempts by leaders to defuse a bitter "set-to."
>
> Ms. M made the point rather insistently that the others (meaning Ms. L) ought to consider that their situation could certainly be worse. Here her man was in a vegetative state, with little prospect that he would recover, and Ms. L was complaining that her husband fussed over not being able to walk again. She ought to feel lucky that he was able to talk and think and that he stood a chance for effective rehabilitation!
>
> The meeting ended by Ms. M going to the elevator angrily denouncing those who did not know how lucky they were.

Usually such a conflict was not generated without an independent personality conflict. In this instance, Ms. L's made-up appearance was a cover for the narcissistic wound inflicted upon her by her husband's illness. She was a fragile, narcissistic personality. Her self-centeredness was offensive to others. Even the group leaders had to struggle to react nonpunitively toward her and to empathize on a dynamic level (i.e., respond to the panic over potential disintegration underneath the exterior [Stolorow & Lachmann, 1980]). In the following meeting a leader tried to be reparative.

> Leader said that last week had been a difficult group and he hoped that despite some tensions they all could learn from one another. He said that everyone was different, and that while they all had something in common—the illness of someone close to them—it was important to keep in mind that everyone had different ways of responding and coping and feeling.
>
> After the meeting Ms. L and Ms. M went down to see Mr. M and half an hour later they were standing in the hall talking.

The leader was setting a norm for the group (let's respect rather than compete with one another) by using "universalization" and "differentiation" (clarifyng what people have in common encourages group cohesiveness and clarifying how people differ encourages differentiation). The implication was that Ms. L belonged in the group because she had a sick relative as others did, and it was all right that she was different and had a different level of tolerance for distress. She probably felt more personally wounded and threatened by her husband's difficulty in walking than others, who were emotionally healthier and who felt less traumatized about having a relative who was brain-damaged. The leader set the boundaries of the group to include Ms. L and validated the range of coping behaviors that were acceptable within those boundaries. Sometimes the leader might say, "This is part of what is so interesting about the group—that people are so different" (Lonergan, 1982).

Contagion. There is a strong pressure in beginning groups to view everyone as the same so that members don't have to deal with differentiation (Garland et al., 1973). If others simply reflect the similarities of the participants, the group is less threatening. This dynamic helps groups become cohesive, but it can be destructive if members have to hide their differences in order to be accepted in the group. As one can see in the following example, if a leader does not intervene, the group interaction can be destructive for the deviant individual. Each person has to be encouraged to find his or her unique optimal coping repertoire.

> Ms. P vividly described her visit to a nursing home. The conditions were disgusting. The patients were lying in their own feces. She would not place her husband in a nursing home no-matter-what.

Ms. S, who had been checking such a placement for her husband, looked panicked.

The leader said that social workers were available to help with placements and that while we are well aware of some horror stories, there were some good nursing homes.

Ms. N said she was determined to take her husband home, virtually at any cost.

This group kept trying to establish the norm that "virtuous people took their relatives home." People who did not do this were "bad." The leaders had to work hard to give credibility and reassurance to those who were constructively arranging placements.

Co-leadership. Roles had to be defined for the interdisciplinary co-leadership team (in this case a nurse and a social worker). The nurse was not trained in group process and felt anxious about assuming a leadership role. Yet she was familiar with the medical aspect of the patients' conditions and adeptly and comfortably could provide valuable information and support. Thus at first the social-work leader "led" the group and the nurse acted as a resource person. Eventually, after a learning period, their roles became less distinct.

The social worker remained the primary leader of the group and attended regularly. The nurse tried to attend regularly, but when she could not other nurses would substitute for her. Nurses throughout the medical-group program at St. Vincent's valued their group experience. Although the voluntary, rotating nurses benefited from and enjoyed attending the group, it was difficult for the primary group leader to be constantly orienting and working with new co-leaders.

The group experience was most satisfying for the social-work group leader when he had a co-leader who consistently attended the group, for then the co-leaders had the opportunity to learn from each other and to develop an effective leadership style. Trust developed between them, and they shared their personal reactions toward emotional material presented by the members.

Countertransference. It is probably impossible to lead a group of this kind without becoming personally moved by the material that emerges. Often the leaders asked themselves, "What if this should happen to me? What if my spouse or child should become seriously ill?" Sometimes a leader would over-identify with one person in the group whose family situation was similar to her own. In one instance a leader became so engrossed with a member that he neglected to bring the rest of the group into the problem-solving process. Thus the leader's emotional reactions can interfere with his judgment in making therapeutic interventions.

Since there is a rapid turnover in this kind of group and a variety of people attend, leaders experience stress in attempting to cope with the personalities as well as the situational problems of the members. It is difficult for leaders to accept their reactions and interpret them dynamically. An example of this is the fragile group member who can be particularly provocative by seeming insensitive to others' woes. Leaders often react negatively to this display of narcissism.

The Leaders' Supportive Techniques

This group was designed to provide emotional support to relatives and friends of seriously ill patients. It was not meant to change long-standing personality patterns but to reinforce existing defense and coping mechanisms. It would have been unrealistic to expect personality changes when most members attended the group only a few times. Members' coping devices might expand by exposure to those of others. Members who did pick up new coping mechanisms were not pushed to do so; they responded naturally to the confrontational aspects of the group process.

The leaders evolved techniques that enabled the group to be supportive. (1) They provided structure and were active in the group. (2) They provided reassurance when they genuinely could do so; they never gave false reassurance. (3) They were empathetic, making an effort to *hear* what the member was describing as *his* particular distress and reflecting that back to him with understanding. (4) The leaders validated members' worth and reinforced their strengths by encouraging mutual support, reinforcing activeness and assertiveness, and respecting peer leadership. (5) Leaders freely shared information so that members were educated and could take more responsibility. (6) The leaders appreciated the value of humor when it arose in the group.

Providing Structure. The leaders gave structure in the group by a purposeful introduction at the beginning of each meeting and a clear summary at the end. Following is a report typifying such an introduction:

> I introduced myself, the nurse, and members of the group and outlined the purpose of these meetings, saying relatives and friends had found it helpful to share feelings and ways of coping. I continued: "For our part, we want to learn from you so that we might have a means for providing better care for the patients. We also will explore ways in which we all differ and look at things that we have in common."
>
> Usually as a way of beginning the group meeting, I go around the room from person to person, asking everyone to introduce himself. But on this occasion I decided to try something different and I asked if anyone had anything particularly pressing to talk about.

Following is a leader's description of a summary:

> As time to conclude neared, I briefly summed up some of the major points we had covered, one of which was the way the stresses of illness affect all family members and disrupt lifelong balances among people in the family.

An important element in structuring the group was using "universalization" and "differentiation" as described earlier. It was often the use of this technique that brought order to what otherwise might have been chaos. Sometimes it was difficult to find a strong enough commonality to balance the number of differences among the members. Finding a commonality was crucial to enable cohesiveness to develop.

The leaders had to intervene quickly when conflict arose in the group. It was the leaders' activity that allowed for constructive (supportive) norms to develop (Lonergan, 1981). The group had to have an atmosphere of acceptance and not one where members feared being attacked.

Giving Reassurance. Since many of the patients had grim prognoses, one wonders how a leader could offer reassurance to a member that was not false. Staff could reassure members that they would try to provide the best possible medical care. Following is an example:

> Ms. A expressed concern about what would happen to her sister when her hospital stay was through. She described in graphic terms the trauma she had suffered when the hospital called to say her sister had had a stroke. She and her sister were very close and dependent on one another. The leader said that he was her social worker and would be working with the family in planning aftercare. At the moment staff was concentrating on the immediate crisis, but when the patient stabilized aftercare planning would begin and medical and financial planning would be considered.

Leaders also provided reassurance when they validated a group member's strengths and worth.

Being Empathetic. It is very difficult to teach the ability to empathize. It demands that a person be able to put himself in another's place and to see things differently as a result. What is insignificant to the leader might be very important to the member or to the group as a whole (Cooper, 1978). For example, it was hard for the leader to understand why relatives would not want to leave the patients alone for an hour to attend the group when they had many other hours to be with the patients. But the staff took the expression of this concern seriously and changed the visiting hours so members would have the same amount of time with the patients.

Validating Members' Worth. When one group of members evaluated the group, they said, "We liked the idea that this group was for us—*we* were the important ones." The leaders learned from this evaluation and began incorporating this validation into their interventions. They would frequently say, "But *you* are important too" or "I'd like to hear how this has been for *you*" or, more specifically, "Is traveling such a long distance to the hospital difficult for you?"

Reflecting on one meeting, a leader described how each member had received some validation:

Ms. P received support for her plan to keep her husband at home and maintain her self-esteem; Ms. O for her sense of being somewhat overwhelmed and anxious; Ms. B for taking care of her own medical and physical needs; and Ms. R for her friendly and helpful attitude toward other relatives and patients on the floor.

Leaders can validate individual members or the group as a whole. Usually members display marvelous adaptive responses to extreme stress, and this can readily be reflected by leaders (Lonergan, 1982). Leaders also observe how members help one another in and out of the group. The leaders reinforce this activity with recognition. Often peer leaders evolve in the group; the group leaders not only respect such peer leaders but often learn from them as well.

In our experience, one peer leader was a model for others. She had taken care of her sick husband at home even though he was terribly incapacitated. She was open about her feelings of anger and frustration, which helped others to accept their ambivalent feelings. She coped beautifully and had many practical suggestions for others who wanted to follow her example (e.g., keeping a bedridden spouse in the living room where there was activity instead of isolated in a bedroom). Although this woman's spouse did not survive, she was an inspiration to the members, and she provided a hope and optimism that others needed desperately. The leaders were as moved by this "model" as the members were. Following is one leader's reaction to this "model":

> She took from me but didn't drain me. She always gave back something and I felt *I* had gotten something from talking to *her*. She had a real sense of humor and I would leave her feeling uplifted. Once I met her on the street and she told me a joke. I went home laughing. Then I thought, "Gee, *she* made *me* laugh and she's the one who has a sick husband!" Since she worked, I would stay at the hospital until 5:30 P.M. so I could see her because I knew she would appreciate seeing me and I would get a lot out of being with her. She was such an enjoyable person.

Part of validating people's strengths included reinforcement of an active rather than a passive approach to problem solving. It is not uncommon to see people respond to trauma and the complex, bureaucratic hospital system with maladaptive withdrawal, passivity, and depression. In the group, members were encouraged to be active and assertive. Often this activity began in the group, where members actively helped one another and the leaders acknowledged their strength. When members complained about staff, leaders reinforced the members for taking the opportunity to convey their concerns to the staff in the group—the leaders—and the members were then encouraged to approach staff outside the group.

Providing Education. When a relative or friend is educated about the patient's illness, community resources, and hospital policy, he or she is in a better position to be an active and responsible participant in the treatment process. The leaders freely answered questions and shared their knowledge. Once members became educated, they began to educate new members. Following is an example of how an educational process was woven into a group meeting:

> I asked how Mr. C was doing and they said he had another stroke over the weekend and could no longer communicate with them, except to say "yeah," which he said in response to any question.

> I asked if they knew what aphasia was, and they said "no." I asked the nurse to explain what that meant, and she explained expressive and receptive aphasia.

> The discussion of aphasia gave Ms. D and Ms. C an invaluable understanding of why their relative was responding as he was to his inability to make himself understood. The nurse and I talked of the enormous frustration that such patients feel when they are unable to communicate their simplest wishes.

> The women wanted to know what the possibility was of recovering some speech function, and the nurse and I said that sometimes the brain rewired itself in a few weeks and sometimes it did not.

> Ms. C said her husband had seemed to be very frightened since his last stroke, and that he wept loudly and frequently, which was not like him. I said that often we found that stroke patients had unusual expressions of emotions, appearing to laugh and cry easily.

> I remarked that anyone who was ill and in the hospital was under tremendous stress. The person was in a strange, threatening environment, and being ill he did not have the usual resources to cope with these pressures of uncertainty and fear.

Appreciating Humor. When any group of people come together, there is the potential of joy over human contact and the production of humor. Some leaders, not expecting this natural occurrence when people are surrounded by morbidity, interfere with its evolution. Members often expressed how wonderful it felt to be part of the group. For many the group (and floor) became the community that they did not feel they belonged to "outside." In the group they were accepted, whereas they often felt rejected elsewhere.

Vaillant (1977) describes humor as a high-level adaptive coping mechanism. Following is an example of humor evolving in the group:

> Ms. D described her husband's problem with his diet and teeth. His teeth had been removed and he refused to wear the uppers because of an ill fit. Somehow this triggered a good-humored discussion of false teeth. Ms. F said her husband had thrown away his lowers. The leader remarked jokingly that this was another way we could see that we all had things in common but were still different. Everyone chuckled.

Results of the Group

Despite the problems in the group that have been alluded to throughout this paper, there were many positive results. Not only did the leaders achieve their stated goals, there were also unanticipated benefits. Among these were (1) development of a mutual-aid network among group members, (2) improved communication between members and staff, (3) improved medical treatment for the patients, and (4) prevention of illness among relatives.

A Mutual-Aid Network

The atmosphere of the unit seemed to change with the development of the group. Visitors were seen talking to one another on the floor, showing an interest in other patients besides their relatives, and often lending a helping hand. Some who came from out of town were no longer so isolated; often members extended themselves to one another outside of group meetings and even outside of the hospital. A few members returned to the group, even when their relative was moved to another floor. People who the leaders originally thought would be excluded were included in the group. One woman alienated the group, but after she had stopped attending because her husband had been discharged, one member had phone contact with her and brought the group up to date on the progress of this woman and her husband, manifesting concern for the missing member.

The change in floor atmosphere seemed to have an impact on members' feelings of isolation and alienation. One patient expressed feeling better about being rehospitalized after the establishment of the group because he knew his wife would also get attention. Thus some patients may have been positively affected by the increasing friendliness on the floor.

Improved Staff-Member Relationships

We have already alluded to the advantage members received from communicating with the two staff members present at group meetings, each representing a different discipline. The social-work leader was able to educate nursing and medical staff about the dynamics of relatives' behavior, which helped them have more compassion and patience. The nursing staff, on the other hand, educated the social worker about the ramifications of disease so that the social worker could take a more active role in member education.

A major help to staff–group member relationships was the fact that, when leaders saw relatives in the group, they learned more about them as people and thus related to them differently and with a greater appreciation of them as individuals. In one instance a nurse leader said that she did not want to come to the group if Ms. T was the only member present because she did not get along with her. Another relative joined Ms. T in the group, so the nurse stayed. She learned that Ms. T had survived a concentration camp, had suffered many losses, and had come to this country two weeks before her daughter was born. During her pregnancy, Ms. T had constantly worried that her years of malnutrition would adversely affect her daughter. Now her husband was ill and she had this additional worry. The nurse felt new compassion for this woman, and their relationship improved considerably.

Improved Medical Treatment

Aside from the fact that group members' comfort and self-esteem must have been soothing to the patients, members at times revealed information that was very relevant for medical management of the patient. For example, one man was in severe pain. When staff asked him how he was feeling, he smiled and said "fine," but he told his wife he wanted to die because the pain in his head was so relentless that he couldn't stand it. After the group meeting his pain medication was elevated. In another instance a patient was hallucinating and staff had known nothing about it:

> Ms. C said that she wanted to ask something that was concerning her. Her husband had been acting strange lately. He asked for a match to light an imaginary cigar. He elaborately struck the match and held it to the "cigar" and enthused about how wonderful it was. The leaders looked at each other and the nurse said that she had heard nothing about that. The social worker asked Ms. C if the medical staff knew and she said "no" because she was afraid staff would think her husband was going crazy.

In two instances histories of patients were clarified by group members. One patient grossly understated his alcohol intake. Another had eaten marshmallows voraciously before his admission and was too ashamed to tell anyone. This information came out of spontaneous group interaction. Often information emerges in this format that would not emerge in a structured individual interview.

Prevention of Relatives' Illnesses

When people are under stress they are more prone to illness (Usdin, 1977). In the group, as members' worth was validated and their self-esteem was elevated, they began to take better care of themselves. Members strongly encouraged one another to take care of their own health problems. As members interacted they would often relish the opportunity to tell about *their* ills, their underlying competition with the patients emerging. They were strongly encouraged to follow through on their own doctor appointments and prescribed medical regimens. At times they were asked to report back to the group the following week with results. Thus relatives not only began to feel better emotionally but to feel better physically as well. (Part of this change was probably due to the group's focus on members' unnecessary guilt, which led the way to permission to take care of themselves and not just the patient.)

Conclusion

We believe that the results of this and later groups warrant consideration of such groups as integral parts of medical care for patients hospitalized in acute-care services. Despite the turnover in the group, the limited number of sessions attended by members, and the erratic composition of the group (sometimes optimal, sometimes not), meetings developed a cohesiveness that was curative and elevated the self-esteem of the participants. With this elevation of self-esteem, relatives and friends could function optimally as members of the treatment team. The reader may wonder how so much could be accomplished with members attending an average of only two meetings. We feel that this can be partially explained by the crisis nature of the group. When people are in a crisis, they are more receptive and responsive to therapeutic intervention.

Groups should be co-led by (1) a psychologically sophisticated leader such as a social worker, psychologist, psychiatrist, or psychiatric nurse and (2) a medically sophisticated person such as a nurse or doctor. Information from the groups can best be integrated into the ongoing care of the patient if the leaders are part of the unit's interdisciplinary team. This group had the best results when the unit's social worker worked with the supervisory nurse as co-leaders.

Every effort should be made by group leaders to involve all members of the treatment team directly or indirectly with the group. Results of the group should be communicated to the entire staff. Quality medical care is contingent on the interdisciplinary team working together.

Positive evaluation of the results of the relatives' group on the neurology and neurosurgery service led the Department of Social Work at St. Vincent's to institute similar groups in other services, including the adult intensive care unit, the neonatal intensive care unit and special baby clinic, and the hospice program and bereavement service.

References

Bardach, J. L. Group sessions with wives of aphasic patients. *International Journal of Group Psychotherapy*, 1969, *19*(3), 361–365.

Barmettler, D., & Fields, G. L. Using the group method to study and treat parents of asthmatic children. *Social Work in Health Care*, 1975–76, *1*(2), 167–176.

Bloom, N. D., & Lynch, J. G. Group work in a hospital waiting room. *Health and Social Work*, 1979, *4*(3), 48–63.

Breu, C., & Dracup, K. Helping the spouses of critically ill patients. *American Journal of Nursing*, 1978, *78*, 50–53.

Cahners, S. S. Group meetings for families of burned children. *Health and Social Work*, 1978, *3*(3), 165–172.

Cooper, E. Beginning a group program in a general hospital. *Group: Newsjournal of the Eastern Group Psychotherapy Society*, July 1976, pp. 6–9.

Cooper, E. The pre-group: The narcissistic phase of development with the severely disturbed patient. In L. R. Wolberg & M. L. Aronson (Eds.), *Group therapy 1977: An overview*. New York: Stratton Intercontinental Medical Books, 1978.

Epperson, M. M. Families in sudden crisis: Process and intervention in a critical care center. *Social Work in Health Care*, 1977, *2*(3), 265–273.

Frey, L. A. *Use of groups in the health field*. New York: National Association of Social Workers, 1966.

Fried, E. *Active/passive: The crucial psychological dimension*. New York: Grune & Stratton, 1970.

Gardner, D., & Steward, N. Staff involvement with families of patients in critical-care units. *Heart and Lung*, 1978, *7*, 105–110.

Garland, J. A., James, J. E., & Kolodny, R. L. A model for stages of development in social work groups. In S. Bernstein (Ed.), *Explorations in group work*. Boston: Milford House, 1973.

Hampe, S. O. Needs of the grieving spouse in a hospital setting. *Nursing Research*, 1975, *24*, 113–120.

Haynes, M. Process recording, St. Vincent's Hospital and Medical Center, New York, 1977.

Johnson, E. M., & Stark, D. E. A group program for cancer patients and their family members in an acute care teaching hospital. *Social Work in Health Care*, 1980, *5*(4), 335–348.

Kornfeld, M. S., & Siegel, I. M. Parental group therapy in the management of a fatal childhood disease. *Health and Social Work*, 1979, *4*(3), 99–118.

La Vorgna, D. Group treatment for wives of patients with Alzheimer's disease. *Social Work in Health Care*, 1979, *5*(3), 219–221.

Lonergan, E. C. Group intervention for medical patients—A treatment for damaged self-esteem. *Group: The Journal of the Eastern Group Psychotherapy Society*, 1980, *4*(2), 36–45. (a)

Lonergan, E. C. Humanizing the hospital experience: Report of a group program for medical patients. *Health and Social Work*, 1980, *5*(4), 53–63. (b)

Lonergan, E. C. *Self-esteem and group intervention*. New York: Jason Aronson, 1981.

Lonergan, E. C. Group for medical patients: Coping mechanisms revealed and mobilized. In L. R. Wolberg & M. L. Aronson (Eds.), *Group and family therapy: 1982*. New York: Brunner/Mazel, 1982.

Moos, R. (Ed.). *Coping with physical illness*. New York: Plenum, 1977.

Stolorow, R. D., & Lachman, F. M. *Psychoanalysis of developmental arrests*. New York: International Universities Press, 1980.

Strain, J. J., & Grossman, S. (Eds.). *Psychological care of the medically ill*. New York: Appleton-Century-Crofts, 1975.

Usdin, G. (Ed.). *Psychiatric medicine*. New York: Brunner/Mazel, 1977.

Vaillant, G. E. *Adaptation to life*. Boston: Little, Brown, 1977.

Wellisch, D. K., Mosher, M. B., & Van Scoy, C. Management of family emotional stress: Family group therapy in a private oncology practice. *International Journal of Group Psychotherapy*, 1978, *28*(2), 225–231.

VIII
WORKING WITH PEOPLE
WITH DEVIANT BEHAVIORS

20

A Therapy Group for Young Felony Offenders in a Residential Treatment Center

Corrine S. Cope, Ph.D.,
and Larry D. Long, Ed.S.

CORRINE S. COPE is a professor in the department of educational and counseling psychology at the University of Missouri—Columbia. LARRY D. LONG is executive director of Reality House in Columbia, Missouri, and a doctoral student in counseling psychology at the University of Missouri—Columbia.

Crime is a major and growing societal problem. Historically, society has dealt punitively with individuals convicted of crimes. Attitudes toward the treatment of offenders change, however, and the effectiveness of traditional methods of punishment is questioned. Innovative programs to rehabilitate offenders emerge and achieve varying degrees of success or failure. Recent trends in the treatment of offenders include the use of community-based correction programs (e.g., Galaway et al., 1976; Hahn, 1975; Killinger & Cromwell, 1978; Perlstein & Phelps, 1975; Solomon, 1976; Wicks, 1974) and the use of therapy groups (e.g., Smith & Berlin, 1981; Stephenson & Scarpitti, 1974). This chapter provides a brief account of one highly successful correctional program that is community-based and has short-term group therapy as the core of treatment.

A group of concerned citizens in a small midwestern city established Reality House in 1970 to "successfully [integrate] the young adult offender back into the community." This community-based residential treatment center for young male felony offenders aims (1) to provide a workable alternative to incarceration and (2) to lessen the likelihood of further criminal activity through early treatment intervention, intensive supervision, and environmental controls.

Reality House is a total group experience encompassing 24 hours a day, seven days a week. The formal therapy-group meetings that are held twice weekly constitute an important part, but only a part, of the total group experience. Reality House offers the three processes of change suggested by Cartwright (1951). First, it is a "medium of change" in that it offers a member support and encouragement as he struggles with changing his behavior. Second, it is a "target of change" in that members continually consider the effectiveness of house activities, rules, and procedures and adapt them for maximum effectiveness. Third, it is an "agent of change," since it uses organized efforts to bring about individual change.

Change in the individual offender's behavior from deviant to law-abiding is the primary goal of the Reality House program. Services at the center provide opportunities for the individual offender to develop responsible community behaviors and self-respect. Residents and staff participate in the formulation of all activities and regulations—that is, the total program. It is believed that for effective behavior change to occur the individual not only must want the change but also must be actively involved in the process through which the change can occur. Although the house as a change agent is important, the individual's role in that change is essential (Yalom, 1980).

Community involvement is an important component of the Reality House program, since the offender must return to the community if treatment is to be successful (National Advisory Commission on Criminal Justice, 1973; Wicks, 1974). Reality House is itself a small community with which the offender can identify and which he can use as a major resource. The larger community also is involved from the beginning in that the offender is immediately required to find employment. At the beginning of the program, however, a member's interaction with the outside community is highly restricted. As he moves successfully through the program this restriction lessens and he gains more freedom and involvement in the community. In the final status or level of the program, the young man lives in the community but continues to see a counselor at Reality House until final discharge from the program.

During a decade of operation, Reality House has proved to be a reliable and effective alternative to jails and penitentiaries for many young offenders. During the last five years 80 percent of the individuals completing the program have been discharged from the courts or are being maintained successfully on probation. Time required for completion of the Reality House program has averaged 183 days or approximately six months.

Residents

Referrals

Local circuit court judges refer young offenders to Reality House to be evaluated for possible placement there in lieu of incarceration. Occasionally probation officers refer young men who are having difficulty adhering to the stipulations and rules of their probations. The offenders referred to Reality House are considered "high risk" by the courts because indications are that these individuals, at the time of referral, would not be able to complete a probationary period successfully. The offenders have the limited choice of either living at Reality House (with the stipulation that the program be completed successfully) or being incarcerated.

Reality House reserves the right of client selection. Referral guidelines developed for agencies in the criminal-justice system are: (1) the individual is 17–25 years of age, and his current difficulty is his first felony conviction as an adult; (2) the court of jurisdiction orders that the individual successfully complete the program; (3) the individual is not experiencing an active psychosis, nor does he have symptoms of physical withdrawal from an addictive drug; and (4) individuals who are mentally retarded are not considered appropriate referrals.

Reality House suggests that individuals who do not fall within these guidelines be referred to facilities more adequately prepared to handle their specific problems.

Characteristics

Sociodemographic data collected since 1976 establish some norms for offenders referred to the program. These data show a consistency explained in part by the population for whom the services are designed—that is, young male felony offenders between the ages of 17 and 25.

The average age of Reality House residents in 1980 and 1981 was 20 years, with ages ranging from 17 to 23 years in 1980 and from 17 to 24 in 1981. Average educational level was tenth grade, with attainments ranging from sixth grade to sophomore year in college. Most of the young men had not completed high school, having either dropped out or been expelled. The majority were single. Those who were not were frequently experiencing severe family turmoil, including separation from spouses and divorce proceedings. Many reported family backgrounds that were disorganized and stressful.

The employment histories of most of the young men in the program in 1980–81 were very poor. Many had been fired numerous times from jobs because of unsatisfactory work behaviors. Traits frequently identified as having caused them difficulty were tardiness, absenteeism, poor motivation, poor work relationships, and a general lack of understanding of job expectations. Their current encounters with the law were generally their first at the felony level, but most had been charged with more than one felony count. Many had received prior inpatient and outpatient psychological services. The most frequent offense for which individuals participating in the program had been convicted was burglary. Drug-related felonies such as possession or sales were the second most common offenses, followed by assault.

Complaints or symptoms reported most frequently by the offenders at the time of admission to the program in 1980 and 1981 were depression, financial problems, and alcohol/drugs. The young men completed a questionnaire as part of the admission procedure and indicated those complaints that applied to themselves from a long list of suggested difficulties. Almost all checked more than one, and some checked many. Less than half reported alcohol or drugs as a symptom or complaint, although many more than that admitted drug use. This discrepancy would seem to indicate that a number who used drugs did not perceive at admission that drugs were a problem for them.

Program

Facility and Staff

Reality House is located in an 18-room, three-story, private residence near the downtown district of the city and only a block from a large university. The city transit system provides easy access to the larger community. Residents can reach vocational, cultural, educational, and social opportunities without a private vehicle. Each resident lives in a furnished, semiprivate room to which he is encouraged to add his own decorations. Kitchen, laundry, and recreational facilities are provided for residents' use.

The staff consists of an executive director (a licensed psychologist), two counselors (one is program director), an administrative assistant/secretary, and four half-time, live-in paraprofessionals (usually university students).

Residents live on the second and third floors of the house with two paraprofessionals on each floor. The first floor consists of offices for staff and a kitchen and a large living room for residents. The facility can accommodate a maximum of 12 residents at any one time.

The Program

The objective of the Reality House program is to develop in residents qualities of responsibility, involvement, and caring. In discussing therapy groups and responsibility, Yalom (1980) states that effective therapy groups are those in which the members are the primary agents of help. He argues that when members assume responsibility for the functioning of the group, they become aware that they have the ability to assume responsibility in all aspects of their lives. The group experience at Reality House substantiates this belief.

The Reality House program comprises six reintegrating statuses or levels through which the offender must progress as he returns to the community: evaluation, restricted (introductory), provisional, group, transitional, and discharge-planning. Table 20-1 presents a detailed outline of the six statuses, including for each status the specific behavioral objectives, restrictions and privileges, time in status, and procedure for moving to a higher status.

The basic principle underlying the Reality House program is democratic self-government. All details of the six statuses—indeed, the statuses themselves—have been formulated, written, revised, and updated by the residents. The current nine-page document, *Reality House Expectations*, is well-written in the language of the residents and reflects careful consideration of the program. This self-government statement is given to each offender immediately upon admission to the house for evaluation. Table 20-1 is abstracted from the most recent revision of the self-government document. Something is lost in the abstraction, but space does not permit inclusion of the complete document. This chapter, however, includes some quotations with specific language used by residents in the conduct of their program.

The program at Reality House has evolved pragmatically over the last 11 years. Incorporated into the program are activities, procedures, and treatment modalities that have "worked" for participants. Success is measured by nonrepetition or nonrecurrence of felony or deviant behavior. Members constantly review, revise, and update the treatment program in view of what they believe works for them to achieve success.

Residents make decisions by voting. Voting is a privilege that must be earned by progressing through the program. Status III, provisional, includes the right to vote. "Voting members," as used in this chapter, means members in status III or above. Staff personnel also are voting members, but not more than three staff members are permitted to vote in any one meeting. This limits the influence of staff in the self-government of the house.

A degree of control and surveillance is necessary in a sound community corrections system. Monitoring is a common intervention strategy used at Reality House. Also, at times of severe group dysfunction the government of the house is removed from the residents and taken over by the staff. The removal of responsibility and authority from members is a powerful tool used very infrequently and only as a last resort. These intervention strategies are discussed in detail below.

Young offenders referred to Reality House undergo a 30-day evaluation (status I) before a decision is made to accept or reject them as members of the program. The residents already in the program actively participate in the evaluation of a prospective member. If an offender is accepted into the program

TABLE 20-1

Outline of Reality House Statuses

Status	Behavioral Objectives	Restrictions/Privileges	Time in Status	Move to Higher Status
I Evaluation	1. Orientation to program. 2. Involvement with other residents and staff. 3. Evidence of desire to use program to change. 4. Evidence of willingness to change. 5. Adhering to restrictions. 6. Seeking employment.	1. Most restrictive status. 2. Sign in and out of house for all movement, and only with approval by staff. 3. May drive private vehicle only to and from work.	1. Thirty days or less. 2. Formal assessment of individual's adjustment is to be completed by end of 30 days. 3. Earlier status change may be requested if requirements of evaluation are met.	1. When requirements of evaluation are met, individual may request change to status II. 2. Requires majority vote of voting members.
II Restricted (Introductory)	1. Maintain intensive involvement with other house members. 2. Adjust to situation. 3. Obtain employment, unless achieved earlier (must talk to employer about residency). 4. Support self responsibility by maintaining job or full-time educational training, or a combination, for 35 hours/week.	1. Sign in and out of house for all movement but need not be approved by staff. 2. May leave house only at specified times for meals or personal business (extended ½ hour if with a status III–VI member). 3. After job is obtained, must return immediately after work each day (exception only with counselor's or group's permission). 4. No voting rights.	1. At least two weeks after employment is obtained, otherwise indeterminant. 2. Voting members consider restricted member's involvement, seriousness, honesty, and evidence of working on problems.	1. Individual requests status change. 2. Requires majority vote of members.
III Provisional	1. Continue and improve activities of statuses I and II. 2. Assume further responsibilities, i.e., high level of caring and involvement with everyone. 3. Vote in group meetings. 4. Maintain full employment for at least three weeks at this status. 5. Keep financial situation in good order, i.e., owe no money to house. 6. Learn to effectively confront those behaving irresponsibly.	1. Right to vote. 2. Curfew is 10:00 P.M. weekdays, 11:00 P.M. Friday and Saturday. 3. Day passes out of town may be requested; they are approved only by group vote. 4. Sign in and out for all movement. 5. May drive private vehicle as sanctioned by group.	1. Maintenance of full-time employment for at least 3 weeks in provisional status, otherwise indeterminant. 2. Voting members consider individual's involvement with other members, financial situation, and other requirements of provisional status.	1. Individual requests status change. 2. Requires majority vote of members.

TABLE 20-1

Outline of Reality House Statuses (Continued)

Status	Behavioral Objectives	Restrictions/Privileges	Time in Status	Move to Higher Status
IV Group	1. Continue to help self. 2. Develop own "plan" for future. 3. Help others in program (a major responsibility) 4. Show willingness to give of free time to organize activities with other residents. 5. Take responsibility for confronting those who are behaving irresponsibly.	1. Curfew is 12:00 midnight weekdays, 1:00 A.M. Friday and Saturday. 2. May request one overnight pass per week, approved only by group vote. 3. Sign in and out for all movement. 4. May drink alcoholic beverages (must be of legal age and have group permission).	1. Maintenance of employment. 2. Member must be meeting all expectations and requirements of house. 3. Member must feel ready to leave house. 4. Member presents and discusses with counselor a reasonable "future plan," to be approved by both member and counselor. 5. Member conducts a staffing of "plan," with at least two staff members and those status members invited by resident.	1. Majority vote of staff and status members at staffing (see #5 in Time in Status column) needed for member to present plan at next scheduled group meeting. Plan must be approved by a majority of voting members at the group meeting. 2. Plan must be approved by a majority of voting members at the group meeting.
V Transitional	1. Increase involvement in outside activities (extremely important). 2. Maintain house responsibilities. 3. Complete plan, including a date for leaving. 4. Choose counselor to work with on discharge-planning, and arrange meeting dates.	1. Curfew is 1:00 A.M. weekdays, 2:00 A.M. Friday and Saturday. 2. Double overnight passes can be requested by member and granted by group vote. 3. Sign out and in once each day, other times optional. 4. Privileges on above statuses are all continued here.	1. Maintenance of employment. 2. Enough time must be allowed for smooth transition from house to community. Average time is about four weeks.	1. Member requests to leave the house in the formal group meeting prior to or on the planned discharge date. 2. Requires two-thirds majority vote for approval to move to discharge-planning.
VI Discharge-planning	1. Make good adjustment in the community. 2. Meet with counselor as needed.	1. No restrictions specified by group.	1. Determined by member and counselor.	1. Discharge from program occurs when both member and counselor agree it is time to do so. (Until that time a member is still in the program and can be discharged as unsuccessful.)

following a favorable decision at the end of the evaluation period, he moves to a restricted level (status II). Each progressive status is designed to be less restrictive and less structured and supervised than the previous one. The authority sanctioning a resident's movement from one status to the next is vested in the voting group.

The time required to successfully complete the in-residence group program (statuses I through V) averages 183 days or approximately six months. Discharge-planning (status VI), the final stage of the program, must be spent living in the community. It is the only out-of-residence status and averages 1½–2 months before final discharge. The young man and his counselor make the decision as to final discharge date, which means successful completion of the program.

Members leave the program in one of two ways: successful completion (i.e., in-program success) or premature termination by the group (i.e., in-program failure). Members can be discharged unsuccessfully from the program at any time from the first day in evaluation status to final discharge data at the end of status VI.

Reality House has been called "one big therapy group." Formal therapy-group meetings are held twice a week, on Monday and Thursday evenings. What occurs in the formal therapy sessions is difficult to separate from what occurs informally throughout the total experience. Much of the rest of this chapter is a description of the formal group meetings, with the understanding that the events in those meetings influence all phases of the experience and vice versa. Topics to be discussed are group-therapy process, goals of group therapy, obstacles to group therapy, and intervention strategies. Outcomes of the program at Reality House will be presented from the findings of a 5-year follow-up study of young male offenders who participated in the groups from 1975 to 1980.

The Group-Therapy Process

Formal therapy-group meetings are scheduled twice weekly, on Monday and Thursday evenings. All residents currently in the program must attend. Meetings typically average four hours. A "full" therapy session on Monday is mandatory. If on Thursday night the members decide that a second full therapy session is not necessary that week, they may substitute recreational events such as volleyball or basketball. The members make this decision at the beginning of the Thursday meeting. Not more than three staff members, generally the program director, counselor, and a live-in paraprofessional, participate in and help facilitate the therapy sessions. Limiting staff participation to three reduces the influence of staff in the therapy process.

Regular therapy-group meetings are held in the facility in a multipurpose area called the Group Room, which is large enough to accommodate everyone. Exceptions to holding sessions in the facility occur periodically when group members decide by consensus to do so. A convenient public park often is used, as a pavilion or secluded open grassy area there offers a relaxed atmosphere for sessions.

Group members and staff sit in chairs in a circle in any order they wish. The atmosphere of the meeting is informal. Smoking and eating while meetings are in progress are forbidden by the group as members believe that such behavior "interferes with good involvement." Everyone is expected to be seated and ready to begin promptly at 7 P.M. Either a member of the group or a facilitator opens the session by saying, "Let's start group." Although the format is flexible, the therapy meetings consist of four distinct parts: members, house business, requests, and closure.

Members

This first part of a full therapy session generally lasts about two hours and focuses on personal problems, current attitudes, and present adjustment difficulties of the members. Members desiring help from the group spontaneously state their concerns, thus inviting consideration and discussion from others. Intense interpersonal feelings about self, family, and others are disclosed. The group respects anyone who cries or becomes upset. Expression of feelings such as anger, sorrow, depression, or reactions to everyday unpleasantness is valued. Members encourage others to share these feelings and reinforce them for doing so.

Periodically the "group" itself is the subject of the therapy meeting. When dysfunction of the group occurs, members and staff become intensely involved in introspection about what needs to be changed.

After several hours devoted to this first segment of the meeting and as members and staff become fatigued, a 15-30-minute break is agreed upon.

House Business

The second phase of the formal group meeting includes discussions of household job assignments, recreational activities, having special visitors, making facility improvements, and general complaints. Periodically members review, revise, and update their self-governing procedures during this part of the meeting. Program expectations, guidelines, rules, and specific consequences for noncompliance are discussed and voted upon. Approval requires a majority voice vote of voting members. This segment devoted to house business generally is short, averaging about 30 minutes. On occasion, however, in order to meet the needs of individuals or the group, this segment has taken a major part of the total meeting time.

Requests

During this third segment members request changes in program status for themselves and for others and also request special privileges. If a member requests a change to a higher status for himself, intense discussion follows during which the individual's progress in the program is carefully scrutinized. Behavioral criteria required to enter the requested status are discussed and confirmed. Overall attitudes, behaviors, and approach to treatment are reviewed by the members. The individual's progress toward achieving stated personal goals, adherence to rules, and group participation are assessed. When both the requester and the group believe that all pertinent information has been shared, a decision is made by the voting members on the status-change request. Voting is by voice, and the first voting member sitting nearest to the requesting member starts the process. Voting proceeds either clockwise or counterclockwise depending on the position of the initiating voter. If the voter is sitting on the requester's left, voting will be clockwise and vice-versa. Voting always proceeds away from the requester and does not cross over his position. Turns in voting go around the group circle until all voters have stated their decisions. Reasons for a "yes" or "no" vote generally are relayed to the requester during each voting member's turn. A majority vote from voting members (residents and staff) is the final authority concerning the individual's requested status change.

Voting members may question, during this status-change period, any member's level or status in the program. If a voting member believes that another member is not abiding by the overall expectations of his status, the voting member may make a motion to call a vote to reduce the person to a lesser level. The motion must be seconded by another voting member of the group or staff. The discussion and voting proceed as described above. Again, a simple majority rules. The individual is placed into a lower status or level if a majority of the members vote to do so.

Removal of a member from the program generally occurs during this third segment. If negative feelings toward the individual, however, are intense, members may deal with the situation at the beginning of the meeting. At either time, a request for removal of a member is very serious. An intense discussion of such an action follows, after which voting members leave the meeting room and cast their vote by secret ballot. Members of the group have adopted the secret ballot to prevent influence on votes when the critical action of program termination for an individual is being considered. A staff member collects the ballots and tallies the vote for treatment termination or continuance. Group members then state orally their decision to the challenged individual. The staff member verifies that the stated vote tallies with the secret vote. A two-thirds majority of eligible voters is required before program removal can occur.

Another type of request considered during this segment is that of members seeking a successful discharge from the "live-in" treatment portion of the program. Their request follows a procedure similar to that for a person removed from the program, with voting by secret ballot and a two-thirds majority required. The only difference between the two procedures is that in the latter situation the member himself initiates the request and no second is required.

After status changes are completed, members may request privileges that the various levels or statuses do not include. Extension of curfew hours for special occasions, driving a vehicle, visiting someone in another city, overnights outside of the facility, and consumption of alcoholic beverages for those over 21 are considered special privileges. A member must ask the group during this part of the meeting to consider his request. The presenting member generally will have discussed the request to be voted on with other members in the house prior to this meeting. Members review the individual's proposal briefly but carefully. If an individual has been vague in presenting his request, members may ask for more definite plans or explanations as to how the privilege is to be used. They question the individual to determine if the request is well thought out, if it will hinder or help the treatment progress, and if the person has been responsible in handling other aspects of the program. The request is granted to the individual if other group members believe that he can be trusted without supervision and that he has achieved "good progress" in the program. This action requires a simple majority supporting the individual's proposal.

The request portion of the group varies from meeting to meeting with no limit set on the number to be handled. Requests can range from none to as many as six, depending upon group size and member status, and average two to three per meeting. This segment requires about 45 minutes of meeting time.

Closure

Closure of the meeting comes with "stamps and warmies." This type of closure has been a tradition in the meetings for years and is similar to closures in transactional analysis (Berne, 1966). "Stamps" are expressions of negative or bad feelings members have about one another. Such feelings can arise from events both inside and outside of the therapy meetings. Anyone, resident or staff, can receive a stamp. Stamp-giving comes first in the period and is introduced by one of the members or staff saying, "Stamps." This signals all participants to present their negative feelings to others in an orderly, structured manner. No two people try to give stamps at the same time to practice courtesy to other participants. The close of stamp-giving is indicated by someone saying, "Does anyone have any more stamps?" If the answer is silence the next part of the period, "warmies," is announced.

"Warmies" represent positive or good feelings that members have for one another. Individuals who receive stamps or warmies do not respond to either criticism or accolade. This helps prevent defensiveness and arguments among members. It encourages reluctant or unconfident individuals to introduce their feelings without fear of being hurt. Stamps and warmies also stimulate members to further explore their feelings outside of meetings. The stamps and warmies part of the meeting is fast-moving, snappy, and short. The formal therapy-group session ends after this period.

Goals of Group Therapy

Three major goals have emerged in the program over the years and have been passed on from one group to the next. Readily accepted by new members as part of the program's creed, these goals are involvement, caring, and responsibility. The responsibility for defining group goals and objectives, however, remains with the group members. Thus goals are based on the group's and the individual members' level of functioning at a given time. The structure and nature of the group permits flexibility in determining goals and in planning behaviors to accomplish these goals.

Involvement

Intense and intimate therapeutic involvement is a goal that must be reached to some degree by each member of the group. The goal of "getting involved" emerged in the early days of the program as the young men interacted in the formal therapy-group meetings. In those days, group members continually challenged each other, claiming lack of involvement on the part of another. The terms "let's get involved" and "good involvement" were used prolifically by everyone. Implementing such words was more difficult. Group members had little understanding of what meaningful involvement was or how to bring it about. They invested many hours and numerous meetings developing their definition of involvement and identifying behaviors, both constructive and destructive, that influenced the process of "becoming involved."

Over the years the groups at Reality House have developed a written statement defining involvement and identifying involvement behaviors. This statement, the product of cumulative group efforts, is given to every new member entering the program and reads as follows:

Involvement

At Reality House, we believe that everyone needs to feel loved and cared for. While we all need this sort of closeness, oftentimes we don't know how to go about getting it. The process by which we get close to others and fulfill this need for love is called involvement. One reason we are here is to help each other learn how to get successfully involved with others.

The group has identified these behaviors and attitudes as ones which bring them closer to others: eye contact; laughter; working together; activities together; caring; warmth; openness and open-mindedness; honesty; sincerity; self-disclosure; confrontiveness; consistency.

These attitudes and behaviors put distance between people: silly, immature gestures; rambling from topic to topic; intimidating looks and body movements; fighting; drug abuse; smoking; hostility; being too intellectual; being too critical; depression; complaining; disinterest; being over-emotional or unemotional.

We believe that what you learn here about getting involved with others applies to people outside of the House as well as to those who live and work here. We encourage you to apply what you learn here to other relationships. It is important. One who has good involvement with others in his world stands a much better chance of staying out of trouble and being successful than one who doesn't. And helping you make it in society is what we're all about.

Although this statement of involvement was derived by group members from their own experiences at Reality House, many elements similar to reality therapy (Glasser, 1965) are evident.

Caring

Caring for oneself and others is another commonly held and valued goal of group members. "Nothing made any difference anymore" or "I just didn't give a . . . " or "I just didn't care what happened" are frequent statements of group members about their earlier experiences. Caring again, or probably learning to care for the first time, is viewed by most members as a very threatening and frightening encounter to be avoided.

To help members learn to care and thus fulfill the group goal, experienced members invite change from the noncaring individual by methods of confrontation mixed with caring concern. The term "carefronting" coined by Augsburger (1980) is descriptive of the practical method that group members at Reality House have developed. In essence, a group member provides a maximum amount of feedback to the recipient but with intimidation held to an effective minimum. Caring is also developed by the individual through such behaviors as obtaining employment, recognizing progress by others in the program, and contributing to the solution of others' difficulties in and out of meetings. The individual's achievement of responsible behaviors provides small successful stepping-stones to a more generalized caring attitude. Offenders learning to care about themselves and others has been, in practical experience, a major milestone in treatment.

The "daredevil," "I have nothing to lose" concept of self lessens as the individual develops a more caring image of himself. Taking risks with socially

395

disapproved behaviors and criminal activities seems to become increasingly difficult, almost proportionately to the development of caring in the offender. The process of developing "caring" for self and others is cumulative and generally extends over much of the time in treatment. The development of care in offenders can be subtle and easily ignored unless group members are sensitive to the process. Steady progress occurs when other members reciprocate with responses of caring and recognize that the individual has changed.

Responsibility

Another important and commonly defined goal of group members at Reality House is "being responsible." "Being irresponsible" is a label often applied during therapy meetings to members and their behavior. Being irresponsible connotes that the individual has not followed through on or perhaps completed an expected task. Familiar terms applied to the irresponsibly acting offender are "lack of respect," "untrustworthy," and "broken promises." Being unable to respond adequately or in an acceptable manner to a given situation is one of the most frequent failures encountered among offender therapy groups (Stephenson & Scarpitti, 1974). Irresponsible behavior is a common characteristic of these young offenders prior to treatment. Learning how to be responsible and then being responsible are not easy tasks for anyone. Among offenders, assuming responsibility for their own behavior is a major difficulty.

Residents of Reality House approach the development of responsibility in several steps. When an individual behaves irresponsibly or fails to respond in an expected manner, other members encourage him to discuss the situation in detail. With reluctant members others may initiate the discussion by pointing out where and in what way the individual has been irresponsible. Alternate ways of behaving are offered by the group members if they believe the individual lacks adequate information. Group members expect, and may demand, that the individual formulate a treatment plan or contract to accomplish change in his behavior.

Treatment plans to accomplish a desired or demanded change may be formulated in several ways—for example, orally or in writing, with group assistance or alone. An individual may choose to develop his plan during one of the formal group meetings with the help of others. A segment of the meeting is then devoted to clarifying the problem, identifying solutions, and exploring possible outcomes. The individual decides on a plan resulting from the general group discussion. Once the choice is made other members declare their willingness to be involved with the individual in accomplishing his plan.

In therapy meetings, members quickly challenge a general, ambiguous plan for change because such plans are often subject to manipulation through "loopholes." A case in point is that of a young man who, when pressured to become more personally involved with group members, declared that he would reveal much more about himself to all concerned before the next meeting. At the next session he was challenged since no one had perceived any change in his behavior. He stated that he had had a long discussion about himself with one member of the group. That member confirmed the discussion but said that the young man in question had revealed only several minor facts about himself and that their talk had been short. Another "loophole" attempted by the young man was the declaration that the plan was indeed fulfilled because no one had come to him after the meeting and said that they were concerned about his lack of involvement. Repeated episodes similar to this have taught group members to request specific, minute details of a treatment plan. They demand that the who's, when's, where's, and how's be clearly defined and understood.

Individuals may choose to formulate a treatment plan on their own without group participation or direct assistance, placing the written action steps on the house bulletin board for inspection or comment. Written plans tend to contain more about goals to be achieved and less about the specific problem to be solved. Written plans are less susceptible to semantic manipulation, "loopholes," or faulty memory than those orally planned.

Regardless of whether the specific plan is oral or written, the choice of the changes that are to be made is left to the individual. Once he makes his choices, other members express their willingness to involve themselves with him in accomplishing his goals. Group members expect the individual to promise to fulfill all aspects of his chosen plan of action. They in turn commit themselves to help him in various ways and to "follow up" to ensure verification of completion. This type of group interaction results in holding the individual accountable for what he says he will do. This "making your word good" is the basic foundation to becoming responsible and builds respect and trust among group members.

If the individual who behaved irresponsibly encounters difficulty in successfully completing his plan, the group (i.e., residents and staff) helps him develop a more realistic plan. These continuing activities occur both in and out of the formal group. If members perceive that an individual is making serious attempts to behave more responsibly, they tend to be tolerant of errors for a time. Their tolerance is limited, however, if an individual is not seriously trying to improve or does not demonstrate progress over a reasonable period. Severe sanctions can be enacted, such as lowering of status, reducing free time, or even terminating his program.

Obstacles in Group Therapy

Certain behaviors exhibited by members in the therapy group meetings result in delaying or preventing satisfactory progress through the program at Reality House. Major obstacles to therapeutic progress that have surfaced are resistance, dishonesty, and manipulation.

Resistance

Most newcomers at Reality House resist the therapy-group meetings. They explain this resistance as resulting from past experiences. Prior to entering the facility, they experienced severe family disruptions, authority conflicts, school failure, and unsatisfying interpersonal relationships. Their past peer groups identified mainly with delinquent and antisocial activities. Most of these peer groups had strong norms requiring a "macho" image or a "lone wolf" role. If signs of vulnerability or weakness were exhibited by an individual, strong consequences often resulted, such as rejection and physical violence. These young men learned that social survival depended on emotional detachment, distrust, and callousness toward life. "Nothing matters" was equated with "being strong."

Experiences with the criminal-justice system frequently compounded or reinforced feelings of detachment, distrust, and callousness. Newcomers often have only a vague understanding of past judicial events, either because of ignorance or because of lack of explanation by authorities or legal counsel. If they attempted to clarify or understand circumstances, their inquiries often were not adequately answered. These young men view themselves as being at the mercy of the system, as victims of whatever happens. Little responsibility or control of situations is perceived by them.

A new participant's past personal difficulties, delinquent peer group norms, life philosophy and criminal-justice exposure are met "head on" during the initial group meetings. The individual initially may assume that the program is just a continuation of the judicial process that has provided unfavorable outcomes so far. He perceives the program at Reality House as being one more event in which he has no control or input. Seasoned group members readily understand this resistant position from their own past experiences. Whenever forms of resistance are expressed or acted out, members explicitly explain to the individual that such behavior and underlying attitudes are no longer appropriate or needed. If the individual is willing to listen, they describe how they have worked through much of their own defensiveness.

The following example illustrates the process of overcoming resistance. A new participant had been in the house for several weeks. He had been ordered by the court to undergo an evaluation at Reality House to determine if placement in the program would be appropriate. In interaction with others in his first four formal group meetings he had been low-keyed and withdrawn. He seldom volunteered any information about himself or voiced any opinion about group issues being discussed. Although he responded to questions directed to him, his responses were guarded and brief.

In the fifth group meeting members stated their concern about his resistant approach to the program and to the meetings. The young man had been convicted of a burglary several months prior to program entrance but he had revealed little to the members about his reasons for committing the offense. Group members told him they were uncomfortable with his silence and lack of effort in exploring with them what had gotten him into trouble. One group member asserted that he was resistant and manipulative. Another countered that he might be shy and afraid to discuss personal things with others. Another insisted that, regardless of the reason, it was time for him to share some things with everyone if he wanted to continue in the program and have a favorable evaluation report sent to the court. It was evident that the group believed it was time for him to discuss with them how he had gotten into trouble.

Sensing the growing resentment of the group and after additional encouragement by several members, the young man described how he had become involved in a felony act. Several months before, after a movie, he and a friend were joyriding in the participant's car. Becoming bored after about an hour, his friend suggested that they drive to a residential section of the city to the home of several girls he knew. The girls were not at home and his friend suggested that they drive around the neighborhood to wait for them to return. After driving several blocks his friend noticed an isolated house that appeared to be unoccupied. The friend speculated that the occupants might be on vacation or visiting and wouldn't it be great if they could get some liquor and money to throw a party when the girls returned. It would be easy to break into the isolated residence.

They drove back to the house and parked around the corner. The young man hid at the back of the house while his friend knocked on the front door. Confident that no one was at home, they broke a back window and entered the dwelling. Once inside they abandoned the idea of securing liquor and money because of the unfamiliar surroundings and darkness. They gathered up anything they believed of value (portable television, stereo, radio, etc.) and quickly left the way they came. They loaded the items into the trunk of the car and drove to a nearby school parking lot to examine what they had taken. As they were looking at the stolen items with the aid of a parking lot light, a passing police patrol became suspicious. The police pulled into the parking lot and surprised them. Both unsuccessfully attempted to escape by running, leaving the car trunk open and the recently stolen property in plain view. The young man paused, then said that was about it.

One group member asked what he believed caused the burglary. His quick response was that none of this would have happened if it were not for his friend and that he was going to stay out of trouble in the future. Most of the group agreed that his so-called friend may not have been a good influence, but there seemed to be other important things to consider besides one's friend as the sole cause of such an act.

Group members suggested things for him to think about and discuss in the future. One member commented that he believed the individual behaved impulsively, used poor judgment, and didn't seem to understand himself very well. Another asked how, since he placed the responsibility for the burglary on his friend, he was going to stay out of future difficulty with other so-called friends. Another wanted him to think about what he had learned and talk to him after the meeting. Another member commented that there was more involved than "just saying you are going to stay out of trouble, since you are the trouble." Other questions stimulated by the individual's account of the burglary were: Were you sorry afterward? Have you gotten away with similar things? Are you easily influenced in most situations? What things are you going to do in the program to prevent such a thing from happening in the future?

This is an example of the group helping a new participant to deal with his resistance and also helping him to begin the process of accepting responsibility for his behavior.

Trust and openness in the interaction among seasoned group members provide a positive model and supportive atmosphere for a resistive individual. Strong resistance to program expectations and interactions in the group typically diminish after several weeks of exposure to the group therapy meetings and the general program. Understanding, support, and the nondefensive posture of other members help the resistive individual to become more receptive of the situation.

Not all beginning participants respond adequately to these expressions of understanding, support, and acceptance. Continued resistance and adamant defensiveness prompt group members to increase confrontation with the individual. The approach of members dramatically changes. Where previously they asked, they now demand. They state that they will no longer tolerate continued resistance to the meetings, to the program, and to themselves. If the individual is not willing to invest trust in them, they can no longer trust his intentions. They demand from the individual a plan of action for reducing his resistance that meets their approval. He may be allowed several days to formulate a plan. Program termination by the group occurs if he does not develop an acceptable plan and continues his strong resistance.

Dishonesty

Dishonesty or deceit is a second common obstacle encountered in group meetings. Forms of dishonesty perceived by group members include lying, purposeful omission, "conning," and "social front." The individual's proclivity to use these coping mechanisms has developed from past experiences in the home, on the "street," and with peer buddies. These techniques of dishonesty become refined and effective through many trial-and-error learning experiences. Use of such measures by the individual is a method of meeting personal needs and keeping emotional distance.

Almost without exception offender participation in group therapy meetings during the initial phases of treatment includes dishonest presentation. Many offenders entering the program begin meetings with the approach of "Mr. Innocent," "Mr. Nice Guy," "Mr. Together," or "Mr. Naive." Such role playing is quickly confronted, often during the first meeting, in a very direct, straightforward manner by other members. The more experienced group members readily perceive the social façade and underlying inadequacies of the beginning participant. Feelings of depression, inadequacy, unworthiness, and lack of control of one's life invariably are painful for the individual to face and to admit. An underlying emptiness or emotional void is a common description presented by offenders (Reid, 1978). Such feelings of self are avoided in interactions with others, and exaggeration and dishonesty are used to achieve an image of social acceptance or approval.

Group members have an old saying that "it's hard to con a con" because most of the tricks of the trade are known. They explain to the new participant that dishonesty is inappropriate and that "conning the program" will be easily detected because of the therapeutic intensity of the program and their knowledge of such methods. They urge the individual to present himself in an honest way. They emphasize the importance of honesty to other members in the group. Group members perceive honesty as a very important element in "getting better," and many view this as the crux of treatment.

The behavior of the beginning participant who chooses to remain dishonest or continues to be "caught" is viewed by members as very serious. It serves as a signal that the individual may not want to make necessary basic changes. Individuals are confronted through procedures similar to those described in the resistance section. An inexperienced group member displaying dishonesty generally is allowed to rectify his behavior without consequence if the infraction is minor. Members show little patience or tolerance, however, if a seasoned member is "caught" behaving dishonestly. The breadth and depth of the individual's dishonesty determines the course of action of the other group members. The individual typically reverts to a lower status in the program if dishonesty is not widespread or severe. If dishonesty becomes generalized and serious (stealing, using or selling drugs, etc.), the individual generally is expelled from the program.

Manipulation

Manipulation is a third major obstacle identified in meetings. Most group participants exhibit hedonistic and narcissistic traits that contribute to an overpowering need to control social events by unfair methods. Personal gratification is achieved at the expense of others. "Fair play" in social interactions is commonly missing from their repertoire. Manipulation may achieve a premeditated purposeful payoff for the individual. The propensity for group members to use

401

their highly polished skills of manipulation can effectively inhibit therapeutic efforts. The potency of meetings diminishes, and the underlying theme of coercion produces distrust and resentment among members.

Manipulation frequently takes the form of an individual reversing a problem, when he is being confronted, by placing it back on the originator. This "switching of the tables" puts an individual trying to be helpful in the role of culprit, as if he were the real problem. The attitude of "I'm right, you're wrong" is common. Such manipulative techniques are sometimes difficult for members to perceive immediately, creating confusion and a momentary pause in meetings. A verbal discourse and heated argument follows between the manipulating individual and other members. Group members quickly learn the numerous techniques used by a manipulating individual. Their refusal to "play into" such events usually is sufficient for the behavior to diminish.

New participants often use manipulation in attempts to integrate into the group successfully. More experienced members sometimes manipulate to "get their way" or "get what they want." Although regression and backsliding are expected to occur among all members, all continually work on developing what they call "dealing straight." "Dealing straight" means being open about one's wants and needs while taking into consideration the effects these have on others. The individual's willingness "to deal straight," "play fair," and "not switch tables" is a valued norm.

Members will confront a persistently manipulating individual. They focus on the individual's disrespect, deception, and selfish motives. A "we don't want to be used" message is clearly expressed to him. If a manipulator does not respond to such warning, the group will demand change. Confrontation methods used by the group in this situation are similar to those previously described for resistance and dishonesty. If no progress occurs within a reasonable length of time, the manipulator is either placed in a lower status or terminated from the program through the democratic voting process.

Intervention Strategies

Intervention strategies described here are the major ones used in the formal therapy-group sessions and in the daily functioning of Reality House. These include democratic self-government, facilitation of therapeutic events, individual counseling, monitoring, restriction, and administrative evaluation. Interventions are used to facilitate progress through the program.

Democratic Self-Government

Democratic self-government is the major strategy of the program. The belief is held that community treatment means living and adjusting in the community and that the offender must participate actively in every level of his return to the community (Solomon, 1976). Participants are expected to assume the responsibility of administering their own treatment. The authority to determine program structure, behavioral limits, and treatment progress is invested in the members in the house. Program expectations, rules, and behavioral consequences for infractions are entrusted to these young men to define and to live by. The staff of Reality House believes that rehabilitation of felony offenders is best realized when treatment is member-centered, not staff-centered. Treatment is a process accomplished "with" the participants rather than being done "to" them.

Democratic self-government places primary responsibility for control and rehabilitation on the offenders themselves. Staff members relinquish control of a program for which they are ultimately held accountable. Such a staff position results not from permissiveness but from intense contact and group interaction with members in the program.

Facilitation of Therapeutic Events

In the formal group meetings the primary role of the staff is to help facilitate therapeutic events. Long and Cope (1980) investigated therapeutic events, or curative factors, perceived by residents at Reality House. They found that felony offenders rated effectiveness of curative factors similarly to members of other groups (Yalom, 1975). Facilitators concentrate on those factors rated most effective (i.e., catharsis, group cohesiveness, and interpersonal learning-input). Factors perceived as least important (i.e., family reenactment and guidance) are not initiated or reinforced. Facilitators praise and encourage members when they express feelings, put the group before themselves, and ask questions to learn about each other. Participants are discouraged by facilitators from excessively focusing on past events, relying on other members to maintain their responsibilities, or having the group make all decisions for them.

The group facilitators actively participate in the meetings and share their perceptions, opinions, and knowledge. They recognize and reinforce specific behaviors and group interactions that are considered conducive to favorable therapeutic outcomes. They monitor group processes and intervene if necessary when obstacles such as dishonesty, manipulation, and resistance are observed.

Individual Counseling

Individual counseling is provided for all program participants. Many individual problems identified and considered during group meetings are further discussed in individual sessions with counselors. In these private meetings the counselor encourages the individual to introduce specific concerns about his problems in the next group meeting. Counselors often suggest that the individual seek help from other members and work for solutions to his difficulties outside of group meetings. Subsequently many one-to-one sessions occur among participants during all hours of the day or night. It is not unusual for several members to band together to work with an individual on specific concerns or difficulties.

Monitoring

Monitoring is an important strategy used by program staff. The whereabouts of residents are checked on a methodical or random basis. A staff member consults other group members, employers, family members, or other relevant persons to confirm behavior or stated whereabouts of an individual. When falsification of whereabouts or other dishonest behavior is uncovered, the staff member may call a "restriction." The staff member informs the group that someone is being dishonest and if he comes forward restriction will be removed. This method frequently brings forward not only the known individual but other residents who "confess" incidents that were unknown. This staff strategy proves to be an effective intervention.

Restriction

A major intervention in group dynamics is necessary when members no longer are assuming responsibility for treatment. Group malfunction is evident when gross rule infractions, cover-ups, inappropriate behaviors, irresponsibilities, or illegal acts by one or more individuals receive little attention from other members. The ignoring of such events by the group gives implicit permission to the perpetrators to continue such acts unabated. Lack of response by group members requires firm intervention immediately by staff.

"Restriction" is the intervention strategy designed by group members, and approved by staff, to counteract group malfunction. Restriction may be called by anyone, member or staff, and markedly constricts all members' outside activities. Status privileges are dramatically reduced. Movement of any member to a higher status is prohibited, and a member may be lowered in status. All group participants revert to hours of introductory status if they are at a higher level. The only exception is a member in transitional status whose "plan" includes essential outside activities that are necessary to complete in order to leave the house by the agreed-upon date.

Restriction produces a very serious attitude among members and staff and extends until sufficient treatment responsibility is assumed by members once again. Efforts are made to resolve a restriction period as quickly as possible since it blocks or greatly reduces program functioning. Program staff and group members explicitly define behaviors, attitudes, or individuals that caused restriction. Plans, goals, and action steps are designed to correct the observed deficiencies. Only the staff may remove a period of restriction. Everyone, however, must be in agreement that remedial actions have been successful and that restriction is no longer warranted. Duration of restriction usually has been about one to two weeks.

Administrative Evaluation

This intervention is a "last resort" to bring back into balance a program no longer functioning. The government of the program shifts from one of group democracy to one of staff authority. This occurs if "restriction," described above, has been tried and has failed. A complete breakdown of positive group norms, member interaction, and responsible self-government can create a program that is no longer therapeutic. Authority invested with group members is completely removed by administrative decision.

Program staff assume an authoritarian role and proceed to remove control from the negative antitreatment group. Staff identify the individuals comprising the negative group and may place each one on "administrative evaluation," which normally lasts one week. If it is evident that these individuals are not willing to change behavior or if staff believes that continuation of services will produce no change, program termination is immediate. If such severe action is required it is not unusual for several long-standing members to be removed during this intervention. Both the authoritarian and the restriction interventions are maintained by staff during this period. These methods continue to be used until the remaining group members reorganize themselves and assume responsibility for treatment once again. Due to the disorganization of the group, restriction is maintained until stability and a positive group core develop. During the past year, this intervention was used only once.

Outcome

Success of treatment of the short-term groups at Reality House is measured by the discharge of an individual by the courts or his maintenance on probation. Failure is measured by recidivism, which means probation has been revoked because of further deviant behavior.

From 1975 to 1980, 111 young male felony offenders were accepted into residency at Reality House, which means they were recommended for and entered the program at the end of their evaluation status. Of these 111, 75 had in-program success. They successfully completed the six statuses and were discharged from the program. Thirty-six had in-program failure. They had their programs terminated before completion. Termination generally occurred by decision of the group through the democratic voting process. Termination before completion results from behavioral evidence that the young man is not using the program constructively to change his deviant behavior. The causes and procedures for termination have been discussed in detail earlier.

Of the 75 who achieved in-program success, 59 (79 percent) had no further difficulty with the law at the time of follow-up. Follow-up reports of the other 16 (21 percent) in-program successes indicated recidivism or revocation of probation. Of the in-program failures, opposite results were found. Of this group of 36 who had been terminated from the program before completion, only 5 (14 percent) had been discharged by the courts or were being maintained successfully on probation. Reports of the other 31 (86 percent) indicated continued difficulty with the law and revocation of probation.

References

Augsburger, D. *Caring enough to confront* (Rev. ed.). Glendale, Calif.: Regal Books, 1980.

Berne, E. *Principles of group treatment.* New York: Oxford University Press, 1966.

Cartwright, D. Achieving change in people: Applications of group dynamics theory. *Human Relations*, 1951, *4*(4), 381–392.

Galaway, B., Hudson, J., & Hollister, C. D. (Eds.). *Community corrections: A reader.* Springfield, Ill.: Charles C Thomas, 1976.

Glasser, W. *Reality therapy.* New York: Harper & Row, 1965.

Hahn, P. H. *Community based corrections and the criminal justice system.* Santa Cruz, Calif.: Davis Publishing, 1975.

Killinger, G. G., & Cromwell, P. F., Jr. *Corrections in the community* (2nd ed.). St. Paul, Minn.: West Publishing, 1978.

Long, L. D., & Cope, C. S. Curative factors in a male felony offender group. *Small Group Behavior*, 1980, *11*(4), 389–398.

National Advisory Commission on Criminal Justice Standards and Goals. *Working papers of the national conference on criminal justice, January 23–26, 1973.* Washington, D.C.: Law Enforcement Assistance Administration, 1973.

Perlstein, G. R., & Phelps, T. R. *Alternatives to prison: Community-based corrections.* Pacific Palisades, Calif.: Goodyear Publishing, 1975.

Reid, W. H. (Ed.). *The psychopath: A comprehensive study of antisocial disorders and behaviors.* New York: Brunner/Mazel, 1978.

Smith, A. B., & Berlin, L. *Treating the criminal offender* (2nd ed.). Englewood Cliffs, N. J.: Prentice-Hall, 1981.

Solomon, H. M. *Community corrections.* Boston: Allyn & Bacon, 1976.

Stephenson, R. M., & Scarpitti, F. R. *Group interaction as therapy: The use of the small group in corrections.* Westport, Conn.: Greenwood Press, 1974.

Wicks, R. J. *Correctional psychology: Themes and problems in correcting the offender.* San Francisco: Canfield Press, 1974.

Yalom, I. D. *The theory and practice of group psychotherapy* (2nd ed.). New York: Basic Books, 1975.

Yalom, I. D. *Existential psychotherapy.* New York: Basic Books, 1980.

21

Short-Term Group Therapy
for Alcoholics

Edward M. Scott, Ph.D.

EDWARD M. SCOTT is clinical director of the Alcohol Treatment and Training
Center in Portland, Oregon, and professor of psychiatry and of medical psychology in the University of Oregon Medical School.

The third edition of the American Psychiatric Association's *Diagnostic and
Statistical Manual of Mental Disorders* (*DSM-III*) distinguishes two levels of
substance use disorders, namely, substance abuse and substance dependence.
Although alcohol abuse may lead to alcohol dependence, it is only the latter
that we identify with alcoholism. This disorder (*DSM-III* does not use the term
"disease") is placed among Axis I Clinical Syndromes.

But the authors of *DSM-III* wisely note: "Frequently, individuals who develop Substance Use Disorders also have preexisting Personality Disorders
and Affective Disorders with concomitant impairment in social and occupational functioning" (p. 164). Personality disorders constitute Axis II in *DSM-
III*'s diagnostic system, the authors explaining: "This separation [of Personality
Disorders from Clinical Syndromes] ensures that consideration is given to the
possible presence of disorders that are frequently overlooked when attention
is directed to the usually more florid Axis I disorder" (p. 23).

In my opinion, treatment of the preexisting personality disorder is the principal task in working with alcoholics, one far more difficult than dealing with the Axis I disorders of alcohol abuse and alcohol dependence. Indeed, alcoholism researchers report considerable success in dealing with Axis I disorders. Thus Polich and associates (1980) write: "At admission, more than 90% [of the sample studied] reported alcohol dependence symptoms or serious adverse consequences of drinking; at the four-year follow-up, almost half of the sample was not affected by such problems" (p. 177). Yet these same authors report: "One important finding from the psychosocial analysis is the lack of improvement in social adjustment . . ." (p. 176). More particularly, they found increases in "depression, anxiety and global dissatisfaction" greater than in comparison groups in the general population.

In dealing with both Axis I and Axis II disorders associated with alcoholism, I have consistently found group therapy to be *the* modality of choice. My approach to group therapy with alcoholics, however, differs significantly from that enunciated by Brown and Yalom (1977). Brown and Yalom began their group work with alcoholics with a number of a priori assumptions. The first was that the intensive group experience would in itself be a powerful vehicle of change and that the process of change would be accelerated if members confined their discussions as much as possible to the "here and now." Further:

> We did not believe that an interactional group (in which conflict as well as acceptance is necessary) would be able to provide the total support needed to maintain abstinence; nor did we set that as the task or goal of the group— we encouraged members to obtain other help if necessary, such as Alcoholics Anonymous and disulfiram therapy. Instead, the group task was formulated as helping members overcome the underlying conflicts which lead to compulsive drinking. We specifically intended to shift the focus of the group's work away from the issue of alcohol. (pp. 427–428)

In my experience, effective treatment of alcoholics must embrace the "there and then" as well as the "here and now." Even more important, I regard the stopping of drinking as a prerequisite to group therapy, the ultimate goal of which is to end the patient's dependence on alcohol. My group practice is based on the following principles:

1. Group therapy must recognize all aspects of the patient's life—drinking, work, intimate relationships, early life factors, leisure, etc., and not turn over some aspects of the treatment effort to another agency. If the patient is unable to stop drinking on his own, Antabuse should be considered.
2. People drink to alter their consciousness. A second task of group therapy, therefore, is to help the ex-user of alcohol to alter his or her consciousness without the use of any drugs.

3. The more "informal" or "spontaneous" factors operative outside of group therapy, the better (Malan et al., 1975).

4. An effort is made to combine two forms of transference: peer-to-peer and parent-child.

Elsewhere, my associates and I wrote (Scott et al., 1977):

> Group therapy is an ideal arena which assembles the above elements with a therapeutic mosaic. Alcoholics, typically, are social and need an arena in which to perform, be recognized, and, as a consequence, feel accepted. A well functioning group therapy helps replace the arena of the tavern and its destructive, yet exciting, atmosphere. Now, instead of out-drinking, out-gambling, and out-talking each other, the patients gather to reflect on the trials and triumphs of the past week, experience the excitement of the here and now, and plan for tomorrow. (p. 145)

Clinical Setting and Group Organization

Portland's Alcohol Treatment and Training Center (AT&TC), established in 1943, is the second oldest in the United States. Its staff numbers 27; its patient load averages 350 per month. All patients are in group therapy. There are currently 22 groups, some of them specialized—for example, groups for couples, schizophrenics, the elderly, the sexually disordered.

A prospective patient is given two psychological tests and a mental health–status examination. These are followed by "staffing," a 15-to-20-minute meeting between the prospective patient and a group of staff members. The prospective patient's spouse or significant other is urged to attend and often does. Staff members from the referring agency are also welcomed. At this meeting, the results of the psychological tests are shared with the prospective patient and an attempt is made to reach mutual agreement on his or her problem and on a treatment plan. This agreement is in effect a therapeutic alliance between the patient and the agency. If the treatment plan goes awry, the patient is brought back for another staffing and possible revision of the treatment plan.

The great majority of prospective patients agree to a therapeutic alliance. In those cases where no problem can be agreed upon, the prospective patient is not accepted for treatment. If he or she has been referred by the court, another agency, or an attorney, a letter is sent informing the referrer that the individual insists he or she has no problem and consequently has been rejected as a patient. Occasionally a few will come "flying back" and be assigned to a specialized group.

An essential element of the therapeutic alliance is cessation of drinking. Where the patient has unsuccessfully tried other modalities—Alcoholics Anonymous, hospitalization, etc.—we suggest Antabuse. In his review of the literature on treatment approaches, Costello (1975) concluded:

> Although the value of Antabuse as a therapeutic aid has been debated for many years, this collation suggests that successful programs have Antabuse available, use it extensively, and that treatment agents are optimistic about its value as an aid. Unsuccessful programs do not have it available, do not use it extensively when available, and when offering it as an adjuvant do so unwillingly or ambivalently. (p. 271)

Certainly this has been our experience at AT&TC. Only with the cessation of drinking can the patient "work on" his or her personality problems—*DSM-III*'s Axis II.

The group described here is a permanent one whose membership changes gradually over time. Membership ranges from 7 to 16; average attendance is 9. Members are of at least average intelligence, not in the later stages of alcoholism, and without residual cognitive dysfunction due to drinking. None have histories of psychotic episodes, and the antisocial element is relatively curtailed. Most are employed. Members generally spend 10 months in group therapy, and the present article covers a recent 10-to-12-month period in the life of this group.

I am the only therapist, and the group meets weekly for 1½ hours in my office. I have a rather large office, with a desk at one end and, at the other, a couch, seven or eight chairs, and a "hypnosis chair," a large easy chair used specifically for hypnosis. In the center of the room is a coffee table with a warming plate for coffee. Members pay 25 cents for coffee. Cigarette smoking is an issue that the group resolves either by choosing a period for smoking "halfway through" or ruling "no smoking" altogether. I do not smoke.

I have a library in my office, and it has been my practice to present to the group material appearing in professional journals. Patients often mention articles they have read in popular magazines and newspapers that are pertinent to them. I do not make psychotherapy a classroom, but I believe that education is part of any treatment effort.

I also believe that psychotherapy must lead eventually not only to a change of feelings, thoughts, and beliefs but to a change of behavior. I am not a behaviorist in the usual sense of that term, but I sometimes prescribe "homework" such as writing a letter, making a phone call, visiting a grave, visiting one's children, taking Antabuse, hugging someone, or "doing a video."

AT&TC has its own video equipment, and group sessions are taped. The tapes are available for group members to view prior to meetings, and they are discussed in the group. My experience suggests that video is a useful adjunctive modality. It provides the patient with a way to view himself (an excellent learning device), a way for the group to "freeze" a certain segment for later discussion, and a means for group members to *admire* those who have "done a video," that is, taped a special session.

Initially, I take an active role in the group—something like a coach. I can't *do* therapy for anyone, but I can provide help and direction. My coaching consists of insisting that the group adhere to a few fundamental rules. For example, no "psychiatric swearing"—that is, no saying "I don't know." I insist that the patient examine himself or herself. Another guideline is to prohibit a patient's "splitting"—that is, saying, "It wasn't me, it was the alcohol." I insist that group members own their behavior.

I have no single approach to therapy. Dreams, transitional objects, exercises, the here and now, the there and then, existential crises: all are employed when a patient or the group presents a particular problem. Like onetime Baltimore Colts quarterback Johnny Unitas, "I use what's offered." That may be a simple inconsistency, like the patient who professed to be shy but wore his shirt completely unbuttoned, showing off his hairy chest. Always, the goal of such confrontations is to make the patient more self-observant.

At first, most alcoholic patients attempt to use the therapist as a "selfobject." As defined by Kohut and Wolf (1978),

> *Selfobjects* are objects which we experience as part of our self; the expected control over them is, therefore, closer to the concept of the control which a grown-up expects to have over his own body and mind than to the concept of the control which he expects to have over others. (p. 414)

The typical alcoholic has treated the significant other in his life as a selfobject and expects to have the same relationship to the therapist. This orientation prevents treatment. Yet a cold, rejecting, noninvolved attitude on the part of the therapist is counterproductive—patients leave. Experience and consultation are necessary before the therapist can acquire an appropriate "treatment stance."

The Initial Phase

The first phase of group psychotherapy with alcoholics is crucial, perhaps more so than in any other type of group. Drinking—whether it's a disease or a symptom, or both or neither—has to be tackled. Some patients struggle to stop drinking; others seem to enjoy the cessation.

Len stopped drinking on his own after 15 years of it and the loss of two wives and children. He was fortunate to find a third wife, a stable woman with two teenaged children. Len, however, had to cope also with an extended period of unemployment, during which his wife was the family breadwinner. Unemployment was a severe blow to Len's masculine ego, but he did not resort to drinking. With his wife's encouragement, he went into business for himself and has done rather well.

Jim, on the other hand, struggled for months to stop drinking, refusing Antabuse. One week he "tied one on," returned to the group, and confessed.

JIM.   I was on vacation and I said, "I'll tie one on." It scared me. I got ripped. I had seven or eight beers, began to feel high and depressed. I went to the tavern to shoot pool, drank some more, and then it hit me. I couldn't get enough. I was asked to leave the tavern. They said I yelled and screamed. Somehow they got my girlfriend's number and called her. I left the tavern, don't remember, almost got hit by a car, I was told. I finally passed out, went to sleep. I—ah—well, just wanted to drink. I'm going to do what I want to do.

DR. SCOTT.   That makes sense. ["Going with" Jim's last sentence. This is a form of confrontation.]

JIM.   No! It doesn't. [Note the immediate effect.] My girlfriend said I embarrassed her. Ah—the drinking—not having to make a decision—or to answer to anyone—and mad—I—also—I was going to have fun. Then, damn it, I drank too much! When my girlfriend saw me at home I said, "I'm Jim and I can do anything I want."

DR. SCOTT.   "Your majesty, the baby," Freud would probably have said.

When questioned about his early life, Jim related:

JIM.   I was on my own. Dad left us and Mom had a nervous breakdown. I was about one year old. I lived with my aunt and uncle, then I was placed in homes, and back to Mom. I can't blame her—she was doing the best she could. But, well—ah—a personality change takes place when I'm drunk—getting away with things, no consequences. I ran away from home a lot. It was exciting. On buses. I'd steal the money. Or jump the train and go anywhere. I started this when I was eight and kept it up until I was fourteen. It was exciting. Mom was—well, she didn't show too much concern.

Jim's abuse of alcohol was another form of exciting running away. His decision to start Antabuse permitted therapy to focus on his personality problems.

Debbie was a typical young alcoholic. Despite a year's treatment three years before, living with a man who drank heavily wore away her abstinence and she started to drink again. During her previous treatment she had said:

DEBBIE.   When drinking, I'm louder. I used to do it with a girl friend and my brother for kicks. I've watched my parents get drunk all my life. It was like a party for everyone—discipline was relaxed and I got Coke and stuff. It was a kick! As I got older, when I drank it was like a rush—a feeling of power and self-confidence. Things changed in my mind. I'm okay for a while—in my mind. Now, that good feeling—aren't—well—just a little to drink and I'm out of it.

Bobbie, a 50-year-old female alcoholic, seemed determined to overcome her alcoholism. Discharged from the hospital, she came immediately to AT&TC. During the first two months of treatment she progressed well. She did not drink, used Antabuse, and participated in group. Most of her contributions, however, concerned her losses—husband, money, etc. She felt lonely and angry. Her fortune changed when she found a job. But suddenly she failed to attend group, stopped Antabuse, and once again had to be hospitalized for drinking. I telephoned her and she assured me she would return to treatment. On the way home from the hospital, however, she got a bottle and, once home, began to drink. She did return to the group two weeks later and explained that her job had been too demanding. Instead of asking her employer for part-time work, she regressed to drinking and was fired.

Len and Bobbie were alike in age, long histories of drinking, and loss of spouses. But Len found support in his wife, whereas Bobbie had no significant other. The presence of a significant other, I have found, is a powerful support in the struggle to stop drinking.

The first phase of group therapy with alcoholics focuses on the cessation of drinking. Treatment of Axis II personality disorders must wait until some level of stability is reached regarding the use of alcohol. In my experience, the average alcoholic requires three to four months for sobriety to settle in, at which point "treatment proper" rather than mere "policing" can begin.

The Middle Phase

Two developments usher in the middle phase of group therapy: (1) group members succeed in abstaining from alcohol for three to four months; and (2) they learn to put themselves under observation. Members do not enter the middle phase in a tightly knit body, but the movement is general with only a few stragglers following behind. Some of the themes that emerge in the middle phase of group therapy have been transitional objects, personality development, confronting reality, and death.

Transitional Objects

Winnicott (1953) introduced the concepts of the transitional phenomenon (for example, thumb sucking) and transitional object ("the first not-me possession"—for example, a favorite blanket). The transitional object (or TO), Winnicott wrote, is gradually decathected and eventually "relegated to limbo. . . .

It is not forgotten and it is not mourned. It loses meaning. . . ." Tolpin (1971) suggested that the TO is internalized as mental structure, and for that reason is neither missed, mourned, repressed, nor forgotten. The child learns to soothe itself, and the external soother is no longer needed.

Some researchers (Arkema, 1981; Horton et al., 1974) have argued that the absence of a TO is a critical diagnostic finding and is at the root of severe personality disorder. In my experience with alcoholics, the TO was not absent but hidden, and it proved to be alcohol.

For many alcoholics, alcohol is employed as a unique TO. It functions, at least initially, as a thumb, a blanket, or a teddy bear. But whereas the TO enabled the child to achieve its effort at separation-individuation from its mother and acquire the ability to face the world, alcohol prevents the alcoholic from making further progress. It keeps him or her at the "intermediate area of experiencing." Structure building, as proposed by Tolpin, does not occur; rather, there is a frantic effort to hold onto alcohol and to use it more and more. Hence, the cessation of drinking is imperative if therapy is to succeed. It "releases" the alcoholic from his primitive cathexis, the alcohol, and offers an opportunity to struggle for personality growth. Here group therapy can become a healthy "intermediate area of experiencing," in which patients learn to trust parental figures—perhaps for the first time—and to cooperate with siblings and peers.

Notes taken at two group sessions reveal the process of obtaining clinical material regarding TOs and, in two instances, of finding patients' "hidden" TOs.

JAY. I didn't suck my thumb, but—well—ah—I burned my brother's teddy bear. He got everything. He was the baby. I ran away from home when I was 3½ years old. Later, when we were grown up, I went to jail for him. He was going into the service. A narcotics beef. I took it for him—I went to jail.

BEN. I had a blanket. I still do. I can't watch TV without it—or sleep. [Ben is 49, married, white, nervous, talkative.]

JAY. I drink to get drunk—to piss on the world—get rid of the world. My marriage went bad. I got into a rut. I've blamed my problems on my wife.

JULIE. We all do a lot of that.

BEN. I've got too much tension.

JAY. When I'm working, I'm a roofer, I look around to find where a tavern is on each new job.

DR. SCOTT. Trying to locate mother's breast?

JAY. Ya, perhaps.

BEN. Not me.

DR. SCOTT. Not mother's breast—but mother's lap. You and your blanket!

BEN. [smiling sheepishly]. Ya—if Mother wasn't home I'd be upset when

I came home from school. My sister and I'd get into an argument. I'd go and sit on Mom's lap. Gosh!

RON.   I had a favorite pillow—that I held onto—maybe—ah—against—well, I hate to say it—I still have the same pillow today! I, well it's—ah—protection.

Time ran out, and at the next session the topic reemerged.

JAY.   Well, too, so you'd like to know more. I took my brother's teddy bear out in the woods, drove a stick in the ground, tied its hands, and set it on fire. It didn't burn completely, so I threw it in the creek. My brother found it. He showed it to the old man and I got a whipping.

LUCILLE.   What kind?

JAY.   Well, he hit me with his belt and asked me, "Are you going to do it again?" I said, "No." He said, "You're lying," and he beat me more. Later, as a young man, I found out why Dad was so mean. Mom didn't want any more kids and cut him off. We're Catholics.

LUCILLE.   How about your brother?

JAY.   Two weeks later he had his little cars lined up. I got a .22 and shot all his cars. I was seven years old.

DR. SCOTT.   Jay, what about you? Did you have a TO?

JAY.   Nothing.

DR. SCOTT.   Think a bit.

JAY [pause].   No, but I ate paper. I'd tear off a piece and chew it—even in school. One time I had to go to the hospital, I was bleeding from the rectum—eating paper.

BEN.   What!

JAY.   I started when I was 3 years old. I'd—ah—tear off a piece of paper, wad it up and chew it—all the juice of it—I'd swallow. I'd take it to bed with me.

RON.   A thumb substitute.

LEN.   The breast?

LUCILLE.   Your brother was getting the attention.

JAY.   Mom wasn't affectionate—she'd push me away. I got a lot of hostility inside, I didn't care for anyone but me.

LEN.   You and alcohol.

JAY.   I'd get drunk, mad, more pissed off, and fight.

LUCILLE.   Today?

JAY.   Not so much the last two or three years. My parents are old now, and I'm taking care of them.

Jay paused, laughed, and said:

JAY.   No more burning of teddy bears. I laugh now, when I look back. I've been in the joint for a couple of years. Last time in court I gave the judge the finger—he added time.

Jay reflected:

JAY.   I want to settle down. I've bought a lot and I'm going to start to build on it.

Several points have to be stressed. Winnicott (1953) wrote: "Less commonly, the wool is swallowed, even causing trouble" (p. 90). It appears that Jay's chewing and swallowing paper is a particular example of this kind of experience. Hong (1978) would classify this as a primary TO. Second, without persistence during the second session, Jay's TO would not have emerged. This suggests the superiority of the treatment situation over research questions asked by unfamiliar persons in discovering hidden TOs. Finally, it is my clinical opinion that Jay presents a severe personality disorder. My finding differs from that of Horton and associates and Arkema, for whom the presence of a TO militates against severe personality disorder.

A second patient, Jim, insisted that he did not have a TO but sucked his thumb until he was 8 years old. Regarding his thumb sucking, he said:

JIM.   I was told not to, but I enjoyed it—peace of mind or security. I'd be lying around listening to the radio, sucking my thumb—it was a big evening.

When questioned further, he connected thumb sucking to booze.

JIM.   Ah—I've never thought of this—ah—feeling blue, I'm devoted to it, I'd tie one on.
DR. SCOTT.   What about the radio?
JIM.   Oh, I had favorites—"The Green Hornet," "The Lone Ranger." It was like I was there—imagining what was happening. It's better than TV. You can imagine it.

In my opinion, this is a kind of combined transitional phenomenon (thumb sucking), which ushered in a transitional object, his favorite radio programs. "Through imagination" he entered "an intermediate area of experiencing," the criterion for any transitional object.

Personality Development

An important theme in the group was personality development. How does one "get to be" what he or she is? A functional approach to this issue was to ask, "What is your earliest memory?" The group reacted eagerly.

Julie was a 52-year-old alcoholic married to an alcoholic who refused to seek help with his problem. Julie was referred to AT&TC by her private physician. She came depressed, somewhat guilty, and appeared to be both indecisive and dependent. She sat silently much of the time for the first three months. The question about her earliest memories stirred her:

JULIE.   My first memory is the stove in the kitchen. My Mom was so proud of it. It was green and white—most stoves were black. I wanted to cook my own eggs. I was 3½. Mom let me do it.

Other group members related their first memories. Julie interrupted excitedly:

JULIE.   My mind is flowing. I was independent then. My life has totally changed. As a teenager I was competitive. My marriage, I'm going to get out of it. For the past ten years, I—ah—thought I'd never have the courage. Group has given me back hope.

It was suggested, "No, we didn't give it back—you rediscovered it." Julie laughingly agreed. This simple technique appeared to "plug" Julie into her own roots. From that time on, Julie became active, assertive, and "sang the praises" of group psychotherapy.

I have found that it is characteristic of my alcoholic patients to root their personalities in negative events. A decade ago, I made a survey of patients and nonpatients that indicated that the latter felt that the happiest events in their lives had been deeper and more meaningful than the saddest (Scott, 1971). The patients, on the other hand, judged the sad events to have been deeper and more meaningful. The earliest memories of this patient group generally seemed to confirm this finding.

Sue, a 35-year-old patient, presented the following first memory:

SUE.   Well, riding in a car—making believe I was smoking a chocolate cigarette. Ah—ah—food—I love food. Food is immediate gratification and—ah—I don't have to work to get the satisfaction. Even today, when I'm upset I like warm potato soup.

DR. SCOTT.   Mother's milk?

SUE.   I've never thought of it. I—ah—remember cuddling up against her bosom [begins to cry]. I want to say I was an independent little girl. I used to be stubborn and do things myself. One day I wanted to wear a dress and Mom said "No." I insisted that I wouldn't get it dirty. I fell into the mud. When I came home, Mom screamed at me. My spirit was broken.

A MEMBER.   Broke your spirit?

SUE.   Ya—a change in me. Maybe I was vulnerable.

417

Lucille remembered skipping along a sidewalk and her mother "yelling at me to stop." She felt her mother's pressure for years, and in high school she began to drink as an act of rebellion. The following exchange between Lucille and Julie is taken from a videotape:

DR. SCOTT. You're doing a good job, Julie.

JULIE. Thanks.

DR. SCOTT. Lucille, how do you about Julie?

LUCILLE. Fine.

JULIE. I saw your video last time, and I think you did well.

DR. SCOTT [to Julie]. How do you feel about me?

JULIE. You! I relate to you like a—ah—father. I can picture your children on your lap. You're—ah—an ideal father—open and honest.

LUCILLE. You're interested in us. As a result, I want to better myself. When I'm approved, I work hard.

DR. SCOTT. Do you want me to be critical or admiring of you?

LUCILLE. Admiring. [Sadly] I'm not getting anywhere in my life.

DR. SCOTT. There's another reason I'm not critical. You're critical enough of yourself. Recall your first memory.

LUCILLE. Oh, yes. Of skipping along the sidewalk and Mother critical of me.

JULIE [surprised]. Your mother didn't approve?

LUCILLE. No.

DR. SCOTT. Why did I want you two to do this video session?

LUCILLE [after some hesitation]. Julie is a mother figure! [Julie and I applaud Lucille's insight.]

JULIE. How simple it is!

DR. SCOTT. How long have you known this, Lucille?

LUCILLE. It just hit me! For years I hated my mother—and all women. I didn't trust my mother. I heard her voice.

DR. SCOTT. Lucille, tell Julie where your mother is located.

LUCILLE. On my left shoulder—I can hear her negative voice.

JULIE. Wow!

LUCILLE. My mother felt inadequate and saw me as inadequate—and pushed and pushed [begins to cry].

JULIE. My mother would crush me like a bug! I hate her. I—ah—have to call her every other day. She's 72.

DR. SCOTT. Could you call her every third day?

JULIE. I'm going to call her once a week. [Lucille and I applaud.]

DR. SCOTT. What about your self-concept?

JULIE. I'm not aggressive enough.

DR. SCOTT. Recall your first memory—as a little girl—making your breakfast of eggs on the green stove.

JULIE. Yes. And in high school I was competitive. Then I began to drink to get away from pressure. I didn't want to drink.

LUCILLE. I drank to spite my mother.

DR. SCOTT. What happened to your mother on your shoulder when you drank?

LUCILLE. I'd drown her out. [Laughs.] I'd say to myself, "I'll show you!"

This particular episode illustrates some of the advantages of "doing a video." In this instance, two patients with similar problems and a potential for transference to one another were selected. The video technique fosters both a therapeutic alliance and a transference, not only between patients and therapist but between the patients themselves.

Confronting Reality

The therapy group is not a comfortable refuge like the seductive tavern but an arena where the members confront the reality of work, illness, death, and especially relationships with significant others. In my judgment, the last is the most persistent and difficult area for the average alcoholic. The literature supports this view. Kurtines and associates (1978) found that even after eight or nine years recovered alcoholics were still troubled by problems of interpersonal relationships. Polich and associates (1980) report: "However much their drinking behavior may have improved after treatment, they did not generally achieve rehabilitation, in the sense of full reintegration into normal social roles" (p. 176).

For a variety of complex reasons, most alcoholic patients make poor choices of their significant others. This was true of those in the present group. Two of the women members indicated that their husbands had rejected them sexually—a painful experience. Many of the women felt that they were used as part objects, objects of male aggressiveness or of the male need for childlike dependency. One female patient stated it well: "I felt he was using his navel cord, not his penis." Male patients frequently spoke of their sexual activity without care or tenderness.

Although group therapy could not "solve" this problem, it provided an avenue for some patients to repair this aspect of their lives. Sobriety made possible new, whole-object interpersonal relations.

Death as a Visitor

The group encountered death on three occasions. Jack, a burly 32-year-old, had killed a man in a bar fight and spent a year in prison. A condition of his parole was that he go for treatment at an alcohol agency. Because I had evaluated Jack for the court and had found him genuinely overwhelmed by what

he had done, I accepted him in the present group. In the group, Jack acknowledged that if his wife—his second wife—had not stayed with him, "I wouldn't
have given a damn." His wife's support during therapy was important for Jack.
This "informal" aspect of therapy cannot be overlooked. During one group
session, I brought this phenomenon to the members' attention. Jack said,
"You're not working with the best of the litter, Doc." This provoked an excellent discussion concerning family origins and early life experiences.

Two years before the present group, Jennie, a 59-year-old woman, had returned home to find "my husband blew his brains out—blood all over." Although she was already an alcoholic, Jennie's intake increased dramatically
after her husband's suicide until she was forced to seek help. During group,
it was found that she had never visited her husband's grave because of her
anger and fear. The group then engaged in a psychodrama in which one member "played dead." Jennie was encouraged to visit her husband's grave "and
say a few words." She did so, and reported that she had experienced new
peace of mind. Thereafter Jennie encouraged other members to "face your
problems—it's not as bad as you think." She was able to terminate treatment
in six months.

May, a daily abuser of alcohol, was an attractive 38-year-old married woman.
Ten months before, she had given birth to a defective child, which soon died.
She had held the dead baby for two hours. Her husband had not been present
at this time. Three months after the baby's death, her husband had yelled at
her, "Don't you hear your baby calling?" In her first group session, May acknowledged that this had been cruel, but she said, "I don't think much of
myself. I hope he'll change." At her second session, she told us that she visited
the cemetery once a month. At her third session, she reported that her husband had rejected her for a new girlfriend.

Two days later, May took her own life. This plunged the group into shock,
depression, and frustration. But it also mobilized the group into a "tighter
family." One member requested a group hug. Members spoke of "not having
enough time to work with May."

Terminations and Results

The members of this group terminated after varied periods of time and under
varied circumstances. Some achieved their goals quickly. Jennie, for example,
experienced a sudden calming of her inner turmoil when she at last visited
her husband's grave; her dependence on alcohol ceased with her anger. Sue's
dependence ended when she terminated a destructive marriage.

For Len, a stable marriage and success as a proficient craftsman in his own
small business provided foundations for a meaningful life without alcohol. Vocational security contributed to Debbie's successful completion of her second

group experience. She obtained training as an auto mechanic and was thus able to provide for herself and her 10-year-old son.

Julie and Lucille represent examples of intrapsychic healing. Each was able to replace self-tormenting introjects of early life with healthy new ones. Julie, however, remained in a troubled marriage. Lucille, on the other hand, having gained a stable sobriety and advancement in her employment, become the support of both her parents when her father became ill with cancer.

Other group members did not fare so well. Jay left the group against my advice to "go fishing" in Alaska; he returned to drinking. Jack, too, left group therapy prematurely, though he still faced a long period on parole for manslaughter. Ben and Bobbie regressed. Ben's wife suffered a psychotic breakdown and had to be hospitalized. Under the stress, Ben drank, was arrested for driving while intoxicated, and was ordered by the court to two years of further therapy. Bobbie was hospitalized for a slight stroke, began drinking again upon her release, and had to be rehospitalized for alcoholism.

Following a year in group therapy, Jim requested private sessions. During this period, which lasted 1½ years, the focus was on early object relations, his schizoid proclivities emanating from early childhood. He developed an excellent therapeutic alliance with me and a moderate degree of transference.

Alcoholism, I believe, is a broad umbrella under which stand a wide variety of individuals with unique problems. The effectiveness of group therapy or any other kind is bound to be affected not only by the nature of the psychopathology that the individual patient presents but also by exogenous factors, both negative and positive. The curative factors in group therapy have been identified and evaluated by many writers. In my own experience, I give special weight to (1) the parental role of the therapist, often the patient's first experience of a supportive, encouraging, admiring parent figure; (2) the sibling roles of group members, not rivalrous as in the conventional portrayal but loving, admiring, and supportive in their ways; and (3) the "informal" extragroup factors, especially supportive significant others.

References

American Psychiatric Association, Task Force on Nomenclature and Statistics. *Diagnostic and statistical manual of mental disorders* (3rd ed.) [*DSM-III*]. Washington, D.C.: American Psychiatric Association, 1980.

Arkema, P. H. The borderline personality and transitional relatedness. *American Journal of Psychiatry*, 1981, *138*(2), 172–177.

Brown, S., & Yalom, I. D. Interactional group therapy with alcoholics. *Journal of Studies on Alcohol*, 1977, *38*(3), 426–456.

Costello, R. Alcoholism treatment and evaluation: In search of methods. *International Journal of the Addictions*, 1975, *10*(2), 251–275.

Hong, K. The transitional phenomena. *Psychoanalytic Study of the Child*, 1978, *33*, 47–49.

Horton, P. C., Louy, J. W., & Coppolillo, H. P. Personality disorder and transitional relatedness. *Archives of General Psychiatry*, 1974, *30*(5), 618–622.

Kohut, H., & Wolf, E. S. The disorders of the self and their treatment: An outline. *International Journal of Psycho-Analysis*, 1978, *59*(4), 413–425.

Kurtines, W. M., Ball, L. R., & Wood, G. H. Personality characteristics of long-term recovered alcoholics: A comparative analysis. *Journal of Consulting and Clinical Psychology*, 1978, *46*(5), 971–977.

Malan, D. H., Heath, E. S., Bacal, H. A., & Balfour, F. H. G. Psychodynamic changes in untreated neurotic patients. *Archives of General Psychiatry*, 1975, *32*(1), 110–126.

Polich, J., Armor, D., & Bracher, H. *The course of alcoholism: Four years after treatment.* Santa Monica, Calif.: Rand Corporation, 1980.

Scott, E. *An arena for happiness.* Springfield, Ill.: Charles C Thomas, 1971.

Scott, E. M., Keener, J., & Manaugh, T. S. Treatment of alcoholism in an out-patient clinic in Oregon. *International Journal of Offender Therapy and Comparative Criminology*, 1977, *21*(2), 141–152.

Tolpin, M. On the beginnings of a cohesive self. *Psychoanalytic Study of the Child*, 1971, *26*, 316–352.

Winnicott, D. W. Transitional objects and transitional phenomena. *International Journal of Psycho-Analysis*, 1953, *34*(2), 89–97.

Index

About the Editor

MAX ROSENBAUM, Ph.D., is a seminal figure in the field of group psychotherapy. He is a past President of the Association for Group Psychoanalysis and Process, as well as the Eastern Group Psychotherapy Society. Former clinical professor of psychology at Adelphi University and clinical professor of psychiatry at New York University, he is co-author of *Group Psychotherapy: Theory and Practice* among numerous other texts. He was editor of *The Intensive Group Experience* and the journal *Group Process,* and co-director of the American Short-Term Therapy Center. Dr. Rosenbaum currently serves as a consultant to different psychiatric centers and is on the Board of Governors, Center for Psychological Studies, Nova Southeastern University, Fort Lauderdale, Florida.